THE ACTS OF PAUL

The Acts of Paul

A New Translation with Introduction and Commentary

Richard I. Pervo

CASCADE *Books* • Eugene, Oregon

THE ACTS OF PAUL
A New Translation with Introduction and Commentary

Copyright © 2014 Richard I. Pervo. All rights reserved. Except for brief quotations in critical publications or reviews, no part of this book may be reproduced in any manner without prior written permission from the publisher. Write: Permissions, Wipf and Stock Publishers, 199 W. 8th Ave., Suite 3, Eugene, OR 97401.

Cascade Books
An Imprint of Wipf and Stock Publishers
199 W. 8th Ave., Suite 3
Eugene, OR 97401

www.wipfandstock.com

ISBN 13: 978-1-62564-171-7

Cataloguing-in-Publication data:

Pervo, Richard I.

The acts of Paul : a new translation with introduction and commentary / Richard I. Pervo.

xviii + 376 pp. ; 23 cm. Includes bibliographical references and indexes.

ISBN 13: 978-1-62564-171-7

1. Acts of Paul—Translation. 2. Acts of Paul—Commentary. 3. Acts of Paul—Criticism, interpretation, etc. I. Title.

BS2880 P3 P35 2014

Manufactured in the U.S.A.

Magistro Meo
Helmut Koester

Contents

Preface | ix

Abbreviations | xi

The *Acts of Paul:* A Translation | 1

Introduction | 41

Translation, Commentary, and Notes | 79

    Chapter 1 | 79

    Chapter 2 | 83

    Chapter 3 | 87

    Chapter 4 | 146

    Chapter 5 | 186

    Chapter 6 | 197

    Chapter 7 | 205

    Chapter 8 | 207

    Chapter 9 | 213

    Chapter 10 | 253

    Chapter 11 | 275

    Chapter 12 | 281

    Chapter 13 | 290

    Chapter 14 | 303

Appendices

    Fragments of Uncertain Location | 327

    The Continuation of Thecla's Story | 329

    The Acts of Titus | 331

Contents

> General Bibliography | 335
>
> Index of Ancient Sources | 353
>
> Index of Modern Authors | 373

Preface

Many find the Apocryphal Acts of the Apostles (ApocActs) fascinating. To others they are strange, even objectionable. I belong to the former group. During the last four decades these texts have constituted one of the three legs upholding my research. The others are ancient popular narrative, broadly construed, and the canonical Acts. The ApocActs are, among other considerations, successors of the canonical book. One of the challenges scholars face when comparing two or more writings is to emphasize both the similarities and the differences. The comparative glass is always half empty and half full. Otherwise stated: when the consensus emphasizes differences, argue for similarities, and vice-versa. (And hope for a great reward in heaven.)

The differences among the so-called major ApocActs, those of Andrew, John, Paul, Peter, and Thomas (*AAndr, AJn, APl, APet, AThom*) are substantial, as are their similarities. Most agree that the *APl* is the earliest; it is, in any case, most like the canonical book. This commentary takes the view that the resemblance is not accidental: *APl* knew the canonical book. Not surprisingly, the book before you views *APl* through the lens of the Pauline legacy and in the context of ancient popular narrative. The past ten years of my career have been devoted to Acts and the Pauline legacy and the various components of this work seem, at least to me, to have cohered. The culmination of the former is Pervo, *Acts*, while *The Making of Paul* represents the latter.

Another apology stems from contrary impulses. The ideal commentator on *APl* will know a good half-dozen ancient languages quite well and roam happily through vales of manuscripts. This commentator is not a skilled paleographer; his Coptic had to be reviewed for the project. For Syriac, Armenian, and Ethiopic he has had to rely upon the work of others. The first full and critical text of *APl* has yet to appear in the handsome CCSA series produced by Brepols. Willy Rordorf, aided by others, will be its editor. Upon his labors, in so far as they are known to date, and those of

Preface

others, I am gratefully reliant. Here English readers will have, for the first time, a translation of all known parts of *APl*, as well as the first commentary upon that text.

In preparation for this project a number of papers were prepared and read to the Upper Midwest Region of the Society of Biblical Literature, a conference on the Centennial of Adolph Harnack's *Mission und Ausbreitung* (Berlin, 2010), The Studiorum Novi Testamenti Societas, the local and national Society of Biblical Literature, and the Minneapolis Area Patristics Society. Work on this ms. was completed in February 2012.

One of the benefits of working with the Christian Apocrypha is the immediate appreciation one has for laborers of earlier generations. The books of Carl Schmidt and Léon Vouaux have been at my side throughout this expedition. Other venerable patriarchs, as it were, include Theodor Zahn, Adolf v. Harnack, and M. R. James. Turning to the recent, I am particularly grateful to the late François Bovon, James Dunkly, Peter Dunn, Julian Hills, Michael Hollerich, Niklas Holzberg, Amy-Jill Levine, Dennis MacDonald, Judith Perkins, Mark Reasoner, Clare Rothschild, Willy Rordorf, and Phillip Sellew.

Note. Citations given under the author's surname or surname and one word only are to be found in the short titles' list following the abbreviations.

Each section of the text includes Comments, Notes, and a distinct bibliography. Comments provide a narrative overview. The notes are largely restricted to technical points, such as terms, and comments on the text. The latter seek to serve two purposes: to demonstrate the instability of the text and, more interestingly, to provide data for the history of *APl*'s reception.

Richard I. Pervo
Saint Paul, Minnesota

Abbreviations

AB	Anchor Bible
ABD	*The Anchor Bible Dictionary.* Ed. David Noel Freedman. 6 vols. New York: Doubleday, 1992. *ABD on CD-ROM.* Version 2.0c., 1995, 1996.
ABRL	The Anchor Bible Reference Library
AAndr	*Acts of Andrew*
ABarn	*Acts of Barnabas*
AJn	*Acts of John*
APl	*Acts of Paul*
APet	*Acts of Peter*
APhil	*Acts of Philip*
AThom	*Acts of Thomas*
ATit	*Acts of Titus*
ACW	Ancient Christian Writers
ANF	Ante-Nicene Fathers.
ANRW	*Aufstieg und Niedergang der römischen Welt.* Ed. Hildegard Temporini and Wolfgang Haase. Berlin: de Gruyter
ApocActs	The Apocryphal Acts of the Apostles
Barn.	*Epistle of Barnabas*
BDAG	Walter Bauer, *A Greek-English Lexicon of the New Testament and Other Early Christian Literature.* Ed. William F. Arndt and F. Wilbur Gingrich. 3rd ed. rev. by Frederick W. Danker. Chicago: University of Chicago Press, 2000.
BHT	Beiträge zur historischen Theologie
BIFCS	*The Book of Acts in Its First Century Setting.* Ed. Bruce W. Winter. 5 vols. Grand Rapids: Eerdmans, 1993–1996.
BIS	Biblical Interpretation Series
BJRL	*Bulletin of the John Rylands Library*
BR	*Biblical Research*
BZNW	Beihefte zur *ZNW*, Supplements to *ZNW*
c.	*circa, approximately*
CBQ	*Catholic Biblical Quarterly*
CBQMS	Catholic Biblical Quarterly Monograph Series
CCSA	Corpus Christianorum, Series Apocryphorum

Abbreviations

CCSL	Corpus Christianorum, Series latina
CD	Cairo (Genizah) text of the *Damascus Document*
CE	*Common era*
1, 2 Clem.	*First, Second Epistle of Clement,*

Clement of Alexandria
    Paed.   *Paedagogus*
    Protrep.   *Protrepticus*
    Strom.   *Stromata*

CSEL	Corpus Scriptorum Ecclesiasticorum Latinorum
DAC	*Dictionary of the Apostolic Church*
DBI	*Dictionary of Biblical Imagery*
DDD	*Dictionary of Deities and Demons in the Bible*. Ed. Karel van der Toorn et al. 2nd rev. ed. Leiden: Brill, 1999.
Did.	*Didache*
Diogn.	*Epistle to Diognetus*
EB	*Études bibliques*
ed(s).	editor, edition, or edited by
Ep.	*Epistle*
ERE	*Encyclopedia of Religion and Ethics*
esp.	especially
et al.	et alii, and others

Eusebius
    H.E.   *Ecclesiastical History*

frg(s).	fragment(s)
FRLANT	Forschungen zur Religion und Literatur des Alten und Neuen Testaments
FS	Festschrift
Gos. Jas.	*Gospel of James*
Gos. Pet.	*Gospel of Peter*
HDR	Harvard Dissertations in Religion
Hermas	*The Shepherd of Hermas*
Man.	*Mandates*
Sim.	*Similitudes*
Vis.	*Visions*

Hippolytus
    Ref.   *Refutatio Omnium Haeresium, Refutation of all Heresies*

HTR	*Harvard Theological Review*
HUT	Hermeneutische Untersuchungen zur Theologie
ibid.	ibidem, in the same place

Abbreviations

Ignatius
   Eph.   Letter to the Ephesians
   Magn.   Letter to the Magnesians
   Phld.   Letter to the Philadelphians
   Polyc.   Letter to Polycarp
   Rom.   Letter to the Romans
   Smyrn.   Letter to the Smyrneans
   Trall.   Letter to the Trallians

Irenaeus
   A. H.   Against the Heresies

JBL   Journal of Biblical Literature
JECS   Journal of Early Christian Studies
JFSR   Journal for the Feminist Study of Religion
JHC   Journal of Higher Criticism

Josephus
   Ant.   Antiquities of the Jews
   Ap.   Against Apion
   Bell.   The Jewish War
   Vit.   Life

JRS   Journal of Roman Studies
JSNT   Journal for the Study of the New Testament
JTS   Journal of Theological Studies

Justin   Justin Martyr
   1, 2 Apol.   First, Second Apology
   Dial.   Dialogue with Trypho

KAV   Kommentare zum Apostolischen Väter
LCC   Library of Christian Classics
LCL   Loeb Classical Library
lit.   literally
LNTS   Library of New Testament Studies
LSJ   Henry George Liddell, Robert Scott, and Henry Stuart Jones, eds. *Greek-English Lexicon*. 9th ed. Oxford: Clarendon, 1940. Reprint, 1966.
LTQ   Lexington Theological Quarterly
LXX   The Septuagint
m.   Mishna tractate
Mart. Perp.   Martyrdom of Perpetua
Mart. Polyc.   Martyrdom of Polycarp
NHC   Nag Hammadi Codex
NPF   Nicene and Post-Nicene Fathers

Abbreviations

NovTSup	Novum Testament Supplements
NRSV	New Revised Standard Version
N.S.	New Series
NTApoc	*New Testament Apocrypha*, ed. Wilhelm Schneemelcher
NTOA	Novum Testamentum et Orbis Antiquus
NTS	*New Testament Studies*
Od. Sol.	*Odes of Solomon*

Origen
    C. Cels.   *Against Celsus*
    Comm. In Ioh.   *Commentary on John*
    Hom. in Jer   *Homilies on Jeremiah*

OTP	James H. Charlesworth, ed. *Old Testament Pseudepigrapha*
par(r).	parallel(s)
PE	The Pastoral Epistles (1–2 Timothy, Titus)
PG	Migne, Patrologia Graeca
PNF	*Post-Nicene Fathers*

Polycarp
    Phil.   *Letter to the Philadelphians*

Ps. Clem.   Pseudo Clementine
    Hom   *Homilies*
    Rec.   *Recognitions*

PTS	Patristische Texte und Studien
RAC	*Reallexikon für Antike und Christentum*
RB	*Revue biblique*
SAAA	Studies on the Apocryphal Acts of the Apostles
SBL	Society of Biblical Literature
SBLDS	SBL Dissertation Series
SBLSP	SBL Seminar Papers
SBS	Stuttgarter Bibelstudien
SC	Sources chrétiennnes. Paris: Cerf, 1943–
SecCent	*Second Century*
SECA	Studies on Early Christian Apocrypha
Sem	*Semeia*
ST	*Studia Theologica*
StudDoc	Studies and Documents
StNT	Studien zum Neuen Testament
Syb. Or.	*Sybilline Oracles*

Tacitus
    Ann   *Annals of Imperial Rome*

Abbreviations

TDNT	*Theological Dictionary of the New Testamen*. Ed. G. Kittel and G. Friedrich. Trans. and ed. Geoffrey W. Bromiley. 10 vols. Grand Rapids: Eerdmans, 1964–1976.

Tertullian
    Adv. Marc.   *Against Marcion*
    Apol.   *Apology*
    De Bapt.   *On Baptism*
    De Res. Carn.   *On the Resurrection of the Flesh*

TextsS	Texts and Studies
trans.	translator, translation
TU	Texte und Untersuchungen zur Geschichte der altchristlichen Literatur
VC	*Vigiliae Christianae*
v. l.	*varia lectio*, variant reading
VT	*Vetus Testamentum*
WGRW	Writings from the Greco-Roman World
WGRWS	Writings from the Greco-Roman World Supplements
WUNT	Wissenschaftliche Untersuchungen zum Neuen Testament
ZBK	Zürcher Bibelkommentare
ZNW	*Zeitschrift für die neutestamentliche Wissenschaft*
ZWTh	*Zeitschrift für Wissenschaftliche Theologie*

Short Titles

Works often cited by shortened title, but not found in the particular bibliographies. Citation is by author's name alone, when possible.

Barrier. Barrier, Jeremy W., *The Acts of Paul and Thecla: A Critical Introduction and Commentary*. WUNT 270. Tübingen: Mohr/Siebeck, 2009.

Cherix. Cherix, Pierre, translator of Coptic in Rordorf.

Crum. Crum, W. E. *Coptic Dictionary*. Oxford: Clarendon, 1939.

Dunn. Dunn Peter, W. "The *Acts of Paul* and the Pauline Legacy in the Second Century." PhD diss., Queens College, Cambridge University, 1996.

Elliott. Elliot, James Keith, ed. *Apocryphal NewTestament*.

Abbreviations

Esch-Wermeling, *Thekla*. Esch-Wermeling, Elisabeth. *Thekla—Paulusschülerin wider Willen? Strategien der Leserlenkung in den Theklaakten*. Neutestamentliche Abhandlungen. Neue Folge 53. Münster: Aschendorff, 2008.

Hovhanessian. Hovhanessian, Vahan. *Third Corinthians: Reclaiming Paul for Christian Orthodoxy*. Studies in Biblical Literature 18. New York: Lang, 2000.

Kasser and Luiser. Kasser, Rodolphe, and Philippe Luisier. "Le Papyrus Bodmer XLI en Édition Princeps l'Épisode d'Èphèse des *Acta Pauli* en Copte et en Traduction." *Le Muséon* 117 (2004) 281–384.

Lampe. Lampe, G. W. H. *A Patristic Greek Lexicon*. Oxford: Clarendon, 1961.

Lipsius. Lipsius, Richard A., and Maximilien Bonnet, eds. *Acta Apostolorum Apocrypha*. 2 vols in 3. Leipzig: Mendelssohn, 1891–1903. Reprint, 1990.

Pervo, *Acts*. Pervo, Richard I. *Acts: A Commentary*. Ed. Harold W. Attridge. Hermeneia. Minneapolis: Fortress, 2009.

Pervo, *Dating*. Pervo, Richard I. *Dating Acts: Between the Evangelists and the Apologists*. Santa Rosa, CA: Polebridge, 2006.

Pervo, *Making*. Pervo, Richard I. *The Making of Paul: Constructions of the Apostle in Early Christianity*. Fortress, 2010.

Pervo, *Profit*. Pervo, Richard I. *Profit with Delight: The Literary Genre of the Acts of the Apostles*. Philadelphia: Fortress, 1987

Rordorf. Rordorf, Willy. "Actes de Paul." In F. Bovon and P. Geoltrain, eds. *Écrits apocryphes chrétiens*, 1:1115–77. Paris: Gallimard, 1997.

Schmidt, *Acta*. Schmidt, Carl. *Acti Pauli: Aus der heidelberger koptischen Papyrushandschrift nr. 1*. 2 vols. Leipzig: Hinrichs, 1905. Reprint, Hildesheim: Olms, 1965.

Schmidt and Schubart. Schmidt, Carl. *Praxeis;* with Wilhelm Schubart, *PRAXEIS PAULOU: Acta Pauli*, Glückstadt: Augustin, 1936.

Snyder. Snyder, Glenn E. "Remembering the *Acts of Paul*." PhD diss., Harvard University, 2010.

Vouaux. Vouaux, Léon, *Les Actes de Paul et ses letters apocryphes*. ANT. Paris: Letouzey, 1913.

Wright. Wright, William. *Apocryphal Acts of the Apostles: Edited from Syriac Manuscripts in the British Museum and Other Libraries*. 2 vols. London: Williams and Norgate, 1871.

The *Acts of Paul*

A Translation[1]

Chapter 1: Damascus

Witness: Textual basis: an unpublished Coptic fragment in the John Rylands Library (P. Ryl inv. 44); APL 9. P. Yale 87. Supplementary texts: APl 9, D-text of Acts 9, Gnostic *Apocalypse of Paul*, The *Epistle of Pelagia, Epistula Apostolorum* 32.

Version based upon Cherix (Rordorf, 1127) [*The glorified Christ is speaking to Paul]* "[...]...today...but now go to [Damascus. *After*]...leave that place and go to Jerusalem." Now when Paul had heard this, he went to Damascus in considerable [fear]. And when he was entered, he found them...[keep]ing...the fast...

Who will be sent away from those...of the sort that...violently, because the one who...treasures..._verso_ your mouth...holy ones...saved by which in Jesus...

Alternative translation: (Crum, "Manuscripts," 501) (Recto?)...today...but go now down to...and when (?) thou hast quitted that place, do thou go to Jerusalem. Now when Paul had heard this, he went to Damascus in great joy (?). And when he was entered in, he found them...ing...the fast... (Verso?) "...Lo (?), God will accept (?)...faith (?), for ye are...ye (have?) received it, it being (inherited) from your fathers; that ye might (not) remain therein as in an iniquitous city, but...the great treasure without (?)"...

---

1. A Note on the *sigla*. An ellipsis...marks a gap (lacuna) in the manuscript. These lacunae may be delineated by brackets [ ]. Proposed restorations are normally *italicized*. Most of these are logical or exemplary (i.e., "something to this effect"), and are the work of other scholars, in particular Schmidt, *Acta*, and Rordorf (et al.). Only controversial cases are discussed. Non-italicized restorations may be regarded as virtually certain. Brackets also mark the beginning and end of mss. Italicized portion of the translation identifies passages suspect as later additions.

The Acts of Paul

Chapter 2: Antioch on the Orontes (in Syria)

Witness: P Heid 1–6, renumbered by Cherix as pp. 9–13. Secondary witnesses: *Acts of Titus* 4; Nicetas of Paphlagonia 82r.

1. (p. 9) [. . .] but [. . .] he [*verb*] . . . He took [. . .] is Anchares [. . .] husband. Paul went into [*the house*] to the place where the [*corpse*] had been laid out. Now Phila [*the wife*] of Anchares was upset [. . .] She [*angrily*] told her husband, "My husband, you have gone off [*because of*] . . . this sorcerer, and you didn't [. . .] the wild beasts. You have not taken [. . .] your son [. . .] whence [. . .]?

(p. 10) [. . .] having [. . .] looked for something to eat [. . .] son placed on [. . .]." But [Paul] stood up in the presence of all. He prayed until the ninth hour, until the crowd came from the city and carried off the young boy. After Paul had prayed for a long time, he lives [. . .] and Jesus, the Messiah [. . .] the [*young*] boy [. . .] [. . .] the prayer [. . .] (p. 11) [. . .] crowd [. . .] eight days [. . .] Paul [. . .] and so that [. . .] this one, so that [*they*] might recall that he had raised the [*young*] man.

2. But after Paul had stayed [. . .] (p. 12) [. . .] seated [. . .] there [. . .] behind him, the people [. . .] sent for Anchares [. . .] they cried [. . .] "[*We*] believe, Anchares [. . .] but save the city." [. . .] Many people expressed these sentiments. [*Anchares*] said to them: "Judge if their [claims] [. . .] (p. 13) [. . .] can [. . .] but I testify [. . .] God [*who has*] son [. . .] salvation, and for me [. . .] [O] my [*brothers and sisters*] [*believe*] that there is no other God than [Jesus,] the Messiah, the Son of [the] Blessed one, to whom be the glory [*for ever,*] amen!"

3. But when they gathered that he would not return to them, they [*thereupon*] chased Paul, seized him and brought [him] back to the city for condemnation. They stoned him and expelled him from their city and their region. As Anchares would not return evil for evil, shut the door of [his house and remained] inside, with his wife [. . .] in fasting *and prayer* [. . .] and [. . . *when night*?] arrived, [*and Paul came*] to him, saying [. . .] the Messiah.

The Story of Thecla, APl 3–4[2]

Chapter 3

3.1–4 Paul Arrives at Iconium

3.1. On his journey to Iconium following his flight from Antioch Paul had as traveling companions Demas and Hermogenes the blacksmith. They fawned over him like devotees, but this was pure deceit. Paul, who attended only to the goodness brought by Christ, wouldn't do anything harmful to them. Rather, he showered them with affection, mellifluously expounding to them all the oracles of the Lord, of the birth and resurrection of the Beloved, and he narrated, point by point, the great deeds of Christ, as they had been revealed to him [*and that the Christ was of Davidic descent and born of Mary*].

2. When he learned that Paul was coming to Iconium, a man named Onesiphorus went out to meet him with his family: Lectra, his wife, and his sons Simmias and Zeno, with the intention of offering him hospitality. Now Titus had told him what Paul looked like, as Onesiphorus had not seen him in person but through spiritual insight.

3. He set out on the king's highway toward Lystra and found a place where he might welcome Paul, evaluating the travelers in accordance with Titus' description. Then he saw Paul coming, short, bald, bow-legged, healthy-looking, single-browed, a bit long-nosed, and bursting with beneficence. Sometimes he looked like a mortal; at other times he had the glowing countenance of an angel.

4. Paul smiled at the sight of Onesiphorus, who responded, "Greetings, servant of the blessed God."

"Grace be with you, and with your household."

This exchange exacerbated the jealousy of Demas and Hermogenes and intensified their deceit. Demas said to Onesiphorus: "Since you did not offer us such a greeting, do we not belong to the blessed one?"

"I don't see the result of proper behavior in you two," replied Onesiphorus, "but, if you are as you say, come in and refresh yourselves."

---

2. Numbers in parentheses ( ) represent the earlier single-chapter scheme for Thecla stories, now divided into chapters 3 and 4.

The Acts of Paul

3.5–6 The Inaugural Sermon.

5. Great joy erupted upon Paul's entrance into Onesiphorus' house. People knelt for prayer, bread was broken, and God's message about self-control and resurrection proclaimed. Paul said:

(1) Blessed are those with unadulterated hearts,
for they shall see God.

(2) Blessed are those who keep the flesh pure,
for they will be God's temple.

(3) Blessed are those with self-control,
for God will speak with them.

(4) Blessed are those who have kissed the world goodbye,
for they will be pleasing to God.

(5) Blessed are those who have wives
but do not have sexual relations with them,
for they will be heirs of God.

(6) Blessed are those who revere God,
for they will become God's angels.

(7) Blessed are those who hold God's oracles in awe,
for they will be consoled.

(8) Blessed are those who have received the wisdom of Jesus Christ,
for they will be called the children of the most high.

(9) Blessed are those who have kept their baptismal vows,
for they will find rest with the father and the son.

(10) Blessed are those who have opened themselves
up to an understanding of Jesus Christ,
for they will be in light.

(11) Blessed are those who, because of their love for God,
have left the fashions of this world behind them,
for they will judge angels and be rewarded
with a place at the father's right hand.

(12) Blessed are the merciful,
for they will obtain mercy and not gaze upon judgment's bitter day.

(13) Blessed are the bodies of virgins,
for they will please God
and not lose the reward for their chastity.

for the father's word will become saving action
>for them on the day of his son and they shall enjoy eternal rest.

3.7 Meet the Heroine

7. While Paul was delivering this message to the church in Onesiphorus' house, one Thecla, the virgin daughter of Theocleia, who was engaged to Thamyris, was seated at the window of her house that was closest to Onesiphorus,' listening without respite to Paul's message about chastity. Thecla did not turn away from the window but progressed in the faith with abundant happiness. Indeed, as she watched any number of women and girls arriving to see Paul, she began to desire that she too might be deemed worthy to hear the message about Christ in Paul's presence, as she had not yet glimpsed his features but only heard his message.

3.8–10 Thecla's Mother Enlists the Fiancé's aid.

8. Since Thecla would not leave the window, her mother sent for Thamyris, who was most pleased to come, thinking that he was about to get a wife.

"Where's my Thecla? [I want to see her]," he asked Theocleia.

"I've got some strange news for you, Thamyris. She hasn't left her window for three days and three nights, nor has she taken a drop or tasted a bite. She is intoxicated by the sight of a stranger and his wily and enticing discourse. I am amazed that such a modest girl can put up with all this."

9. "Thamyris, this fellow is agitating Iconium, specifically your Thecla. All the women and young people are coming to him for instruction. 'You must,' he says, 'revere the one and only god and live chastely.' And here is my daughter, in the grip of a novel lust and frightening emotions, trapped in her window by the web of his message. All her attention is fixed upon his utterances. She has been swept away. Look, she's your fiancée. You go and talk to her."

10. Thamyris, approached Thecla caught between his attraction for her and fear of her unbalanced state. He said, "Thecla, dear fiancée, why are you sitting like this? What kind of feeling has got you so wrought up? Behave yourself! Come back to your Thamyris!" Her mother chimed in with similar statements, such as, "My child, why are you sitting that way, downcast, without a word, as if you were catatonic?"

Everyone wept bitterly: Thamyris because he was losing a wife, Theocleia her child, the slaves a mistress. The house was disrupted by sorrow. Nonetheless, Thecla did not budge an inch but remained riveted on Paul's message.

3.11–14 Thamyris Seeks and Finds a Way to Stymie Paul

11. Thamyris jumped up and ran out into the street, where he could take careful note of whoever was going to see Paul or leaving. He saw two men engaged in a bitter argument. "Tell me who you are, gentlemen," he asked, "and who is this fellow with you inside, the one who leads young men astray and deceives young women, so that they do not marry but stay single? I, who am one of the leading men of this city, can promise you a good deal of money if you tell me about him."

12. "We don't know who this fellow is," Demas and Hermogenes replied, "but he would deprive young men of wives and young women of husbands, saying, 'You will possess no resurrection if you do not remain chaste and do not defile the flesh but keep it chaste.'"

13. Thamyris said to them, "Gentlemen. Come to my place and accept my hospitality. They went and found a splendid banquet, with abundant wine, conspicuous extravagance, and a brilliant table. Thamyris plied them with drink because of his fondness for Thecla and his desire to gain her hand in marriage. As the meal wore on he said, "Gentlemen, tell me what he teaches, so that I too may know it. I'm all torn up about Thecla, for she is quite swept away by the stranger, leaving me without a bride."

14. "Present him before Governor Castellius on the grounds that he is trying to entice the public to embrace the alien doctrine of the Christians," they advised. "By that means you will do away with him and have Thecla to be your wife. Further, we shall teach that what he calls 'resurrection' has already taken place through the children we have."

3.15–17 The Arrest and Trial of Paul

15. Thus informed by them, Thamyris, brim-full of jealousy and rage, arose early and went to Onesiphorus' house, accompanied by magistrates, public servants, and a mob armed with clubs, and addressed Paul: "You have corrupted Iconium, specifically my intended, so that she won't have me. Let us proceed to Governor Castellius."

The mob howled: "Away with this magician! He has corrupted all of our women!"

The public found this persuasive.

16. Thamyris stood before the bench and loudly declaimed: "Proconsul, this man, whose origins we do not know, does not allow young women to marry. Let him explain why he teaches thus." Demas and Hermogenes urged Thamyris: "Say that he is a Christian. That way you will take care of him."

Unswayed by the mob, the governor summoned Paul to the bench and said: "Who are you and what is it that you are teaching? These are grave charges."

17. Paul spoke loudly, "If, proconsul, I am being examined today regarding my teaching, listen. The living God, the avenging God, the jealous God, the God who requires nothing yet needs that humanity be saved has sent me to draw people away from corruption, impurity, every pleasure, and death, so that they may cease erring. Therefore God sent his son, who alone has compassion for a world gone astray, whom I proclaim and in whom I teach that people should locate their hope, so that they may not be subject to condemnation but rather have confidence in and reverence for God, as well as intimacy with majesty and passion for truth. So if I teach matters revealed to me by God, what law am I breaking, Proconsul?"

The governor then ordered that Paul be secured and held in custody until he might have the opportunity for a more thorough hearing.

3.18–19 *Thecla Escapes and Expresses Her Love*

18. That night Thecla took off her bracelets, gave them to the porter, and, once the door had been opened for her, went to the prison, where, after rewarding the jailer with a silver mirror, she went to Paul and sat at his feet to hear him speak of God's great deeds. Paul exhibited no fear but conducted himself with a boldness that came from God. With growing faith Thecla kept kissing Paul's shackles.

19. Thecla's household and Thamyris were looking for Thecla. Presuming her lost, they sought her frantically in the streets. One of the porter's fellow slaves reported that she had gone out at night. They thus interrogated the porter, who stated that she had gone to see the foreigner in jail. There they went and found matters as he had reported. Thecla was held in the bonds, so to speak, of affection. They left to stir up the mob and alert the governor to what had happened.

The Acts of Paul

3.20 Trial of Paul and of Thecla

20. The governor directed that Paul be conducted to the bench. [*After he had been removed from the prison*] Thecla rolled about on the spot where Paul had sat teaching in jail. The governor additionally directed that she, too, be brought before the bench. She went jumping with joy. The return of Paul to court stimulated the mob to continue shouting more vehemently: "He's a wizard! Away with him!" For his part the governor listened with pleasure as Paul spoke of Christ's holy deeds. After consulting with his staff he summoned Thecla and asked her: "Why do you not marry Thamyris in accordance with Iconian law?" She did not respond but stood there, her gaze locked on Paul. At this her mother Theocleia shrieked: "Burn this outlaw! Burn this enemy of matrimony in the middle of the theater, so that all the women who have been instructed by this fellow might learn some respect!"

3.21–22 Thecla faces immolation in the theater

21. Strongly moved, the governor had Paul flogged and expelled from the city. As for Thecla, he condemned her to be burned. He arose and proceeded directly to the theater. The entire mob also headed for the violent spectacle. Thecla kept looking for Paul, as a lamb in the wild looks for the shepherd. Glancing about the crowd she saw the Lord, looking like Paul, seated there. "Paul has come to watch over me, as if I could not otherwise endure this." She continued to hold her eyes fast upon him, but he went up into heaven.

22. The young boys and girls carried in logs and straw with which to burn Thecla. When she was brought in naked the governor wept, amazed at the force within her. The executioners arranged the wood and directed her to mount the pyre. After making the sign of the cross she mounted the wood, which they ignited. Although a great blaze broke out, the fire did not touch her, for God out of compassion had set off a subterranean rumble. A cloud full of rain and hail overshadowed the place and discharged its contents, bringing fatal danger to many, but it quenched the fire and rescued Thecla.

3.23–26 Reunion

23. Meanwhile, Paul and the Onesiphorus family were fasting in an unsealed tomb on the road *outside of* Iconium. As day after day passed foodless, the children said to Paul: "We're hungry." They lacked the wherewithal to purchase food as Onesiphorus had abandoned worldly affairs and followed

Paul with his entire family. Paul took off his coat and said, "Go, my child, buy a substantial amount of bread and bring it here." While the son was shopping, he saw, to his astonishment, his neighbor Thecla. "Thecla, where are you going?" he asked.

"Since my delivery from the fire I've been looking for Paul."

"Come, I'll take you to him. He has been distraught with worry about you, praying and fasting for six days now."

24. At the tomb she came upon Paul praying on bended knee, "Father of Christ, let not the fire touch Thecla, but be with her, for she is yours."

Standing behind him, she exclaimed, "Father, the maker of heaven and earth, the father of your beloved son Jesus Christ, I praise you because you have delivered me from fire so that I might see Paul."

Paul arose, saw her and prayed, "God, to whom all hearts are open, the father of our lord Jesus Christ, I praise because you heard me and hastened [to do] what I asked."

25. Love abounded in the tomb. Paul rejoiced, as did Onesiphorus and everyone else. They had five loaves, vegetables, and water and were celebrating the holy deeds of Christ, when Thecla said to Paul: "I shall cut off my hair and follow you wherever you go."

He replied, "The times are so ugly and you are so pretty. Another trial, worse than the first, may overtake you, a trial that you will not be able to withstand but be conquered by fear."

"Just give me the seal in Christ," she countered, "and no adversity will touch me."

"Be patient, Thecla. You will receive the water."

26. Paul sent the Onesiphorus family back to Iconium.

Chapter 4

4.1–2 Thecla Confronts Alexander

1 (26b). Taking Thecla, Paul traveled to Antioch. Just as they were entering the city the head of the Syrian chapter of the Empire League named Alexander saw Thecla and became passionately enamored of her. He plied Paul with offers of money and gifts, but Paul said, "I do not know the woman about whom you speak; she is definitely not mine." Alexander, with his considerable strength, embraced her in the middle of the street. She would not put up with this but kept on looking for Paul. She cried out, sharply,

The Acts of Paul

"Don't assault a visitor; don't assault God's slave. I am a prominent citizen of Iconium, from which I was expelled because I was unwilling to marry Thamyris."

She grabbed Alexander, tore his cloak, knocked the crown from his head and turned him into an object of derision.

2 (27). Both desiring her and ashamed at what had happened to him, Alexander arraigned Thecla before the governor. When she admitted what she had done he condemned her to the beasts, since Alexander was going to provide games. This astonished the women, who shouted, in the presence of the court: "Wicked judgment! Impious judgment!" Thecla asked the governor that she might remain a virgin until her encounter with the beasts. So a wealthy woman of royal lineage named Tryphaena, whose daughter had died, took her into protective custody, viewing Thecla as a consolation.

4.3–4 Thecla Paraded in Public

[(3) 28. For the opening parade of the animals Thecla was bound to a fierce lioness. *Queen Tryphaena followed her. The lioness kept licking the feet of Thecla who was seated atop her. The crowd marveled at this. The charge inscribed on a sign was,* "Thecla, the sacrilegious violator of the gods, who dashed the imperial crown from the head of Alexander." In contrast, the women and children began to shout once more: "O God, an impious judgment is being carried out in this city!"

[[*Tryphaena then took her back home after the procession, for her late daughter Falconilla had told her in a dream,* "Mother, take this abandoned stranger Thecla in place of me, so that she may pray for me and I may be translated to the place of the righteous."]]

(4) 29. When Tryphaena took Thecla back to her home after the procession, she felt grief because of the next day's combat with the animals and deep affection for her like that for her daughter Falconilla, asking her, "My second child Thecla, please pray for my child, so that she might live forever. For I saw this in my dreams."

Thecla immediately raised her voice: "Heavenly God, son of the most high, give her what she wants: that her daughter Falconilla live for ever."

After these words Tryphaena grieved as she considered that such beauty was going to be tossed to beasts.]

4.5–6 Thecla to the Arena

5 (30). *In the morning Alexander (who was the sponsor of the hunt) arrived to take Thecla, announcing,* "The governor has taken his seat and the crowd is growing restive at our failure to get the show on the road. Give me the one condemned to the beasts so that I might take her away."

But Tryphaena routed him, shouting, "My household is experiencing fresh mourning for my Falconilla, and there is no one to help, not a child—she is dead, nor any relative. I am a widow! God of Thecla, my child, help her."

6 (31). The governor dispatched soldiers to convey Thecla, but Tryphaena did not leave her, but personally took her by the hand and escorted her, with these words: "I escorted my daughter Falconilla to the grave; you, Thecla, I am escorting into battle with wild beasts."

Thecla wept with bitter groans to the Lord: "Lord God, in whom I believe, to whom I have fled for refuge, who delivered me from fire, reward Tryphaena, who has taken pity upon your slave, because she kept me chaste."

4.7–10 Baptism

7 (32). *When they arrived* the place was in an uproar, with bellowing creatures and competing calls for action from the People and the women. The latter sat together. The former shouted, "Bring in the defiler of the sacred," while the women rejoined: "Down with the city for this lawlessness. Kill us all, governor! A wretched spectacle! A wicked judgment!"

8 (33). Thecla was taken from Tryphaena, stripped [given a sash], and thrust into the arena. Lions and bears were set upon her. A savage lioness ran up and up but lay down at her feet. The crowd of women let loose a loud shout. A bear dashed up against her, but the lion ran toward the bear, encountered it, and ripped it to shreds. Now another lion, one that had been provided by Alexander and had been schooled to attack people, rushed toward her. Lioness grappled with lion. Both died. The women redoubled their laments now that the lioness that had helped Thecla was no more.

(9) 34. While Thecla stood praying with outstretched arms, they launched numerous beasts at her. Her prayer finished, she turned and saw a large pit filled with water. "This is my opportunity to wash," [*throwing herself into the water with these words: "In the name of Jesus Christ I am baptized on my last day."*]

The women spectators—as well as the whole crowd—shouted, "Don't jump into the water!" Even the governor was reduced to tears at the thought that such beauty would become a meal for seals. She threw herself into the water in the name of Jesus Christ. The seals floated dead upon it after seeing a flash of fiery lightning. A fiery cloud surrounded her, preventing the beasts from touching her and shielding her nudity from sight.

(10) 35. When additional, more fearful beasts were loosed, the women raised a piercing lament. Some threw flower petals, others nard, others cassia, still others amomum. The resultant abundance of aromas reduced all of the attacking animals to unconsciousness. They did not touch her.

Whereupon Alexander said to the governor, "I have some very scary bulls. Let's tie the condemned to them."

The governor gave his unhappy consent: "Do what you want."

So they tied her by the feet between two bulls and applied red-hot irons to their genitals so that, greatly provoked, they would kill her. The bulls were galvanized, but the scorching flame had burnt through the ropes, leaving Thecla effectively unbound.

4.11–14 Vindication

11 (36). At this Tryphaena, who was standing near the field, by the facing around the gate, collapsed, leading her servants to cry: "Queen Tryphaena is dead!"

The governor called a halt to the games; the whole town was in a tizzy. Alexander prostrated himself before the governor and said: "Have mercy on me and upon the city. Release the condemned woman, so that the city will not perish as well. If the Emperor learns about this he may well destroy the city along with us, since Queen Tryphaena, his relative, died at the gate."

12 (37). The governor summoned Thecla from the menagerie and asked: "Who are you? What powers are associated with you that not a single animal touched you?"

"I am a slave of the living God. As for my powers, I have come to believe in God's son, in whom God is well pleased, because of whom none of the animals touched me. He is the sole definition of salvation and the basis of immortal existence, a refuge for the storm-tossed, relief for the oppressed, a haven for the desperate, and, in sum, any who do not believe in God's son will not live but die forever."

13 (38). At this the governor directed that clothing be brought and told her: "Put on these clothes."

"The one who clothed me while I was naked among the beasts will clothe me with salvation on the day of judgment," she rejoined. Thecla then took the clothes and put them on. The governor thereupon issued a decree: "I release to you Thecla, the reverent slave of God." All the women shouted unison praise to God loud enough to make the whole city shake: "There is one God, who saved Thecla."

14 (39). When she had been apprised of the welcome decision, Tryphaena met Thecla with a large entourage, embraced her, and exclaimed: "Now I believe that the dead arise! Now I believe that my child lives! Come in; I shall convey all of my property over to you." So Thecla went with her into her house, where she rested for eight days, instructing her in the word of God, with the result that most of her female staff also became believers. Joy abounded in her household.

4.15–16 Reunion with Paul

15 (40). Thecla continued to long for Paul and kept trying to find him. She sent out inquiries in every direction and was advised that he was in Myra. Collecting some young people of both sexes, and belting herself into a coat that she had sewn into a man-styled garment, she set out for Myra, where she found Paul engaged in proclaiming God's message. When she approached him he was amazed to see her—and her entourage. When she perceived that he thought that some new trial had come upon her, she said: "I have received the bath, Paul. For the one who has worked with you for the gospel has also worked with me for the washing."

16 (41) Taking Thecla by the hand Paul led her to Hermias' house, where she told him everything. He was quite amazed, while the other auditors found their faith strengthened and offered prayers for Tryphaena. Thecla arose and announced to Paul: "I shall go to Iconium."

"Go and teach God's message," he replied.

Tryphaena sent her a large amount of clothing and gold. She left these things to Paul for the care of the poor.

The Acts of Paul

4.17–18 Wrapping up Thecla

17 (42) Thecla went on to Iconium, entered Onesiphorus' house and knelt down on the floor where Paul had sat teaching the oracles of God. In tears she exclaimed:

"My God, and God of this house, where the light illumined me,
Jesus Christ, the son of God,
> my deliverance in prison,
> my deliverance with governors,
> my deliverance from the fire,
> my deliverance from wild animals,
> you indeed are God.
> To you be glory for ever. Amen."

(18) 43. She learned that Thamyris was dead, but her mother still alive. Summoning the latter, she said: "Theocleia, mother dear. Can you believe that the Lord lives in heaven? If you desire possessions, the Lord will give them to you, on my behalf. If a child, look: here I am!"

Following this exhortation she went to Seleucia, where, after enlightening many with God's word, she enjoyed a noble death.

Chapter 5

Primary source: P.Heid; pp. 35–39/49–61; secondary sources: Ephrem Syrus (probably), the *Acts of* Titus (see the note), and possibly the *Acts of Barnabas*. (See the note on the latter.)

5.1 Hermippus Healed

When He Had Left Antioch and Was Teaching in Myra

(p. 38) 1. While Paul [*was proclaiming*] the word of God at Myra, a man named Hermocrates, who suffered from edema, stood in the presence of all and said to Paul: "Nothing is impossible for God, especially for the god whom you proclaim. Ever since the arrival of the one whom you serve, many have been healed. Now we cast ourselves at your feet, I, my wife, and my children. (p. 39) [*Have mercy on me*] so that I also may believe, as you have come to believe, in the living God."

[*Paul*] said to him, "I shall give you [. . .] without charge, but [*by the name*] of Jesus the Messiah you will be [*healed in*] the presence of all these

The Acts of Paul

persons." [...] As he pressed his hand downward [...], a huge amount of water gushed [*out of him* ...], he collapsed like [...] so that some said, "It would have been better for him to have died rather than suffer so." But when Paul had quieted the crowd, he [*took*] Hermocrates by the hand, lifted him, and asked, "Hermocrates, [*what*] do you want?"

"I want to eat."

Paul took some bread and gave it to him to eat. Hermocrates was healed at that moment. Together with his wife he received the grace of the seal in the Lord.

5.2–3 The Wrath of Hermippus

2. His son Hermippus, however, was angry with Paul and was alert for the opportunity to spring into action with his peers (p. 40) to do away with Paul. He had not wanted his father to be restored, but to die so that he could quickly get control of his estate. The younger son, Dion, on the other hand, heard Paul gladly.

So those allied with Dion's brother plotted to [*start a fight*] with Paul, with the intention that [*Hermippus*] [...] and try to kill him. He fell and ... Hermippus gave Dion to drink [...] Hermocrates [*loved*] Dion more. [He was] seated at Paul's feet [...] unaware that Dion was dead.

3. At the death of Dion his mother Nympha tore her dress and went to Paul. She took a place next to her husband and Paul. Concerned at her arrival, Paul said, "What is it, Nympha?"

"Dion is dead." The whole crowd wept at the sight of her. Paul looked at the distraught crowd and dispatched some youths, with these words: "Go and bring him here to me." They set out, but Hermippus [seized] the body en route and shouted, "[...]

(A leaf is missing, with two pages of text. Paul revived the dead Dion.)

5.4 Paul's Arrest and Miraculous Vindication. The Punishment of Hermippus.

4. (p. 43) [...] he [...] the word to [him].

Now a messenger of the Lord had said to him that night, "Paul, [...] this day there will be a great assault against your body, but God, [the father of] his son Jesus, the Messiah, [...]" When Paul awoke he went to the believers, but remained downstairs (?) while asking, "What is this [*vision*]?" While he was so occupied he saw Hermippus approaching with a sword in

The Acts of Paul

his hand, accompanied by young men armed with clubs. Paul [*said to them*] "I am [*not*]a robber; no murderer am I. The God of the universe, [the father] of Christ, will turn aside your arms, put your sword back in its sheath, and transform your strength into weakness. For I am a slave of God, alone and a stranger, small and meaningless among the polytheists. But you, O God, look down upon their plots and do not let them annihilate me."

(p. 44) [...] Hermippus [...] his sword [...] upon Paul [...] [but] he became [*blind*], and [*cried out*] "[ ] [*my*] friends do not forget [...] Hermippus! I have [*pursued*] Paul; I have persecuted [*innocent*] blood. Learn, you people, whether you are dull or perceptive: the world is nothing. Money is nothing. All possessions are nothing. I once overindulged myself with all manner of goods; now I am a beggar. I implore all of you: Hear me out, my friends and all residents of Myra. I mocked a man [*who has*] [*healed*] my father, I have [*reviled*] [...] a man who revived my brother [...] a man who did me no injury. But, ask him! The one who saved my father and revived my [*brother*] will have the power to save me also." Paul stood weeping, mindful of God, since God had heard him so quickly, mindful also of the people, because pride had been corrected. He turned and went (p. 45) [*to Hermocrates' house?*]

5.5–6 *The Family Is Restored and the Mission Concludes*

5. [...] And the sons [...] feet. They carried Hermippus [...] to the place where Paul [...] They left him at the door of [...] the house. When they were [...], a large crowd was proceeding [...], another [*crowd*] to see the blinded [*Hermippus*]. For his part he would entreat everyone who entered to intercede for him. Now [*when those who entered saw Hermocrates and*] Nympha rejoicing [*at*] the revival of Dion and bringing in food for his wellbeing and money for the widows, they saw their son Hermippus, looking like the second [...] He touched the feet of all, including those of his parents, and implored them, like a stranger, for healing. His parents were astonished by this and lamented to all who entered. [*Some of the latter*], however, asked, "Why are they weeping?" [...]

Hermocrates (p. 46) set out [and] blessed the goods; he then took them and distributed them. Thereafter [...] Hermocrates was upset [...], primarily because they had eaten their fill, "[...] and so let's leave the [food] [...], and let us attend to [...] Hermocrates [...] Nympha [...] much [...] upset [...] he has [...] because [...] Hermocrates [...] to the [...] so that

The Acts of Paul

[...] Hermippus may see and stop [...] and fighting against Christ and [...] But they, with Paul, have [*sinned*] against God. "

Once he had regained his sight Hermippus turned to his mother and said, "Paul came and laid a hand on my hand while I was weeping. From that moment I could see everything clearly." Nympha took him by the hand and led him inside into the presence of the widows and of Paul. As Paul wept bitterly, Hermippus [...] said, "Whoever [believes] ... "

6. (p. 49) [...] a word [...] in the manner [...] [*for the church*], in [*the peace of God*] Amen. [*Paul, together with*] the believers who [*were with him in*] Myra, left for [*Sidon*].

Chapter 6: Sidon

Primary source: P.Heid; pp. 35–39/49–61; secondary sources: Ephrem Syrus (probably), the *Acts of* Titus (see the note), and possibly the *Acts of Barnabas*. (See the note on the latter.)

After leaving Myra, [Paul Goes to Sidon]

1. [*Paul*], after[*leaving Myra*] went to[*Sidon*]. Great distress beset the believers in [Cilicia] and Pamphylia, because they longed for his message and his holy Christ-given grace. Some couples from Perga [*followed*] Paul: Thrasymmachus and Aline, as well as Cleon and Chrysa. In the course of the journey they fed Paul. While they were sharing bread [*beneath*] a tree, as they were about to say "amen," there came *(p. 50)* [...] the believers [...] to partake of it, were [...] on them [...] images [...] [*eternal*] become [...] [*the*] table of demons [...] for that reason s/he dies. [*But whoever*] [...] believes in Jesus Christ[*the one who has cleansed us from*] all stains, [*from*] all impurities[*and from*] all wicked [*thoughts*] shall eat[*of it*] [...] they have approached [*the table*] in an impure state [...] images [...] stand upright [...] tutelary [*images*].

2. An elderly man [...] stood up among them and [said] to them "Men, [*wait*] a little while to see what happens to the priest who approaches our god. Now when our fellow citizen Charinos had listened to this and attacked the gods, he died, along with his [...]. Thereafter Xanthos also died, as did Chrysa and [...] died of dropsy, [*with*] his wife

3. [...] *(p. 55)* like a stranger [...]

17

The Acts of Paul

4. [unknown speaker] "Why do you presume to undertake actions that are unacceptable? Have you—yes, you—really not heard what happened when God wrought [judgment] upon Sodom and Gomorra, because [*they had*] seized [*others*], including (?) strangers and women [. . .] God [had no pity on them], but cast them down into the underworld. Now, however, we are not people of the [sort] that you say or think; we are proclaimers of the living God and his [*well-beloved.*] [*And*] never be able to [accomplish] evil. For this matter, [. . .] those who bear witness for [*him*] . . . "

5. They did not listen to him, but they [*were seized*] and cast into the [*temple of*] Apollo to be secured until [. . .], so that the [*whole*] city might gather. They were given large amounts of expensive food, but Paul, fasting for the third day, was exhausted after preaching all night. Falling prostrate, he prayed, "God, take note of their threats, do not let us stumble and permit not our enemies to lay us low *(p. 56)*, but deliver us and bring down your justice quickly upon us." Just after Paul, with the believers Thrasymmachus and Cleon, had thrown himself to the ground, the temple collapsed. He [. . .] so that the guards [*informed*] the magistrates, who were [. . .] some others among them in [. . .] fell on the ground [. . .] fell to the ground [. . .] turned [. . .] in the midst of the two [parts] [. . .]. They [*entered*] [*to see what had*] happened [*and*] marveled [that] [. . .] in their [. . .] and that they [. . .][were] rejoicing [at the collapse] [. . .]. They cried out: "Truly the [. . .] people of a mighty god!" They left and proclaimed throughout the city: "Apollo, the god of the Sidonians, has fallen, together with half of his temple." All the residents dashed toward the temple and saw Paul and his colleagues weeping at this trial, which would make them a spectacle for all. The mob shouted, "Bring them to the theater." The magistrates came to fetch them. And they groaned bitterly in their hearts. [. . .]

6. *(p. 61)* [. . .] from my hand. Remember [. . .] Do not ask [. . .] They cannot do such things [. . .] The behavior of Christ [. . .] not in faith [. . .] and that you [. . .] as for you [. . .] long-suffering [. . .] of the Egyptians [. . .] of the hail [. . .] the crowd [. . .] followed Paul [*saying*] "Blessed be the god [. . .] who has sent Paul [. . .] so that we are not [. . .] [of] death." Theudes [. . .] begged Paul [. . .] he grasped his feet [. . .] for the seal in the lord. [. . .] *[He]* commanded them to go to Tyre. [. . .], Before they [. . .] [*They*] put Paul [*aboard a ship*] with [*them*].

Chapter 7: Tyre

Primary source: P. Heid, p. 40/62; secondary: The *Acts of Titus* 3.

The Acts of Paul

After leaving Sidon, Paul resolved to set out for Tyre

7.1 Arrival and Exorcism

1. *(p. 62)* Following [the arrival] of Paul [at Tyre, a] crowd of Jews [approached] him. The latter [...] and they heard the [...] The [...] were astonished [...] that Amphion [...] [saying] "Chrysippus [...] demons with [*him*] [...] numerous [wonders] [...]" As Paul [...], saying, [...] God. And no one [...] with Amphion. They have [...] through the demon [...] So no one has [...], saying to him: "Save [me] [...] of the dead." While the crowd [...] the demon also appeared [...] in the [...] and immediately the demons [...] So the crowd [...] of God, they glorified the one who had [...] for the benefit of Paul. One person had a [son] who had never had the ability to speak.

Chapter 8: Jerusalem (to Smyrna)

Primary sources: P Heid, pp. 67–82 (Cherix); secondary: *Acts of Titus*, Nicetas of Paphlagonia, *Life of Polycarp* (?)

1. *(p. 67)* [...] to my house [...] in the [...] of Cilicia [...] so that [...] to them, so you say [...] to proclaim the savior [...] the son of God [...] look [...]

2. *(p. 68)* [...] in [...] he who is [...] who is [...] be [...] numerous [...] large [...] these [...] of Cilicia [...] in order to place [...] for which I run [...] Moses [...] with me [...] move forward [...] move forward [...]after [*he*] [...]

3. *(p. 69)* [...] For what we are saying has already been realized [...] look, we shall bring you to this place [...] so that [...] for you, for hearing [...] your [holy] thoughts [...] fulfilled [...] outside of . . .

4. *(p. 70)* [...] to God whose will has been fulfilled [...] by him. [*In this*] manner [...] the father [...] Jesus the [Christ] [...] outside of [...]

5. *(p. 73)* [...] You are face to face with Jerusalem [...]. As for me, I trust in the Lord [...] in truth [...] so that you [e.g., *turn*]. to him, to him who has [...]

The Acts of Paul

6. *(p. 74)* [...] [He who was crucified,] on whom the [blame] [...] afflicted [...] chosen because [...] he who has [...] our flesh [...]

7. *(p. 75)* [...] outside of [...] Paul [...] Paul [...] of the person [...] Cleanthes [...] the law [...] that which is called [...] way, haven't we followed him *[in]* all the cities? And after they [...] he turned to [...] to this [...] ancestors. And he [...] exists [...] nothing [...] words of this type, nor does he preach [...] as you preach [...] O Paul, so that you won't [...]

8. *(p. 76)* [...] Christ [...] hidden [...] who has [...] [but] [...] that I may go [...] who have [...] with [...] by him. But were water [...] being thirsty [...] so that they might not be [...] among the wild beasts [...] out of the ground, but so that they may not be burned by the fire. They have begotten these works for the age which [...] The one who was a persecutor.

9. I *(p. 77)* [...] [...] to him [...] great glory [...] to you [...] what I have taught [...] nor [...] he will come [...] [...] in [...] Israel [...] necessity [...] he has not [...] [...] much [...] [...] outside of [...] But he [...] a freedom [...] and, having placed [...] with the yoke [...] all flesh [...] [...] those who [...] of whoever confesses [...] he is the Christ who is the glory of the father [...]

10. *(p. 78)* [...] [...] we [...] in Syria [...] in Cyrenaica [...] to ruin them [...] in [...] in [...] you [...] because [...] [...] Moses [...] [...] I die [...] an abomination [...] Again, I tell you [...] I am the one who does [...] me [...] [...] because the person will be justified [...] but because he will be justified [... the] deeds of righteousness and he [...]

11. *(p. 81)* [...] *[the]* Christ. [...] all of you. The [...] to them. This [...] exists for him [...] Paul, he who has [...] while they take [...]. The day when [...] to persecute/pursue the apostles who are with me outside of Jerusalem. I have [...] I have comfort and we [...] They are content [...] The message according [...] I have fallen [...] in numerous troubles [...] [I have submitted] to the Torah, as [...] you. Now [...] night and day in my [struggles] [...] Christ. While I [...] a lamb [...] of his [...] He opposes the [...] He abuses [...] *(p. 82)* Paul ... shepherds [...] concerning/over [...] by Paul [...] because of the search [...] concerning Peter [...]. He cried out "[...] God is one, there is no [other god] than He. Christ is also one [...] his son [as] we have [...], he whom you have [...] proclaimed [...] he whom we have crucified, he whom the [...] views with great [...] Now you yourselves say [that] [...] he is God. And the [...] he the judge [of] the living and [the

The Acts of Paul

dead] [. . .], king of [. . .], while you [. . .] of his [. . .], the person [. . .] about [. . .] thus as I say [. . .] in the manner that [. . .]

Chapter 9: Ephesus

Primary sources: P Hamb (Greek); P Bod (Coptic); secondary sources: "Hippolytus," *Commentary on Daniel*, *Acts of Titus*, Commodian, *Carmen Apologeticum*, Jerome, Nicephoras Callistus, the *Letter of Pelagia*.

I. 1–10. Pastoral and Missionary Activity in Ephesus.

1. When he had finished speaking, Paul left Smyrna for Ephesus. He went into the house of Aquila and Priscilla, where he was happy to see the believers whom he most happily loved. They also rejoiced that they had been deemed worthy for Paul to set foot within their house. Joy and gladness abounded.

2. They devoted the night to a prayer vigil, seeking, with gladness and unanimity, discernment in complete assurance. The angel of the lord came into Aquila's house and stood in the sight of everyone. The angel spoke with Paul to the discomfiture of all, for, although he was seen by everyone, they could not hear what he was saying to Paul.

3. After the angel had ceased speaking with Paul in tongues, the onlookers, filled with fear and trembling, kept silent. Paul looked at the believers and said: "Brothers and sisters, the angel of the lord has come to me, visible to all of you, and said: 'A great fire will descend on you during Eastertide [. . .] but take [*courage*], because many distresses are coming from the Evil One. [*But*] trust in the God Jesus Christ and hand over everything to him. Give him all (your) anxiety and your every deed and he will sustain you.'"

4. But Paul could not be unhappy, on account of Eastertide, as it is a festival for those who have come to believe in Christ, catechumens no less than (full) believers. Great joy and abundant love prevailed, accompanied by songs and praises addressed to Christ, all of which strengthened those who heard.

5. Paul said: "My brothers and sisters, listen to what happened to me, when I was in Damascus, when I persecuted the faith in God, when mercy struck me, mercy from the father who proclaimed the message of his son to me, so that I might live in him, having no other life but that in Christ. I entered

The Acts of Paul

into a large assembly with the support of blessed Jude, the brother of the lord, who gave me from the beginning the sublime love bestowed by faith.

6. "I conducted myself then in grace, with the support of the blessed prophet and through the revelation of Christ *who was begotten before all the ages*. As he was being proclaimed I rejoiced in the lord, nourished by his words. But when I was able to be worthy of the Word, I spoke to the believers—Jude encouraged me, and I became dear to those who heard me.

7. "When evening arrived I left the agapē prepared by the widow Lemma and her daughter Ammia. I intended to reach Jericho in Phoenicia by this night hike. We covered a lot of ground, so that when dawn came I perceived that Lemma and Ammia, who had provided the agapē, had been following me all along, for they were so enamored of me that they wished to be close to me. Then a huge and famished lion came out of the valley of the field of bones. As for us, we were praying fervently; Lemma and Ammia *fell before the beast in prayer*. When I had finished praying, the beast was crouched at my feet. Filled with the spirit, I looked at it and said, 'Lion, what do you want?'"

"'I want to be baptized.'

8. "I praised God who had given speech to the beast and safety to God's servants. That spot featured a large stream; I went down into it, the creature following. As pigeons gravely threatened by eagles seek protection in a house, so Lemma and Ammia, who were clinging to me would not let me go until I blessed and praised God. I was also seized by ordinary fear, wondering how I was going to drag the lion and toss it into the water. I stood on the bank of the river, sisters and brothers, and cried out, 'You who dwell in the heights and take notice of the downtrodden, You who give respite to the oppressed, You who stopped the jaws of the lions set against Daniel, You who have sent me our lord Jesus Christ, grant us also a means for escaping from the beast and accomplish the established divine plan!'

9. "Following this prayer I grabbed it by the mane and immersed it three times in the name of Jesus Christ. When he had come up out of the water he shook out his mane and said to me, 'Grace be with you.'

"'And also with you,' I replied.

"When the lion dashed off into the country, rejoicing—this was revealed to me in my heart—a lioness encountered him, but he would not even look at her but turned away and headed for the forest.

The Acts of Paul

10. "So you also, Aquila and Priscilla, who have come to faith in the living God [. . .] That which you have received proclaim like me."

I. 11 Transition

11. In response to Paul's message a large crowd was added to the community of faith, resulting in jealousy and opposition to Paul *from leaders throughout Asia*, who wanted to put him to death.

A woman in the city named Procla did many good works for the Ephesians. Paul baptized her together with her entire household. The renown of grace, with abundant praise, spread abroad between [. . .] and Eastertide. The crown of Christ grew by large numbers, so that jealousy arose [*giving impetus*] to a widespread rumor in the city: "This stranger has destroyed the gods, saying, 'you will see them consumed by fire.'"

II. A. 9.12 Arrest

12. As Paul was setting out for a place in the country, the citizens, together with magistrates, seized him, hauled him to the theater, and urged the governor to come. When he arrived he questioned Paul: "Why do you offer these [*ideas*] and teach what monarchs have condemned and the world has rejected? Nor have we been taught these things. We are given to understand that you exalt your god and have destroyed [*our gods*], those of the Romans and of this people here. Say now what you proclaim when you would persuade the public."

9.13 II. B. Defense Speech

13. Paul said [to him], "Proconsul, do as you will, for your authority extends only to my body, which you can destroy, but you have no power to kill my soul. Listen now how you can be saved. Take all that I say to heart. This is the one who created the sky and the land. This is the one who created the sun, the moon, the stars, authorities, dominions, and the world with its adornment, and fashioned all the good things that are in the world for the sake and use of humankind. God has not rejected his creature, i.e., humankind. But (*people reject God*) when they have been led astray through moral inversion and aberration, captured by their lust for gold, silver, precious stones, sexual misconduct, the drunken revels that are congenial to the pursuit of pleasure, and the life of darkness that leads to evil. People have obtained all

that we have mentioned and are dead. Now, however, because of the deceit resident in the world, the Lord wills us to live in God and not die in sins; he saves us through those who preach the unalloyed Word, so that you might repent and come to believe that Jesus is the Messiah and that there is no other (god). Your gods are worthless, bronze, stone, and wooden objects, which cannot eat, see, hear, or stand erect. Make the right choice and be saved, lest God become angry and burn you with inextinguishable fire and the very memory of you be eradicated."

9.14. II. C. Judgment; Reaction of the faithful

14. When the governor, as well as the crowd in the theater, had heard this, he said, "Gentlemen of Ephesus, We know that this man speaks well, but this is not the proper occasion for learning such matters. We are well aware of the unsuitable character of this (settting). Judge for yourselves what should be done."

"Burn him in front of the temple," shouted some.

But the goldsmiths countered with the unison shout: "To the beasts!" In the midst of a substantial uproar Hieronymos judged that Paul should be whipped and thrown to the beasts. For their part the believers, since this took place during Eastertide, did not weep, nor did they kneel, but they rejoiced, praying with [. . .]

9.15 II. D. The Lion

15. Six days later Hieronymos provided an exhibition of animals to impress all the spectators with the size of the animals. Although he had been placed in custody . . . Paul did not avert his eyes [*e.g., from the spectacle*], but he drew as close as he could, heard the hiss of the wagons [*and the racket of those*] transporting the animals. When [*a lion*] . . . entered through the side gate of the stadium in which Paul was incarcerated, it roared loudly, and [everyone] hollered, "The lion!" It roared so harshly and seve[*rely that even Paul*] was frightened enough to interrupt his prayers.

III. 16–21. Subplot: Eubula and Artemilla.

16. The wife of Diophantes, a freedman of Hieronymos, was a disciple of Paul and attached herself to him day and night. This made Diophantes jealous and eager to expedite the animal fight. Now Artemilla, the wife of

The Acts of Paul

Hieronymos, wanted to hear Paul at prayer. She said to Eubula (Diophantes' wife) "[*I wish*] to hear (the) prayer [and message] of the beast-fighter."

Eubula wen[t] and reported this to Paul. Filled with joy he said: "Brin[g h]er." After changing into rather somber clothes, Artemilla went with Eubula to see Paul.

17. When he saw her, he groaned and said, "Madam, ruler of this world, mistress of much gold, citizen possessing abundant luxury, you who boast about your wardrobe, sit down on the floor and forget your wealth and beauty and adornments, for none of these will help you, unless you implore God, who views what is considered great in this realm dung but bestows what is marvelous in that realm. Gold perishes, wealth is consumed, clothing wears out, beauty fades, great cities fall, and fire destroys the world because of human lawlessness. God alone abides, and the adoption bestowed through him, the only path to salvation. Now then, Artemilla, hope in God who will deliver you, hope in Christ who will give you forgiveness of sins and bestow upon you the crown of freedom, so that you will cease worshiping images and with offerings but (worship) the living God and father of Christ to whom be glory forever and ever. Amen." In response Artemilla (with Eubula) begged Paul that he would baptize her immediately. (The beast fight was scheduled for the next morning.)

18. Diophantes advised Hieronymos that their wives were seated next to Paul night and day. Hieronymos was infuriated with Artemilla and the freedwoman Eubula. He retired early from the table in order to speed up the show. The women asked Paul: "Do you want us to bring a blacksmith so that you can get free and wash us in the sea?"

"No. For I have confidence in God, who has rescued the whole world from chains."

19. It was Sabbath and the Lord's day was approaching, the day on which Paul was to be thrown to the beasts. He cried out "My God, Christ Jesus, who has delivered me from so many perils, grant that these shackles may be shattered and fall from my hands, in the presence of Artemilla and Eubula." While Paul was vigorously entreating for this, a very attractive youth came in, released Paul's shackles, and promptly left, smiling. Because of this celestial manifestation that he had received and the exceptional miracle of the shackles, Paul's grief about the beast-fight evaporated and he leapt in joy as if in Paradise.

20. Taking Artemilla (by the hand) he exited the cramped a[nd gloo]my [place in which the in]carcerated were held. When, after eluding the guards,

The Acts of Paul

they were outside and safe, Paul solemnly invoked his God: "The d[oors opened] [...] to praise your providence [...] so that Artemilla might be initiated with the seal of the lord..." [...] the outer [g]ates flew open immediately at the n[a]me of God [...] the guards were held in a deep sleep. The mistress left first, followed by the blessed Paul, with [Eubula] into the [thick] darkness. A yout[h physically resembling] Paul preceded them to the [seashore], illuminating (the path) not with a lamp but by the brightness of his body.

21. At that point the illuminator came to a stop. After praying, Paul laid a hand upon Artemilla, descended into the water [*e.g., with her and, after she confessed her faith, baptized her*] in the name of Christ Jesus. [*e.g., When they had come up*], the water glowed, which so terrified Artemilla that she nearly fainted. Anxious, Paul prayed, "You who illuminate and reveal, help, lest the gentiles say that the prisoner Paul escaped after killing Artemilla." Just as the youth smiled again, the matron revived and set out for home. Dawn was breaking. When Paul went back indoors the guards were still asleep. He broke bread, offered water, and after quenching her thirst for the word, sent Artemilla to her husband Hieronymos. Paul then returned to his prayers.

9.22–26 IV. Judgment in the Arena.

22. At dawn the citizens began to cry, "Let's go to the spectacle. Let us go and see the one who 'possesses God' fighting with beasts." Hieronymos was present in person, driven both by suspicion of his wife and determination that Paul not escape. He directed Diophantes and the other slaves to bring Paul into the stadium. As he was being dragged about he said nothing but kept his head bowed down and groaned because he was being led in triumph by the city. After being paraded, he was tossed directly into the field. His dignity exacerbated the multitude.

Because Artemilla, not to mention Eubula, had fallen ill to the point of mortal danger because of the ruin of Paul, Hieronymos was very unhappy. On top of this was the widely circulated story that she was no longer in harmony with him.

23. When Hieronymos had taken his place, he commanded that a very fierce lion, recently taken, be let loose upon Paul, leading the entire crowd to shout: "Let the rapacious lion devour the one who 'possesses god!'"

So when the cage was opened and the lion came forth, Paul set out to meet it as a suppliant, praying to the lord Jesus Christ. The attendants who urged the lion to attack were astonished at the size and ferocity of the creature. Meanwhile, Paul paid no attention but continued with his responsibility of prayer and witness. The lion, puffed up to full size, looked around the stadium, then came at Paul on the run, reclining by his legs, like a trained lamb... When Paul had finished praying, the lion got up on its paws and said to Paul, in a human voice, ["*Grace be with you!*"] Unperturbed, Paul replied, "Grace be with you, lion," and put his hand on its head. At this the crowd hollered in unison: "Get rid of this sorcerer, get rid of this magician!"

24. Paul and the lion looked at one another, Paul reckoned that this was the lion that had come [*and been baptized*]. Supported by his faith, Paul greeted the lion [*with a kiss*] and said, "Are you the one that I baptized?"

"Y[es]."

Paul spoke again: "How were you captured?"

"Just like you, Paul" replied the lion [...]

25. Hieronymos sent many wild animals to kill Paul and archers to dispatch the lion. Despite the clear sky a huge and voluminous rain of hail plummeted down from the sky, so dense that it killed many and sent the rest fleeing for shelter. Both Paul and the lion were unharmed, but the other animals perished from the volume of hail. Hieronymos' ear was hit and sliced, and the fleeing crowd kept shouting: "Save us, O God! Save us, God of the one who fights the beasts!"

26. Paul then said farewell to the now silent lion, left the stadium, went down to the harbor, and boarded a ship bound for Macedonia. Many were sailing away, supposing that the city was about to fall, so Paul went aboard in the guise of a refugee. For his part, the lion set out for his accustomed haunts in the hills.

9.27–28. V. Resolution of the Subplot.

27. Artemilla and Eubula were dreadfully upset and occupied themselves with fasting and [*weeping*] in their anxiety over what had happened with Paul [*and the lion*]. That night [*the handsome youth*] appeared manifestly in the bedroom where the women were comforting one another and Hieronymos lay with a suppurating ear. Artemilla had not gone to tend to him because of her grief. The youth said to them, "Don't be upset or ill, but be secure in the name of Christ Jesus and in his might. For Paul, the slave of Christ, the prisoner, has left. He has gone to Macedonia to accomplish the

The Acts of Paul

lord's plans entrusted to him. But you . . . the father's grace . . . will encourage." This news left them beside themselves with amazement.

Hieronymos, brought to his senses by a night of agony, cried out: "God who came to the help of the beast-fighter, save me through the youth who appeared in the closed bedroom via a vision."

28. When the youth saw the attendants [fleeing] in terror, he called back the physicians and cried loudly: "Through the will of Christ Jesus heal his ear!" It became well. The youth then directed him, "Treat it with honey."

Chapter 10: Philippi

Primary sources: P.Heid 45–50, 41–42; 44a; P.Bodmer 10; Secondary sources: cf. Nicetas of Paphlagonia.

Chapter 10

When he had departed from [. . .] and went [to Philippi]

1. Now when Paul came to Philippi [. . .] he went [*into the house of* . . .] great joy abounded [*among the believers*] and to all [. . .] the lawless one [. . .] the reward. They [. . .] in [. . .] single prayer [. . .] All and each [. . .] Paul to comfort [. . .] [*Philippi*]

3 Corinthians

I . . . The Corinthians were gravely concerned about Paul because he was going to leave the world before the proper time. Simon and Cleobius had come to Corinth with this message: "There is no resurrection of the flesh but [only] of the spirit, and the human body is not a divine creation, and, with regard to the world, God neither created it nor knows it, nor has Jesus Christ been crucified—he was mere appearance, he was neither born of Mary nor was he of Davidic descent." In sum, they taught many things in Corinth, deceiving themselves and many others. When therefore the Corinthians heard . . . they sent [*a letter to Paul*] in Macedonia [*by the hand of the deacons*] Threptus and Eutychus. The letter read:

The Acts of Paul

[*The Corinthians to the Apostle Paul*]

(2) II. 1. Stephanas and his fellow-presbyters Daphnus, Eubulus, Theophilus, and Zeno to Paul, who is in Christ: greetings. 2. Two individuals have come to Corinth, Simon and Cleobius; they overthrew the faith of some with corrupt words. 3. These you will examine, 4. for we never heard such things either from you or from the others. 5. But we maintain what we have received from you and from them. 6. As the Lord has shown us mercy, we should hear this from you again while you are still in the flesh. 7. Either come to us or write to us, (8) for we believe, as it was revealed to Theonoe, that the Lord has delivered you from the hand of the lawless one. 9. They say and teach as follows: 10. The prophets are not to be utilized; (11) God is not almighty; (12) there is no resurrection of flesh; (13) God did not fashion the human race; (14) The Lord neither came in the flesh nor was he born of Mary; (15) the world is not of God but of angels. 16. Therefore, brother, please hasten here, so that the Corinthian church may continue without stumbling and the foolishness of these men may be exposed. Farewell in the Lord.

(3) III 1. The deacons, Threptus and Eutychus, took the letter to Philippi. 2 When Paul received it, although he was in prison because of Stratonike, the wife of Apollophanes; he became quite upset, 3 and exclaimed, "It would have been better had I died and were with the Lord than to remain in the flesh and to hear words that heap sorrow upon sorrow. 4 How dreadful it is to be in prison while Satan's wiles flourish!" 5. And in considerable affliction Paul wrote this reply to the letter.

IV. The Letter of Paul

Paul to the Corinthians

Concerning the Flesh

(4) IV. 1. Paul, the prisoner of Jesus Christ, to the believers at Corinth: greetings. 2. Since I am undergoing numerous misfortunes, I am not surprised that the teachings of the evil one are experiencing rapid success. 3. The Lord Christ will quickly come, since he is rejected by those who falsify his teaching. 4. For I delivered to you first of all what I received from the apostles before me who were always with Jesus Christ, (5) that our Lord Christ Jesus was of Davidic descent, born of Mary, into whom the Father sent the spirit

The Acts of Paul

from heaven (6) that he might come into this world and liberate all flesh by his own flesh, and that he might raise us in the flesh from the dead as he has shown us by example. 7. Humanity was created by his Father (8) and was thus sought by God when lost, so that it might become alive by adoption.

9. For the almighty God of the universe, maker of heaven and earth, sent the prophets first to the Jews to deliver them from their sins, (10) as he desired to save the house of Israel; therefore he distributed some of the spirit of Christ and apportioned it to the prophets who proclaimed the true worship of God over a long period.

11. Yet the [evil] prince wished to be god himself and laid his hands on them and bound all human flesh to lust. 12. But the almighty God, who is just, did not wish to nullify his own creation (13) and sent Spirit through fire into Mary the Galilean, [v. 14: see p. 269] (15) that the evil one might be conquered by the same flesh by which he ruled and be convinced that he is not god. 16. For by his own body Jesus Christ saved all flesh, (17) so that he might exhibit a temple of righteousness in his own body (18) by which we are liberated. 19. Those who impede the providence of God by denying that heaven and earth and all that is in them are works of the father are children of wrath, not of righteousness. 20. They possess the accursed faith of the serpent. 21. Avoid them and keep your distance from their teaching. [vv. 22–23: see 272]

(5) 24. For those who tell you that there is no resurrection of the flesh there will be no resurrection—(25) Those who do not believe the one who thus [*in the flesh*] rose. 26. For they do not know, Corinthians, about the sowing of wheat or other seeds that one casts naked upon the ground and dies, then rises by God's will, in a body and clothed. 27. God not only raises the sown body but also bestows upon it abundant blessings.

28. If we cannot develop a parable from seeds, (29) you know of Jonah, the son of Amathios who, when he refused to preach to the Ninevites, was swallowed up by a sea-monster. 30. After three days and three nights God heard the prayer of Jonah from the depths of Hades. No part of him was corrupted, not even a hair or an eyelid. 31. How much more, you of limited faith, will he raise those who have believed in Christ Jesus, as he himself was raised up? 32. When some Israelites threw a corpse on the bones of the prophet Elisha, the person's body was raised. So also will you, upon whom the body, bones, and Spirit of Christ have been thrown, will be raised on that day with a whole body.

The Acts of Paul

6) 34. If, however, you receive any different teaching, do not trouble me, (35) for I have shackles on my hands so that I may gain Christ and marks on my body so that I may attain to the resurrection of the dead. 36. Whoever abides by the rule which we have received through the blessed prophets and the holy gospel, shall receive a reward, (37) but whoever transgresses these, and those who did so earlier will receive fire, (38) since they are godless persons, a generation of vipers. 39. Rebuff them by the power of Christ. 40. Peace be with you.

Chapter 11 Philippi

Sources: P.Heid 41–42/117–19. Nicetas of Paphlagonia. Secondary: *Acts of Titus*

1. [...] Longinus [...] Longinus [...] Paul [...] "Since [...] the mine [...] Nothing good has happened for my house." He determined that, as Frontina, his daughter, was going to be thrown [*from a cliff*] that Paul also should be thrown with her, alive. Paul was aware of this, but he continued to toil with the other convicts [*and fast*], in great good cheer, for two days.

2. They [...] on the third day [*brought forth*] Frontina. The [*whole city*] followed. Firmilla, Longinus and [*the*] soldiers [*lamented*]. The prisoners carried the bier. When Paul saw the elaborate mourning spectacle, with the young woman and eight [...] (*gap of several lines*)

3. and without [...] heart [...] Paul alive with the young woman. When Paul had taken the young woman in his arms, he sighed to the lord Jesus Christ because of Firmilla's grief. He threw himself to the ground on his knees [...] praying for both mother and daughter. At that very moment Frontina arose. The onlookers fled in terror. Paul took her by the hand [*and led her*] through town to the house of Longinus. The crowd cried out in unison: "There is one God, the creator of heaven and earth, who has given life to [this young woman through the agency] of Paul. [...]"

4. [a loaf] He blessed it [...] so that they might bless [...] without [...] then [...] Paul [...]

The Acts of Paul

The Passion of Paul: APl 12–14

Chapter 12 Corinth

Sources: P.Hamb pp. 6–7; P.Heid pp. 51, 52, 71

From Phi[*li*]ppi to Corinth

12.1–6

1. Paul's arrival at Stephen's house in Corinth after his journey from Philippi produced joy on the part of all our people, joy coupled with tears, as he related what he had undergone in the workhouse at Philippi, as well as what had happened to him in every other place, until his tears finally brought relief, and all made fervent prayer for Paul, so that he deemed himself privileged because they daily referred his concerns to the lord in prayer with such spiritual unanimity. As a result the magnitude of his joy was boundless, and Paul's spirits were elevated because of the believers' affection. He taught for forty days about what he had endured, what he had experienced in various places and the sundry marvels accorded to him. In every account he praised God the almighty and Christ Jesus who had been well pleased with Paul in every place.

2. When the time had come for Paul to leave for Rome, grief gripped the believers over when they would see him again. Filled with the Holy Spirit, Paul said: "Sisters and brothers, Devote yourselves to fasting and charity, for I am headed for a fiery furnace—I am speaking of Rome—and I should not be able to endure it if the Lord did not empower me. For David took the same path as Saul [. . .] overcome with anger he [*would have*] killed Nabal, convinced [. . .] Nabal; for the God Christ Jesus was with him [. . .] this valuable fast. The Grace of the Lord [P.Heid 51 begins here] will be with [*me so that I might accomplish the*] divine plan [*in store for me*] with patient endurance.

3. [*When they heard this*], the believers were troubled and resumed their fasting vigil. Cleobius, speaking through the Spirit said to them, "Sisters and brothers, Paul must fulfill the entire plan of God and go up to the [*place*] of death [. . .] with impressive instruction, knowledge, and dissemination of the message, until, having stirred up jealousy, he leaves this world." [P.Heid p. 51 ends] When the believers and Paul heard this, they raised their voices

and prayed: "God of our lord, father of Christ, come to the aid of your slave Paul, so that he may remain with us because of our weakness."

4. These words crushed Paul. He brought his fast with them to an end and offered the eucharist (P.Hamb p. 7) [*The bread broke*] into pieces of its own accord [. . .] When they asked what this [sign] might mean and what he was going to say about it, he [P.Heid. p. 52 begins here] would not respond.

5. But the Spirit fell upon Myrta, who said: "Brothers and sisters, why do you regard this sign with fear? Paul, the slave of the lord, will deliver many in Rome and will nourish so many with his message that their number will exceed calculation and he will become the most noteworthy of the faithful. The glory [of the Lord Christ Jesus] will clothe him with splendor, a magnificent grace in Rome." Once the Spirit within Myrta had subsided, each took some food and they feasted in accordance with the practice of fasting, singing psalms of David and other songs. Even Paul enjoyed himself. [P.Heid. 52 ends]

6. The next day, after they had kept an all night vigil following God's will, Paul said, "My fellow believers, I shall sail out on Friday [P.Heid. 71 begins] and make for Rome. I have no wish to hinder what has been ordained and imposed upon me. This is why I was appointed." All the believers were quite upset at this message; [P.Heid 71 ends] each made as large a contribution as possible so that Paul would not be troubled beyond his separation from them.

Chapter 13

Sources: P.Hamb. 7–8, P.Heid. 79–80, P.Mich. inv. 1317, 3788, P. Berlin 13893.

13.1–2 Voyage and Christophany

1. When Paul boarded the ship, attended by the prayers of all, its captain, Artemon, who had been baptized by Peter, [*greeted*] Paul with joy . . . and so, because so many things had been entrusted to Paul [*Artemon treated him as if, in him,*] the lord had come aboard. Once the ship had gotten underway, Artemon, by divine grace, joined Paul to glorify the lord Jesus Christ, who had fashioned in advance his plan for Paul. When they had reached the

The Acts of Paul

high sea and quiet prevailed, Paul fell asleep, exhausted by his fasting and nightlong vigils with the believers.

2. At that time the lord came to him, walking on the sea He nudged Paul and said, "Get up and see!" Upon awakening he said, "You are my lord Jesus Christ, the king [...] But why are you so sad and gloomy, Lord? If you are troubled, [*tell me clearly what it is*], lord, for seeing you like this is quite upsetting."

"Paul, I am going to be crucified again."

"God forbid, lord, that I should ever see that!"

"Paul, go to Rome and exhort the believers to remain faithful to their heavenly calling."

[...] walking on the sea the lord went ahead of them, pointing out the way like a [guiding s]tar.

13.3–4 Arrival and Pastoral Address

3. When the voyage was over [...] Paul left the ship, burdened with considerable sadness. [*He saw*] a man in the harbor area who welcomed captain Artemon with a greeting when he saw him: (p. 8) "Claudius, Look at who is here with me [*Paul, the be*]loved of the lord." [P.Mich. 1317 begins here] Claudius greeted Paul with a warm embrace. [Berl 13893 begins here] and promptly, with Artemon, carried the baggage from the boat to his place.

4. Claudius quite joyfully advised the believers about Paul, so that his house was quickly filled with joy and grace. They took note of how Paul dropped his unhappiness and began to teach the authentic message:

5. "My fellow believers, soldiers of Christ, Hear me out. How often God delivered Israel from some lawless person! So long as they observed what God required, he did not desert them. For example he delivered them from Pharaoh's lawless claws and from the utterly unsanctified king Og, from Arad, and the foreigners. So long as they observed God's requirements, the almighty, since he had promised them the land of the Canaanites, granted them offspring, and subjected the foreigners to them. After all that he had provided for them in the uninhabited country and the waterless territory, (6) he also sent them prophets to announce our lord Jesus Christ. They also received, in accordance with their station, lot, and portion some of the Spirit of the Christ and consequently suffered much and were put to death by the people. Because their lawlessness led them to rebel against the living God, they lost their eternal inheritance.

The Acts of Paul

7. "At present, brothers and sisters, a great trial impends. If we endure it we shall have access to the lord and receive a sanctuary and a source of good will, [P.Mich. 3788 begins] Jesus Christ, who gave himself for us. He is indeed God's son, in accordance with the message you have received. In the last times God sent for us a spirit of power into flesh, that is, into Mary the Galilean, in fulfillment of the prophetic message. He was conceived and carried by her until she delivered and gave birth to Jesus our king, in Judean Bethlehem. He was reared in Nazareth, went to Jerusalem and all Judea teaching, 'The kingdom of heaven is at hand. Abandon the darkness; accept the light, you who haunt the shadows of death. A light has risen for you.'

8. "He did splendid and marvelous things, (and so selected twelve men from the tribes whom he kept with him, men of [intel]ligence [...] and faith), raising the dead, healing the sick, cleansing lepers, healing the blind, curing the crippled, raising up the paralyzed, cleans[ing] the demon-possessed, and, in a word, he went about ministering to the entire region along the shore [...] heal[ing] [...] the river. [Isra]el. For [A] woman with a flow of blood [came] to him [but I] not other than [...] of our Lord Jesus Christ [...][...] [he/I was brought to a] meeting and [...] cemeteries [...] greatly by [...] glorious king. The other seed that the glorious king [sowed] for the price of/upon [the twelve men] [...] receiv[ing?] Israel [... P.Heid. 79 begins here]

9. "... the deeds [...] wondered considerably and [*pondered*] internally. [*He said to them*] [*After all the powerful deeds and works that he did*] 'Why are you surprised that I raise the dead or make cripples walk or purify lepers or revive the sick or heal paralytics and possessed people or that I distributed a little bread and satisfied a multitude or walked on sea or commanded the winds? If you believe these things, then you [*know*] that they are extraordinary. For truly [*I say*] to you, if you tell [*this mountain*], "Get going and throw yourself [*into the sea*]." This will take place if you do it without a shred of mental reservation. This [...]'

10. "One of them, named Simon, was sufficiently convinced to say, 'Lord, the deeds you accomplish are truly magnificent, for we have never heard nor have we [*ever*] seen someone other than you who raises the dead. [...]'

11. "[The Lord said] '[...], but the other works [...] these I perform as a temporary deliverance, while they are here, so that people may believe in the one who sent me.'

Simon said, 'Lord, direct me to speak.'
'Speak, Peter.' (For thereafter he always addressed them by name.)

'What work is greater than these [...] other than raising the dead [...] [*and*] feeding a multitude?'

'There is something greater than this. Blessed are those who have believed with all their heart.'

Philip then said angrily, 'What sort of stuff are you trying to teach us?'

'You...'"

Chapter 14: The Martyrdom of the Holy Apostle Paul

Sources: Three complete Greek mss, one of the ninth and two of the eleventh centuries. P.Hamb, Latin, Coptic (P.Heid, which is fragmentary), Syriac, Arabic, Ethiopic, Armenian, and Georgian versions; secondary source: Nicetas of Paphlagonia.

14.1–3 New Life Brings the Threat of Death to Believers

1. Awaiting Paul at Rome were Luke, who had come from Gaul, and Titus, from Dalmatia. The sight of them brought joy to Paul. He therefore rented a barn outside of Rome in which he taught, along with the believers, the message that introduces truth. He achieved fame; many persons joined the community. The word reverberated through Rome. A large number of the imperial staff came to him and became believers. Joy abounded.

Patroclus, an imperial cupbearer came late to the barn and, since he could not get close to Paul because of the crowd, perched in a high window and listened to him as he taught God's word. Because the Devil, that wicked creature, was aroused to jealousy by the believers' love for one another, Patroclus fell from the window and died. News of this quickly reached Nero.

When Paul learned of this through the Spirit, he said, "My fellow believers, the evil one has contrived an opportunity to test you. Go outside to find a boy fallen from a height. He is about to expire. Pick him up and bring him to me here. They went and did as he said. The sight of the body wrenched the attendant crowds. Paul said, "Brothers and sisters, show your faith. Come, let us implore our Lord Jesus Christ with tears that he may live and we remain unmolested." After all had uttered profound sighs, the boy began to breathe again. They put him upon an animal and sent him home alive with the other members of the imperial staff.

2. News of Patroclus' death upset Nero a great deal. Upon returning from the bath he directed someone else to serve the wine. His servants, however, said, "Caesar; Patroclus is alive and has taken his place at the table." This

information made the emperor initially hesitant to go in. When he finally did so, he saw the lad and said, "Are you alive, Patroclus?"

"I am, your majesty."

"Who brought you back to life?"

Uplifted by the enthusiasm of his faith, the youth said, "Christ Jesus the king of the ages."

Upset, Caesar said, "Is he therefore going to rule the ages and abolish every kingdom?"

"Yes. He will destroy all kingdoms. He alone will be eternal and no kingdom will elude him."

Nero struck him on the face, saying, "Patroclus, are you also a soldier of that king?"

"Yes, Lord Caesar, for he raised me after I had died." Then Barsabas "Flatfoot" Justus, Orion the Cappadocian, and Festus the Galatian, Nero's leading men, said, "We too serve in the army of the king of the ages."

Despite his great affection for them, Nero imprisoned these men and subjected them to brutal torture. He directed that all the soldiers of the great king be sought out and promulgated an edict that all exposed as Christians and soldiers of Christ were to be killed.

3. Among the many taken into custody was Paul. The other prisoners paid careful attention to him. Observing this, Caesar concluded that he was in charge of the soldiers and addressed him, "Agent [P.Hamb 9 begins] of the great king, albeit my prisoner, why did you come up with the idea of surreptitiously entering Roman territory and recruiting from my dominion?"

Inspired, Paul responded, with the entire audience in mind, "Caesar, we do not recruit from your dominion alone, but from every inhabited place, for we have been directed to exclude no one who wishes to enlist in the service of my king. If enrolling in his service should actually appeal to you, neither wealth nor the splendors of present existence will avail you, but if you submit and entreat him, you will experience deliverance. For on a single day he will destroy the world."

Caesar thereupon ordered that all the prisoners be burned at the stake, excepting Paul, who was to be decapitated, in accordance with Roman law. This did not silence Paul, who continued to share the message with Longinus the prefect and Cescus the centurion. Because of the machinations of the evil one many Christians were being executed at Rome without trial, so many in fact that the citizenry gathered in front of the palace shouting, "Enough, Caesar. These are our people! You are ruining Roman power!" He desisted on the grounds that no Christian should be touched until he had investigated the facts of the case.

The Acts of Paul

14.4–7: The Execution and Vindication of Paul

4. Subsequent to this direction Paul was brought forward. Nero persisted in his claim that he should be decapitated. Paul said: "Caesar, my life for my king is not ephemeral. Even if you decapitate me, I shall do this: rise and appear to you, because I shall not have died but remain alive in my Lord Christ Jesus, who will come to judge the earth."

[*After Paul had been sent off to be executed*] Longinus and Cescus said to Paul: "Where do you get this king from, in whom you so trust that even death will not change your mind?" Paul shared the message with them, "Gentlemen, living in ignorance and deceit, change your minds and be saved from the conflagration that will inundate the world. We are not enrolled, as you imagine, in the service of a terrestrial king, but one from heaven, the living God, who because of the lawless things done in this world is coming as judge. Blessed are those who will have trust in him and live forever, when he comes to purify the world with fire!"

They thereupon begged him, "Please, please help us and we shall let you go."

"I am no deserter from Christ, but a loyal soldier of the living God. If I knew that I was going to die, I would have tried to save myself, Longinus and Cescus, but since I live for God and love myself, I am going to the lord, so that I might come back with him in the glory of his father."

"How shall we live if you have been beheaded?" asked the two.

5. Nero sent one Parthenion and Feritas to learn whether Paul had been decapitated. They arrived to find him alive, still speaking with the two officers. He invited them: "Believe in the living God, who raises me and all who believe in him, from the dead!"

"We're returning to Nero now," they replied. "We'll believe in your God after you have died and arisen."

To the inquiries of Longinus and Cescus about salvation, he said: "Come promptly here to my tomb at dawn. You will find two men praying, Titus and Luke. They will seal you in the Lord." Paul stood, facing east and prayed at some length, communing via prayer in Hebrew with his forebears. Without another word he stretched out his neck. When the executioner lopped off his head, milk spewed out onto the soldier's clothes. When the soldier and all the bystanders saw this, they praised the God who had given Paul such glory. They then returned to report to the emperor what had happened.

The Acts of Paul

6. While he was amazed at this report and still at a loss for words, Paul came, at 1500, when many philosophers, as well as the centurion, were assembled with the emperor. Visible to all, he said to the Emperor, "Caesar, behold Paul, the soldier of God. I have not died, but live. Many dreadful things will happen to you because of the righteous you have killed." Nero was upset and directed that the prisoners be released, including Patroclus and Barsabbas' circle.

7. Longinus and the centurion Cescus set out with anxiety for Paul's tomb as he had told them. Upon their rival they saw two men at prayer, Paul between them. The sight astonished them. Titus and Luke, swept away by mortal fear, turned and ran away. Their pursuers cried, "We are not chasing you with death in view but life, as Paul—who was praying between you a moment ago—promised."

Titus and Luke were glad to hear this and sealed them in the Lord.

Introduction

I. Overview

The *Acts of Paul* appeared in the second half of the second century, between c. 160 and c. 190, probably c. 170–75. The works now designated "Apocryphal Acts of the Apostles" are a disparate group united by a biographical frame that follows an apostolic missionary from his original commission to his death, usually by martyrdom. Five of these books—those featuring Andrew, John, Paul, Peter, and Thomas—are called "major," although a case can now be made for adding the *Acts of Philip* to that category. Only the *Acts of Thomas* is complete, and all of these acts were subjected to frequent editing. Of the major Acts the piece devoted to Paul was the most acceptable in catholic circles, particularly on doctrinal grounds, and was ultimately condemned more because of its use by heretics, notably the Manichees as well as followers of Priscillian, than for its doctrines. Nonetheless, the *APl* continued to be read and utilized as an historical and edifying source throughout the Middle Ages.

Perhaps two-thirds of the entire work survives; several sections are quite fragmentary. The existence of some scenes can be identified or outlined by reference to use by later authors (Section III). Although the work was composed in the late second century, the edition now reconstructed is not earlier than c. 300. Three components of the *APl* enjoyed a separate existence. One, the martyrdom, was used liturgically on the appropriate feast, and was thus subject to considerable editing. Another, *3 Corinthians*, was not an original part of the *APl*. The third is the material featuring Thecla (or Thekla) of Iconium, who became an immensely popular saint in antiquity and later eras, as well as a more recent feminist heroine. The residue of the work must be pieced out from incomplete papyrus texts.

APl represent what most would find a quite old-fashioned viewpoint. The apostle is an itinerant missionary of the sort characterized in Mark

6:1–12 and its parallels, an itinerant who remains in a town as guest of householders until expelled by officials. The Paul of these non-canonical Acts, like the Paul of Acts, is a wandering missionary, who works wonders and converts large numbers to the faith. Differently from the Paul of Acts, his message has, as the following commentary will show, a strongly anti-establishment edge, rejecting the official forms of authority, notably the Empire and its institutions, particularly the family. He is, like the Paul of the Deutero-Pauline letters (Colossians, Ephesians, 2 Thessalonians, 1–2 Timothy, Titus), but unlike the Paul of Acts, a "loner," with no apparent connections to a community in Jerusalem or to other leaders, such as Peter and James. See Pervo, "Hospitality."

As is the case with all of the ApocActs except those of Thomas, the opening of the *APl* is not extant. The logical and standard place to begin was the call of the particular apostle. In the case of Paul that means his "conversion" in the vicinity of Damascus. The span of *APl* thus extended from that event to his martyrdom in Rome under Nero and subsequent resurrection. The intervening material narrates visits to various sites. In the more complete passages, these visits are not always explicitly initial, church-founding visits. The emphasis is upon the apostle's pastoral role. This is in keeping with much of the Deutero-Pauline tradition, which honored Paul as a great missionary, but focused upon his role as a teacher for the extant church, as in, most notably, the PE. The balance of this introduction will seek to flesh out and argue for these assertions.

II. The Reception of APl

This survey includes not only the identification of witnesses to the existence of the *APl* but also the chronological and geographical extent of knowledge of the text, the portions of *APl* attested in various texts and writers, the use to which it was put, and the various evaluations of this work. Direct allusions mention the title *Acts of Paul* (or a variant thereof). Most of these are primary, i.e., the source comes directly from *APl*. Indirect references often consist of the name of a character from *APl*. By far the most common example is Thecla. Not all such references demonstrate use of *APl*, or even of the Thecla portion (chaps. 3–4). Only references that mention a specific incident constitute evidence. In general, *APl* were accepted as historical from the early third century until the late Middle Ages (and beyond).[1] See the surveys of Holzhey, Schmidt, *Acta*, 108–16, and Vouaux, 24–64.

---

1. Thecla's name was removed from the Roman Catholic Sanctorale (Church calendar) in 1969, based upon doubts of her historical existence. She remains on various Eastern calendars.

1. The first, and probably earliest, extant example deviates from the aforesaid generalization. Tertullian, in his *On Baptism* 17.5, condemns *APl*. This reads, in accordance with the most likely text:

> Now should certain *Acts of Paul*, which are a fabrication, appeal to the example of Thecla as authorizing women to teach and to baptize, note that the Asian presbyter who concocted that document, aspiring to enhance Paul's standing, was exposed and, despite his plead that he acted out of love for Paul, renounced his office. (author's trans.)[2]

The alternative text omits "Acts" and could refer to other writings falsely attributed to Paul. Even were this alternative preferred, Tertullian would almost certainly have the *APl* in mind. The shorter text may attempt to improve cloudy syntax or possibly even to remove an aspersion upon the *APl*. See MacKay, "Response"; Ng, "Acts"; Rordorf, "Tertullien"; Hilhorst, "Tertullian," 150–58 (probably the most detailed discussion); and Snyder, "Remembering," 158–61. On the basis of the extant text "baptizing" must refer to Thecla's own irregular initiation. (See the comments on 4.9.)

Tertullian disapproved of Thecla. From that stance one may conclude that at least some women read the text and viewed it as a model. He is a witness both to the existence of *APl* and to the threat it could pose. One should therefore view with caution his claims about the work's origin. (See sec. V.) Tertullian's rejection of *APl* was theological in nature, rather than historical. From his exhortation in the face of martyrdom, *Scorpiace* 15, which refers to Paul's resurrection after execution by Nero, it is most probable that Tertullian knew the entire *APl* (rather than the martyrdom as a distinct work). He does not (and would not) cite his authority for the claim about Paul, but it is *APl* 14. Tertullian is the earliest witness for *APl*, probably for the entire text. He is also the earliest authority for the use of Thecla as an example of women's authority. Tertullian offers a theory of composition, by a single author who sought to enhance Paul's standing.

2. A rather different viewpoint emerges in the *Commentary on Daniel* long attributed to Hippolytus of Rome. This is probably the oldest largely extant commentary upon a biblical book by a Christian author (if it is dated 203–204. See Moreschine and Norelli, 1:242–43). Hippolytus, *In Danielem* 29.3:

---

2. *quod si quae Acta Pauli, quae perperam scripta sunt, exemplum Theclae ad licentiam mulierum docendi tinguendique defendant, sciant in Asia presbyterum qui eam scripturam construxit, quasi titulo Pauli de suo cumulans, convictum atque confessum id se amore Pauli fecisse loco decessisse.*

The Acts of Paul

> Then accordingly when the angel appeared in the den, the wild beasts were tamed and the lions, wagging their tails at him, rejoiced as being subjected by a new Adam. They, licking the holy feet of Daniel, rolled *around* to taste the soles of his feet and they longed to accompany him. 29.4. For if we believe that, after Paul was condemned to beasts *and that* a lion was set upon him, it reclined at his feet and licked him all around, how do we not also believe what happened to Daniel, which even Darius himself described to all, having dispatched *it* through scribes? And in the books of the Persians and Medes it is read up to today that these *things* really occurred, so that not only the Hebrews nor only the Babylonians, but also the Medes and the Persians and all the nations who live under heaven, having heard the *things* which happened, they themselves feared God. (Trans. Thomas. C. Schmidt, at files/Hippolytus Commentary on Daniel by T C Schmidt. pdf [last accessed 10 January 2012].)

The source of this indirect witness is *APl* 9, in which the apostle relates how he had come to baptize a lion shortly after his conversion. In due course Paul is condemned to the beasts in that very city of Ephesus (cf. 1 Cor 15:32). By a stroke of fortune so good that it seems providential, the lion selected to lunch on Paul was that very same creature. See the comments on chap. 9. The commentator on Daniel does not report the lion's gift of speech or subsequent baptism. Several points merit attention. One is that the commentator, who is not aware of the general credulity presumably shared by ancient common people, expects (and has evidently experienced) doubts about the credibility of the tale of Daniel in the lions' den. Skepticism about wondrous events reported in Scripture is not an invention of more recent godless times.

Even more notably, the author makes his point through an *a maiori* argument, based upon an apposite religio-historical parallel. The greater is the *APl*. The commentator presumes that the audience knows *APl* 9 and takes it as fact. Without those assumptions his argument is utterly futile. The *APl* is evidently scarcely thirty years old, but it has attained the status of "gospel truth," as it were, at Rome.

3. Origen's (c. 185–c. 254) views on official and non-official Scripture vary. See Hanson, *Tradition*, 141. *APl* exemplify this generalization. The first example is indirect. It comes from Origen's *De pascha*, discovered in 1941 and edited in 1979. (See Bovon, "A New Citation.") Nautin, *Origène*, 411, dates this text c. 239–242. For a translation, see Daly, *Origen*. Origen, characteristically, takes the injunction to eat the Passover "with girded loins" (Exod

Introduction

12:11) in an ascetic sense. At the minimum it prohibits sexual intercourse before Communion. The maximum is more rigorous. In support whereof Origen invokes John the Baptizer's girded loins (e.g., Mark 1:6) and the apostle: "The married man who eats the Passover 'shall gird' also his 'loins' because the Apostle has said, 'Blessed are those who have wives [*if they live*] as those who have none.'" Behind this lies 1 Cor 7:29, but its immediate source is the transformation of that verse in *APl* 3:5, where it is formulated as a beatitude. Origen cites the *APl* without identifying his source. The quotation formula attributes these words to Paul. A parallel would be someone who said, "As Paul said, 'Athenians, I see how extremely religious you are'" (Acts 17:22). Contemporary critical scholars would characterize those words as placed in Paul's mouth by the author of Acts. For Origen the words of Paul's sermon in *APl* can be attributed directly to the apostle. The citation is both authoritative and cogent. The next two examples are direct, although a bit puzzling.

Origen, *On First Principles* 1, 2, 3, dated by Nautin, *Origène*, p. 371, c. 229. The discussion focuses upon the relation of Wisdom to Word. The former is identical to the latter, which is called Word "because she [wisdom] is as it were an interpreter of the mind's secrets. Hence I consider that to be a true saying which is written in the Acts of Paul, 'He is the word, a living being.' [*unde et recte mihi dictus videtur sermo ille qui in Actibus Pauli scriptus est, qui 'hic est verbum animal vivens.'*] John, however, uses yet more exalted and wonderful language" (Trans. Butterworth, *Origen on First Principles*, 16–17). The expression "which is written in the *Acts of Paul*" is characteristic of quotations of authoritative documents. The location of this citation is unknown. It probably comes from a speech. The speeches of the ApocActs are less likely to survive than are the narrative, as speeches were more likely to be victims of abridgement and censorship. See Appendix 1.

Commentary on John 20.12 (c. 239–242, according to Nautin, *Origène*, p. 411): "If any care to accept what is written in the *Acts of Paul* as a saying of the savior, 'I am going to be crucified again . . .'"

Readers immediately note that, in this milieu, Origen may be aware of objections to the *APl*. This is not to suggest that *APl* has lost standing in the exegete's eyes. He continues to value the work, not because of its stirring stories of rebellious young women or celibate lions, but because of its theological ideas. Each of his citations is of sayings material. Whether one can construct a history of the reception of *APl* from contrasting views of its status is dubious. The source is *APl* 13.2. (For the question of the relation between this passage and the APtr, see the comments on chap. 13.)

From these citations and allusions one can deduce that Origen had a "full" text of *APl,* including chapters 3 and 13 (and thus two of the

The Acts of Paul

"independent" sections). For that famous exegete *APl* was a source of Paul's *ipsissima verba*. He can quote it just as he cites the letters. *APl* is a useful resource that provides theological data for the interpretation of other scriptures. One may also postulate that Origen's career witnessed crescent attention to the establishment of textual boundaries, i.e., that limits were being set on the number of authoritative texts of the formative era.

4. Commodian (probably second half of third century; see Moreschini and Norelli, *Early Christian Greek and Latin Literature*, 1:381–82). In his *Carmen Apologeticum* 624–30, Commodian mentions talking animals: Balaam's donkey, and sandwiched between the talking dog and the articulate infant of APtr 9–12; 15, a reference to the lion that spoke "with divine voice" ("at divine urging"?, *voce divina*). This early Christian poet utilized Numbers and the two ApocActs as historical sources of equal value. See James, *Apocrypha*, 54–56. This witness is interesting because he lived in North Africa and was strongly influenced by Cyprian, who made no reference to *APl*. The indirect reference is probably to chap. 9 (although chap. 1 is possible). Commodian very probably utilized a Latin translation. This is the earliest evidence for that version.

5. The *Didascalia*. This Syriac work of c. 250 may have utilized 3 Cor. This would not be surprising because Ephrem and other Syrian authors accepted this letter. Utilization of 3 Cor does not prove that *APl* was the source, as it was (also) included in the Pauline corpus from an early date.

6. Methodius (died 311–312). Circa 300 Methodius of Olympus issued a *Symposium* based upon that of Plato, which he wished to replace. See Moreschini and Norelli, *Early Christian Greek and Latin Literature*, 1:313–15. Thecla has the climactic contribution. This indirect witness indicates the extent to which Thecla was admired in celibate circles in the third century.

7. *The Physiologus*. This prototype of the medieval bestiary appeared c. 300 or slightly earlier. See Curley. *Physiologus*, chapter 17, which includes a catalogue of those saved by praying: Moses, Daniel, Jonah: "Thecla was thrown into the fire and into the pits of the beasts and the figure of the cross saved her" (Curley, 26), followed by Susanna, Judith, Esther, and the three young men condemned in Daniel. Chapter 31 (pp. 45–46) notes those who fled from evil: Joseph from Mme. Potiphar, Thecla from Thamyris, Susanna from the wicked elders, Esther and Judith from Artaxerxes and Holofernes, respectively, the three youths from Nebuchadnezzar, and Sarah from "Nasmodeus" (Tobit). Thecla will frequently appear in catalogues with Susanna, Esther, and Judith. (Examples include Isidore of Pelusium, 440, *Epistles*

Introduction

1.160, who compared Thecla with Susanna, the daughter of Jephtha, and Judith. Monophysites of the sixth century place Thecla with Ruth, Susanna, Esther, and Judith among prominent women, and Gregory Nazianzus, *Contra Julian* 1.69, associates her with Susanna.) The specifics indicate that chaps. 3 and 4 were known to the author of the *Physiologus*.

8. Eusebius of Caesarea (c. 260–c. 340). Eusebius belongs to the early stages of efforts to determine and establish a *canon* of sacred Christian writings. From the late first century some writings, notably the letters of Paul, were viewed as authoritative. Inspiration was a broad category. Decisive personal statements notwithstanding, even individual writers were not consistent, and manuscripts contain texts condemned or rejected in "canon lists." At *H.E.* 3.25 Eusebius lists "the writings of the New Testament." The first category includes those accepted by all, although Revelation, included in this category, is not undisputed. Next are disputed books, although "most" accept them: James, Jude, 2 Peter, 2–3 John. The third category of NT writings are "spurious," probably to be taken as meaning pseudonymous: *APl*, the *Shepherd* [*of Hermas*], the *Apocalypse of Peter*, as well as *Barnabas* and the *Didache*. Revelation may belong here, as may the *Gospel according to the Hebrews*. Eusebius then adds, confusingly (3.25.6), that these would belong among the disputed. They differ from the "canonical" (*endiathēkous*, "covenanted") but are known to most Christian authors. The historian then lists heretical writings, including gospels attributed to Peter, Thomas, Matthias, etc., and the AAndr, AJn, and other Acts. These do not even belong to the category of the spurious. Eusebius evidently has three broad categories: writings accepted by all, disputed writings, in two groups, and heretical texts. The major distinction within the disputed is between those of apparently genuine authorship and those written by others. Paul did not write *APl* (and narrate his own death and resurrection). The major point is that Eusebius sharply distinguishes between *APl* and the other ApocActs. The latter are heretical. This view was rather general, Tertullian and Jerome being the two major exceptions.

At the beginning of that same book 3 of his *Ecclesiastical History* Eusebius discusses (3.3) writings of Peter. There he accepted 1 Peter, but judged 2 Peter "uncanonical," although some study it "along with other scriptures" (3.1). The *Acts, Gospel, Preaching,* and *Revelation* of Peter are rejected because not used by right-thinking believers (3.2). In 3.4 Eusebius admits fourteen Pauline epistles, again noting that some reject Hebrews. At the close of sec. 5 he states that he does not acknowledge his so-called Acts as an undisputed book. Eusebius then turns to *Hermas*, which receives a mixed review, not unlike Hebrews or 2 John. Perfect consistency was not

47

The Acts of Paul

a Eusebian hobgoblin. One example of this refusal to be controlled by his stated principles occurs two chapters earlier. 3.1 begins with the "Apostolic lottery," in which each apostle receives a missionary region by lot. This is found, for example, in AThom. At the end of that section the historian notes that Peter was crucified head down at his own request. 2.25.5 states that Paul was beheaded under Nero. The sources of these two statements are the respective Acts of Peter and Paul. Like others, Eusebius was prepared to draw upon *APl* for historical data.

9. The Codex Claromontanus. This fifth- to sixth-century Greco-Latin ms. contains at its close a list in Latin of biblical books, with the number of lines in each. This counting of *stichoi* intended to serve as a mark of authenticity and as an indication of tampering. (Unfortunately the length of these lines was not fixed with perfect consistency.) After listing the books of the OT, the text notes four gospels, then epistles of Paul: Romans, 1–2 Corinthians, Galatians, Ephesians, 1–2 Timothy, Titus, Colossians, Philemon. (Philippians and Hebrews are omitted, probably by error.) Then come 1–2 Peter, James, 1–3 John, Jude, *Barnabas*, Revelation of John, Acts, *Hermas*, *Acts of Paul*, and the *Revelation of Peter*. This fascinating list reflects a viewpoint like that of Eusebius, in which disputed books are set apart from others. It also shows that manuscript Bibles do not always conform to rules, including conciliar decisions.

10. Other manuscript data. Most of these use *APl* for details of historical background.

2 Timothy 3:11 (Paul is speaking): ". . . my persecutions, and my suffering the things that happened to me in Antioch, Iconium, and Lystra. What persecutions I endured! Yet the Lord rescued me from all of them." In the margins of several witnesses, K (ninth century), 181 (eleventh century), and the Harclean Syriac (sixth century or later), after "Antioch" appear: "[W]hat he suffered because of Thecla and from the Jews against those who believed in Christ." The first addition derives from *APl* 3 (Iconium). The second evidently stems from the canonical Acts. The origins of this gloss evidently go back to at least the fifth century, given attestation from Syrian monophysites and Byzantine Chalcedonians. An ancient commentator thus used both the apocryphal and canonical books to detail the sufferings, in much the same manner as modern commentators will refer to Acts to specify 2 Cor 11:24–28.

2 Timothy 4:19 "Greet Prisca and Aquila, and the household of Onesiphorus." 181 (above) and 460 (thirteenth century) insert, after "Aquila": "*Lectra, his wife, and his sons Simmias, and Zeno.*" The ineptly placed

interpolation evidently derives from a gloss. Its purpose is pedantic enough: to supply the names of Onesiphorus' family. The source is *APl* 3.2. This glossator is among those who long ago recognized links between the Pastoral Epistles and the *APl*, links that continue to bear scholarly fruit. (That the Pastorals place Onesiphorus in Ephesus and the *APl* in Iconium evidently does not matter.) These examples demonstrate that data from the *APl* were deemed wholly reliable sources for the elucidation of 2 Timothy and continued to serve that purpose for over a millennium.

11. Some Representative Commentators. Ambrosiaster, as the Latin commentator of the last third of the fourth century is known, remarks, regarding 2 Tim 2:17-18, which says of the unlovable Hymenaeus and Philetus, that they "have swerved from the truth by claiming that the resurrection has already taken place": "These persons, as we learn in another writing, said that resurrection comes about as a result of children."[3] The unidentified "other writing" is the *APl* 3:13. The two persons are not directly named here; they are Demas and Hermogenes. This comment was repeated by subsequent commentators, including Pelagius, Theodore of Mopsuestia, and Theodoret. See Lalleman, "The Resurrection," 138-39.

With reference to 2 Tim 4:14 ("Alexander the coppersmith did me great harm; the Lord will pay him back for his deeds") Ambrosiaster says: "This creature Alexander and the aforementioned Demas were cronies. Previously they had been companions of Paul and feigned friendship for him."[4] This increases the probability that Ambrosiaster was reading *APl*, rather than cribbing the data from an earlier commentator, for he summarizes 3.1.

Regarding 2 Timothy 1:15 ("You are aware that all who are in Asia have turned away from me, including Phygelus and Hermogenes") Ambrosiaster observes: "These people, whom Paul mentions, were jam-packed with hypocrisy, for they feigned friendship with the apostle, so that they might affiliate with him and learn more, whence they might do him injury or incite others to do so. When they found their plans exposed, they separated from Paul."[5] Despite the differences in names, Ambrosiaster identifies the enemies of Paul in the Pastorals with his opponents in *APl* 3. In the late fourth century the *APl* was a valuable resource for elucidating the background of the Pastorals, despite such minor matters as the use of different names.

3. Hi, ut ex alia scriptura docemur, in filiis fieri resurrectionem dicebant

4. Alexander iste, et Demas supradictus, collegae fuerunt. Hi prius cum apostolo errant, simulantes illi amicitiam

5. Hi, quos memorat [Paul] fallacia pleni errant; simulabant enim amicitias apostoli, ut adhaerentes ei addiscerent, unde illi calumniam facerent aut per alios immiterent. Qui posteaquam viderunt manifestatos se recesserunt ab eo.

The Acts of Paul

John Chrysostom (c. 347–407). In his comments on Acts 11:27–30 (collection for famine relief) he cites as an example of giving: Hear . . . her concerning that blessed Thekla, how, that she might see Paul, she gave even her gold: and thou wilt not give even a farthing that thou mayest see Christ: thou admirest what she did, but dost not emulate her (trans. Morris et al., *Homilies*, 167).

The reference is to *APl* 3:18. Thecla was not making a contribution for the relief of the poor but bribes to guardians of doors. Besides their value to the plot and, as the good patriarch implies, marks of the depth of her desire for intimacy with Paul, these bribes demonstrate her renunciation of worldly wealth and beauty. The most important point is that Chrysostom did not deem himself obliged to summarize the story. He could assume that his faithful hearers knew it.

Chrysostom's utilization of *APl* 14 is complex but certain. (See Mitchell, *Heavenly Trumpet*, 364–68.) The initial motive for Nero's action against Paul in *APl* 14 is the conversion of Patroclus, the emperor's Ganymede (cupbearer and lover). See the comments on chap. 14 and Pervo, "(Not) Appealing."

Chrysostom's speech against the opponents of the monastic life, 1.3, states that conversion of a concubine got Paul in hot water (Vouaux, 37). This looks like confusion with APtr, but see the reference to Romans 16 below. His *Homily on 2 Timothy* 10 says, à propos of 4:16: "He had appeared before Nero, but had escaped. Afterwards, because he had converted his cup-bearer, he was beheaded" (author's trans.). John therefore knew *APl* 14.

The *Homily on Acts* 46 states "that Paul was said to have saluted both Nero's cupbearer and his concubine." The exegetical context is Paul's arrest in Acts 21. Evidently an earlier commentator on Romans 16 had attempted to flesh out some of the names in the greeting list by reference to *APl* 14. Such enterprises, a staple of the commentator's art, presume general acceptance of the historical accuracy of *APl*, regardless of its canonical status. Just who was in mind is a difficult question. One possibility for the cupbearer is Narcissus (Rom 16:11). A former slave with this name was an official during the reign of Claudius. Chrysostom was familiar with *APl* 3 and 14. It is possible that he knew these as separate works, but this is no more demonstrable than the hypothesis that he knew the entire book.

12. Various patristic authorities. Jerome (c. 345–420), next to Tertullian, the most vigorous ancient critic of *APl*, proclaimed (*Vir. Ill.* 7): "We therefore classify the *Journeys of Paul and Thecla* and the entire fable of a baptized lion with the apocryphal writings." Although he has taken from Tertullian the story that a presbyter wrote the text, Jerome was familiar with it, for he,

Introduction

like many more recent critics, was particularly incensed by chap. 9, to which Tertullian did not refer. Jerome utilizes the term "journeys" (*periodoi*), reserving "Acts" (*praxeis*) for the canonical book. He asks if it were possible that Luke (Paul's constant companion) had overlooked this incident. That question will be answered by Nicephorus Callistus (below). Responsive animals were not a legitimate issue, for in his own egregiously fictional biographies of Paul, Malchus, and Hilarion Jerome did not hesitate to introduce thoughtful, considerate, and obedient animals as helpmeets to the ascetics. Moreover, in the climax of his letter on virginity to Eustochium (*Ep.* 22.41), Jerome introduces Thecla after Mary and Miriam. She will happily dash into Eustochium's arms. The story of Thecla was exemplary for this difficult and brilliant author. In sum: Jerome knew of chaps. 3, 4, and 9 of the APl.

Augustine of Hippo (354–430). In the account of Augustine's dispute with the Manichean Faustus (*C. Faustum* 30–31), Faustus concedes that Augustine will not accept evidence based upon the Acts of Andrew, John, Peter, and Thomas, but he presumes that arguments utilizing the story of Paul and Thecla will be mutually acceptable. The Manicheans had a corpus of five Acts used in place of the canonical book. In this context it is unlikely that Faustus was contrasting four apostolic acts to a "martyrdom" of Thecla (chaps. 3–4). *APl* is set against the others because it was generally acceptable in Catholic circles. See Vouaux, 46–50, who notes a reference to Thecla also in Augustine's *De sancta virginitate* 45.

13. Other Texts. The fourth-century *Life of Polycarp*, attributed to Pionius, 2. (Lightfoot, *Apostolic Fathers* 2/3:433–44) may be a witness to *APl*. Paul arrives at Smyrna from Galatia. *APl* 9 (P.Heid) has Paul depart from Smyrna for Ephesus. Nothing can be discovered of his activities there from P.Heid. Rordorf (1149) proposes that he went to Smyrna from Jerusalem. The *Life* is (unlike Polycarp) strongly anti-Quartodeciman. "Pionius" introduces a brother of Timothy, Strateas. These tantalizing data provide no help for the reconstruction of *APl*. See also Rordorf, "Was Wissen wir," 73.

The *Cena Cypriani. The Dinner Party*, which appeared in northern Italy or southern Gaul c. 360–70 (roughly contemporaneous with Ambrosiaster), resembles in technique the then popular cento, in which authors told the story of salvation in hexameters entirely derived from Virgil, for example, as well as parodic, even satiric, literature. On introductory questions, see Modesto, *Studien*, 72–77, whose edition is utilized here. Harnack, "Drei wenig," introduced this text into the discussion of *APl*. The specific genre is a symposium, linked to the wedding at Cana (John 2:1–12). Perhaps the work was composed as an entertainment associated with Epiphany. In any case it is a patent example of early Christian humor.

The Acts of Paul

The text names more than 450 biblical characters, about three-fourths of whom come from the Latin version of the LXX (OL), many more than once. Thecla is among the most popular, with nine references (16.5; 18.8; 24.8, 23; 28.15, 30.17, 19; 32.11; 34.17), all of which can be attributed to *APl* 3-4. For comparison Jesus receives one fewer than Thecla while Peter merits a dozen. In four places (16.9; 18.22; 24.17; 32.13) Paul is named. One of these could refer to the canonical Acts. Other characters are Onesiphorus (24.6) and Tryphaena (34.5), from *APl* 3-4, Hermocrates (20.12; 20.27; 26.16), and Hermippus (26.9), *APl* 5. Some of the statements about Paul could derive from other chapters: 16.9 *patiens stabat Paulus* ("Paul stood suffering"), 18.22 *Paulus candidam* ("Paul [wore] bright white), 24.17 *omnia perministravit Paulus* ("Paul administered everything") are quite general. A likely reference for 16.9 is *APl* 4.16. 16.9 might refer to his conversion (according to the accounts in Acts 9, 22, and 26 he fell to the ground).

The *Cena* is important for reconstruction of the *APl* in three ways. It attests to the existence of a fourth-century Latin translation that included not only the chapters about Thecla but also material for chap. 5 (Myra) and perhaps other portions of the work. For the author *APl* enjoyed more or less biblical status. No single reference can be positively attributed to the canonical Acts, although at least one is possible. Examples of this material, with glosses and comments:

16.5 *Tecla super fenestram, Susanna in orto*. Thecla in a window, Susanna in a garden. (These two women are often found together. See above.).

16.9b *Patiens stabat Paulus*. Paul stood suffering.

18.8 *Tecla flammeam, Danihel leoninam*. Thecla [wore] fiery red.

18.22 *Paulus candidam*. Paul [wore] bright white. The author uses tropes to indicate what the guests were wearing. Thecla's color comes from burning at the stake. Paul's gleaming white attire represents the blinding flash attending his conversion.

20.12b *Ventrem aperuit Hermocrates*. Hermocrates opened his stomach.

20.20-21 *Tunc intulit panes Saul, fregit Iesus*. Paul offered the loaves; Jesus broke them. See, e.g., 12.4.21, *Tradidit omnibus Petrus*. Peter distributed (bread) to everyone. The source may be APtr.

20.27b *Panem petebat Hermocrates*. Hermocrates asked for bread.

Introduction

24.8 *Araneum Tecla*. Among dishes contributed this plays on the spider imagery of 3.9. The word could mean "spider," but it also refers to a kind of fish.

24.17 *Omnia perministravit Paulus*. Paul took care of everything. Cf. *APl* 3.4.

24.23 *Arsinum Tecla*. "burnt wine" (from fire, again, as at 18.22).

26.9 b *Murmurabat Hermippus*. Hermippus was murmuring.

26.16 *Effudit Hermocrates, linteum porrexit Petrus*. Hermocrates poured [it] out; Peter spread the table cloth. Hermocrates suffered from dropsy and gushed. There are several possibilities for the reference to Peter.

28.15. *In fornacatore Ananias, in bestiario Tecla*. Ananias in the oven; Thecla as beastfighter.

30.7 *Taurum Tecla*. Thecla [contributed] a bull.

30.19b *Speculum argenteum Tecla*. Thecla (had) a silver mirror.

32.13 *Flagellatur Paulus*. Paul is whipped. (Could be Acts 17 but *APl* 3 fits the singular.)

24.6 *Attendebat Onesiforus*. Onesiphorus attended (3.3).

34.5a *Plorabat Trifena*. Tryphaena wept.

34.17 *Vestem detraxit Tecla*. Thecla removed her dress (she plays most of her scenes in the nude).

This work remained quite popular. A ninth-century edition by Rhabanus Maurus removed all of the references to the *APl* (Modesto, *Cena*, 122–75). This shows that he did not believe that such references belonged in a biblical parody. This work demonstrates shows that in popular circles, in which the rules and boundaries of ecclesiastical authorities were not viewed as sacrosanct, *APl* could be viewed as a biblical text in the late fourth century.

14. In 384 Egeria, probably a Spanish nun, visited the sacred sites of the East. One of these was the complex at Seleucia devoted to Thecla. Egeria describes her arrival at the martyr's shrine, "[W]e had a prayer there, and read the whole Acts of holy Thecla" (23.5; trans. Wilkinson, 141). The term "whole acts" would probably include the supplements to chap. 4 added to round off her life and enhance the shrine in Seleucia. Egeria did not have

to tell her sisters in religion who Thecla was; one may reasonably infer that they were familiar with the Acts.

15. Doubts about *APl*. By the late fourth century official views were hardening. Conflict with the rigorous followers of Priscillian and the existence of the Manichean corpus of Acts brought *APl* into disrepute. (*APl* was a source, like other ApocActs, of Manichean hymnody: Allberry, *Psalm-Book*, 2:143.5–10; 32; 192.25–193.32:143.) Innocent I (bishop of Rome) indicated, c. 405, that ApocActs were employed by Manichaeans and Priscillianists in Spain. Philaster, Bishop of Brescia, c. 390, views the various Acts as suitable only for the elite. The portions of *APl* with a liturgical home, chaps. 3–4, and 14 survived, as did the secondary 3 Cor; the rest seems to have disappeared in the West. The so-called "Gelasian Decree," a sixth-century piece from Spain or Gaul (France), seeks to demarcate canonical from apocryphal books. Among the latter is "a book which is called the Acts [*actus*] of Thecla and Paul" (6, 22). See Vouaux, 53–58, for details on various authorities. In the East matters were different.

16. The supersession of *APl* 14 at Rome. Under Roman influence the martyrdom chapters of *APl* and APtr were gradually coordinated, revised, and combined with Acts 27–28. The goal was to present and describe the joint martyrdom of Peter and Paul at Rome. See Tajra, *Martyrdom*, 143–65, and Pervo, *Making*, 168–69. (This amalgam was the only form reflective of *APl* known to the ancient Irish Church, McNamara, *Apocrypha*, 99–102, although the story of Thecla may also have been familiar, 113.)

17. Other Acts. *APl* were utilized directly by APtr, directly or indirectly by other ApocActs, and influenced such books as the *Acts of Titus* (Appendix 3), which contains clues about partially or entirely missing chapters of *APl*, and the *Acts of Polyxena and Xanthippe*. See Pervo, *Making*, 166–74.

18. *APl* in art. The amalgamation of the respective stories of Peter and Paul is well represented in art. See Cartlidge and Elliott, *Art*, 134–38. The fourth-century sarcophagus of Junius Bassus (Cartlidge and Elliott, fig. 5.4) and another sarcophagus of the same era (fig. 5.5) depict the arrest of Paul, an event not narrated in *APl*. An ivory of the fifth or sixth century has two scenes from chap. 3: Thecla listening to Paul (fig. 3.7) and Paul being stoned (fig. 3.21). A famous fragment of a sarcophagus from Rome depicts Paul steering a ship named "Thecla." She may be a trope for the church, often depicted as a ship and as a pure virgin. Perhaps the most famous image of Thecla is a limestone carving now in Kansas City, Missouri, which is a

Introduction

stylized portrayal of Thecla among the wild animals (*APl* 4; fig. 5.10). For discussion of these and other material remains, see Cartlidge and Elliott, *Art*, 143–62, and Castelli, *Martyrdom*, 157–71. Artistic representation echoes literary testimonies in showing preference for chaps. 3–4 and 14. See also van den Hoek and Herrmann Jr., "Thecla the Beast Fighter: A Female Emblem of Deliverance in early Christian Popular Art."

19. Byzantine witnesses. On the seventh-century Homily on St. Thecla wrongly attributed to Chrysostom see pp. 140–41 (chap 3).

Nicetas of Paphlagonia, a tenth-century orator wrote a panegyric of Paul that utilized *APl*. Nicetas was a pupil of Photius, a vigorous critic of ApocActs. (On the views of Photius, see Junod, "Actes Apocryphes.") In 1931 Vogt published panegyrics on Saints Peter and Paul by Nicetas of Paphlagonia, a pupil of Photius. Although he was a learned man at home with Scripture and established patristic authorities, Nicetas did not hesitate to use apocryphal sources in his panegyric, including the *APl*. Nicetas follows Acts and the epistles closely until he comes to Paul's departure from Damascus. Immediately following the description of his escape in the basket (which does not appear to be a component of the extant portions of APl), he reports that Paul went to Syrian Antioch (82r; these numbers are those of the ms.). There Paul preached, was imprisoned, and subsequently rescued. The chief of the city saw in a vision his son, who had died. His wife was also restored. This is presumably a summary of the episode of Anchares and Phila (*APl* 2).

Thence the apostle went to Iconium. Nicetas summarizes the deeds of Thecla, whose authority he underlines. The oration then records a(n initial) Jerusalem visit inspired by a desire to interview Peter, whom Paul had not previously seen (83r). At this juncture (84r, *ad fin.*) Nicetas reverts, apparently, to Acts 13, for 84v reports that, with Barnabas, he returned to Antioch again. Thereafter the orator takes up the mission to the Anatolian cities, Myra and Lystra, with a suitable apostrophe on the apostle's experiences. Ephesus is the next destination. The orator thus appears to describe an itinerary that moved from Antioch through southern Asia Minor to Ephesus. There Paul delivers a public address, summarizing, after an appeal to natural revelation (cf. *APl* 9), the stories of the fall and the redemption (85v–86v). It is worthy of note that this is the only speech of Paul quoted *verbatim* in the entire panegyric. The text continues to follow *APl* 9. Nicetas refers to an "apostolic act" (*praxis*) and argues that the one who had delivered Thecla would also save Paul from the beasts, referring to 1 Cor 15:32.

Nicetas then generally follows Acts, with an initial acquittal of Paul at Rome followed by more evangelizing and a second arrest that appears to

The Acts of Paul

derive from later sources that integrated the stories of Peter and Paul. His work shows continued use of multiple sources. The *APl* serve not only to fill gaps in the canonical account but also to supersede it at points, particularly in the narrative reported in Acts 9–15; 19. The Pauline itinerary revealed in this oration is as follows: Damascus, Syrian Antioch, Iconium, Jerusalem, Antioch, Myra, Lystra, Ephesus, Philippi, Thessalonica, Athens, Beroea, Corinth, Macedonia, Troad, Ephesus, and the other cities of Asia, Jerusalem, Caesarea, Rome, Italy, East and West, Rome. Nicetas appears to have had at his disposal the entire *APl*, as he refers to chaps. 2, 3, 4, and 9, at least.

Nicephorus Callistus (c. 1256–c. 1335) composed a church history in eighteen books that covered the period from Christ's birth to 610, based upon various sources. *Ecclesiastical History* 2.25 reads:

> Now they who drew up the travels of Paul have related that he did many other things, and among them this, which befell when he was at Ephesus. Hieronymus being governor, Paul used liberty of speech, and he (Hieronymus) said that he (Paul) was able to speak well, but that this was not the time for such words. But the people of the city, fiercely enraged, put Paul's feet into irons, and shut him up in the prison, till he should be exposed as prey to the lions. But Eubula and Artemilla, wives of eminent men among the Ephesians, being his attached disciples, and visiting him by night, desired the grace of the divine washing. And by God's power, with angels to escort them and enlighten the gloom of night with the excess of the brightness that was in them, Paul, loosed from his iron fetters, went to the sea-shore and initiated them into holy baptism, and returning to his bonds without any of those in care of the prison perceiving it, was reserved as a prey for the lions.
>
> A lion then, of huge size and unmatched strength, was let loose upon him, and it ran to him in the stadium and lay down at his feet. And when many other savage beasts, too, were let loose, it was permitted to none of them to touch the holy body, standing like a statue in prayer. At this juncture a violent and vast hailstorm poured down all at once with a great rush, and shattered the heads of many men and beasts as well, and shore off the ear of Hieronymus himself. And thereafter, with his followers, he came to the God of Paul and received the baptism of salvation. But the lion escaped to the mountains.
>
> And thence Paul sailed to Macedonia and Greece, and thereafter through Macedonia came to Troas and to Miletus, and from there set out for Jerusalem.

> Now it is not surprising that Luke has not narrated this fight with the beasts along with the other acts: for it is not permitted to entertain doubt because (or seeing that) John alone of the evangelists has told of the raising of Lazarus: for we know that not every one writes, believes, or knows everything, but according as the Lord has imparted to each, so does he perceive and believe and write spiritually the things of the spirit. (trans. James, *The Apocryphal New Testament*, 292)

It is noteworthy that (in the last paragraph) Nicephorus defends the authenticity of the story of Paul and the lion by analogy with the different accounts found in the intracanonical gospels. Both traditions (Acts and the APl) are valid. Nicephorus regards the "travels" as supplemental to Acts. The extent to which he made direct use of *APl* is disputable, since he may have garnered material from Nicetas or another source, but once again there is evidence that a later authority viewed *APl* as parallel ("when he was at Ephesus") to Acts rather than as a sequel. For additional witnesses, see Vouaux, 58–64.

The penultimate example is "The History of the Contending of Saint Paul," part of an Ethiopic collection. This selection exemplifies the rather extravagant growth of tradition. Researchers peruse this text in hope of discovering a trace of a missing portion of *APl*, but with no clear success. The "Contending" is a hagiographic hodge-podge, the object of which appears to have been the utilization of all possible sources before exploiting the less possible. There are many items of interest not germane to this inquiry. An instance is an alternate description (to *APl* 3.3, p. 438, chap 2): "[A] . . . vigorous man of fine, upright stature, and his countenance was ruddy with the ruddiness of the skin of the pomegranate, his complexion was clear, his nose was high and large, his eyes were dark, and his cheeks were full, and bearded, and of the colour of a rose." This is one indicator of ancient lack of enthusiasm for the famous description and a good indicator of fidelity to *APl*.

Chapter 9, for example, takes Paul to Ephesus, with a scene reminiscent of the *Acts of John*, as the temple of Artemis contains many sick people. On p. 483 Demetrius, properly, as it were, located in Ephesus and correctly identified as a smith, although as "the smith of the idol Artemis." Page 484 sees the arrival of a lioness, a mixture of *APl* 4 and 9. This creature speaks, and licks while kissing the feet of the accused, Paul and Trophimus. With p. 485 arrives another savage creature, associated with an Alexander (*APl* 4). A speech with many features like that of Paul in *APl* 9 (p. 485) precedes another lion attack (486–87), at which the creature is a very lamb. All of this, p. 438 makes clear, is what 1 Cor 15:32 was about. The story of Thecla, an immensely popular saint in Egypt, is omitted. The narrator wishes to defend Paul against the charge of fracturing marriage. Those who wished to tell the whole story of Paul, the full story of Paul, and more than the full story of Paul utilized *APl* to fill gaps in Acts. It is also an example of mutual contamination among the traditional ApocActs.

The "Letter of Pelagia," translated by Goodspeed in 1903, was an important source for reconstructing *APl* before the discoveries of the twentieth century. See Schmidt, *Acta*, xxi–xxix. This describes, in the style of *APl*, Paul's mission to Caesarea (which Caesarea is not specified; Maritima, the coastal capital, is probably in view). The apostle was arrested but released after preaching a sermon on God the creator. The baptism of the lion follows. The raising of a dead brother (see chap. 5) occasions a long sermon with OT examples.

Among those following Paul was Pelagia, the king's [!] daughter, who left her husband. The example of Thecla looms large. (See also Goodspeed, "Book.") Arrested, Paul is condemned to the lion, which, of course, is the one he had baptized. This follows *APl* 9 closely. Paul and the lion are released, but Pelagia is condemned to be cast into a red hot, hollow cow. (This kind of torture is familiar in the "Contending" previously reviewed.) Rain ruined this plan, in a somewhat inept borrowing from *APl* 3. The husband took his own life. Schmidt (*Acta* xxv–vi) notes contamination with the known legend of Pelagia of Tarsus. Behind this story can be seen an edition of *APl* that included chaps 4 and 9. Judgment balances between two poles: the *APl* as stimulation for creative hagiography and/or as the basis of tawdry and unimaginative imitation. The same work, as the two representatives of Ethiopic Christianity suggest, may contain both.

20. Manuscripts and versions of *APl*. These witnesses of the specific text of *APl* are the subject of the following section. They also constitute evidence for the popularity and distribution of APL The existence of at least eleven papyri, in Greek and Coptic, from Egypt, is a respectable number. For the canonical Acts thirteen Greek papyri are known.

Concluding summary. The *APl* were known from Spain in the West to Mesopotamia in the East, from France in the North to Ethiopia in the South, and translated into many languages. *APl*, in one form or another, never ceased to be viewed as historical. Theological objections were raised by two famous Latin writers: Tertullian, who fulminated against the text's authorization of women, and Jerome, who took great exception to the baptism of a lion. The latter indicates that at least some readers did not understand the symbolic nature of this story and ancient debates about the qualities of animals. Of

Introduction

the former the most important fact is that Tertullian was not joined by nearly every other ecclesiastical authority.

APl was tainted in the West because of its use by followers of Priscillian and its presence in the Manichaean corpus of five Acts, but, like most such decisions, it was not universally honored. The Codex Claromontanus list and the *Cena Cypriani* attest to APl's presence in a broad collection of biblical books. A parallel to this is the continuing presence of 3 Cor in some biblical mss. and of Laodiceans in Latin mss. until the Renaissance. These were the most Catholic of the ApocActs and often distinguished from the others because of a lack of speculative theology.

APl nevertheless suffered a fate common to ApocActs in general: the opening was lost and the final chapter was detached (and edited) to serve as reading for the apostolic feast days. Two factors contributed to the loss of the initial chapter. One is mechanical: the beginning (and closing) parts of codices were the most vulnerable. Another is a deviation from the eventually canonized Gospels and Acts. *APl* is distinctive in that three portions survived in independent forms: the story of Thecla (chaps. 3-4), 3 Cor, a later addition then detached to become a part of the Corpus Paulinum, and the Passion.

III. The Materials for the Reconstruction of the Acts of Paul.

This list includes two parts, direct witnesses, with actual texts, and other documents useful for determining the original shape and content. The abbreviations used in this commentary are placed in parentheses. For more details see Geerard, *Clavis,* 117-26.

1. A Greek papyrus of third to fourth century (P.Hamb). Eleven leaves. (Schmidt and Schubart, *Praxeis*). Shorter Greek papyri include:

1a. P. Michigan 1317, 3788, P. Berlin 13893, P. Oxy. 6, 1602, P. Bodmer 10, fourth century, mostly overlapping with P.Hamb. Cf. also Gronewald, "Einige Fackelmann-Papyri," 274-75.

2. A Coptic papyrus of fifth to sixth century, P.Heid. This includes 2000 fragments, ranging from tiny fragments to sections of consecutive pages, of parts of the entire work. (Schmidt, *Acta*)

3. Paul and Thecla (Chaps 3-4), available in over forty Greek mss. and various versions. Conybeare, *Apology,* 49-88, judges (59) that the Latin

The Acts of Paul

tradition is superior to the Greek, the Syriac to the Latin, and the Armenian to Syriac. His arguments, 49–60, are still worth consulting. For a translation of the Syriac, see Wright, *Apocryphal Acts*, 2:116–45. The variant traditions indicate, at the very least, that this story experienced considerable editing.

4. The Martyrdom (chap. 14), available in several Greek mss. and various versions. Additional bibliography on various versions can be found in Elliott, *Apocrypha*, 358–59.

5. P. Rylands inv. 44 (chap. 1). A short but valuable Coptic papyrus, yet unpublished. See Crum, "New Coptic Manuscripts in the John Rylands Library," 497–503, 501.

6. Coptic Bodmer Papyrus XLI (chap. 9). See Kasser and Luisier, "Le Papyrus Bodmer XLI."

The following texts are of use in reconstructing the shape of *APl* and in identifying missing or fragmentary chapters:

7. The *Acts of Titus*. See Appendix 3

8. Nicetas of Paphlagonia. See above, II.18

9. Nicephorus Callistus. See above II.18

10. The *Cena Cypriani*. See above II.13

11. The *Life of Polycarp* attributed to Pionius. (See under II.13.)

Fragments of unknown location:

12. A citation from Origen [above]. See also Appendix I.

13. P.Yale 87 (inv. 1376, in Stephens, ed., *Yale Papyri in the Beinecke Rare Book and Manuscript Library II*, 3–7). See Appendix I.

Excursus: Did *APl* Originate as a Single Text?

Prior to 1900 only the three distinct segments, chaps. 3–4 (Thecla), 10 (3 Cor) and 14 (Martyrdom) were known. Some astute critics, notably Zahn (e.g., *Geschichte* 2.2:880n2), proposed a unified *APl*. The discoveries of the twentieth century have filled out the text. Scholarship has assumed that a single text had been fragmented. Scholarly assumptions benefit from challenges. Snyder ("Remembering") has challenged the notion of a single, original *APl*. His arguments should be considered.

At some point a unified *APl* existed. Nicetas (II.18) shows that this was the case in the tenth century. P.Hamb and P.Heid are good evidence that this was also the case much earlier. All of the items noted in section II that include more than one section are evidence for a unified Acts. Tertullian and Origen both knew of a work entitled "The *Acts of Paul*." Tertullian refers only to chap. 4, but he does not suggest that it constituted the entire book (for which *Acts of* Paul would scarcely be a suitable title). He also knew chap. 14. Origen knew at least chaps. 3 and 13. It is quite likely that he had access to the entire text. The existence of a work that included at least two of the sections known today existed in the early third century.

The other major point is literary. The different sections show parallels that reflect the work of a single hand. The most notable of these are between chaps. 3–4 and 9. For details consult the comments on those chapters. Another distinct parallelism can be seen between Thecla (chap. 3) and Patroclus (chap. 14). Although it is possible that a later author created 3 or 14 to correspond with the other, this is not as likely as the hypothesis of a single author. Themes and styles are recurrent, despite the ravages of editing. Finally, the various sections of *APl* exhibit a general plan. Such plans can be discovered or contrived after the fact, but, again, it is more probable that a single mind has devised this plan. The book was not left intact. In addition to excerpts, 3 Cor was added (chap. 10) and both expansion and abridgement may be suspected at various points in the work. The extant material points to a single work developed by a single author on the basis of various sources and ideas.

The Acts of Paul

Table 1.1: Contents of the Acts of Paul

Chapter	Location/Subject	Condition
1	Damascus to Jerusalem (conversion)	D
2	(Syrian?) Antioch	C--
3	Iconium (Paul converts Thecla)	A
4	Antioch (Thecla)	A
5	Myra	C
6	Sidon	C (-)
7	Tyre	C-
8	Jerusalem, Cilicia, Smyrna (?)	C--
9	Ephesus	B+
10	Philippi (*3 Corinthians*, a later addition)	A-
11	Philippi	C-
12	Corinth	B+
13	Voyage to Italy	B
14	Rome (martyrdom)	A

Key
A: Attested in multiple witnesses.
B: Fairly complete attestation (B+= 2 witnesses, for at least part).
C: Fragmentary attestation.
D: Little data available

IV. Genre; structure, style.

Generic classification is one means of determining the function of a work (which is not the same as its purpose: the function of an automobile engine, e.g., is to run; its purpose is to drive a vehicle). For example, nearly every scholar would classify *APl* as a work of fiction. Formally, it may share many features with a work of fact. This is how many would contrast the canonical Acts to APl: formally similar but different on the question of fact. On the practical plane genre determines comparability: Where would one place this on her bookshelf? For many, the question would today be determined by fact: canonical Acts merits an LC designation while *APl* is filed alphabetically by author (or would be if the author were known), for non-fiction and fiction respectively.

Since *APl* is incomplete, hypotheses about genre may play some role in reconstruction of the text. *APl* belongs to a group, the ApocActs. Groupings often promote views about genre. This approach may also be misleading. Bovon recommends a holistic approach: *all* of the Acts spring from the canonical Gospels ("Canonical," and "Synoptic Gospels"; see also Brock,

Introduction

"Genre"). This is fundamental, but it does not bring the quest to an end, for the canonical gospel type is generically malleable and complex, with a number of constituent forms. Mark and John, for example, are similar in their lack of stories about Jesus' birth, but Mark is more like Matthew, which has an infancy narrative, than like John, although both Matthew and John include more long speeches than does Mark. To posit Mark as the point of departure also raises the questions about the cultural, political, and religious factors that promoted the gospel as the characteristic vehicle of the Christian message. These factors coalesced around the biographical: the message of Jesus and the story about Jesus are intertwined. This is one reason why the heroes of the Acts tend to become "Christ-figures." (On the canonical Acts, see Pervo, *Acts*, 644–67, e.g.; on *APl*, see below.) Narrative fiction focusing upon an individual as a means of affirming identity in a minority religious context emerged in the Hellenistic era. See Braun, *History and Romance*, and Pervo, "*Testament of Joseph*." One characteristic of the several acts is that they take up the heroes and heroines when they begin their careers, so to speak. This is a feature of monographs that distinguishes that genre from biographies proper. The canonical Acts, for example, begins with Paul as a "young" persecutor of the Jesus people (Acts 7:58b; 8:1a; 9:1–2), although the story of Jesus devoted 132 verses to his birth and childhood. (Because information about birth and education was an essential part of claims to social status, Acts has Paul supply these data in a speech [22:3].)

One genre that contributed to the Acts was the ancient novel. Novels in antiquity were generally historical in form. (Comic novels constitute the major exception.) Restricting the term to romantic novels is questionable. (See Schmeling, ed., *Novel*.) A major reason for comparison of various novels to the several acts is to show that the acts were intended as popular writings. Links between the ApocActs and the Greek romantic novels—love stories that focused upon the trials and tribulations of a young couple—have been explored for more than a century. Both Acts and romantic novels flourished in the second century. Brown characterizes these links by judging the acts as

> Epic Christianity, a Christianity of impact. Wandering Apostles pass through proud cities wreaking havoc with the established pagan order—altars explode, temples collapse, storms bring to an ignominious halt the evil roar of the circus ... The Apocryphal Acts explored with zest and attentiveness the issues of vocation, of vulnerability and of survival in a dramatically hostile environment. For this reason, the choice of the late classical Romance as a model for so many Acts was a stroke of genius. For the pagan Romances had already developed a narrative form that overlapped with the central concerns of a Christianity of

> impact and vocation. They had frequently begun with a moment of love at first sight. Time stood still as two souls, destined for each other, met for the first time. (Brown, *Body*, 155)

"Stroke of genius" is doubtless correct in the long view. At the time it may have required much more conscious thought than does the contemporary (2012) commingling of news and entertainment and the deliberate confounding of fact with fiction. People watch "reality" shows to see who will go home this week and political primary returns to learn who will be eliminated this week.

The best example of direct imitation of/competition with romantic novels is *APl*. Romantic elements are concentrated in chap. 3; they are the means by which the author fashioned Thecla into a disciple of Paul. Whereas the lovers in romantic novels are equals, the lover as disciple is inferior to the master. Greek education had long included a possible sexual element in which a mature man initiated a boy into the adult world, while the ideal marriage partner for a married man was an utterly inexperienced and unformed girl. (For examples, see Dover, *Homosexuality*, 47, 91, and 202–3; Pomeroy, in eadem, ed., 33–57.) In so far as it utilizes the genre, *APl* belongs to the reception of the romantic novel; to the extent that its approach is creative it represents the opening of a new chapter in ancient fiction. Reflection on the relations between the romantic novel and *APl* has produced much research of good quality. On the specific question of genre see, e.g., Brock, "Genre," and Aubin, "Reversing."

APl may be classified, logically enough, as an acts (*praxeis*; see Pervo, *Acts*, 14–18). The broader category to which it belongs is the historical novel. The major model is the canonical gospel (see below). Unlike the canonical Acts, this book does not just have a major character who emerges in the course of the narrative; Paul is the major character from the outset, to all intents and purposes the only apostle. No need to legitimate gentile Christianity and its chief apostle is visible. *APl* also provides a "proper" conclusion: Paul's martyrdom and post-mortem vindication.

Structure. More recent studies of this issue include Rordorf, "Was Wissen wir?"; and Dunn, "Pauline Legacy," 26–49. All who work on the structure of *APl* are indebted to the patient labors of the pioneer researchers, among whom Carl Schmidt stands out. His essays in *Acta* remain valuable more than a century later.

Table 1.2: Acts of Paul as a "Gospel"

Element	APl	Gospel Parallel (Blank = Mark)	Acts et al.
1. [Initial Epiphany commission]	Cf. 9.5–6, repeat (?)	1:9–11	9:1–19a (repeated: 22; 26) cf. Gal 1:17
2. Wilderness	Cf. 9:7	1:12–13	
3. Ministry			
A. proclamation B. wonders C. persecution	A 2, 3 B 2 C 2	A 1:14–15; 1:21 B 1:23–34 C 2:1–22; cf. Luke 4:16–30	9:20–22 13:6–12; 9:23–25
Inaugural sermon, opening macarisms	3.5–6	Matt 5:3–12	
4. Recruits followers who renounce all and are persecuted and Forerunners	3 3 3–4; 14 3.1	1:16–20; 10:28 13:9–13; Matt 10:17–25 Luke 10:1	14:20 14:1–6
5. "Passion Predictions"	12.2, 3, 5; 13.2	8:31; 9:31; 10:33–34	20:35; 21:4, 11–13
6. Passion A. Message in capital B. "Gethsemane" C. Arrest D. Trial E. Execution	13:5–14:1 14.4 14.3 14:3–4 14:5	11–13 13:32–42 14:43 14:53–15:15	28:17–31 21:10–14 21:33 22:30–25:12
7. Vindication A. Appearance B. Empty Tomb	14.6 14.7	15:16–37; John 19:34 Luke 24; Matt 28 16:1–8	-- Note

<u>Note</u>. Pervo argues that Acts 27–28 symbolically represent the "death" and vindication of Paul (Pervo, *Acts*, 644–54).

Table 1.2 shows that *APl* both contains many of the leading structural features of a canonical gospel and presents them in roughly the same order. The "strong" statement of the significance of this structure is that the text presents Paul as a "Christ figure" (Pervo, "Christ Figure"). Stated less strongly, but not contradictorily, the story takes the proper shape for a "perfect" imitator of Jesus. The fourth column indicates that Acts followed much the same pattern. This is also the pattern of the other acts (granting that Paul's story cannot begin in Jerusalem after the Ascension).

The Acts of Paul

Chapter 1 is extremely fragmentary. From the "flashback" in chap. 9 it is clear that, after some time spent in ministry at Damascus, Paul set out for Jerusalem. It is not indisputably certain that he arrived there. The narrator may have related the story of the converted lion in chap. 1, repeating it in 9, or the story may have first been related in 9. The latter seems slightly more probable. Two distinct structural features are clear. The episodes featuring Thecla portray a convert who became a disciple of Paul and a missionary in her own right. The other is the "Passion Narrative" of chaps. 12–14. Ancient editors did not mark these as separate components of the narrative.

Otherwise, the narrative may have moved, like Acts, toward Jerusalem at the center. The course of action proceeds from Damascus to Jerusalem (if Acts was followed at this point), to Antioch, then southern Asia Minor (the provinces covered in Acts 13–14), to coastal Palestine, Jerusalem, and then to Cilicia (? Cf. Gal 1:21; Acts 9:30). Thereafter Paul visits the Asian coastal cities of Smyrna (on which there is no data) and Ephesus (chap. 9), sailing thence to Philippi, Corinth, and Italy. Building upon a precedent established by the historical Paul, *APl* tends to focus upon one city per province. The narrator prefers detailed development of a single mission to brief, if lively, summaries of many. Although some of these sites are new foundations, the primary focus is upon Paul's role in nurturing established communities. This is appropriate to the date of composition. Paul was the pastor and teacher of communities wrestling with a host of problems, as well as joys. Although the apostle is rarely the first believer on the scene, he, as in Acts (Acts 19; 28), effectively founds the church wherever he goes. Paul's arrival ignites conflict. Believers may have been going about their business in tranquility, but, upon Paul's advent, trouble explodes. He is a travelling volcano. Trouble is not regularly attributable to Jews. Conflict with or attempts to convert Jews are not part of the general picture. Christian false teachers (as in Paul but not in Acts) can stir up trouble (chap. 3, later expanded by the interpolation of 3 Cor), but polytheism is the standard opponent.[6] Behind polytheism stands the civic leadership. Paul is a moral threat to the community and its long established values and traditions. At the micro level the threat is to the family; disloyalty to the empire embraces the macro level. Although the narrative evidently attended to some cities given minimal

---

6. Both "polytheism" and "paganism" have defects as labels for ancient religions other than those of Israel and of the Christians. "Paganism" has fallen out of favor because of its pejorative connotations. "Polytheism" does not in this book imply a fixed contrast between belief in many deities vs. belief in a single god. Most often it means non-exclusive religion(s). Ancient intellectuals who preferred to speak of a single god rarely attacked the various gods or their cults. For an airing of the limits of this term, see Fredriksen, "Mandatory Retirement," 231–46.

Introduction

attention in Acts (Myra, Sidon, Tyre, Smyrna, chaps. 5–8), the author does not seem to have looked for blank spots, as it were. The chief sites are those of Acts. The source question therefore requires attention.

V. Sources and Editing.

APl made use of the Synoptic Gospels and John, as well as Pauline letters. See Vouaux, 113–24, as well as the notes and comments on the text. In the early decades of the twentieth century critics generally assumed that the author knew and used the canonical Acts (e.g., Schmidt, *Acta*, 198–217, Vouaux, 113–24). Later, other views came to prevail. Schneemelcher states, "I have attempted to explain the agreements and the differences between the *APl* and Acts on the basis that the author of the *APl* probably did know Acts, but is not literarily dependent on it; rather he used traditions that were in circulation about Paul and his work" ("Acts of Paul," 232). For details, see "Apostelgeschichte." Rordorf has vigorously upheld the position that *APl* did not know Acts. See also Dunn, "Legacy," 49–57. In the last decade of the twentieth century the question was decisively settled: *APl* utilized Acts as a major source. See Bauckham, "Replacement"; Hills, "Legacy"; Marguerat, "Rereading"; and Pervo, "Hard Act."

The major objection to the use of Acts was content. In brief, if the author of *APl* used Acts, how could he have been in such disagreement with it? This objection does not take *APl* seriously as fiction. It presumes that Acts was always and everywhere an authoritative (and accurate) work. Neither assumption is valid. When faced with the alternatives of unattested oral traditions that happen to agree with the written text of Acts or Acts, probability resides with the latter. That probability increases when the evidence for specific linguistic borrowing (Hills, "Legacy") is introduced. The current question is not whether *APl* knew Acts, but the author's view of Acts.

Bauckham proposed that *APl* is a sequel to Acts ("Sequel"). Pervo developed the case for viewing *APl* as a replacement of Acts. Marguerat opted for a mediating view, which, in the end, is a mild form of the replacement hypothesis. Two analogies may be explored. Can one compare the difference between Acts and *APl* to that between Mark and Matthew? The initial reaction may be that the contrast between the two acts is greater. What after all, did Matthew change from Mark? The beginning and the end, without doubt. To these must be added extensive expansions and revisions of the middle. The debate could be extensive. The purpose here is to stress that an unfamiliar work, like *APl*, will seem more unlike a familiar writing, than will one familiar work to another (e.g., Mark and Matthew). The second analogy is with the Pastoral Epistles (1–2 Timothy, Titus = PE). All agree that *APl* knows and uses the PE and that contrasts between the two can be discovered. See, most notably, MacDonald, *Legend*. The author of *APl* used the PE both to enhance his credibility, as it were, and to discredit the PE.

Those who view *APl* as a work of edification and entertainment presume that the author did not expect readers to view his work as factual. For them use and misuse of Acts and the PE raise no problems. Alas, these books are precisely the problem. It is likely that the writer of *APl* wanted his book to enjoy greater authority than either Acts or the PE. This is a preferable way to state the matter, for what authors wish their readers to believe—a slippery term—is extremely difficult to discover and may have little to do with what said readers may or may not believe. Modern readers do not believe that *APl* is "true" because they do not believe that Paul demanded perfect celibacy—or baptized animals. Many, including myself, do not believe that Paul wrote the PE because of their views about women, for example. Belief structures and history do not correlate. For example, if someone were to publish a story describing Sherlock Holmes as a sadistic serial killer of children, fans would not "believe" it, despite accuracies in background, characterization, and style (not to mention the irony of "believing" any Sherlock Holmes story).

If all will not agree that *APl* seeks to supersede Acts, as Matthew and Luke sought to supersede Mark, or that the author of *APl* thought that he or she could "do it better," there will be agreement that *APl* seeks to "do it" differently. The first indisputable use of Acts, together with the attribution of both the Third Gospel and Acts, is by Irenaeus of Lyon, c. 180 (see Pervo, *Acts*, 1). Irenaeus was also the first writer to identify the PE as Pauline. Some doubted their genuineness, including Basilides and Marcion (Tertullian, *Against Marcion* 5.21), Tatian (1–2 Timothy, according to Jerome, Preface to his *Commentary on Titus*), and others, according to Clement of Alexandria, *Strom.* 2.11. All of these doubters were classified as heretics in emerging Christian orthodoxy. The author of *APl* was not engaged in attacking widely accepted and "canonical" books.

APl is a witness to the D-Text (also known as the "Western Text") of Acts. From the perspective of literary development the D-Text is a kind of intermediary between the conventional text of Acts and the *APl*. See Czachesz, "Between"; Head, "Problem"; and Hills, "Legacy." This is not to posit an evolutionary model, but to locate *APl* within a world of thought and upon a line of literary history.

Another category is that of unwritten or unavailable sources. These have been a stimulus of long standing. One possibility is chap. 14, a legend or legends about the death of Paul. See Snyder, "Remembering," 10–66, and

Rordorf, "Christenverfolgung." One basis for a hypothetical source is the militant apocalyptic tone of this chapter. Upon examination, however, this intensifies themes and motifs found throughout the text. Nothing in the text indicates local knowledge of Rome. The chapter is most prudently viewed as an authorial composition.

Critics since Ramsay (*Church*, 375–428; Jensen, *Thekla*) have found in chapter 4 the strongest claim for a historical basis in *APl*. This chapter is quite likely the oldest narrative section of the book. The material about Paul in chap. 4 is improbable, unflattering, and readily identified as secondary. The most apposite and defensible reconstruction is to posit that a legend about Thecla, quite probably in written form, antedated *APl*. The author composed chap. 3 as a preface and revised chap. 4 to translate Thecla from a quite independent Christian confessor and missionary into a disciple of Paul (Esch-Wermeling, *Thekla*). The composition of chap. 3 was quite skillfully managed, but the editing of chap. 4 was less than distinguished. Having got Paul out of the way by expulsion from Iconium, the author may have hesitated to use the same device twice, but nearly anything would have been superior to the appearance of cowardly flight. In the end Thecla evaded subordination to Paul and flourished at Seleucia.

With this key it is possible to understand an important element of the compositional technique, for the parallels between Paul and Thecla in chap. 9 derive from chap. 4, while those between Thecla and Patroclus (chap. 14) are to chap. 3. Thecla's story appears to have inspired the structure of much of the work. Artistically, her story made an important contribution. This does not explain why the author sought to absorb and incorporate the Iconian into his book. Was Thecla already so popular that her presence lent cachet to Paul? Was he seeking to induce independent women into the Pauline circle? Here some data are available, since one contribution of *APl* is to oppose the views of Paul and Thecla to those of the Pastor. This answer can gain some traction. At least one probable explanation for introducing the story of Thecla into the tale of Paul is to say that the "real Paul" welcomed energetic celibate women, unlike the creature responsible for the PE.

For the rest, the author is essentially responsible, with the important assistance of hints and bits from Acts and the epistles. Local and other traditions are not prominent. Subsequent editors sought to keep *APl* up to date. The addition of 3 Cor, which pits the apostle against contemporary "heresies," is the most widely recognized addition. Examination of the versions reveals tendencies to abbreviate and to expand. Many of these changes are described in the notes. Some changes are ideological or doctrinal. A widely recognized example is the costume of Alexander (4.1), modified in the Byzantine world to eliminate an insult to the Emperor. Chapter 9 exhibits expansions probably made by a later editor. Editorial additions are probable in chap. 13 and possible in the case of chap. 14. *APl* was not a highly stable text, given the detachment and expansion of chaps 3–4, the separation of chap. 14 as a martyrdom reading, and the interpolation of chap. 10, to note the highlights.

The style of APL may be characterized as "popular," in several senses. The Greek, where preserved, is simple; the structural and plotting devices do not demand sophistication; suspense is frequent, but gratification is rarely delayed; good and evil characters are drawn with broad strokes, and so forth. "Popular" does not mean mass-produced, which requires technology not available until c. 1840 for light reading, nor does it mean only for the less-educated. For discussion of the subject with regard to ancient literature, see Hansen's definition, in the introduction to his *Anthology of Ancient Greek Popular Literature*, xi–xxiii and Pecere's comments in Pecere and Stramaglia, eds., *La letteratura di consumo nel mondo greco-latino*, 5–7.

VI. The Date and Provenance. Author.

See Vouaux, 104–12; and Dunn, "Legacy," 21–24. Tertullian's discussion of *APl* (above, II.1) establishes a date of composition before 200. The work can scarcely be earlier than 150, as indicated by knowledge of multiple gospels, a Pauline corpus inclusive of the PE, and other texts, probably including *2 Clement*. The issue is not the date of any one of these texts, but the availability of a large number. The spirit of the work shows that it belongs to the era of the apologists without deep immersion in their theologies. Similarly, the author is not engaged in polemic. *APl* has no sympathy with the speculative theologies known as "Gnosis." The writer may be sympathetic to the New Prophecy ("Montanism"), but does not discuss this controversy, or others, such as that surrounding the date of Easter (Quartodeciman controversy). The book is reasonably dated slightly before Irenaeus, i.e., c. 170–75.

Consensus agrees with Tertullian that *APl* was written in Asia, the Roman province including much of what is now western Turkey. Affinities with the *Martyrdom of Polycarp* have suggested Smyrna (Vouaux, 99–104; Schmidt, *Acta* 205n1). That *Martyrdom* assumes strong antagonism between the Jewish and Christian communities (although these features may be later: Campenhausen, "Bearbeitungen"). On those grounds a location in Galatia would probably suit. In truth, the absence of a special interest in a particular city and the failure to display accurate data about nearly every community make it difficult to formulate a cogent argument about a particular locality. Readers did not, one hopes, pick up *APl* to learn geography.

Introduction

Tertullian's claim that *APl* was written by an Asian presbyter is widely accepted. This may be because the location is reasonable and the motivation of love for Paul irresistible, but for those familiar with polemical writings it has the earmarks of an attempt to discredit a work by reference to the character of its author and the circumstances of its composition. A relevant example is the so-called Jewish Christian material found in Epiphanius' *Panarion* 30.16.7–9, which claimed that Paul was a pagan gentile who converted to Judaism in order to marry a priest's daughter. Failing to achieve this ambition, he began to attack circumcision and Torah. The excuse of "Love of Paul" is probably sarcastic on the lips of Tertullian. Modern critics are likely to wonder what hatred of Paul would have produced if the story about Paul and Thecla manifests love for him. One must also ask why Tertullian alone learned this story, which would have been a useful arrow in his quiver of rejection. The story is too suspect to serve as helpful information. *APl* was an anonymous book that seemed to later scribes (if not to the author) to have been issued under the authority of Paul.

VII. The Theology of *APl*

References and details supporting the following general statements will be found in the body of the commentary.

In 1916 Lake ("Acts," 33) said that, theologically, APl

> has exceptional value as giving a presentment of the ordinary Christianity of Asia at the end of the 2nd cent., undisturbed by polemical or other special aims.
>
> So far as the doctrine of God is concerned, the teaching of the Acts is quite simple—it is that 'there is one God, and his Son, Jesus Christ,' which is sometimes condensed into the statement that there is no other God save Jesus Christ alone ... [*This is*] ... distinctly not Nicene. It is also definitely not Gnostic, for the Supreme God is also the Creator, and the instigator if not the agent of redemption. The general view ... is that the world was created good ... From [*the Fall*] history became a struggle between God, who was repairing the evil of the Fall, through His chosen people Israel and through the prophets, and the prince of this world, who resisted His efforts, had proclaimed himself to be God (in this way heathen religion was explained), and had bound all humanity to him by the lusts of the flesh. The result of this process was the existence of [*ignorance and error*] followed

by [*decay, impurity, pleasure and death*[7]], and the need of an ultimate judgment of God, which would destroy all that was contaminated. But in His mercy God had sent His Holy Spirit into Mary, in order in this way, by becoming flesh, to destroy the dominion of evil over flesh. This Holy Spirit was (as in Justin Martyr) identical with the spirit which had spoken through the Jewish prophets, so that the Christian faith rested throughout on the Spirit, which had given the prophets to the Jews and later on had been incarnate in the Christ, who had given the gospel.

Lake observes that Logos and Spirit are not distinguished. "Father, Son and Spirit" has several meanings. "[T]his is the popular theology out of which the Sabellian and Arian controversies can best be explained." Eschatological hope is centered upon the establishment of a glorious kingdom. The means of salvation are "asceticism and baptism." The ascetic eucharist is a community celebration of uncertain meaning.

Lake has been cited at some length not only because of the clarity and brevity of his summary but also because this précis, made decades before the publication of P.Hamb and P.Bod XLI, showed the relative unity of the theology of *APl* and thus of its text, for, with some clarifications and additions, this abstract still stands. (For a more detailed summary of no less enduring value, see Schmidt, *Acta*, 183–98.) One qualification is that the Monarchian sentiments ("One God, Jesus Christ") have been reduced through subsequent editing. Chaps. 3 and 4 (Thecla), contain no references to the Spirit. Another is that the "Spirit Christology" is arguably secondary to the text. See the comments on chaps. 10 and 13.

The more recently unearthed narrative segments show that the Spirit was active in the worshiping communities of *APl*, inspiring women in particular toward prophetic speech. This illuminates the environment in which the New Prophecy would flourish. Like the prophetic movement, *APl* offers a vigorous eschatology in which vengeance is left to God but without detriment of its ferocity. In its asceticism the *APl* are more rigorous than the followers of Montanus were. Most importantly, the prophecies recorded do not bear upon doctrine. Celibate women prophets and renunciation of marriage are also features of the canonical (Luke and) Acts, where they must, however, be discovered by inference. The unmarried are to avoid matrimony, evidently. The ideal is that couples live together in celibacy. The periodic practice recommended by Paul (1 Cor 7:2–5) has become a rule. Similar developments occurred elsewhere: Pervo, *Making*, 147, 187, as did

---

7. Lake's Greek terms have been translated.

the opposite. Colossians and Ephesians view marriage as the norm, and the PE regard it as a requirement.

The text does not offer a theological or other rationale for asceticism. (An example of a non-dualistic theological ground would be that abstinence from sex restores the original human state, prior to the fall.) Desire, pleasure, and lust for various earthly goods and experiences is denounced (e.g., 3.17; 9.13), but such sentiment is typical. Cf. *2 Clement* and *Hermas*. The goal is to subdue fleshly desire through discipline, not because matter is evil, but because the flesh has been corrupted. This is to say that, although asceticism is congenial to a dualistic system, *APl* is monistic—and the later monastic Christian asceticism flourished in an officially monistic theological environment.

A pressing question is whether radical asceticism, including a sparse vegetarian diet, frequent fasts, and complete sexual abstinence constituted a norm that all were to follow or an ideal toward which the faithful were to aspire. Granting that all believers fast and keep prayer vigils, the latter is nonetheless more likely. Those who could not achieve perfection were to do the best they could, with the goal of ongoing growth and improvement. *Didache* 6.2 comes to mind: those who can bear the whole yoke will be perfect; those who cannot will do their best. One interpretation of that "whole yoke" is sexual renunciation (Niederwimmer, *Didache*, 121–22).

The place of grace in redemption is not carefully worked out. The danger of post-baptismal sin seems to overshadow the understanding of baptism as empowerment, although much of the explicit expression of this view is related to the particular requirements of chaps. 3 and 4. (Since Paul did not baptize Thecla, the narrator states that he hesitated to do so.) Baptism is a seal, but it does not come with a lifetime guarantee. The seal is so frangible and permeable that more effort is devoted to protecting it than to acquiring it. As in the era of Ambrose and Augustine, baptism was the introduction to an ascetic life. Augustine would not, to be sure, have approved the sentiment of 8.10 that people are not justified through the law, but through righteous deeds. Grace has made the playing field level. The rest is up to believers. An anthropology can be inferred and extracted from these data. In brief: the Fall yielded a pessimistic anthropology; redemption reverses this. The most widespread quality of Christians is joy. This charismatic quality is one that not all subsequent Christians have regarded as paramount, or even desirable.

The death of Jesus receives little attention. As in Irenaeus the Incarnation is the means of redemption. Jesus is a model martyr whose post-mortem return to life vindicated his life and teaching. Paul will share a martyr's death and a savior's victory. Resurrection is central. The gospel can be summarized in two words: self-control and resurrection (3.5), to be understood as self-control that brings resurrection.

Those who come to *APl* with the advance notice that the apostles of ApocActs are supermen may be disappointed. Paul is a bit more of a superman in the canonical Acts than here, where he frequently expresses varied emotions and suffers degrading punishments of some duration. Paul's outstanding characteristics are great courage and even greater fidelity to his vocation and mission. To that extent he is an example *par excellence*. Miracles of various types also abound. Their primary link is to providence. See Pervo, "Planning." These wonders are beacons illuminating the vast realm of divine power and care. Miracles rescue believers, in particular missionaries. They also inaugurate missions. Without any more need for theoretical reflection than is found in the canonical Gospels and Acts, miracles manifest God's power and partiality. As is characteristic of the ApocActs in general, resurrections become the most common type of healing. This is the result of reflection upon the symbolic significance of miracles. Resurrections best represent the gift of new life.

The ecclesiology of *APl* is anachronistically primitive. Communities are house-based, as they probably still were at the time of composition, but structure consists of house churches led by heads of households. No officers are mentioned. Once again, it is possible that the author was attempting a historical reconstruction, as it were, but it is also possible that traces, at least, of the view of itinerants as ideal believers endured and were considered worthy of presentation.

Because of its incomplete state and editorial history, any attempt to give a precise profile to *APl* will require some qualifications and reservations. That stated, the text presents two commingled "popular" theologies: an unreflective propensity toward Modalistic Monarchianism and a somewhat debased form of Apologetic Logos theology. Two ultimately condemned theologies are characterized as Monarchian. "Dynamic Monarchianism" is a form of adoptionism, the view that Jesus was a human adopted and promoted by God through an infusion of divine power (*dynamis*). "Modalistic Monarchianism," often labeled as "Sabellianism," views the functions of the Trinity not as separate persons of a single godhead but as modes of action in creation, redemption, and sanctification. Hereafter "Monarchian/ism" refer to the modalistic variety.

Coherence among Christology, soteriology, moral theology, sacramental theology, and ecclesiology is generally lacking. The value of the theology of *APl* is that the author was not a theologian. This gives scholars views of popular, less systematic, religious views. Affinities are found less in other ApocActs than in works classified among the Apostolic Fathers, particularly *2 Clement* and *Hermas*.

VIII. The Scope and Plan of This Commentary

This commentary seeks to present the surviving *APl* as a whole, into which the best-attested and most studied parts were once integrated. The approach is broadly and eclectically literary, i.e., the examination of APL as a (now fragmentary) work of prose fiction. The methods are primarily historical and comparative: the place of *APl* among the writings of its era, with particular emphasis upon similar works. A leading danger in working with incomplete writings is that one reconstructs the text to fit one's notions and discovers that one's notions are correct. The interpreter must be constantly alert to this danger. Other disciplines are ancillary to this task, but they are not optional.

Bibliography

Allberry, C. R. C., ed. *A Manichaean Psalm-Book, part II, vol. 2*. Stuttgart: Kohlhammer, 1938.
Aubin, Melissa. "Reversing Romance? The *Acts of Thecla* and the Ancient Novel." In *Ancient Fiction and Early Christian Narrative*, edited by R. F. Hock, 257–72. SBL Symposium Series 6. Atlanta: Scholars, 1998.
Bauckham, Richard. "The *Acts of Paul* as a Sequel to Acts." In *The Book of Acts in Its Ancient Literary Setting*. Vol. 1 of *The Book of Acts in Its First Century Setting*, edited by Bruce W. Winter and Andrew D. Clarke, 105–52. Grand Rapids, MI: Eerdmans, 1993.
———. "The *Acts of Paul*: Replacement of Acts or Sequel to Acts?" *Semeia* 80 (1997) 159–68.
Bovon, François. "Canonical and Noncanonical Acts of the Apostles." In *New Testament and Christian Apocrypha: Collected Studies II*, by François Bovon, edited by Glenn E. Snyder, 197–222. WUNT 237. Tübingen: Mohr-Siebeck, 2009.
———. "A New Citation of the *Acts of Paul* in Origen." In *Studies in Early Christianity*, 267–70. Grand Rapids: Baker, 2005. Originally published as "Une nouvelle citation des *Actes de Paul* chez Origène." *Apocrypha* 5 (1994) 113–17.
———. "The Synoptic Gospels and the Noncanonical Acts of the Apostles." *HTR* 81 (1988) 19–36.
Braun, Martin. *History and Romance in Greco-Oriental Literature*. Oxford: Blackwell, 1938.
Brock, Ann Graham. "Genre of the *Acts of Paul*: One Tradition Enhancing Another." *Apocrypha* 5 (1994) 119–36.
Brown, Peter. *The Body and Society*. New York: Columbia University Press, 1988.

Budge, E. A. Wallis. *The Contendings of the Apostles: Being the Histories and the Lives and Martyrdoms and Deaths of the Twelve Apostles and Evangelists* 2nd ed. London: Oxford University Press, 1935, 435–582.

Butterworth, G. W. *Origen on First Principles*. 1936. Reprint, New York: Harper & Row, 1966.

Cartlidge, David R., and J. Keith Elliott. *Art and the Christian Apocrypha*. London: Routledge, 2001.

Campenhausen, Hans von. "Bearbeitungen und Interpolationen des Polykarpmartyriums." *Aus der Frühzeit des Christentums*, 253–301. Tübingen: Mohr/Siebeck, 1963.

Castelli, Elizabeth. *Martyrdom and Memory. Early Christian Culture Making*. New York: Columbia University Press, 2004.

Conybeare, Frederick C. *The Apology and Acts of Appolonius and Other Monuments of Early Christianity*. London: Swan Sonnenschein, 1894.

Crum, W. E. "New Coptic Manuscripts in the John Rylands Library." *BJRL* 5 (1920) 497–503.

Curley, Michael J. *Physiologus*. Chicago: University of Chicago Press, 2009.

Czachesz, István. "The Acts of Paul and the Western text of Luke's Acts: Paul between Canon and Apocrypha." In *The Apocryphal Acts of Paul and Thecla*, edited by Jan Bremmer, 107–25. Kampen: Kok Pharos, 1996.

Daly, Robert J., ed. *Origen: Treatise on the Passover and Dialogue of Origen with Heraclides and His Fellow Bishops on the Father, the Son, and the Souls*. ACW. New York: Paulist, 1992.

Dover, Kenneth J. *Greek Homosexuality*. New York: Random House, 1980.

Esch-Wermeling, Elisabeth. *Thekla–Paulusschülerin wider Willen? Strategien der Leserlenkung in den Theklaakten*. Neutestamentliche Abhandlungen 53. Münster: Aschendorff, 2008.

Fredriksen, Paula. "Mandatory Retirement." *Studies in Religion/Sciences religieuses* 35 (2006) 231–46.

Geerard, Maurice. *Clavis apocryphorum Novi Testamenti*. Corpus Christianorum. Turnhout: Brepols, 1992.

Goodspeed, Edward J. "The Book of Thekla," *American Journal of Semitic Languages and Literatures* 17 (1901) 65–95.

———. "The Epistle of Pelagia." *AJSL* 20 (1903–1904) 95–108.

Gronewald, M. "Einige Fackelmann-Papyri." *ZPE* 28, no. 3 (1978) 274–75.

Hansen, William, ed. *Anthology of Ancient Greek Popular Literature*. Bloomington: Indiana University Press, 1998.

Hanson, R. P. C. *Origen's Doctrine of Tradition*. London: SPCK, 1954.

Harnack, Adolf von. "Drei wenig beachtete cyprianische Schriften und die Acta Pauli." TU n.f. 4, 3–34. Leipzig: Teubner, 1899.

Head, Peter. "Acts and the Problem of Its Texts." In *The Book of Acts in Its Ancient Literary Setting*, edited by Bruce W. Winter and Andrew D. Clarke, 1:415–44. Grand Rapids: Eerdmans, 1993.

Hilhorst, A. "Tertullian on the Acts of Paul." In *The Apocryphal Acts of Paul and Thecla*, edited by Jan N. Bremmer, 150–63. Kampen: Kok Pharos, 1996.

Hills, Julian V. "The *Acts of Paul* and the Legacy of the Lukan Acts." *Semeia* 80 (1997) 145–58.

Holzhey, Carl. *Die Thekla-Akten. Ihre Verbreitung und Beurteilung in der Kirche.* München: Lentner, 1905.
James, Montague Rhodes. *Apocrypha Anecdota.* Vol. 2. TextsS. Cambrige: Cambridge University Press, 1893.
Jensen, Anne. *Thekla—Die Apostolin: Ein apokrypher Text neu entdeckt.* KT 172. Basel: Herder, 1995.
Junod, Eric. "Actes Apocryphes et Hérésie: le jugement de Photius." In *Les Actes apocryphes des Apôtres: christianisme et monde païen*, ed. François Bovon et al., 11-24. Publications de la Faculté de Théologie de l'Université de Genève 4. Geneva: Labor et Fides, 1981.
Kasser, Rodolphe, and Philippe Luisier. "Le Papyrus Bodmer XLI en Édition Princeps l'Épisode d'Èphèse des *Acta Pauli* en Copte et en Traduction." *Le Muséon* 117 (2004) 281-384.
Lake, Kirsop, and J. de Zwaan. "Acts of the Apostles (Apocryphal)." In *Dictionary of the Apostolic Church*, edited by James Hastings, 1:29-39. Edinburgh: T. & T. Clark, 1919.
Lalleman, Pieter J. "The Resurrection in the Acts of Paul." In *The Apocryphal Acts of Paul and Thecla*, edited by Jan N. Bremmer, 126-41. Kampen: Kok Pharos, 1996.
Lightfoot, Joseph Barber. *The Apostolic Fathers.* 2 parts in 5 vols. 2nd ed. London: Macmillan, 1889.
MacDonald, Dennis R. *The Legend and the Apostle: The Battle for Paul in Story and Canon.* Philadelphia: Fortress, 1983.
Mackay, Thomas W. "Response [to S. Davies]." *Semeia* 38 (1986) 145-49.
Marguerat, Daniel. "The *Acts of Paul* and the Canonical Acts: A Phenomenon of Rereading." *Semeia* 80 (1997) 169-83.
McNamara, Martin. *The Apocrypha in the Irish Church.* Dublin: Institute for Advanced Studies, 1975.
Mitchell, Margaret M. *The Heavenly Trumpet. John Crysostom and the Art of Pauline Interpretation.* HUT 40. Tübingen: Mohr/Siebeck, 2000.
Modesto, Christine. *Studien zur Cena Cypriani und zu deren Reeption.* Classica Monacensia 3. Tübingen: Narr, 1992.
Moreschini, Claudio, and Enrico Norelli. *Early Christian Greek and Latin Literature: A Literary History.* Trans M. J. O'Connell. 2 vols. Peabody, MA: Hendrickson, 2005.
Morris, J. B, et al. *The Homilies of St. John Chrysostom on the Epistle of St. Paul the Apostle to the Romans.* In *A Select Library of the Nicene and Post-Nicene Fathers*, edited by P. Schaff, 11:329-564. Grand Rapids: Eerdmans, 1979.
Musurillo, Herbert, S. J. *St. Methodius: The Symposium. A Treatise on Chastity.* ACW. Westminster, MD: Newman 1958.
Nautin, Pierre. *Origène. Sa vie et son oeuvre.* Christianisme antique 1. Paris: Beauchesne, 1977.
Niederwimmer, Kurt. *The Didache.* Trans. Linda M. Maloney. Hermeneia. Minneapolis: Fortress, 1998.
Ng, Esther Y., "Acts of Paul and Thecla. Women's Stories and Precedent." *JTS* 55 (2004) 1-29.
Pecere, Oronzo, and Antonio Stramaglia, eds. *La letteratura di consumo nel mondo greco-latino.* Cassino: Università degli studi di Cassino, 1996.

Pervo, Richard I. "God and Planning: Footprints of Providence in Acts and in the *Acts of Paul.*" In *Method and Meaning: Festschrift for Harold Attridge,* edited by Andrew McGowan, 259–77. Atlanta: SBL, 2011.

———. "A Hard Act to Follow: *The Acts of Paul* and the Canonical Acts," *Journal of Higher Criticism* 2, no. 2 (1995) 3–32.

———. "The Hospitality of Onesiphorus: Missionary Styles and Support in the Acts of Paul." In *The Rise and Expansion of Christianity in the First Three Centuries of the Common Era,* edited by Clare K. Rothschild and Jens Schroter, 341–51. Tübingen: Mohr/Siebeck, 2013.

———. "(Not) Appealing to the Emperor: Acts (and The *Acts of Paul*)." In *Paul and the Heritage of Israel: Paul's Claim upon Isaraels's Legacy in Luke and Acts in Light of the Pauline Letters,* edited by D. Moessner et al., 165–79. London: T. & T. Clark, 2012.

———. "The *Testament of Joseph* and Greek Romance." *Studies on the Testament of Joseph,* edited by G. Nickelsburg Jr., 15–28. Missoula, MT: Scholars, 1975.

Pomeroy, Sarah B., ed. *Plutarch's* Advice to the Bride and Groom *and* A Consolation to His Wife. New York: Oxford University Press, 1999.

Ramsay, William M. *The Church in the Roman Empire.* London: Hodder and Stoughton, 1897.

Rordorf, Willy. "Die neronische Christenverfolgung im Spiegel der Apokryphen Paulusakten." In *Lex Orandi, Lex Credendi: Gesammelte Aufsätze zum 60. Geburtstag,* 368–77. Paradosis 36. Freiburg: Universitätsverlag Freiburg, 1993.

———. "Tertullien et les *Actes de Paul.*" In *Lex Orandi, Lex Credendi: Gesammelte Aufsätze zum 60. Geburtstag,* 475–84. Paradosis 36. Freiburg: Universitätsverlag Freiburg, 1993.

———. "Was wissen wir über Plan und Absicht der Paulusakten?" In *Lex Orandi, Lex Credendi: Gesammelte Aufsätze zum 60. Geburtstag,* 485–96. Paradosis 36. Freiburg: Universitätsverlag Freiburg, 1993.

Schmeling, Gareth, ed. *The Novel in the Ancient World.* Rev. ed. Memnosyne 159. Boston: Brill Academic, 2003.

Schneemelcher, Wilhelm. "Die Apostelgeschichte des Lukas und die Acta Pauli." In *Apophoreta: Festschrift für Earnst Haenchen,* edited by W. Elster and F. H. Kettler, 236–50. BZNW 30. Berlin: Topelmann, 1964.

Snyder, Glenn E. "Remembering the *Acts of Paul.*" PhD diss., Harvard University, 2010.

Stephens, Susan A., ed. *Yale Papyri in the Beinecke Rare Book and Manuscript Library II.* Chico, CA: Scholars 1985.

Tajra, Harry W. *The Martyrdom of St. Paul.* WUNT 67. Tübingen: Mohr/Siebeck, 1994.

van den Hoek, Annewies, and John J. Herrmann, Jr. "Thecla the Beast Fighter: A Female Emblem of Deliverance in early Christian Popular Art." *The Studia Philonica Annual* 13 (2001) 212–49.

Vogt, A. "Panégyrique de St. Pierre; Panégyrique de St. Paul. Deux discours inédits de Nicétas de Paphlagonie, disiple de Photius." *Orientalia Christiana* 23 (1931) 5–97.

Wilkinson, John. *Egeria's Travels.* 3rd ed. Oxford: Aris & Phillips, 1999.

Wright, William. *Apocryphal Acts of The Apostles, Edited from Syriac Manuscripts in the British Museum and Other Libraries.* 2 vols. London: Williams and Norgate, 1871, 2:116–45.

Zahn, Theodor. *Geschichte des neutestamentlichen Kanons.* 2 vols. in 4 parts. Erlangen: Deichert, 1888–1891.

Translation, Commentary, and Notes[1]

Chapter 1: Damascus

Witness: Textual basis: an unpublished Coptic fragment in the John Rylands Library (P. Ryl inv. 44); *APl* 9. P. Yale 87. Supplementary texts: *APl 9, D-text of Acts 9, Gnostic *Apocalypse of Paul*, *The *Epistle of Pelagia*, Epistula Apostolorum 32.

> *Version based upon Cherix* (Rordorf, 1127) [*The glorified Christ is speaking to Paul*] "[...]... today... but now go to [Damascus. After]... leave that place and go to Jerusalem." Now when Paul had heard this, he went to Damascus in considerable [fear]. And when he was entered, he found them... [keep]ing... the fast...
>
> Who will be sent away from those... of the sort that... violently, because the one who... treasures... *verso* your mouth... holy ones... saved by which in Jesus...
>
> *Alternative translation:* (Crum, "Manuscripts," 501) (Recto?)... today... but go now down to... and when (?) thou hast quitted that place, do thou go to Jerusalem. Now when Paul had heard this, he went to Damascus in great joy (?). And when he was entered in, he found them... ing... the fast... (Verso?) "... Lo (?), God will accept (?)... faith (?), for ye are... ye (have?) received it, it being (inherited) from your fathers; that ye might (not) remain therein as in an iniquitous city, but... the great treasure without (?)"...

1. A Note on the *sigla*. An ellipsis... marks a gap (lacuna) in the manuscript. These lacunae may be delineated by brackets [ ]. Proposed restorations are normally *italicized*. Most of these are logical or exemplary (i.e., "something to this effect"), and are the work of other scholars, in particular Schmidt, *Acta*, and Rordorf (et al.). Only controversial cases are discussed. Non-italicized restorations may be regarded as virtually certain. Brackets also mark the beginning and end of mss. Italicized portion of the translation identifies passages suspect as later additions.

Comments

As is the case with all the ApocActs save *AThom*, the opening is lost. The position taken here is that *APl* opened with an account of his "conversion" near Damascus. See also Rordorf, "Conversion." Chapter 9 refers to the event. This does not exclude an earlier account, for the canonical Acts, a major model for *APl*, reported the experience in chap. 9 and repeated it in first-person speeches by Paul in chaps. 22 and 26. The two texts may disagree about the place where Paul's change took place, but this is not certain, since the flashback account in chap. 9 is not quite specific. Although the Rylands fragment lacks any context, it is usually presumed, with good reason, to stem from chap. 1.

Summary of the (presumed) Events. Paul was in the vicinity of Damascus, whither he had possibly come from *Tarsus*. (*APl* does not present Paul as an agent of Jerusalem.) He was persecuting followers of Jesus (chap. 9). Outside of the city Paul had a vision of the risen Christ, in which he was commanded to go to Damascus and then to Jerusalem (P. Ryl.). After some time under the tutelage of Jude the brother of Jesus (the name comes from Acts 9:11; the author has identified this person with Jesus' brother), Paul experienced success as a preacher. He then set out, evidently in accord with the Lord's command, for Jerusalem. In the course of that journey he baptized a lion (chap. 9). According to a document kindly supplied by Rordorf in 1994 ("Reconstitution du contenu des *Actes de Paul*," presumably a draft for his forthcoming commentary), Cherix has calculated that eight pages are missing from the beginning of P.Hamb, six prior to chap. 2. This calculation is welcome but far from certain. It would allow for an episode of modest length. It is not clear how much the report of the events after Paul's conversion in chap. 9 repeats chap. 1 and how much there is new.

An important question is whether chap. 1 contained the story of the baptized lion. Ancient popular literature in general and *APl* in particular are not likely to leave gaps of this nature for later narration to fill in. Chap. 1 probably had some form of the lion story. This would put Paul ahead of Thecla, who will encounter a lion in chap. 4. Moreover, it conforms to the gospel parallel (Mark 1:12–13. See Table 1.1, p. 62). Little space would have been available for more than a summary of Paul's visit to Jerusalem. The Coptic *Apocalypse of Paul* may reflect that report.

It transpires that Paul is upon a mountain (a favored site for epiphanies), "the mountain of Jericho." That site evokes the apparent initial scene of the *APl*. Paul asks the youth the road to Jerusalem—a feature not in harmony with Galatians, although it could fit the *APl*. The child says, "I know who you are Paul. You are he who was blessed from his mother's womb. For

I have [come] to you so that you may [go up to Jerusalem] to your fellow [apostles]" (18, 14-19, trans. MacRae and Murdock, 257). Nicetas (82_r) reports that Paul went from Damascus to Syrian Antioch (although he reports the escape in accord with Acts 9).

Rordorf (who holds that *APl* does not use Acts) stresses that Galatians is the major source of this story ("Conversion"). He is correct. It is also true that Acts prefers Galatians 1 to the source used in Acts 9. Each account of Paul's encounter with the risen Christ in Acts is a bit closer to Galatians 1. Assuming that the author knew Acts 9, some details may have been borrowed from it, especially those providing dramatic detail.

Czachesz ("Between") seeks to find traces of both the D-Text of Acts 9 and the *APl* 1 in the work of Ephrem Syrus. His object is to identify a three stage development from the early text of Acts to the D-Text to *APl*. This is an important insight into the history of early Christian literature. See also Pervo, *Acts*, 233 and 249. One rather clear feature of the D-Text is emphasis upon Paul's great fear in the face of the christophany. It is likely that *APl* would adopt and possibly intensify this emotion. Czachesz identifies these features: Paul's ignorance, his confession of sins, and his acceptance of Christ's message. These items shift the narrative in the direction of a "conversion story" proper. Attribution of "ignorance," applied to gentiles in Acts 17:30, Eph 4:18, and 1 Peter 1:14, is applied also to Paul in 1 Tim 1:13, for example. See Pervo, *Making*, 14–15.

P. Yale 86 mentions Damascus three times in fourteen lines of the verso (ll. 3, 8, 13) and Jerusalem in ll. 4–5. Line 11 has the phrase "the manifestation (*epiphaneia*) of the lord." This may be in a speech from a later chapter reporting the conversion; it does not seem to come from chap. 1.

Notes

Crum ("Coptic Manuscripts," 501) describes Rylands inv. 44 as probably the oldest in their collection. It is part of a vellum leaf, c. 15 x 12 cm. (and thus not a papyrus), written in small square uncials, like a fourth-century papyrus in form. The dialect is Achmimic.

Tarsus. See *Epistle of the Apostles* 32, where Paul proceeds to Damascus from Tarsus rather than Jerusalem.

"Go to Damascus." Cf. Acts 9:6; Acts 22:10.

Fast. The practice, both individual and communal, is common in *APl*: 2.3; 3.23; 6.5; 9.27; 10.2–4; 13.1. Fasting, for several purposes, was widespread

The Acts of Paul

among early Christians, with variety regarding the length and frequency of the fast.

Fear. Crum supplied *joy.* Cherix prefers *fear,* based upon the D-text of Acts 9:5: "I am Jesus, whom you are persecuting." Overcome with fear at what had happened to him, he said, "Lord, what do you wish me to do?" Czachesz ("Between," 111), however, prefers "pride," based upon Ephrem's commentary.

Bibliography

Ephrem Syrus. *Commentary on Acts.* Quoted in *The Beginnings of Christianity,* edited by Frederick J. Foakes Jackson, and Kirsopp Lake, 3:373–453. New York: Macmillan, 1920–1933.

Crum, W. "New Coptic Manuscripts in the John Rylands Library." *BJRL* 5 (1920) 497–503.

Czachesz, István. "The Acts of Paul and the Western Text of Luke's Acts: Paul between Canon and Apocrypha." In *The Apocryphal Acts of Paul and Thecla,* edited by Jan N. Bremmer, 107–25. Kampen: Kok Pharos, 1996.

Klauck, H.-J. *The Apocyphal Acts of the Apostles. An Introduction.* Translated by Brian McNeil. Waco: Baylor University Press, 2008.

Murdock, William R., and George W. MacRae, eds. "The Apocalypse of Paul." In *Nag Hammadi Codices V 2–5 and VI with Papyrus Berolensis 8502, 1 and 4,* edited by Douglas M. Parrott, 47–63. Nag Hammadi Studies 11. Leiden: Brill, 1979.

Pervo, R. "A Hard Act to Follow: *The Acts of Paul* and the Canonical Acts," *Journal of Higher Criticism* 2, no. 2 (1995) 3–32.

Rordorf, W. "Paul's Conversion in the Canonical Acts and in the *Acts of Paul.*" *Semeia* 80 (1997) 137–44.

Translation, Commentary, and Notes : Chapter

Chapter 2: Antioch on the Orontes (in Syria)

Witness: P Heid 1–6, renumbered by Cherix as pp. 9–13. Secondary witnesses: *Acts of Titus* 4; Nicetas of Paphlagonia 82r.

1. (p. 9) [...] but [...] he [*verb*] ... He took [...] is Anchares [...] husband. Paul went into [*the house*] to the place where the [*corpse*] had been laid out. Now Phila [*the wife*] of Anchares was upset [...] She [*angrily*] told her husband, "My husband, you have gone off [*because of*] ... this sorcerer, and you didn't [...] the wild beasts. You have not taken [...] your son [...] whence [...]?

(p. 10) [...] having [...] looked for something to eat [...] son placed on [...]." But [Paul] stood up in the presence of all. He prayed until the ninth hour, until the crowd came from the city and carried off the young boy. After Paul had prayed for a long time, he lives [...] and Jesus, the Messiah [...] the [*young*] boy [...] [...] the prayer [...] (p. 11) [...] crowd [...] eight days [...] Paul [...] and so that [...] this one, so that [*they*] might recall that he had raised the [*young*] man.

2. But after Paul had stayed [...] (p. 12) [...] seated [...] there [...] behind him, the people [...] sent for Anchares [...] they cried [...] "[*We*] believe, Anchares [...] but save the city." [...] Many people expressed these sentiments. [*Anchares*] said to them: "Judge if their [*claims*] [...] (p. 13) [...] can [...] but I testify [...] God [*who has*] son [...] salvation, and for me [...] [O] my [*brothers and sisters*] [*believe*] that there is no other God than [Jesus,] the Messiah, the Son of [the] Blessed one, to whom be the glory [*for ever,*] amen!"

3. But when they gathered that he would not return to them, they [*thereupon*] chased Paul, seized him and brought [him] back to the city for condemnation. They stoned him and expelled him from their city and their region. As Anchares would not return evil for evil, shut the door of [his house and remained] inside, with his wife [...] in fasting *and prayer* [...] and [... *when night?*] arrived, [*and Paul came*] to him, saying [...] the Messiah.

83

The Acts of Paul

Comment

Nicetas and *ATit* provide a vague outline of the story. The fragments add a few bones, not all of which seem to fit the outline. According to Nicetas (82r) Paul preached at Syrian Antioch, was imprisoned, and subsequently rescued. The chief magistrate of the city saw in a vision his son, who had died. His wife was also restored. *ATit* 4 speaks of Barnabas, the son of *Panchares*, whom Paul raised.

These authorities are not summarizing Acts, in which Barnabas is an early diaspora Jewish believer, who took Paul under his wing, so to speak (Acts 4:36; 9:27; 11:25–26). To reiterate what was stated in the introduction (sec. V), failure to follow Acts does not mean that *APl* does not know Acts. *APl* wishes to view Barnabas as a dependent follower of Paul. That he was of polytheist background is not anti-Jewish. The author is largely indifferent to Jews. The typical convert comes from a polytheist background. The imprisonment and rescue noted in Nicetas, however, do not fit comfortably into the surviving fragments.

As §1 opens, Paul appears to be a free agent, evidently summoned to the home of Anchares because their son has died. Anchares might well have been the chief magistrate, a character far from unusual in ApocActs. What is unusual is that Anchares seems to have been attracted by Paul's message before his wife was converted. Her labeling of the apostle as a "sorcerer" suggests that he has been working miracles and/or enticing members of households to follow him. Paul had been arrested and condemned, perhaps to the beasts, by the chief magistrate, Anchares (although Syrian Antioch was in fact the seat of the governor of Roman Syria). After the death of his son, Anchares had a vision of the youth that led him to release the apostle.

His wife Phila was angry with him because of his attention to Paul and his evident neglect of his son's corpse. The body had been laid out in a house, evidently theirs, to which Paul goes. This residence evidently lay outside of the city. (Antioch was notable for its suburbs.) The apostle stood, presumably by the bier, and engaged in continuous prayer. At 1500 mourners came to transport the corpse to its place of burial.

After this lengthy build up, the resuscitation of the boy was announced rapidly. The subsequent reference to *eight days* is not clear. It may refer to eight days during which Paul was incarcerated or to eight subsequent days. Section 1 closes with action, presumably verbal, by which Paul recalls public attention to the wonder.

Phila evidently collapsed in shock at the miracle and had also to be rehabilitated. §2 opens with an indication that strong hostility to Paul endures. Many of the populace confront him. This may not be a formal trial.

The chief magistrate, Anchares, is summoned. General expressions of faith usually signal mass conversions motivated by a miracle. In this instance the crowd may affirm the raising of the young man but still judge Paul to be a menace to the civic order, possibly as a magician. Cf. Mark 5:1–20. Anchares invites the public to reach its own conclusions about the charges laid by Paul's antagonists while making a firm confession of faith. The crowd's specific wish is not clear. This desire is evidently related to the claims of Paul's adversaries. They may see him as an opponent of traditional religion. Anchares responds with an affirmation of Christian faith.

§3 is a rather more typical example of a pattern known from various Acts. The apostle's frustrated adversaries must resort to pursuit and capture of their prey, who is returned to the city to receive his due, which includes stoning and expulsion. Anchares refused to retaliate and remained inside his home, where he and Phila fasted and prayed. Paul, neither debilitated nor intimidated by stones, returned, probably that evening, to console the couple. Cf. Acts 14:18–20. A less likely alternative is that he returned in the form of a vision.

Notes

Antioch. Many cities (including, for a period, Jerusalem) in the ancient world were given the name Antioch (after Antiochus, founder of the Seleucid dominion, an empire that, at its greatest extent, reached from present day Pakistan to the borders of Egypt). According to Acts 11:19—14:23, Syrian Antioch was the center of the early mission to gentiles.

(P)anchares. The name "Anchares" in Coptic is due to two ways of reading *panchaes*: "p.Anchares," in which "p" is the definite article, thus "Anchares," and "Panchares."

Sorcerer. See, e.g., Poupon, "L'accusation."

Wild Beasts. The link to chaps. 1, 4, and 9 is apparent. Anchares may have condemned Paul, who was released prior to execution.

Ninth hour. This time (1500) has symbolic value as the hour at which Jesus died (Mark 15:34). Cf. also Acts 10:3, 30.

The Crowd. Cf. Luke 7:11–17.

Eight days. This number is also symbolic. From the perspective of Genesis 1–2, the eighth follows the seventh, the day of weekly rest, and is thus the time of ultimate rest. Astronomical theory identified the eighth sphere as that of rest (which was judged superior to motion). Within this were the spheres of the seven "planets" (which means "moving bodies"). (Ancients included earth's moon and the sun among the seven.)

No other God than [Jesus]. Anchares' initial statement is Monarchian, followed by the claim that Jesus is the son of God.

Evil for evil. This is an ethical commonplace in Greco-Roman (e.g., Musonius Rufus, ed. Lutz 76–80), and Jewish (Prov 17:13; *Asen.* 28.4 *et passim;* 2 Enoch 50.1–4), as well as Christian (e.g., Rom 12:17) thought. By this single example the narrator illustrates Anchares' moral transformation.

They stoned him and expelled him from their city and their region. The themes are borrowed from Acts: expulsion, 13:50 (Pisidian Antioch); stoning: see 14:5 (Iconium); and return after stoning, 14:19–20 (Lystra).

Bibliography

Poupon, Gérard. "L'accusation de magie dans les Actes Apocryphes." In *Les Actes apocryphes des Apôtres: christianisme et monde païen,* ed. François Bovon et al. 71–93. Publications de la Faculté de Théologie de l'Université de Genève 4. Geneva: Labor et Fides, 1981.

Rordorf, Willy. "In welchem Verhältnis stehen die apokryphen Paulus akten zur kanonischen Apostelgeschichte und zu den Pastoralbriefen?" In *Text and Testimony. Essays on New Testament and Apocryphal Literature in Honour of A. F. J. Klijn,* edited by T. Baarda et al., 225–41. Kampen: Kok, 1988.

———. "Was wissen wir über Plan und Absicht der Paulusakten?" *Oecumenica et Patristica,* 71–82. FS W. Schneemelcher. Stuttgart: Teubner, 1989.

Chapter 3

For chapters 3 and 4 attestation changes radically. These chapters are extant in 3 fragmentary papyri, forty-three Greek manuscripts, and a number of versions, of which Coptic, Latin, Syriac, and Armenian are the most important. (Greek mss. are identified by letters, Latin with L and a subscript letter, e.g. L_c.) These witnesses represent several editions, the major examples of which are (1) as an integral part of *APl* (attested by P.Heid); (2) as a detached story centered upon Thecla, as in various mss and versions, notably the Syriac; and (3) in a fully independent edition supplied with endings designed to complete the saint's story and associate her with her cult site in Seleucia (Davis, *The Cult of Saint Thecla*).

This commentary propounds the view that chap. 4 was a freestanding story about *Thecla*, taken up by the author, who composed chap. 3 and modified 4 to show that Thecla belonged to the Pauline circle. In its earliest (oral or written, probably the latter) form, Paul was not a character in chap. 4. As Lipsett (*Desiring Conversion*, 64–66) proposes, the story of the marriage-rejecting virgin is framed by that of a married householder. Although the narrator's rejection of sexual activity implies that the sons of Onesiphorus will not marry and have children in turn, the goal of *APl* is not to produce a movement composed entirely of itinerants. See also Pervo, "Hospitality of Onesiphorus." Thecla is not the only model for converts. In chap. 3 Thecla has courage but she is not a "strong" character. She does not utter a reported word until §23 and that is to announce her quest for Paul. In chap. 4 matters invert: Paul is weak to the point of cowardice, while Thecla is the center of action and attention.

Excursus: *The Acts of Paul and the Acts of Thecla*

These chapters, provided with new and sometimes discordant endings (see below) constituted a separate work best entitled the *Acts of Thecla*, tracing her career to her eventual death. This material has constituted a basis for Gender Studies, Cultural Studies, and related disciplines, the history and vicissitudes of which can be aptly traced by those who peruse the literature of *APl*. This commentary will scarcely contribute to this fruitful discussion, for its object is the entire *APl*, the author of which sought to capture and subordinate Thecla, presented as a disciple of the apostle. Without denying the merits of the "final text" or derivative texts, for those who subscribe to the editorial theory here accepted (the evidence for which is quite compelling), the story of Paul and Thecla deconstructs. Chap. 4 *is* about women;

> females of every species introduced into the story are arrayed against the opponents. Chap. 3 locates her in a male world, albeit not an especially repressive environment. The ultimate message is: if you like Thecla, you'll love Paul, as she in fact did.

The text of chaps. 3–4 shows that many hands sought to make improvements. Syriac, with support from the Armenian version, derived from it, and some agreement in the Coptic and Latin witnesses, often offers a longer text. As so often, critics are torn between two familiar processes: expansion and abbreviation. When longer and shorter forms of a text occur, New Testament scholars are inclined to suspect expansion, but abbreviation was also common in late antiquity. Although many of the longer readings in the Latin tradition, for example, are readily attributable to the propensity to expand, in other cases the shorter text scarcely makes sense. See the comment on 3.18–19. It is arguable that the Syriac edition of chaps. 3 and 4 represents an early, longer, stage of the text. A valuable study of the malleable textual tradition is Haines-Eitzen, *Gendered Palimpsest*.

The two chapters have the same structure, beginning with Thecla in conflict with a socially prominent male, followed by her arrest and attempted execution. See Aubin, "Reversing," 261. The author probably composed chap. 3 as a doublet of 4.

3.1–4 Paul Arrives at Iconium

3.1. On his journey to Iconium following his flight from Antioch Paul had as traveling companions Demas and Hermogenes the blacksmith. They fawned over him like devotees, but this was pure deceit. Paul, who attended only to the goodness brought by Christ, wouldn't do anything harmful to them. Rather, he showered them with affection, mellifluously expounding to them all the oracles of the Lord, of the birth and resurrection of the Beloved, and he narrated, point by point, the great deeds of Christ, as they had been revealed to him [*and that the Christ was of Davidic descent and born of Mary*].

2. When he learned that Paul was coming to Iconium, a man named Onesiphorus went out to meet him with his family: Lectra,

his wife, and his sons Simmias and Zeno, with the intention of offering him hospitality. Now Titus had told him what Paul looked like, as Onesiphorus had not seen him in person but through spiritual insight.

3. He set out on the king's highway toward Lystra and found a place where he might welcome Paul, evaluating the travelers in accordance with Titus' description. Then he saw Paul coming, short, bald, bow-legged, healthy-looking, single-browed, a bit long-nosed, and bursting with beneficence. Sometimes he looked like a mortal; at other times he had the glowing countenance of an angel.

4. Paul smiled at the sight of Onesiphorus, who responded, "Greetings, servant of the blessed God."

"Grace be with you, and with your household."

This exchange exacerbated the jealousy of Demas and Hermogenes and intensified their deceit. Demas said to Onesiphorus: "Since you did not offer us such a greeting, do we not belong to the blessed one?"

"I don't see the result of proper behavior in you two," replied Onesiphorus, "but, if you are as you say, come in and refresh yourselves."

Comment

3.1–4. The Onesiphorus family welcome Paul, recognized via a description supplied by Titus, to Iconium. Paul is characterized as charitable nearly to a fault and as a missionary whose proclamation is unceasing. His companions, on the other hand, lacked these virtues.

Demas. Demas and Hermogenes form an inseparable pair in *APl.* They function as one character. The name Demas comes from the Pauline tradition. Demas is one of four named in the greeting list in Phlm 24, which is picked up by the author of Colossians (4:10–14). He is thus associated with communities in the Lycus valley. The Pastor, as the author of 1–2 Timothy and Titus is called, states that Demas, "in love with this present world," deserted Paul (2 Tim 4:8). He fulfills this description in *APl*, since pursuit of gain is his major motive. Hermogenes is associated with one Phygelus in 2 Tim 1:15. The most probable solution is that the author selected the names Demas and Hermogenes from 2 Timothy. The contrasting figure is

89

Onesiphorus (2 Tim 1:16; 4:19), a role he will presently reprise. The author has blithely relocated Onesiphorus from Ephesus to Iconium, substituted the known apostate for Phygelus, a cipher, and equipped Paul with two faithless companions. This inattention to detail makes it less likely that the author has utilized independent tradition, as proposed by MacDonald, *Legend*, 65–66. According to 2 Tim 4:14, Alexander was a coppersmith. Other unsavory characters are Hymenaeus and Philetus (2 Tim 2:17–18). The author has simplified these to a single, undifferentiated pair, characterized as deceiving creatures.

2. The narrative presumes that Paul has never been to *Iconium*, but that Titus has visited and, perhaps, founded a community in the home of Onesiphorus. This method reflects Pauline practices implied in the letters (e.g., 1 Thess 1:8), but not in Acts. The narrator displays no interest in how Onesiphorus learned of Paul's coming arrival. The presence of the entire family constitutes a welcoming party for Paul. Their reappearance at the end of the chapter forms a kind of bracket or inclusion. Hospitality was essential for itinerant missionaries, who depended upon householders to supply both room and board and a base of operations. As is typical of the various acts (cf. Acts 19; 28:16–31), Paul essentially founds the Christian mission despite its previous existence.

Titus is mentioned without further introduction. *APl*, probably deducing from 2 Corinthians that Titus undertook delicate assignments to places that Paul was going to visit, shows him as Paul's advance man at both Iconium and Rome. Other data may have been lost. The author of the *Acts of Titus* views him as Paul's regular precursor who went before him as a messenger to prepare his way.

The reference to the King's Highway has been viewed as an opportunity to unravel the geographical setting of *APl*. The task is to identify a royal (imperial) road leading from Syrian Antioch to Iconium. A difficulty is that, although the *APl* presumably locate chap. 2 in Syria, it is possible that a hypothetical source of chap. 3 envisioned Paul as coming from Pisidian Antioch. Ramsay (*Church*, 30–35), convinced of the historical value of this passage, was quite specific: "Onesiphorus went out from Iconium till he came to the point a few miles south of Misthia" (33). He thus envisions a relatively lengthy journey (omitting the accompanying family). One must ask why the prospective host would go so far rather than take a station before the proper gate into Iconium. For the continuation of the Ramsay tradition, with up-to-date information on topography, see Mitchell, *Anatolia*, 1:7, 70, 76–78.

Ramsay wrote before the discovery of P.Heid and was not aware of the possibility that Paul could have been depicted as coming from Syrian

Antioch. There was no royal road linking Syrian Antioch with Iconium in the first two centuries. The Via Sebaste ("Imperial Highway") linked Roman colonies, such as Pisidian Antioch and Iconium (French, "*Road System,*" 707–15). Either the author erred or merged incompatible traditions. It is noteworthy that the Syriac tradition speaks simply of a highway (Wright, 117). Ebner, who summarizes the difficulties, asks whether the term may have endured because of its symbolic associations. Philo spoke of the royal road to truth: philosophy (*Poster. C.* 101; *Migr. Abr.* 146). See also Esch-Wermeling, *Thekla*, 92–94. It appears that the King's Highway creates more problems than it solves. Onesiphorus' search introduces the theme of gazing at/looking for Paul that plays a prominent role in the book, especially in the embedded story of Thecla. See Lipsett, *Desiring Conversion*, 64.

The Description of Paul

The description of Paul is adeptly placed by the narrator to foreshadow the hero's appearance. Scholars of a sentimental bent have suggested that it may be a historical reminiscence. For example Ramsay: "This plain and unflattering account of the Apostle's personal appearance seems to embody a very early tradition" (*Church*, 32). Today such judgments reveal nearly as much about their author as about the subject. Consider: (a) "Red hair and figure, lots of both"; and (b) "She was a tall voluptuous woman with long, elaborate red hair, wearing a blue dress that was too tight and too short, and black, open-toed, spike heel shoes." (a) probably came from a man who focused upon what he regarded as the subject's most prominent features. A woman is a likely source of (b). She took note of the subject's vulgar display.

Detailed ancient descriptions are more like those of the hypothetical woman: their major purpose was to reveal character. People in the Greco-Roman world believed, on the one hand, that external appearance revealed internal qualities, and, on the other, that appearances could be deceiving. Literature prefers the former. Not all descriptions needed to be detailed. Since *APl* 3 has many points of contact with romantic novels, the initial descriptions of two heroes are worthy comparisons:

> Now there was a certain youth named Chaereas, whose handsomeness surpassed all, resembling the statues and pictures of Achilles and Nireus, and Hippolytus and Alcibiades. His father was Ariston, second only to Hermocrates [the father of Callirhoe] in Syracuse. (*Callirhoe* 1.1.3; LCL, trans. G. P. Goold, 29–31)

The Acts of Paul

> In Ephesus there was a man named Lycomedes, one of the most powerful people in the city. This Lycomedes and his wife Themisto, also a local, had a son Habrocomes, a paragon of handsomeness without precedent in Ionia or anywhere else. This Habrocomes grew handsomer by the day, and his spiritual values blossomed along with his physical excellences. (*Xenophon of Ephesus* 1.1; LCL, trans. Jeffrey Henderson, 213)

The narrator of the *Ephesian Tale* is content to say that Habrocomes is the best looking man in creation, and not devoid of subdermal attractions. Chariton makes a common comparison to artistic representations of men acknowledged to possess extraordinary good looks. Each notes two other essential qualities: citizenship in an important place and membership in the local nobility. These descriptions are noteworthy for their brevity (as are those of heroines). One could not tell someone how to pick Chaireas out of a crowd by saying, "He looks like Achilles or Alciabides." The description of Paul is, on the contrary, ostensibly intended to be recognizable.

Such a description can be seen in a warrant for the arrest of a runaway slave (*P. Parisiensis* 10, of the Ptolemaic era, cited by Fitzmyer, *Philemon*, 26–27). This begins with his name, alias, nation and place of origin, continuing: "His age is about 18, of medium height, clean-shaven, sturdy of leg, with a dimple in the chin, a mole to the left of the nose, a scar above the mouth to the left, branded on the right wrist with two foreign letters."

P. Grenf. ii. 23 (a) (= *Select Papyri* 1; trans. Hunt and Edgar, LCL, 81–83) records a land sale by three sisters, each described in detail, as is their guardian, the husband of one ("Psennesis also called Krouris son of Horus, Persian of the Epigone, of the village of Gotnit in the lower toparchy of the Latopolite nome, aged about 45 years, of medium height or under, dark-skinned, rather curly-haired, long-faced, straight-nosed, with a scar on the under lip"), and the chief purchaser. This material is the ancient equivalent of the data on a current driving license.

If the body is the window of the soul, it provides clues to character. In service of this ancients developed a pseudo-science of physiognomy. For data, see Parsons, *Body and Character*; Malina and Neyrey, *Portraits*, 100–152; Bollók, "Description," 6–9; Bremmer, "Magic," 38–39; and Malherbe, "Physical Description." Pseudo-sciences are rarely exact; physiognomy conforms to this convention. Interpreters cannot simply find a value for each item and issue the results. Physiognomy, which evidently reached its peak during the second century, supplies a number of details and establishes the grounds and range of interest in description.

The classical model, exhibited in the citations from *Callirhoe* and *An Ephesian Tale*, presumes that the physically and morally beautiful cohere. The notion is both elitist and convenient, as any who have ever watched B movies can affirm. One great exception to this tradition was a lover of the aforementioned Alcibiades. Socrates was universally viewed as ugly in face and figure (see Alcibiades on this subject [as Plato would have it: *Symposium* 215D–217A]), but he was no scheming villain. (See, Zanker, *Mask*, 32; and Cartlidge and Elliott, *Art*, 139–43.) Closer in time and spirit to the *APl* is the *Life of Aesop*, whose hero is described in these words: "He was truly horrible to behold: worthless, pot-bellied, slant-headed, snub-nosed, hunchbacked, leather-skinned, club-footed, knock-kneed, short-armed, sleepy-eyed, bushy-lipped—in short, an absolute miscreant" (1.2–6; trans. Wills, 181).

Aesop was no matineé idol, but he was a benefactor. Similarly, the apostle described in *APl* need not be handsome to possess admirable qualities. Grant did not give priority to the physiognomic literature, but he realized that the portrait was not intended to be homely and thus realistic, but laudatory. He proposed Archilochus' (*Frg.* 58) portrait of a general ("Description"). This is apt, as Barrier (75) observes, in the light of chap. 14, in which Paul is a "general" recruiting soldiers for Christ. Malherbe argued for Heracles, noting the numerous Christ parallels found in the second century ("Physical Description," 168–70). He demonstrated that the features of a hooked nose, bowed legs, and continuous eyebrow should not be viewed simply as homely features but signs of virtue. Bollók tries to summarize the often ambiguous language of the physiognomic literature (see the notes) before suggesting the possibility that 2 Corinthians (i.e., 10:10) helped inspire the description ("Description," 6–12). He also identifies (Ps.-) Dares' book on the Trojan War as a good example of low-brow literature influenced by the canons of physiognomy. Ebner ("Schein," 58–60) argues that the final items reflect spiritual truth, whereas the physical features pertain to the "fleshly" realm. The wide-ranging study of Malina and Neyrey (*Portraits*, 100–52) provides a great deal of background data and a methodological model, although it seeks answers from a range of Pauline texts rather than from the specific terms, compromising its own approach. The presumed philosophical reference was not universally grasped. Manuscripts and versions show many mollifying "improvements" of the data, an indication that readers in late antiquity often found the portrait discomforting.

Cartlidge and Elliott (*Art*, 138–42) correctly stress that ancient portraits, whether iconic or verbal, sought to portray inner virtue. They find resemblance to portraits of Socrates, who was portrayed with a receding hairline and pointed beard. These features become components of the iconic portrait of Paul. Only the hairline could be linked to *APl*, and that not completely.

The description is suitable for an itinerant teacher, emanating both wisdom and the rigors of life on the road. The phrase "bursting with beneficence" (lit. "full of grace") serves as a transition. Its meaning is debatable. One possibility is "filled with God's grace," whatever that might mean, as a variant makes explicit. Acts 6:8 is probably a hendiadys and thus not fully pertinent. The context, however, suggests a less theological meaning: Paul generously bestowed what he had, the message about God's grace. The portrait is, however, qualified by two ironies.

The end of §2 reports that Onesiphorus had not seen Paul in person but spiritually (lit. "had not seen him in the flesh but only in spirit"). This cannot refer to a vision of Paul, for that would make the description unnecessary. To see Paul spiritually was to perceive his charismatic power, active in his teaching. The description is superseded by its final words, which succinctly observe that Paul could be *transfigured*. The translation seeks to suppress the nearly indelible image of angels impressed upon us. The narrator is not attempting to say that the apostle often looked like the ideal Siegfried. The Christian iconography of angels derives from the Greek personification of Victory (*nikē*) and does not antedate the fourth century. The emphasis is upon the heavenly glow (artistically standardized in the halo).

Although the ApocActs often ascribe polymorphy to Christ (Cartlidge, "Metamorphoses"), it is less frequently a characteristic of apostles. Transfiguration is another quality that Paul shares with Christ. The essential notion is that those transfigured, such as Moses and Stephen, reflect heavenly reality. See Acts 6:15 and Pervo, *Acts*, 170 (to which add Gregory Epit 11 [*Acts of Andrew*]). The D-text of Acts 24:10 and 26:1 reports a similar phenomenon. In each case this precedes a speech, as with Stephen. This is an example of overlap between the D-text of Acts and the *APl*, on which see chap. 1.

The other remarkable irony emerges in comparison with the romantic novels, in which typically the boy and girl are briefly described, see one another, and fall in love at first sight. Thecla falls for Paul at first hearing and does not see him until §18. Readers may suspect that this is just as well, since Paul is not on anyone's list of Heracles look-alikes, but it is a perfect little illustration of the similarities and differences between *APl* and the Greek romantic novels.

§4. In their initial meeting Onesiphorus' display of his spiritual insight sets Demas and Hermogenes on the path to explicit opposition. Onesiphorus does not inquire, "Are you Paul of Tarsus," etc., nor does Paul so much as ask his name before treating Onesiphorus to a celestial smile (see Notes). Their reciprocal greetings utilize the same Greek stem (*chaire, charis*).

Onesiphorus' attention to Paul and neglect of his companions excites jealousy, a basic motivation in popular literature. See Pervo, *Acts*, 177. Demas alone speaks here, although Onesiphorus views them as a pair. (Two Latin witnesses have them speak in unison.) Onesiphorus displays more insight than Paul has, but he is equally charitable, accepting the pair's claim at face value. (Despite the claim of hypocrisy, the two appear to have sincere religious beliefs at variance with those of Paul.)

Notes

On the popularity of Thecla, see, e.g., Pesthy, "Thecla"; and Johnson, *The Life*, 1–14. Johnson's study focuses upon a fifth-century paraphrase of her life, which was issued with a collection of miracles worked at her shrine. For a review of recent thought, see Matthews, "Thinking."

The opening words are marked as a title in P.Heid.

Unlike the previous chapters, 3 and 4 are richly attested, with more than forty Greek mss. and numerous versions. The symbols used are those of Lipsius and Bonnet, eds., *Acta Apostolorum Apocrypha* (hereafter Lipsius-Bonnet), 1:xciv–cvi. In most cases, however, textual notes are general (e.g., "some witnesses"). Unless otherwise marked (e.g., "Latin"), the witnesses are Greek.

The Title: Only A entitles the work "The Acts of Paul and Thecla." This is unlikely to be original, as the two rarely act in concert. Greek witnesses B E F offer "The Martyrdom of the holy protomartyr Thecla." Others include "The martyrdom of St. Thecla, peer of the apostles and first female martyr." Another witness identifies her as an "apostle."

Journey. Some Latin witnesses provide an opening phrase like "in those days" to indicate the opening of a new work.

Iconium. See Acts 14:1–6. Iconium, known for at least a time as Claudiconium, was an old and important city of Lycaonia, with a Phrygian populace. It lay c. 150 kilometers from Antioch. Travelers would probably proceed southeast through Neapolis and take the Via Sebaste east, a journey of at least five days. This city had the characteristics of a typical Pauline missionary center, for its location on crossroads linking several regions made it an important and prosperous commercial center in the early Christian era. See Gasque, "Iconium," *ABD* 3:357–58. Note also the dated but detailed account of Ramsay, *The Cities of St. Paul: Their Influence on His Life and Thought*,

317–82; and Taylor, "St Paul," 1211–16, who gives evidence for the presence of Phrygian language and culture.

Antioch. Some Latin mss. delete Antioch, perhaps in the interest of presenting a coherent account of Paul's adventures with Thecla. One Latin witness adds "after the persecution," indicating that it continues chap. 2.

Companions. Mss. exhibit some interesting variety in the names. E reads "Demas, Cephas, and Hermogenes." Two Latin witnesses add Alexander (cf. 2 Tim 4:14). Cephas is the Aramaic equivalent of Peter.

Great deeds of Christ. See Acts 2:11. Cf. also *T. Job* 51.4; *AJn* 37.4; *APet* 5.19.; *AAndandMatt* 10:2.

Like devotees. Two Greek witnesses omit these words.

Goodness. Lit. "of Christ." The expression refers not to Christ's nature but to his gift. Although orthodox (Lampe, 74), the phrase could seem marcionite. Variants include "G. of God," and, harmonizing, "G. of God and Christ," while some Latin versions remove any reference to the divine.

Affection. Some Latin witnesses temper this into a statement of concern.

Oracles of the Lord. For the phrase see, e.g., Polycarp Phil. 7.1. *Logia* is often better rendered as "oracles" than as "sayings" (*logoi*). Probably secondary are: "and the instruction and the interpretation [of the gospel]." These expand the series of genitives, which is awkward with or without them. A, B, and M omit "instruction." G reads "of the gospel." M smooths matters out by replacing birth and resurrection with "ascension and including "great deeds" within the genitives.

Beloved. Cf. Eph 1:6.

[*Davidic descent*] The phrase is read by Vouaux (148) and Rordorf (1129, and Rordorf, "Orthodoxie," 397).The basis is Rom 1:3. G and some Latin mss. omit it. One explanation for omission is its awkwardness. It is not characteristic of the christological summaries in *APl* and may well be based upon 3 *Corinthians* (10:4–5). Variants include "Virgin" with Mary.

B lacks the phrase about Paul's coming to Iconium. Lc identifies Onesiphorus as a "just man." The same epithet is applied to Paul in the *Acts of the Scillitan Martyrs* 12. G assures that he moved quickly. For further development of the Onesiphorus legend, with some borrowing from *APl*, see the *Acts of Peter and Andrew*.

Translation, Commentary, and Notes : Chapter

On the sons of Onesiphorus, see pp. 48–49. Their names vary in the ms. tradition of *APl*, probably due to error. Ebner ("Schein" 56) observes that the sons' names are related to the philosophical tradition, Zeno as founder of the Stoa and Simmias from the Socratic circle (*Phaedo;* cf. Plutarch's *De genio Socratis*).

Bald. This characteristic may derive from Acts 18:18, where Paul (evidently) shaves his head as part of the ritual of a vow. Iconography normally portrays Paul as bald. The Syriac, as translated by Wright, limits potential extremes: "of middling size . . . hair was scanty, and his legs were a little crooked, and his knees were projecting (*or* far apart), and he had large eyes, and his eyebrows met, and his nose was somewhat long" (Wright, 117). From various Latin revisions (Vouaux, 150) it is apparent that believers of the Middle Ages found some of the descriptive terms upsetting.

Transfigured. Other examples include Esther 5:2, 1 Enoch 38:4; 2 Baruch 51:3; cf. 2 Macc 6:18; *Didascalia* 19; *Mart. Polyc.* 7:3; 12.1; Eusebius *H. E.* 5.1.35; and the *Acts of Marianus and James* 9.2. See also Betz, *Lukian*, 132–33.

4. *Smiling* can be a sign of a divine epiphany and of special knowledge. Cf. also *APl* 9.19; 21; *Acts of Andrew* (Epitome of Gregory 16 [dl 3]); *Acts of John* 73.1; *Acts of Peter* 6.13; Pseudo-Clementine *Recognitions* 1.47.3; *Hom.* 2.50.1 Classical examples include *Ody.* 16.476; 20.201; Euripides, *Bacchae* 439. Some Latin witnesses revise or paraphrase this clause.

Servant (hypēretēs). This term is important to Luke (1:2), who applies it to Paul (Acts 26:16). Among the wide range of applications were cultic titles and usages. See Spicq, *Theological Lexicon* 3:398–402, esp. 401–2. Syriac reads "apostle."

Blessed God. Cf. Rom 13:4; 9:5.

Household. Ms. E eliminates the household.

Demas. Syriac directs this statement to Paul.

result of proper behavior. Lit., "fruit of righteousness." Cf. Phil 1:11. Syriac witnesses prefer the more concrete "works."

Are as you say. The translation is a guess, supported by some variants, of the intended meaning.

Come in. Cf. Acts 21:8. Note Mark 6:31.

The Acts of Paul

Bibliography

Aubin, Melissa. "Reversing Romance? The *Acts of Thecla* and the Ancient Novel." In *Ancient Fiction and Early Christian Narrative*, edited by R. F. Hock, 257–72. SBL Symposium 6. Atlanta: Scholars, 1998.

Betz, Hans Dieter. *Lukian von Samosata und das Neue Testament*. TU 76. Berlin: Akadamie, 1961.

Bollók, János. "The Description of Paul in the Acta Pauli." In *The Apocryphal Acts of Paul and Thecla*, edited by Jan N. Bremmer, 1–15. Kampen: Kok Pharos, 1996.

Bremmer, Jan N. "Magic, martyrdom and women's liberation in the Acts of Paul and Thecla." In *The Apocryphal Acts of Paul and Thecla*, edited by Jan N. Bremmer, 36–59. Kampen: Kok Pharos, 1996.

Cartlidge, David R. "Transfigurations of Metamorphosis Traditions in the Acts of John, Thomas, and Peter." *Semeia* 38 (1986) 53–66.

Cartlidge, David R., and J. Keith Elliott, *Art and the Christian Apocrypha*. London: Routledge, 2001.

Ebner, Martin. "Sein und Schein auf dem 'Königsweg': Figurenaufstellung und 'Einspurung' des Lesers (ActThecl 1–4)." In *Aus Liebe zu Paulus? Die Akte Thekla neu aufgerollt*, edited by Martin Ebner, 52–63. SBS 206. Stuttgart: Katholisches Bibelwerk, 2005.

Fitzmyer, Joseph A. *The Letter to Philemon*. AB 34c. Doubleday: New York, 2000.

Foster, Paul. "Polymorphic Christology: Its Origins and Development in Early Christianity." *JTS* 58 (2007) 90–93.

French, David H. "Acts and the Roman Roads of Asia Minor." In *The Book of Acts in Its Graeco-Roman Setting*, edited by David W. J. Gill and Conrad Gempf, 49–58. BIFCS 2. Grand Rapids: Eerdmans, 1994.

———. "The Roman *Road-system* of Asia Minor." *ANRW* II 7.2 (1980) 698–729.

Grant, Robert M. "The Description of Paul in the Acta Pauli." *VC* 36 (1982) 1–4.

Haines-Eitzen, Kim. *The Gendered Palimpsest: Women, Writing, and Representation in Early Christianity*. New York: Oxford University Press, 2012, 95–112.

Lipsett, B. Diane. *Desiring Conversion: Hermas, Thecla, Aseneth*. New York: Oxford University Press, 2011.

Luke, T. S. "The Parousia of Paul at Iconium." *Religion and Theology* 15 (2008) 225–51.

MacDonald, Dennis R. *The Legend and the Apostle*. Philadelphia: Westminster, 1983.

Malherbe, Abraham J. "A Physical Description of Paul." In *Paul and the Popular Philosophers*. Minneapolis: Fortress, 1989, 165–70.

Malina, Bruce J., and J. H. Neyrey *Portraits of Paul*. Louisville: Westminster John Knox, 1996.

Mara, M. G. "I macarismi di Paolo." *Augustinianum* 47 (2007) 87–108.

Matthews, Shelly. "Thinking of Thecla: Issues in Feminist Historiography." *Journal of Feminist Studies in Religion* 17 (2002) 39–65.

Mitchell, Stephen, *Anatolia*. 2 vols. Oxford: Oxford University Press, 1993.

Omerzu, H. "The Portrait of Paul's Outer Appearance in the *Acts of Paul and Thecla*: Re-considering the Correspondence between Body and Personality in Ancient Literature." *Religion and Theology* 15 (2008) 252–79.

Parsons, Mikeal. *Body and Character in Luke and Acts: The Subversion of Physiognomy in Early Christianity*. Grand Rapids: Baker Academic, 2006.

Pesthy, Monika. "Thecla in the Fathers of the Church." In *The Apocryphal Acts of Paul and Thecla*, edited by Jan N. Bremmer, 164–78. Kampen: Kok Pharos, 1996.

Ramsay, William M. *The Church in the Roman Empire.* London: Hodder and Stoughton, 1897.
Rordorf, Willy. "Hérésie et Orthodoxie selon la Correspondance apocryphe entre les Corinthiens et l'apôtre Paul." In *Lex Orandi, Lex Credendi: Gesammelte Aufsätze zum 60. Geburtstag,* 380–431. Paradosis 36. Freiburg: Universtitätsverlag Freiburg, 1993.
Taylor, Joseph. "St Paul and the Roman Empire: Acts of the Apostles 13–14." *ANRW* 2.26.2 (1995) 1190–1231.
Wills, Lawrence M. *The Quest of the Historical Gospel. Mark, John, and the Origins of the Gospel Genre.* Routledge: London, 1997.
Zanker, Paul. *The Mask of Socrates: The Image of the Intellectual in Antiquity.* Translated by A. Shapiro. Berkeley: University of California Press, 1995.

3.5–6 The Inaugural Sermon

5. Great joy erupted upon Paul's entrance into Onesiphorus' house. People knelt for prayer, bread was broken, and God's message about self-control and resurrection proclaimed. Paul said:

> Blessed are those with unadulterated hearts,
>> for they shall see God.
> Blessed are those who keep the flesh pure,
>> for they will be God's temple.
> Blessed are those with self-control,
>> for God will speak with them.
> Blessed are those who have kissed the world goodbye,
>> for they will be pleasing to God.
> Blessed are those who have wives
>> but do not have sexual relations with them,
>> for they will be heirs of God.
> Blessed are those who revere God,
>> for they will become God's angels.
> Blessed are those who hold God's oracles in awe,
>> for they will be consoled.
> Blessed are those who have received the wisdom of Jesus Christ,
>> for they will be called the children of the most high.
> Blessed are those who have kept their baptismal vows,
>> for they will find rest with the father and the son.

The Acts of Paul

> Blessed are those who have opened themselves up
> > to an understanding of Jesus Christ,
> > for they will be in light.
>
> Blessed are those who, because of their love for God,
> > have left the fashions of this world behind them,
> > for they will judge angels and be rewarded
> > with a place at the father's right hand.
>
> Blessed are the merciful,
> > for they will obtain mercy
> > and not gaze upon judgment's bitter day.
>
> Blessed are the bodies of virgins,
> > for they will please God and not lose
> > > the reward for their chastity.
> > for the father's word will become saving action
> > > for them on the day of his son and they shall enjoy
> > > eternal rest.

Comment

3.5–6 proceed without further ado to Paul's mission, opening with an address that might be entitled "The Sermon in the House." This is quite probably Paul's initial sermon. In the canonical Acts Paul is described as preaching from chapter 9, but the text of a sermon does not appear until chap. 13. The obvious parallel to this address is Jesus' inaugural sermon in Matthew 5–7, with which the author is familiar and the initial macarisms of which are repeated and developed. See Table 1.2, p. 65. The house-based community is the norm in *APl*, as it probably was at the time of composition. On this setting, see Osiek and Balch, *Families*, 193–214.

The scene is like a dramatic stage, such as in New Comedy, which depicts proximate buildings. In *APl* the walls are transparent, as it were, allowing the audience to see and hear what is going on inside the houses as well as on the street. The reference to joy is characteristic of the beginning of Paul's missions. See 4.14 (Thecla, in fact), 9.1.4, 10.1, 12.1, 13.4, and 14.1.

The section opens with a description of Paul's mission and continues with a verbatim report of his message. The first sentence looks like a summary and would be taken as such, were not specifics of the message presented in direct speech. The sentence evidently describes a service consisting

Translation, Commentary, and Notes : Chapter

of prayer, sacrament, and word (not necessarily in that order). Kneeling seems to be the normal posture for prayer (3.24), except during Eastertide (if that is not a later modification), 9.14. There is no reference to reading from scripture (or other texts).

A prepositional phrase specifies the content of God's message. The message is not about salvation or any overtly christological topic. The essence of the message is "self-control and resurrection." This is not a hendiadys. A probable meaning is "self-control that leads to resurrection." The subsequent macarisms serve as explication. "Self-control," a classic Greek virtue with a wide range of applications, acquired in early Christianity the sense of "chastity." See Pervo, *Dating Acts*, 268. Note Acts 24:25. "Resurrection" is the essence of Christian hope for both present and future. Paul favored celibacy but accepted marriage. In the second century some Paulinists favored celibacy to the point of requiring it. The Pastoral Epistles essentially demanded marriage. On this point *APl* and the PE occupy, as so often, opposite points on the spectrum. Luke is closer to the radicals. Luke 20:34-36, for example, also associates worthiness for resurrection with celibacy. See Pervo, *Profit*, 181n79. Ebner aptly characterizes the difference between the PE and the *APl*: the key virtue for the former is *eusebeia* (conventional piety; see Pervo, *Dating Acts*, 236-37); the *APl* proclaim *enkrateia* (self-control; see Ebner, "Seligpreisungen," 72).

The opening macarisms/beatitudes of the Sermon in Matthew 5 and Luke 6 turn the world upside down. That is precisely the function of the beatitudes here, with the exception that they generate a prompt and explicit disruption of the social order. It is as if the Gospel of Luke described, in reaction to "Blessed are the poor" (6:20), poor people who began to appropriate food, clothing, and shelter.

Macarisms occupy a rich field in the history of religion. The blessed state is a quality possessed by gods that can be bestowed upon humans. In his summary of a vast amount of material Betz (*Sermon*, 92-105) identifies these characteristics: macarisms originate in worship, are declarative, pertain to present and future, and have ethical and moral dimensions (*Sermon*, 93). In the course of time beatitudes could be applied to various spheres, notably wisdom. Aphorisms and proverbs are readily recategorized as beatitudes. An invented example of this process is "Blessed are those who eat an apple a day, for they will keep the doctor away."

The thirteen macarisms that constitute this sermon (numbered here for convenience in parentheses) are uniformly of two members, the second of which gives a reason, through (10). (11) provides two explanations, (12) presents its reason in antithetic parallelism, and (13) has two sets of reasons, each with two parts. In this end-loading the author imitates Matthew, the major source. Both sets of macarisms conclude with the idea of an eschatological reward.

Theologically, macarisms announce salvation. This is counter to their appearance, especially in the two-part form found here, which represent an act-consequence orientation at home in the wisdom tradition. (If you eat an apple a day, you will keep the doctor away.) Macarisms offer reward for virtuous conduct. The concomitant theology is manifest in chap. 3. Baptism is not empowerment for life or armor against evil, as in the Pauline tradition. Paul declines to baptize Thecla because he fears that she will backslide. This is in part literary, to raise suspense (not to mention frustration with Paul on the part of many readers), and, in part, due to the sources, as Thecla will undergo a *martyr's baptism*, but the passage exhibits a view of baptism that emphasizes fidelity rather than grace.

Reliance upon Matthew 5:1–11 does not stem from poverty of imagination. The author expects readers to recognize these parallels, which enhance the authority of his hero as well as his status. In short, Paul sounds like Jesus. The author evidently composed the macarisms on the basis of Matthew and other material, 1 Corinthians in particular. For a comparison of the lists in Matthew and *APl*, see Chart 1 in Barrier, p. 54. These beatitudes were probably not extracted from a pre-existing source, as Merz (*Selbstauslegung*, 320–33) proposed.

The nature of lists of macarisms is such that the number does not particularly matter. Two may be as good as twenty, while two hundred could not begin to exhaust the possibilities. The variety breaks the chains of concrete interpretation, urging readers to release their imaginations. Find a form of righteous life that inspires you and fill in the blank for the desired reward. The overlap among the macarisms supports this understanding. See the use of pure/purity in (2) and (13), divine utterance in (3) and (13), "judgment day" in (12) and (13).

The structure is not haphazard. The text exhibits a loose ABA arrangement; five macarisms focus upon renunciation, with particular reference to renunciation of sexual activity, followed by general themes in (6) through (10), returning to renunciation in (11) through (13). Ebner ("Seligpreisungen," 71) observes that the basis for theological reflection is essentially charismatic. Quite unlike the emphasis of the PE and 2 Thessalonians, there is no appeal to tradition and no resort to Scripture. (7) could refer to prophetic Scripture, but this is not necessary. Whereas proto-orthodoxy emphasizes the institution as the setting for interpreting revelation, these macarisms are devoid of institutional sanctions.

Translation, Commentary, and Notes : Chapter

(1) The macarisms begin with an exact parallel to Matt 5:8, the sixth beatitude. This sums up the message. Purity will lead to the eschatological vision of God. The modifier "in heart" (lit.) clarifies that ritual purity is not the subject.

(2) specifies the nature of the purity that is desired. The trope of the community as a temple is found in the Qumran literature (1QS 8.5–9) and utilized by Paul (1 Cor 3:16–17; 6:19) and the Pauline tradition (Eph 2:20–21). The closest parallel, however, is *2 Clem* 9.3: "We must, therefore, guard the flesh as a temple of God" (trans. Holmes, *Apostolic Fathers*, 149). 1 Cor 6:19 uses the theme in the context of sexual activity (Ebner, "Paulinische Seligpreisungen," 63). Cf. also *1 Clem* 38:2; *2 Clem* 8:4; 14:3, Ignatius *Phil* 7:2.

(3) This macarism takes up the announced subject. Sexual abstinence as a prerequisite for revelation ("God will speak to them"), especially for females, is a widely attested phenomenon. See Pervo, *Acts*, 536. Examples include *2 Clem* 4:3; 15:1; *Hermas* 35.

(4) Renunciation of the "world," i.e., wealth, possessions, family, home, and all types of security, is the essential vocation of the itinerant missionary. Paul, Thecla, the Onesiphorus family, and others undertake this life. The Pastorals envision the church, as God's household, in hierarchical terms. Proper subordination, in which particular persons and groups are subordinate to others, is the model. The *APl* call for subordination of the self to God's will. See Ebner, "Seligpreisungen," 70. According to 1Tim 3:1, aspiration for the tip of the hierarchical pyramid (the episcopate) is pursuit of a "good work." This term (*ergon*) appears in (13) with regard to divine activity. Cf. also *2 Clem* 6:5; 16:2; *Hermas* 36.

(5) modifies 1 Cor 7:29. This form was preferred by Origen. (See Introduction, pp. 45–46). Lit. "As if they do not have [wives]." The phrase is quite androcentric, as is 1 Cor 7:29. See the notes. The second clause derives from Matt 5:3 ("the meek will inherit the land"). For this meaning, see BDAG 547 1 (b), but, as the notes indicate, scribes found the sentiment too radical.

(6) is a conventional sentiment. Proper reverence for the divine was ubiquitous in the ancient world. The second clause is uncertain. The simplest interpretation is that the redeemed will become celestial beings unimpaired by sexuality. Cf. Luke 20:36; *APl* 3.9; 17; *Barnabas* 1:7; 2:24; 11; 19:5; 20:2; *Hermas* 35; 37; 40.

(7) may refer to Scripture, but the oracles (*logia*) in mind are probably prophetic revelations, especially those about lifestyle. Cf. the revelations about second marriage and other matters of behavior that characterized the New Prophecy ("Montanism"). The second clause repeats, less appropriately (see notes), the promise made to the "mourners" in Matt 5:4 (the second beatitude).

(8) The wisdom praised is probably the teaching *of* rather than *about* Jesus Christ. Both (7) and (8) are most probably to be understood as references to charismatic rather than institutional wisdom. The second clause closely resembles the promise to peacemakers in the seventh beatitude of Matt 5:9. The *APl* has limited interest in peacemakers. Neither Paul nor Thecla would be so classified. They will make no peace with oppression.

(9) reads, lit., "have kept their baptism." For the meaning, see 2 *Clem* 6:9, "[W]hat assurance do we have of entering the kingdom of God if we fail to keep our baptism pure and undefiled? Or who will be our advocate, if we are not found to have holy and righteous works?" (trans. Holmes, *Apostolic Fathers*, 147). "Rest" is one of the most poignant terms for the eschatological reward, as in the term *requiem* ("Grant *them* eternal rest"). In speculative and philosophical theology rest appealed because it represented a state superior to motion (cf. "the unmoved mover). The locus is "binitarian" (see the Notes). Although "charismatic" in several senses, chaps. 3–4 of *APl* make no place for the Spirit. Cf. also 2 *Clem* 6:9; 7:6; 8:6, *Hermas* 72.3.

(10) amounts to a paraphrase of (8) and is omitted by some witnesses. Such redundancy is normal in lists of macarisms, on which see above.

(11) is similar to (4). 1 Corinthians has contributed to both members: 7:31 for "worldly fashions," and 6:3 for judging angels.

(12) repeats Matt 5:7, the fifth beatitude, with a clarifying addition: God will be merciful to them at the final judgment.

(13) is the climactic macarism, accompanied by four promises. It is as if the author did not wish to abandon the declaration. The final position is also literarily apposite, for the first respondent to Paul's message will be a virgin, whose body will be a center of attention. This blessing need not be limited to female virgins. B reads "those who practice the discipline of virginity," using the masculine, which includes females but does not exclude males. (The so-called "masculine gender" often functioned, when it refers to biological sex, as common or inclusive.) The macarisms have returned to their original

and central subject. This works as a foreshadowing of the plot of Thecla's story. Her virginal body will remain pure, come what may—and a great deal will come.

Notes

The description begins with four crisp, euphonious two-word phrases consisting of a noun and a modifier: *chara megalē, klisis gonatōn, klasis artou, logos theou*. The translation seeks to evoke the meaning.

Joy is the basic Christian response to the message of salvation.

One Latin edition omits "kneeling," probably because it was viewed as penitential and in conflict with joy. Several Latin mss. eliminate the reference to resurrection.

Martyr's Baptism. From very early times Christians have held that uninitiated martyrs were "baptized in their own blood." Since Thecla was presumably leaping to her death, this understanding would apply to her case.

(2) Some Latin mss. alter to "souls will be temples," or, in conformity to 1 Cor 3:16, "temple of holy spirit."

(3) Some Latin mss. read a redundant "who abstain from all impurity."

(4) A variant for the second clause, "they will be called upright," is difficult to explain.

(5) G omits "wives," making the mental renunciation general. This unusual object second clause is avoided by variants: "Kingdom of Christ," "earth/land," or "life." One element of the Latin tradition omits this macarism. Cf. Rom 8:17.

(6) A variant replaces "God" with "Christ." Syriac (Wright, 18) reads "they shall be called angels," with the variant "they shall be as angels."

(7) A Latin variant promise that "they will be exalted," evidently more apt than "consoled."

(9) One variant promises a vision of the Son of God. A Latin witness states that believers will rest in light. Other witnesses add the Holy Spirit.

(10) Syriac (Wright, 119) reads "Blessed are they who have received the exhortation of the Messiah." Variations in the tradition indicate that the participle *chōrēsantes* ("be open to") was difficult. Cf. 2 Cor 6:12; 7:2.

(11) has "Christ" as a variant for "God." Syriac (Wright, 119) reads "Blessed are they who for the love of God have gone out of this body." This understood *schēma* in the sense of "outward appearance." Here it is taken in the sense of "life style," based upon 1 Cor 7:31. M expands: "because of the friendship and love of God . . . turmoil and pomp of this world." Some witnesses read the more common "shall stand at God's right hand."

(12) The mss. exhibit substantial alterations. Syriac (Wright, 119) completes: "[O]n the Day of Judgment they shall receive the kingdom." This is clearer and less vivid than the Greek. M contains this attractive second clause: "For the merciful serve Jesus Christ, who is himself poor."

(13) Syriac (Wright, 119) reads: "Blessed are the bodies and souls of virgins, for they shall be pleasing unto God, and the reward of their holiness shall not be lost, for, according to the word of the Father, there shall be found for them works unto life at the day of His Son." This shifts the understanding of "work" from divine action, as the Greek evidently intends, to good deeds performed by believers.

Bibliography

Betz, Hans Dieter. *The Sermon on the Mount*. Edited by A. Y. Collins. Hermeneia. Minneapolis: Fortress, 1995.

Ebner, Martin. "Paulinische Seligpreisungen à la Thekla: Narrative Relecture der Makarismenreihe in ActThecl 5." In *Aus Liebe zu Paulus? Die Akte Thekla neu aufgerollt*, edited by Martin Ebner, 64–79. SBS 206. Stuttgart: Katholisches Bibelwerk, 2005.

Merz, Annette. *Die fictive Selbstauslegung des Paulus. Intertextuelle Studien zur Intention und Rezeption der Pastralbriefe*. NTOA 52. Göttingen: Vandenhoeck & Ruprecht, 2004.

Osiek, Carolyn, and David L. Balch. *Families in the New Testament World: Households and House Churches*. Philadelphia: Westminster John Knox, 1997.

Pervo, Richard I. *Dating Acts: Between the Evangelists and the Apologists*. Santa Rosa, CA: Polebridge, 2006.

———. *Profit with Delight: The Literary Genre of the Acts of the Apostles*. Philadelphia: Fortress, 1987.

Translation, Commentary, and Notes : Chapter

3.7 Meet the Heroine

7. While Paul was delivering this message to the church in Onesiphorus' house, one Thecla, the virgin daughter of Theocleia, who was engaged to Thamyris, was seated at the window of her house that was closest to Onesiphorus,' listening without respite to Paul's message about chastity. Thecla did not turn away from the window but progressed in the faith with abundant happiness. Indeed, as she watched any number of women and girls arriving to see Paul, she began to desire that she too might be deemed worthy to hear the message about Christ in Paul's presence and hear the message, as she had not yet glimpsed his features but only heard his message.

Comment

3.7 introduces Thecla. As in the case of Paul, comparisons with non-Sophistic romantic novels are appropriate:

> Hermocrates, ruler of Syracuse, victor over the Athenians, had a daughter named Callirhoe, a marvel of a girl and the idol of all Sicily. In fact her beauty was not so much human as divine, not that of a Nereid or mountain nymph, either, but of Aphrodite herself. Reports of this incredible vision spread far and wide: suitors came pouring into Syracuse, potentates and princes, not only from Sicily, but from Italy, the continent, and the peoples of the continent. (Chariton, *Callirhoe* 1.1.2; LCL, trans. G. P. Goold, 29)

Anthia, heroine of *An Ephesian Tale*, first appears in a religious procession at Ephesus, in which young men and women of marriageable age marched in separate groups, an event that served as a marriage market.

> Heading the line of girls was Anthia, daughter of Megamedes and Euippe, locals. Anthia's beauty was marvelous and far surpassed the other girls. She was fourteen, her body was blooming with shapeliness, and the adornment of her dress enhanced her grace. Her hair was blonde, mostly loose, only [A] little of it braided, and moving as the breezes took it. Her eyes were vivacious, bright like a beauty's but forbidding like a chaste girl's ... [*her clothing is described*] Often when seeing her at the shrine,

The Acts of Paul

> the Ephesians worshiped her as Artemis, so also at the sight of her on this occasion the crowd cheered; the opinions of the spectators were various, some in their astonishment declaring that she was the goddess herself. (Xenophon of Ephesus, *Anthia and Habrocomes* 1.2.5–7; LCL, trans. Jeffrey Henderson, 217)

Chariton begins by stating that Hermocrates (an historical character) had a daughter. As in the case of the hero, Chaireas, her beauty is proclaimed rather than described. This set off an international competition for her hand. Readers might expect that the lucky man would have to win an athletic competition (possibly against her, as in the story of Atalanta), perform various feats or labors, or solve riddles. In any case competition would be fierce. Family standing comes first. Anthia receives different treatment. Although this novel is much shorter than *Callirhoe*, substantially more space is devoted to the heroine here, including information about her looks.

The introduction of Thecla ignores her looks. Her father is not mentioned. Theocleia, the mother, is either a widow or a divorcée. Chap. 3 will pit daughter against mother, acting out Luke 12:53. Thecla need not be identified as a virgin. This status was assumed. The word connects with the final macarisms, which honored the bodies of virgins, an outstanding example of which is about to come on stage. The other datum is about marital status: Thecla is engaged to one Thamyris, of whose status readers are not yet informed. The ancient audience would probably place Thecla at about fifteen years or under, as her single mother would be unlikely to delay the nuptials. The narrator requires no explanations, of course. Thecla must be a virgin and thus unmarried.

She is also a proper stay-at-home girl. The narrative is most intriguing. Without leaving her house, Thecla can hear Paul's message (and see admiring females arriving), but, as he is inside the home, she does not see him. The result is a stimulating twist on the conventions of romance (love at first sight) that also gives center place to the key issue: the power of the word, the message proclaimed rather than the appeal of the proclaimer. That notion is authentically Pauline (cf. 2 Cor 10–13, e.g.). Thecla also assumes, equally ironically, the image of "the woman in the window." That motif was ubiquitous in antiquity. Women, confined to the home, gazed from a window for the sight of their menfolk returning from war or some other activity. Examples of various types include Judg 5:28 (the mother of Sisera); 2 Sam 6:16, and 2 Kgs 9:30 (Jezebel). See Bovon, "Woman at the Window." Glimpsing Joseph (whom she has refused to meet) from her window: "At the sight of Joseph in his chariot Aseneth's heart was shattered. Her soul was crushed; her knees gave way; she trembled all over with great anxiety. Sighing deeply, she thought . . ." (*Aseneth* 6.1) Aseneth was a victim of the lightning bolt, love at first sight. The reader is uncertain about Thecla. She has felt no *coup de foudre*. Perhaps this will change when she sees the object of her interest. The author has managed to raise a bit of suspense at the end.

Notes

Non-Sophistic. The term "Second Sophistic" is utilized to describe rhetorically sophisticated composition during the Roman Imperial era. The novels of Chariton and Xenophon of Ephesus are relatively simpler in style than other, later romances.

Aphrodite . . . Artemis. Aphrodite was the patron goddess of Chariton's hometown, Aphrodisias, as was Artemis the patron of Ephesus. The comparisons are thus appropriate to their settings.

Virgin. One could render "unmarried," but news of her engagement follows immediately. Well-to-do girls normally married at about fourteen to sixteen. Legally they were then matrons, even if only twelve. For some studies of the age of marriage, see Horn, "Suffering Children," 119n8. No one protests that Anthia is too young for marriage.

Without respite. Lit. "night and day." Cf. 1 Thess 2:9.

Chastity. Mss. E, I, K, and G are longer: " . . . the message about God and about chastity and the faith in Christ, and prayer." Some Greek witnesses read "love" (*agapē*) instead of "chastity" (*hagneia*). This longer text is preferred by Vouaux, 160, and Rordorf, 1130. The short text rendered here is that of Lipsius, 240. Barrier, 85, reads the short text, without discussion.

Women and girls. Parthenoi (virgins, unmarried women) is omitted by Syriac (Wright, 120) and some other witnesses, probably because its presence raised the question of why Thecla did not walk over to Onesiphorus' house. One Latin witness mentions her desire to go in. Thecla is still a properly behaved young woman who would not leave the house without escort or permission. (Barrier's claim [86] that "arrive at" [*eisporeuomai*] has a sexual connotation is baseless here.)

Deemed worthy . . . presence. Syriac (Wright, 121) shortens to, "[S]he was longing to hear the words of Paul."

His features. "Seen him/Paul" would be good Greek. The term "character" stresses external appearance.

Bibliography

Aubin, Melissa. "Reversing Romance? The *Acts of Thecla* and the Ancient Novel." In *Ancient Fiction and Early Christian Narrative*, edited by R. F. Hock, 257–72. SBL Symposium 6. Atlanta: Scholars, 1998.

Bovon, François, "The Woman at the Window: A Study in Intertextuality between Aeschylus and the Book of Judges." *Scripture and Interpretation* 4 (2010) 113–20.

Bremmer, Jan N. "Magic, martyrdom and women's liberation in the Acts of Paul and Thecla." In *The Apocryphal Acts of Paul and Thecla*, edited by Jan N. Bremmer, 36–59. Kampen: Kok Pharos, 1996.

Calef, Susan A. "Thecla 'Tried and True' and the Inversion of Romance." In *A Feminist Companion to the New Testament Apocrypha*, edited by A.-J. Levine, 163–85. Feminist Companion to the New Testament and Early Christian Writings 11. New York: T. & T. Clark, 2006.

Horn, Cornelia B. "Suffering Children, Parental Authority and the Quest for Liberation? A Tale of Three Girls in the *Acts of Paul (and Thecla)*, The *Act(s) of Peter*, The *Acts of Nerseus and Achilleus* and the *Epistle of Pseudo-Titus*." In *A Feminist Companion to the New Testament Apocrypha*, edited by A.-J. Levine, 118–45. Feminist Companion to the New Testament and Early Christian Writings 11. New York: T. & T. Clark, 2006.

3.8–10 Thecla's Mother Enlists the Fiancé's aid

8. Since Thecla would not leave the window, her mother sent for Thamyris, who was most pleased to come, thinking that he was about to get a wife.

"Where's my Thecla? [I want to see her]," he asked Theocleia.

"I've got some strange news for you, Thamyris. She hasn't left her window for three days and three nights, nor has she taken a drop or tasted a bite. She is intoxicated by the sight of a stranger and his wily and enticing discourse. I am amazed that such a modest girl can put up with all this."

9. "Thamyris, this fellow is agitating Iconium, specifically your Thecla. All the women and young people are coming to him for instruction. 'You must,' he says, 'revere the one and only god and live chastely.' And here is my daughter, in the grip of a novel lust and frightening emotions, trapped in her window by the web of

his message. All her attention is fixed upon his utterances. She has been swept away. Look, she's your fiancée. You go and talk to her."

10. Thamyris, approached Thecla caught between his attraction for her and fear of her unbalanced state. He said, "Thecla, dear fiancée, why are you sitting like this? What kind of feeling has got you so wrought up? Behave yourself! Come back to your Thamyris!" Her mother chimed in with similar statements, such as, "My child, why are you sitting that way, downcast, without a word, as if you were catatonic?"

Everyone wept bitterly: Thamyris because he was losing a wife, Theocleia her child, the slaves a mistress. The house was disrupted by sorrow. Nonetheless, Thecla did not budge an inch but remained riveted on Paul's message.

Comment

Despite the efforts of her mother, her prospective husband, and the household staff, Thecla will not budge from her position. The scene ends as it began, with Thecla at her window. Theocleia evidently hopes that the personal presence of her intended will bring her daughter back to her senses, perhaps with a bit of male superiority added to physical attraction and the prospect of marriage. Thamyris, who thinks that today may be the day (see Notes), will be lashed by disappointments. The narrator will ascertain that any sympathy for him will be quashed by dastardly actions.

Thecla is in the clutches of love sickness (see Tohey, "Love") and addicted to the words of Paul. The malady also carries symptoms proper to a convert preparing for initiation. Cf. Acts 9:19, where Paul spends three days without food or drink. Aseneth provides a closer parallel:

> She ran back up to her chambers by herself and collapsed exhausted, for she felt joy, distress, and considerable fear and trembling. She was also covered with sweat while she reflected upon all that Joseph had said to her in the name of God Most High. She wept loudly and bitterly, repudiated all the gods she had been worshiping, spurned all their images, and waited for evening to arrive ... So Aseneth was left alone with her seven maids. She was depressed and wept constantly until sunset, taking no nourishment, solid or liquid. (*Aseneth* 9.1–10.2, author's trans.)

The Acts of Paul

One of the infelicities of fictional love sickness is that no one, with the possible exception of the victim, who will not admit it, recognizes it. At this point Theocleia abruptly changes the subject. Thecla's seducer is a menace to civilized life. One may not ask why this missionary phenomenon has escaped Thamyris' attention. It gives information to the audience. Paul, whose name remains unknown to Theocleia, is subverting the social structure by enticing women and young people to abandon their religious and reproductive responsibilities. Greco-Roman political theory tended to view the family as the microcosm of the state (*polis*). To disrupt the family and interfere with its functions was to threaten the state. The effects of the various "revolutions" of the 1960s challenging most institutions and all authority continue to reverberate through western nations. Thecla's mother faces just such a revolution and its potentially ruinous effects upon her family. By one means or another she has learned Paul's message: one god + no sex = resurrection. See, in general, Francis, *Subversive Virtue*, e.g., 173–76. On anti-family rhetoric in early Christianity, see Clark, "Antifamilial"; and Jacobs, "Family Affair."

Theocleia implies that her daughter has been bewitched. "Binding" is a technical and ubiquitous term in magical recipes. The language is also appropriate for love-sickness, often suspected to be the cause of that malaise. See Faraone, *Love Magic*; and Jackson-McCabe, "Women." This circumstance hints at the accusation that will be raised in §20. She is prepared to blame everything on Paul. That view will change when her daughter takes action.

The image of Paul as a spider feminizes him, since spiders weave, a primary activity of women in antiquity. Cf. the label "black widow" for women who attract and marry men and then kill them for their money. He is repeatedly "feminized" in the course of the story, the inverse of Thecla, who will be "masculinized." See Aubin, "Reversing." Scholarship has viewed Thecla as a spider, but "web" is a more suitable translation in this context. Thecla is utterly inactive. Theocleia's invitation might mean, "See if you can do anything," but she is probably handing over responsibility to Thamyris, whom she has summoned. He is a male with authority over Thecla.

First fiancé then parent try to bring Thecla to her senses, without success. The entire household is reduced to tears: intended, mother, slaves. Rending the social fabric produces social tragedy. Amidst all this anxiety and sorrow Thecla remained a rock. Three times she is characterized with the verb *atenizō*, indicating intense concentration. The world is in chaos; Thecla, unmoved, unmoving, is unaffected by it all.

Translation, Commentary, and Notes : Chapter

Notes

Get a wife. B makes this explicit: "Take her home as wife." The circumstances are not clear. If they were awaiting a birthday, Thamyris would presumably know that date. A developmental stage, such as menarche, may be in mind, or it could be that the marriage would take place when mother said so. The readers would have understood.

See her. The bracketed phrase is widely attested, but otiose. It may be a pedantic expansion. One Latin witness reads "kiss" instead of "see," indicating that a scribe found it meaningless.

Strange news. P.Oxy. 6 reads *theōrēma*. Later mss. and versions have the equivalent of "story." "novel sight," the meaning of P. Oxy., is the kind of sensational language found in light reading. ("You won't believe what you're going to see.")

All this. Syriac (Wright, 120) reads the final phrase as a plural: "[A]nd accordingly I am surprised how discreet young women are quickly (and) evilly led away after him." This edition is wrestling with the problem of how other women can visit Paul's mission, but that Thecla cannot or will not do so.

Tasted a bite. A Latin witness picks up the love sickness theme, adding: "Restrained by the love of Christ, whoever he is."

Discourse. Cf. Titus 1:10. P.Oxy. 6 adds "vain."

Modest girl. The text is uncertain. P.Oxy. 6 and some Latin witnesses eliminate *aidōs* (modesty), possibly misunderstanding the Greek. Syriac (Wright, 120) blends this sentence into the next.

Agitating. The verb (*anaseiō*) appears in the charges against Jesus at Mark 15:11; Luke 23:5.

Women and young people. The term is evidently inclusive, but P.Oxy. 6 does not agree, for it adds "with the young women," Latin versions run the gamut.

Revere. E adds "venerate"; F "know." Cf. 1 Cor 8:4.

Chastely. Cf. 1 Tim 2:2. One Latin witness adds "always" (i.e., not just until marriage); another shifts away from celibacy to "genuinely and prudentially."

And here is. The narrative repeats the three Greek particles (*eti de kai*) applied to Thecla in the previous sentence.

The Acts of Paul

Web. Spittler (*Animals*, 162–68) makes a strong case for reading *arachnē* as "web" rather than "spider," and as an instrumental dative (most mss. at that time would not have marked the difference between the nominative and dative cases). Comparison to a spider might have focused upon her firm adhesion to the window, but the image of web suits her passive and captive behavior, as well as the connotation of "trapped" (*dedemenē*), with its intimation of magic "binding" (cf. 3.20).

Remained. C and Coptic add "in her window."

Lust . . . emotions. These two nouns appear in a list of vices at Col 3:5. Many Greek witnesses apply "frightening" to both nouns. Some Latin witnesses omit the phrase, others read "empty desire." "Empty" is read instead of "novel" by several witnesses. The two words (*kainē, kenē*) would have sounded the same.

Taken in. The last phrase has generated a number of variants. It was evidently viewed as too strong. These include the suggestion that fasting has done her in (K), that she hopes to remain a virgin (C), and that she fears for her life (Latin versions). Syriac lengthens: "And moreover Thecla is bound *to him* like a spider on its web *on the window* and is seized with a new desire and with an evil corruption, and her eyes are intently fixed on whatsoever comes out of that chamber/*on the words that are heard from the chamber* and she does not quit that window either to eat or to drink, and the virgin is quite absorbed (in thought) [*corrupted*] (Wright, 121, with variants in italics).

Attraction. Elliott (366) renders *philōn* as "kissed" (see note above under "see her"). This is possible, but the balanced construction speaks against it. The versions have difficulty with the implication that Thecla is mentally disturbed. Syriac, e.g., reads: "And Thamyris her betrothed drew nigh unto her, firstly, because he loved her, and secondly, because he had respect for her modesty" (Wright, 121).

Behave yourself. That is, "Exhibit the sense of shame appropriate to young women."

Catatonic. The adjective *paraplēx* can mean "paralyzed," which fits the sense of not moving. More often it refers to mental illness. The versions vary, although Syriac (Wright, 121) is frank: "mad woman."

Translation, Commentary, and Notes : Chapter

Bibliography

Aubin, Melissa. "Reversing Romance? The *Acts of Thecla* and the Ancient Novel." In *Ancient Fiction and Early Christian Narrative*, edited by R. F. Hock, 257–72. SBL Symposium 6. Atlanta: Scholars, 1998.

Clark, Elizabeth. "Antifamilial Tendencies in Ancient Christianity." *Journal of the History of Sexuality* 5 (1995) 356–80.

Faraone, Christopher A. *Ancient Greek Love Magic*. Cambridge, MA: Harvard University Press, 1999.

Francis, James A. *Subversive Virtue: Asceticism and Authority in the Second-Century Pagan World*. University Park: Pennsylvania State University Press, 1995.

Jackson-McCabe, Mattthew. "Women and Eros in Greek Magic and the *Acts of Paul and Thecla*." In *Women and Gender in Ancient Religions: Interdisciplinary Approaches*, edited by Stephen P. Ahearne-Kroll et al., 267–78. Tübingen: Mohr/Siebeck, 2010.

Jacobs, Andrew S. "A Family Affair." *JECS* 7 (1999) 105–38.

Spittler, Janet, E. *Animals in the Apocryphal Acts of the Apostles*. WUNT 247. Tübingen: Mohr/Siebeck, 2008.

Toohey, Peter. "Love, Lovesickness, and Melancholia." *Illinois Classical Studies* 17 (1992) 265–86.

3.11–14 Thamyris Seeks and Finds a Way to Stymie Paul

11. Thamyris jumped up and ran out into the street, where he could take careful note of whoever was going to see Paul or leaving. He saw two men engaged in a bitter argument. "Tell me who you are, gentlemen," he asked, "and who is this fellow with you inside, the one who leads young men astray and deceives young women, so that they do not marry but stay single? I, who am one of the leading men of this city, can promise you a good deal of money if you tell me about him."

12. "We don't know who this fellow is," Demas and Hermogenes replied, "but he would deprive young men of wives and young women of husbands, saying, 'You will possess no resurrection if you do not remain chaste and do not defile the flesh but keep it chaste.'"

13. Thamyris said to them, "Gentlemen. Come to my place and accept my hospitality. They went and found a splendid banquet, with abundant wine, conspicuous extravagance, and a brilliant table. Thamyris plied them with drink because of his fondness for Thecla and his desire to gain her hand in marriage. As the meal

The Acts of Paul

wore on he said, "Gentlemen, tell me what he teaches, so that I too may know it. I'm all torn up about Thecla, for she is quite swept away by the stranger, leaving me without a bride."

14. "Present him before Governor Castellius on the grounds that he is trying to entice the public to embrace the alien doctrine of the Christians," they advised. "By that means you will do away with him and have Thecla to be your wife. Further, we shall teach that what he calls 'resurrection' has already taken place through the children we have."

Comment

Luck is with Thamyris in his attempt to identify Paul's adherents, for he stumbles upon the dissident Demas and Hermogenes, who will, for a consideration, reveal a means for removing Paul from the picture. Lau ("Enthaltsamkeit," 80–82) observes that this section has two little parallel scenes. Each opens with a question by Thamyris, followed by an answer from the pair. Question and answer are formally similar in each scene, the first of which takes place in the street, while the second is at Thamyris' home. Characteristically of popular literature, the two function as a single unit.

Thamyris is able to stifle his grief and take action. Outside Onesiphorus' he will be able to interrogate or apprehend those coming and going. At that very moment two men are quarrelling. The narrator does not reveal the subject of their argument. People like this will fight one another if they cannot find someone else to fight. Thamyris assumes, possibly inspired by their quarrel, both that they know Paul and also that they take exception to his teaching. Furthermore, he suspects that they are open to tenders of thirty pieces of silver. In Demas and Hermogenes he has found the only two people in Iconium who could meet his requirements.

After summarizing the single feature of Paul's teaching that matters to him (and, one is sometimes tempted to suspect, the author), Thamyris points out his status, implying that they would do well to manifest cooperation, followed by the carrot: he is prepared to recompense them for their services.

The two add the denial of Peter to the betrayal of Judas, while not rejecting the role of Simon the magician (Acts 8:18). They claim not to know who Paul is. Cf. Mark 14:68. At 4.1 Paul will similarly deny Thecla. This could be prudent, lest they be taken as colleagues (as they, in fact, had been). His teaching they can summarize. A forthright attack on marriage (rather than an essay on the merits of matrimony, such as Juvenal's sixth satire) may be, as Barrier (98) says, actionable, although it is not pressed. The theological warning that resurrection requires sexual abstinence would probably have been unintelligible to most contemporaries, for whom resurrection was viewed as impossible, undesirable, or both. Two contrasting views emerge. For Paul resurrection is future and depends upon celibacy; Demas and Hermogenes locate it in the present and require child bearing. Dunn argues that these two misrepresent Paul's views on celibacy ("Influence"), but what they say is quite consistent with the opening macarisms. See also Barrier, 99; and Lalleman, "Resurrection."

3.13 is a parody of 4–5. Thamyris, like Onesiphorus, invites these two to refresh themselves (*anapauō*) in his home. Unlike the vegetarian, teetotaling Christian fare, seasoned with prayer and godly discourse, is an extravagant and far from abstemious repast. (On the meals in *APl*, see Merz, "'Tränken'"; and, in general, McGowan, *Ascetic Eucharists*.) Their indulgence coheres with their eschatology, for it reflects the vulgar "Epicureanism" of "eat, drink, and be merry, for tomorrow you may die." See the Notes.

The narrator does not wish readers to overlook Thamyris' intent: to loosen the pair with alcohol so that they will freely divulge. His promise of a large payment receives no further mention. The motivation of Thamyris' conduct is explicit and not dishonorable. He wants to marry Thecla, whom he loves. This generates his second question, the answer to which he has, in fact, already heard. His guests ignore it, while answering a query that Thamyris is too discreet to ask, at least just yet. They tell how he may have Paul killed, quite legally and expeditiously.

From the anachronistic perspective of the text it would suffice to have Paul arraigned as a Christian. That status was a capital offense. Christian literature of the second century, apologetic and martyrological, redounds with proud confessions and bitter complaints illustrating its centrality. The pair's proposal implies that blotting out the apostle will also erase Christian doctrine, restoring Thecla to her previous loyalty and love. The proposal is utterly without logic, but more than one official has attempted to suppress a view by executing its promulgator.

Almost as an afterthought, the duo offer their own doctrine: Resurrection (i.e., immortality) results from bearing children. Their views about marriage and diet reflect 1 Tim 4:3, while their language about resurrection having already occurred amounts to a citation of 2 Timothy 2:18, where the notion of present resurrection is denounced. Lau ("Enthaltsamkeit," 88–89) calls this a "narrative trick" of transforming the Pastor's regulations for Christian life into a theology. This is true in the sense that the pair makes the requirements for marriage and a non-ascetic diet look like articles of faith. The author is not representing an actual early Christian view about marriage and children. He is exploiting the PE both by associating his story with theirs and by ridiculing the Pastor's anti-ascetic stance. (For another view, see Lalleman, "Resurrection," 134–39, who concludes that the author attacks Judaism.)

Notes

Leaving. Some witnesses omit "leaving." Those persons would make the best subjects.

Stay single. Witnesses vary in details, but the thesis is consistent.

Leading men. Thus does the narrator inform the audience that Thamyris belongs to the local aristocracy. Thecla will reveal a similar status at 4.1. Syriac exhibits the development of the tradition. After mentioning payment, Thamyris says that he is the chief person of Iconium (Wright, 122). Syriac also identifies the pair by name, as does Coptic. On the term, see Pervo, *Acts*, 343n125.

Tell me about him. The Greek witnesses C, E, and F add a statement, evidently derived from 13 (where C does not repeat it) about Thamyris' anxiety about his fiancée and his marital prospects. This provides a motive for Thamyris' interest in Paul.

Who. Coptic is more credible: "Where he is from."

Brilliant table. Witnesses vary in their account of the banquet's details.

Drink. Greek mss. E, F are explicit: "got them drunk."

"Epicurean." For the notion of "enjoy life now," see, e.g., Isa 22:13. Eccles 8:15; Tob 7:10; Luke 12:19; 1 Cor 10:7. Greco-Roman examples include Euripides, *Alcestis* 788, and a number of epitaphs, on which see Lattimore, *Themes*, 260–61. See also Malherbe, *Paul*, 85–87. (The notion is a parody of Epicurus' philosophy.)

Alien doctrine. The variant *kenēn* ("vain," "baseless") is based upon similar sounds.

Children. The Greek tradition (and the Coptic ms., but not Latin or Syriac), includes the closing phrase "and we rise when we have come to know the true God." Most of the Latin tradition omits these terms. The two expressions, one affirming that resurrection takes place naturally through the generation of children, the other that it is present and "spiritual" are in tension. In the dramatic context the former would appeal to Thamyris, for whom a notion like resurrection would be nearly incomprehensible. The latter expresses the "gnostic" ("know God") view attacked by the Pastor. This is at variance with the "this worldly" views of Demas and Hermogenes and is therefore probably secondary. See Bauckham, "Acts of Paul," 128; and Lau, "Enthaltsamkeit," 84.

Governor Castellius. The term *hēgemōn* can be applied to a range of rulers. Here it presumably applies to the provincial governor ("proconsul," 3.16), who would exercise capital jurisdiction, but his later decision to expel Paul (§21) would have been within the jurisdiction of the leaders of the colony. The name Castellius is otherwise unknown. On the orthography, see Barrier, 106n14.

Bibliography

Bauckham, Richard, "The Acts of Paul as a Sequel to Acts." In *The Book of Acts in its First Century Setting*, edited by Bruce W. Winter and A. D. Clarke, 1:105-52. Grand Rapids: Eerdmans, 1993.

Dunn, Peter W. "The Influence of 1 Corinthians on the *Acts of Paul*." In SBLSP, 438-54. Atlanta: Scholars, 1996.

Lalleman, Pieter J. "The Resurrection in the Acts of Paul." In *The Apocryphal Acts of Paul and Thecla*, edited by Jan N. Bremmer, 126-41. Kampen: Kok Pharos, 1996.

Lattimore, Richmond. *Themes in Greek and Latin Epitaphs*. Urbana: University of Illinois Press, 1962.

Lau, Markus. "Enthaltsamkeit und Auferstehung: Narrative Auseindersetzungen in der Paulusschule." In *Aus Liebe zu Paulus? Die Akte Thekla neu aufgerollt*, edited by Martin Ebner, 80-90. Stuttgart: Katholisches Bibelwerk, 2005.

Malherbe, Abraham. *Paul and the Popular Philosophers*. Minneapolis: Fortress, 1989.

McGowan, Andrew. *Ascetic Eucharists. Food and Drink in Early Christian Ritual Meals*. Oxford: Oxford University Press, 1999.

Merz, Annette. "Tränken und Nähren mit dem Wort." In *"Eine gewöhnliche und harmlose Speise?" von den Entwicklungen frühchristlicher Abendmahlstraditionen*, edited by Judith Hartenstein, Silke Petersen, and Angela Standhartinger, 269-95. Gütersloh: Gütersloher, 2009.

The Acts of Paul

3.15–17 The Arrest and Trial of Paul

15. Thus informed by them, Thamyris, brim-full of jealousy and rage, arose early and went to Onesiphorus' house, accompanied by magistrates, public servants, and a mob armed with clubs, and addressed Paul: "You have corrupted Iconium, specifically my intended, so that she won't have me. Let us proceed to Governor Castellius."

The mob howled: "Away with this magician! He has corrupted all of our women!"

The public found this persuasive.

16. Thamyris stood before the bench and loudly declaimed: "Proconsul, this man, whose origins we do not know, does not allow young women to marry. Let him explain why he teaches thus." Demas and Hermogenes urged Thamyris: "Say that he is a Christian. That way you will take care of him."

Unswayed by the mob, the governor summoned Paul to the bench and said: "Who are you and what is it that you are teaching? These are grave charges."

17. Paul spoke loudly, "If, proconsul, I am being examined today regarding my teaching, listen. The living God, the avenging God, the jealous God, the God who requires nothing yet needs that humanity be saved has sent me to draw people away from corruption, impurity, every pleasure, and death, so that they may cease erring. Therefore God sent his son, who alone has compassion for a world gone astray, whom I proclaim and in whom I teach that people should locate their hope, so that they may not be subject to condemnation but rather have confidence in and reverence for God, as well as intimacy with majesty and passion for truth. So if I teach matters revealed to me by God, what law am I breaking, Proconsul?"

The governor then ordered that Paul be secured and held in custody until he might have the opportunity for a more thorough hearing.

Translation, Commentary, and Notes : Chapter

Comment

The hitherto formally personal problem of the households of Theocleia and Thamyris becomes, in response to the urging of Demas and Hermogenes, a public issue and civic crisis. In a scene characteristic of elements of various episodes in the canonical Acts, an aggrieved jealous rival has Paul arrested. After a short speech the apostle is remanded to custody for further examination. A difference is that, whereas in Acts the charges are notoriously slanderous and false, the accusation that he opposes and prevents marriage is correct.

Motivated by jealousy (of Paul's ability to entice Thecla?), fueled by rage (typical features of fiction, on which see p. 95), Thamyris arises bright and early to bring the apostle to justice. He does not go alone, but arrives at Onesiphorus' equipped with both officialdom and the flower of thuggery. So large a crowd was quite unnecessary; the narrator wishes both to show what a great threat Paul seemed to be and to evoke the arrest of Jesus (Mark 14:43).

The narrative is quite compressed. The text may have been abbreviated. Textual variations indicate the dissatisfactions of many readers with the brevity of the account. Readers may imagine that Paul appeared voluntarily at the command of this mob of quasi-official character. Ancient cities—even Rome—lacked the apparatus of law and order. See Nippel, *Order*. Thamyris, acting in his private character as a member of the local aristocracy, advises Paul of the charge and directs him to accompany them to the governor. He frames the issue both generally (all of the women have been seduced) and personally (his fiancée has been alienated). The former charge would justify criminal action, while a lawsuit would be appropriate for the second. The narrator does not wish to suggest that Paul had but one convert; Thecla is nonetheless the only one of interest. When she is condemned she has no support whatsoever; the young men and women, evidently including those once drawn by Paul participate in her execution.

One construal will understand that the party arrives at the governor's bench, to which the general populace has also been attracted. (In popular literature judges are always seated and ready when a mob drags in an alleged criminal. See, for example, Acts 16:19–21; 17:6–9; 18:12–13.) From the trial of Jesus onward, Christian texts portray the urban mob as the prime mover of persecution, while gentile officials often seek to moderate their demands. This picture may have been accurate, at least on occasion, but it is apologetic. In short: "Judge us by the quality of our enemies." See Pervo, *Dating Acts*, 179–82, and Pervo, "Meet Right." The mob incites the public with its incendiary charges, placing the responsible official in a precarious position.

The Acts of Paul

"The charge of magical practice is so frequent in the Apocryphal Acts that one might treat it as a proper *topos*." With this sentence Poupon begins his study ("Magie," 71). The charge is particularly suitable when, as here, the Christian message stresses sexual renunciation. As noted, Thecla's entranced state (see the comment on §9) is highly suitable for arousing expectations that she has been a victim of magic. Surviving recipes, narratives, and discussions indicate that erotic interests played a major role in ancient magic. See Faraone, *Love Magic*. The apologetic tradition labored to distinguish Jesus and the apostles from mere "magicians," a pejorative term. See Pervo, *Acts*, 207–9. The African writer Apuleius, a near contemporary of *APl*, had to defend himself against the charge of using magic to win the heart of the wealthy widow Pudentilla. See Harrison, *Apuleius*, 39–88.

Thamyris, noting in rather Johannine (e.g., John 9:29) language uncertainties about Paul's origin and identity, offers a single charge: Paul instructs young women not to marry. Nothing is said about young men or the married women who attended his lectures in person (cf. §7, 9, and 11). If this is accidental, it helps to explain the acceptability of *APl* in catholic circles, which frowned upon episodes in which apostles broke up lawful marriages.

Demas and Hermogenes appear once more to urge that Thamyris charge Paul as a Christian. That advice is ignored. The two have fulfilled their mission of betraying him. The narrator has no more need of these scoundrels, who vanish from the story. Thamyris evidently assumes that all that is required for conviction is to let Paul speak. The closest model is Acts 24, where Paul is arraigned before a provincial governor, Felix, who is advised that the prisoner will provide evidence of his guilt, if questioned (Acts 24:8). At the conclusion he is returned to custody for further investigation.

Paul's speech (on which see also the comment upon its parallel in 4.1–2) includes a number of elements common to the second-century Christian apologetic tradition. Another feature is a clearly stated formulation of the "gospel" in common early Christian language: out of love God sent the son to save (evidently) the world. This is so at variance with the message of celibacy and resurrection that opened Paul's Iconian mission that current readers might question the character's integrity. Paul is certainly being discreet. Further inquiry might have exposed the implications of avoiding impurity and pleasure, but, as it stands, one ground of the defense is that Paul's message proclaims a strict morality like that of such philosophers as Musonius Rufus. No harm is likely to come from the broadcast of such sentiments. His other defense is that he was acting in response to divine revelation. This may seem immaterial and irrelevant, but it is a venerable defense, attributed to Socrates (Plato, *Apology* 21–23) and utilized to explain his mission by Dio of Prusa (Chrysostom, *Or.* 13.9) in the late first century. The outcome is favorable. Rather than immediate condemnation as a witch, Paul is detained for further investigation. Matters are looking up.

Notes

Public servants. *Dēmosioi* were probably municipally owned slaves or employees who could serve as police.

Governor. Coptic states "the tribunal of..." specifying the legal nature of the visit. This is probably taken from §16.

Addressed Paul. A number of Latin witnesses state that the crowd made loud shouts. Other mss. add a demand that Paul come outside. These cover gaps in what is probably a dramatically terse narrative (but see the note under *mob*).

Have me. Witnesses paraphrase this statement.

Mob. A number of Latin witnesses, perceiving a gap between arrest and arrival at the bench, state here that they seized Paul and dragged him before the governor. Syriac reads: "And the whole city said: 'Drag him along, he is a magician; for he has corrupted all our wives.' And the whole people let themselves be persuaded. And when Paul had gone, they holding him..." (Wright, 124). It is possible that the Greek text has been abbreviated here.

That way. Witnesses are divided between "quickly" and "thus."

Origins. C and Syr add "who he is."

Teaching. Some witnesses omit this part of the question, perhaps because some might think that Paul did not answer it. The Latin tradition adds "Where do you come from?"

Charges. Some Latin witnesses and Syriac state that there are many accusers. The tradition evidently viewed the litotes "not small" as either large numbers or major crimes.

Examined today. An imitation of Acts 4:9, where Peter and John, following a night in custody, are charged with apparently magical practice (healing in the name of Jesus). Cf. also Acts 24:21.

Living, avenging, jealous. "Living" contrasts with "dead idols." Cf. Acts 14:15. "Avenging" (Ps 94:1) and "jealous" (Exod 20:5) serve to distance this work

The Acts of Paul

from Marcion. Creation, however, receives no attention. The last is absent from several Greek witnesses, Cop and Syr and may be secondary. In a missionary speech the audience would be invited to renounce the vanities of idolatry.

Requires nothing. The philosophical critique of ancient cults often noted that a real god was not dependent upon humans for nourishment and care. See Pervo, *Acts*, 434, on Acts 17:25. Here the dogma is paradoxically linked to the pleasant notion that God does "need" to be a savior. Some versions lighten the paradox. Syriac almost falls back into the dilemma: "a God who does not require anything, but to whom the life of men is useful" (Wright, 125). For adverbial modifiers of the divine "need," see Barrier, 111.

Sent me . . . sent Son. In Acts "send" usually refers to Paul. In Gal 4:4, 6 it is used first for the sending of the Son, then of the Spirit.

Corruption. This list of vices culminates with death. The meaning is that these activities are deadly, will culminate in death. Cf. 2 Tim 4:18; 2 *Clem* 17.1. Variants are numerous.

Son The term *pais* can elsewhere mean "servant." Paul does not name this son as that would make liable to the charge proposed by Demas and Hermogenes.

Compassion. Less likely: "suffered with." Cf. Ignatius *Rom* 6:3.

World gone astray. Cf. Heb 4:14.

Locate their hope. Cf. Col 1:27–28.

Condemnation. Cf. John 5:24.

Passion for truth. Cf. 1 Tim 4:12.

The entire speech exhibits many variants. Note Syriac: "That in [God] shall be the hope of all . . . who has taken providential care and delivered the nations from error, that they might sin no more, and might not walk in sedition, but that fear might be in them through belief in God, and (that) they might know fear and love in truth" (Wright, 125).

Translation, Commentary, and Notes : Chapter

Bibliography

Faraone, Christopher A. *Ancient Greek Love Magic*. Cambridge, MA: Harvard University Press, 1999.
Harrison, S. J. *Apuleius. A Latin Sophist*. Oxford: Oxford University Press, 2000.
Leinhäupl-Wilke, Andreas. "Vom Einfluss des lebendigen Gottes: Zwei Bekenntnisreden gegen den Strich gelesen." In *Aus Liebe zu Paulus? Die Akte Thekla neu aufgerollt*, edited by Martin Ebner, 139–58. Stuttgart: Katholisches Bibelwerk, 2005.
Nippel, Wilfred. *Public Order in Ancient Rome*. Cambridge: Cambridge University Press, 1995.
Pervo, Richard I. "Meet Right—and Our Bounden Duty." *Forum* N.S. 4, no. 1, (2000) 45–62.
Poupon, Gérard. "L'accusation de magie dans les Actes Apocryphes." In *Les Actes apocryphes des Apôtres: christianisme et monde païen*, ed. François Bovon et al. 71–93. Publications de la Faculté de Théologie de l'Université de Genève 4. Geneva: Labor et Fides, 1981.

3.18–19 Thecla Escapes and Expresses Her Love

18. That night Thecla took off her bracelets, gave them to the porter, and, once the door had been opened for her, went to the prison, where, after rewarding the jailer with a silver mirror, she went to Paul and sat at his feet to hear him speak of God's great deeds. Paul exhibited no fear but conducted himself with a boldness that came from God. With growing faith Thecla kept kissing Paul's shackles.

19. Thecla's household and Thamyris were looking for Thecla. Presuming her lost, they sought her frantically in the streets. One of the porter's fellow slaves reported that she had gone out at night. They thus interrogated the porter, who stated that she had gone to see the foreigner in jail. There they went and found matters as he had reported. Thecla was held in the bonds, so to speak, of affection. They left to stir up the mob and alert the governor to what had happened.

Comment

§18–19 reveal the hitherto mute and motionless Thecla springing into action. Using the means at her disposal she escapes from the prison of her home to enter the jail in which Paul has been incarcerated, where she will hear his message in person. After a (presumably) frantic search and investigation by her household (including Thamyris), Thecla is located. Rather than have her restored to their custody, the family resorts to those twin agents of justice: mob and proconsul.

This passage has much in common with romantic novels: a love-sick girl gains access to the wrongfully imprisoned object of her affection. It also evokes the door miracles that constituted a widespread theme of ancient religious symbolism. Thecla's ability to pass through barriers establishes one of the parallels between her and Paul in chap. 9 (9.19–20). Symbolism is important here. Thecla's use of her possessions illustrates the transformation she is experiencing.

Although Thecla has thus far appeared utterly passive, she has attained her heart's desire: the message of Paul. When that has been removed, she will take any steps to restore it. Readers will assume that some member of the household, which includes Theocleia, possible siblings, other relatives, and slaves, learned what had happened to Paul after he had been dragged off, and advised Thecla.

Her passage through locked barriers is not formally a "door miracle," with gates that open of their own accord and angels to guide the way, but these incidents serve the same function, which is to effect and symbolize liberation (see Pervo, *Acts*, 142–43; 301–15). Thecla's home is, in effect, a prison, which she rarely leaves and even then, not without a chaperone. From this domestic prison she escapes, only to bribe her way into an actual jail. The truly wise are free even while incarcerated.

Thecla uses her personal possessions—items of precious metal often embodied much of a family's wealth. By so doing she shows what value she places on being with Paul. She is also renouncing the world (macarism 4, 3.5; Esch-Wermeling, *Thekla*, 55, cites 1 Tim 6:17–19). In particular she is renouncing items of adornment that proclaim her as an upper-class female. Her bracelets correspond, as Aubin suggested, to Paul's shackles ("Reversing Romance," 264). She is casting off the shackles of gender.

The mirror was not only an object of value; some were works of art. Mirrors usually represented one or more gods, while the subject matter was often erotic (for examples, see Clarke, *Sex*, 40–46). Mirrors were important items of the female toilet. Giving up one's mirror is an even stronger renunciation of gender. The face reflected in a mirror was not the true self (cf. 3.3). Thecla is discarding the appearance of freedom and wealth for the reality of authentic spiritual liberty and riches.

The statement about Paul's courage need be no more than an expression of his refusal to allow incarceration to have a chilling effect upon him

Translation, Commentary, and Notes : Chapter

(see, e.g., Acts 4:13, 29, 31; 28:31), but this typical statement is compromised by the context, which depicts the apostle alone with a frankly adoring pretty girl. The Syriac relieves the absence of chaperonage by placing a number of prisoners in Paul's audience, here and in the next section (Wright, 126).

§19 demands the use of imagination. The possibility of abbreviation arises once more. See the Notes. The first requirement is the discovery that Thecla is missing. Why should they presume that she was lost? Is her presumed mental status justification for this idea? Their actions are possibly comic. As the domestic slaves and Thamyris search the streets for a missing girl of high status, someone comes up with the idea of interrogating the slaves. It did not require a Sherlock Holmes to identify the porter as a person with potentially useful knowledge. Still, it took prompting by another slave to bring this about. The Syriac may represent a superior text:

> And the companion of the doorkeeper came, and informed against him, and said: "I saw Thecla by night give her bracelets to the doorkeeper, and he opened the door for her, and she went out." And when they had scourged the doorkeeper, he confessed and said to them: "She went out, and said to me, 'Lo, I am going to the stranger, where he is imprisoned.'" (Wright, 126)

Admirers of logic may ask why, in addition to random searches of the streets, someone did not wonder whether Thecla, obsessed with Paul, may have sought him out. For that matter, one may ask why "they" did not attempt to remove her forcibly from Paul's presence. Such glitches were common to popular narrative, which rushes so quickly that readers tend not to stop and ask questions. It will presently transpire that the family has changed from searching for a lost daughter to seeking her condemnation.

Notes

Door. Doors are barriers to love, famously celebrated in the type of poem known as a *paraklausithron*. In the elegiac tradition the frustrated man (*exclusus amator*) finds himself locked out by his would-be one and only. See Reitzenstein, *Wundererzählungen*, 156. Door openings were also suitable subjects for magical recipes, e.g., PGM XIII 326–34. For ancients doors and gates were weighted with heavy symbolic freight. (A vestige survives in the tradition of a groom carrying his bride across the threshold of their home.) On the theme of the difficult gate-keeper, see Trall, "Knocking."

Bracelets. The word could mean "anklet." A variant is "earrings." Versions show that "bracelets" is best. In much of the Greek world such jewelry was worn chiefly by women.

Rewarding the jailer. According to Lucian, *On the Death of Peregrinus* 12, Christian leaders bribed guards in order to remain in the jail with their hero while he slept. Visiting was not, in general, permitted at night, requiring, or motivating, bribery. See Cicero, *Verrines* 2.5.112; Lucian, *Toxaris* 30; *AThom* 9.118; 13.154; and *Acts of Perpetua* 3.7. On bribing porters for the purpose of nocturnal assignations, see Juvenal, *Sat.* 6.235.

Silver mirror. Some witnesses provide it with a gold rim. Syriac makes the entire object gold (Wright, 125). Others replace it with a gold ring, more easily concealed but symbolically inferior.

Feet. To sit at someone's feet is the posture of learning. Cf. Luke 10:39; Acts 22:3.

Deeds. Cf. Note at 3.1

Fear. This reference to Paul's boldness, evidently to the free expression of his views, troubled some editors, who offered different expressions, such as, "as since he seemed to suffer not at all" (F, G), and Latin renderings that suggest an underlying text with "suffer" or the like. Syriac (Wright, 126): "Paul was not distressed, but was teaching the commandments of God openly."

Growing faith. The juxtaposition of sentiment and activity is difficult to translate. Some Latin witnesses omit the phrase about faith. Syriac reads "with great joy," a considerable improvement (Wright, 126).

Kissed shackles. Cf. Luke 7:38; *An Ephesian Tale* 2.7.5.

Looking for. The Syriac (Wright, 126) and Armenian (Conybeare, 71) are more circumstantial, but not adequate. Latin versions supply more details.

She had gone. Recent editors, including Rordorf (1134) and Barrier (115, who supplies no evidence), put the statement in direct speech. Versions and some mss. support this. (In Greek the difference is a matter of two letters: *-etai* vs. *-omai*.) Direct speech is suitable to the longer text but somewhat intrusive in the shorter.

Foreigner. It suffices to identify Paul as a "foreigner," i.e., not a citizen of Iconium. He is what used to be known in American society as an "outside agitator" (people from elsewhere who took it upon themselves to disrupt the allegedly profound racial harmony of communities in the American South, splendid relations between owners and workers, and the like). The term also conveys ironic truth: Paul is an alien insofar as he rejects the world with its trappings and projects.

Affection. G and some Latin witnesses omit or revise this clause to speak of her desire for Christ or to reiterate her role as a devout listener. *Held in the bonds* represents the participle *syndedmenē* that can be evocative of magic. See on 3.19. The word *storgē* is the least erotic of the various Greek terms translated by love, but it is not exclusively non-erotic. Cf. the *Palatine Anthology* 5.165; 190; 7.476.

Mob. Cf. Acts 13:50. Syriac (Wright, 126) omits the mob.

Governor. The texts vary, but all involve advising the proconsul.

Bibliography

Aubin, Melissa. "Reversing Romance? The *Acts of Thecla* and the Ancient Novel." In *Ancient Fiction and Early Christian Narrative*, edited by R. F. Hock, 257–72. SBL Symposium Series 6. Atlanta: Scholars, 1998.
Clarke, John R. *Roman Sex. 100 BC–AD 250.* New York: Abrams, 2003.
Reitzenstein, Richard. *Hellenistische Wundererzählungen.* Leipzig: Teubner, 1906.
Trall, A. "Knocking on Knemon's Door." *TAPA* 131 (2001) 87–108.

3.20 Trial of Paul and of Thecla

20. The governor directed that Paul be conducted to the bench. [*After he had been removed from the prison*] Thecla rolled about on the spot where Paul had sat teaching in jail. The governor additionally directed that she, too, be brought before the bench. She went jumping with joy. The return of Paul to court stimulated the mob to continue shouting more vehemently: "He's a wizard! Away with him!" For his part the governor listened with pleasure as Paul spoke of Christ's holy deeds. After consulting with his staff he summoned Thecla and asked her: "Why do you not marry Thamyris in accordance with Iconian law?" She did not respond but stood there, her gaze locked on Paul. At this her mother Theocleia shrieked: "Burn this outlaw! Burn this enemy of matrimony in the middle of the

theater, so that all the women who have been instructed by this fellow might learn some respect!"

Comment

Paul and Thecla face trial. The apostle's second hearing is like the first. While the crowd wants him executed for witchcraft, the governor finds his message appealing. Since readers have already been shown what he has to say (§17), it need not be repeated. Thecla refuses to respond to the proconsul's question about her reluctance to marry. Silence is typical of martyrs (e.g., Mark 14:4–5); in this case an honest answer would also implicate her teacher. Then comes a shocking dénouement: rather than offer to take her daughter home and teach her the error of her ways or propose that she be forcibly married to Thamyris, who would undertake her reeducation, Theocleia calls for Thecla's public immolation as a salutary lesson that will achieve deterrence. The narrator is depicting in the most vivid terms the absolute conflict between Pauline Christianity and the social order. Thecla would rather burn than marry and her mother is willing to oblige her in this matter.

Once again the narrative is very brief. Compare the Syriac:

> And Thamyris went forth thence with many persons, and they went in a great rage and informed the hēgemōn of what had happened. Then the hēgemōn said: "Fetch Paul." And the young men ran and unbound Paul, and were dragging him from the prison until (they came) before the hēgemōn. And Thecla was prostrating herself and weeping on the spot where Paul had been sitting bound and teaching the commandments of God. And again of a sudden the hēgemōn commanded and said: "Bring Thecla, the betrothed of Thamyris." And Thamyris ran with many men, and they laid hold of Thecla, and were dragging her up to the hēgemōn. And when the hēgemōn saw her, he was very sorry for her; but Thecla was standing before him with great joy, and was not sorry . . . [*crowd demands Paul's death*] But he [the hēgemōn] did not say anything concerning Paul. Then the hēgemōn sat in council, and he arose, he and his companions, and they called Thecla, and say to her . . . (trans. Wright, 126–27)

Although this version changes the reference to her rolling about (see the Notes), it makes better sense, whereas the Greek requires some supplementation, as in the second sentence.

The entry of each into court is exactly parallel. For Thecla it was a real thrill. The mob, thoughtfully invited by Thamyris and company, turned up the volume of their chant. Through such demonstrations crowds were able to express their will and influence decisions. See Pervo, *Acts*, 494nn80–86. The demand "away with him!" is that of the crowd at the trial of Jesus (Luke 23:18) and at the arrest of Paul (Acts 21:36; 22:22). While centering the dramatic interest upon Thecla, the author makes Paul a Christ figure in this chapter. Cf. §21.

The governor's question raises difficulties. Thecla has not verbally refused to marry Thamyris. She has maintained silence on the subject. To what Iconian law does Castellius refer? Is failure to honor an engagement to marry a criminal offense? What jurisdiction does a Roman governor have over this matter? See the Notes. Any need to consider these problems is obviated by the intervention of Theocleia. Thecla maintained her resolute silence (cf. §10) and her fixity upon Paul (cf. §8).

Theocleia demands that her daughter be sacrificed for the public good. In effect, it is better that one virgin should die than that dozens of others refuse to perform their civic duties. Patriot she may be, but the demand evokes the world of tragedy and myth, in which children murder parents (e.g., Electra) and prospective fathers have their sons' betrothed executed (Antigone). Contrast this with the conflict between Vibia Perpetua and her father (*Acts of Perpetua and Felicitas* 3, 5, 6). Their meetings are painful because her father tries to dissuade her out of love, as she acknowledges. Rather than call for her death the old man is beaten for trying to dissuade her (6.5).

Notes

Rolled. There is a very close parallel to this fetishistic behavior in *An Ephesian Tale*, where the soon to be sold away Anthia visits her imprisoned husband: "With this she kissed him, embraced him, clung to his chains, and rolled at his feet" (*Xenophon of Ephesus* 2.7.5; LCL, trans. Jeffrey Henderson, 263). Xenophon of Ephesus uses a compound, *proukylieto*, of the verb *ekylieto* in *APl*. Some Latin witnesses omit the phrase or paraphrase it.

Return. C and some versions omit "again," which seems to imply that the crowd was in continuous session.

Listened with pleasure. The verse is evidently indebted to Mark 6:20, where King Herod, whose matrimonial history displeased John the Baptizer, nonetheless appreciated his message. See Hills, "The Acts of the Apostles in the Acts of Paul," 24–54, 36. Another possibility is the D-Text of Acts 13:8 (D E syr[hmg] cop[G67]). This is a closer parallel in that Paul is preaching to a Roman proconsul. For other parallels, see Barrier, 120. The adverb, however, is superlative (*hēdista*, as opposed to *hēdeōs*, in Mark and *APl*). Without citing evidence Barrier (118) inserts, after "with pleasure," two conjunctions: "for" and "when" (*gar, hōs*). This yields a broken sentence. (See, however, the text cited by him at 119n9, which differs.)

Holy deeds. Paul recited miracles and other wondrous actions. Cf. 3.25, where the phrase relates to Thecla's deliverance.

Consulting with his staff. The primary meaning of *symboulion* is the expert body that provided legal counsel to governors (who were not jurists). Cf. Acts 25:12 (after Paul's appeal). It is not clear whether Castellius is to be imagined as seeking advice about Paul or about Thecla. The latter may be more likely, and marital law the subject.

Law. The variants show some discomfort with the formulation by reference to "obeying" (your spouse).

Outlaw. Theocleia knows the value of assonance. Her epithets are two adjectives *anomos* and *anymphos*. The former picks up the governor's appeal to Iconian law (*nomos*). The second means "unbride," applied tragically to girls who died before marriage because of catastrophes (e.g., Euripides, *Hecuba* 612).

Women. "Wives" may be a better translation, as the word "virgins" is absent (cf. §7). Latin witnesses hasten to erase the reference to Paul's teaching. One (lca) states: "so that other virgins might learn not to take lovers."

Bibliography

Hills, Julian V. "The Acts of the Apostles in the Acts of Paul." In SBLSP, 24–54. Atlanta: Scholars, 1994.

3.21–22 Thecla faces immolation in the theater

21. Strongly moved, the governor had Paul flogged and expelled from the city. As for Thecla, he condemned her to be burned. He arose and proceeded directly to the theater. The entire mob also headed for the violent spectacle. Thecla kept looking for Paul, as a

lamb in the wild looks for the shepherd. Glancing about the crowd she saw the Lord, looking like Paul, seated there. "Paul has come to watch over me, as if I could not otherwise endure this." She continued to hold her eyes fast upon him, but he went up into heaven.

22. The young boys and girls carried in logs and straw with which to burn Thecla. When she was brought in naked the governor wept, amazed at the force within her. The executioners arranged the wood and directed her to mount the pyre. After making the sign of the cross she mounted the wood, which they ignited. Although a great blaze broke out, the fire did not touch her, for God out of compassion had set off a subterranean rumble. A cloud full of rain and hail overshadowed the place and discharged its contents, bringing fatal danger to many, but it quenched the fire and rescued Thecla.

Comment

Castellius issues two judgments: Paul is to be given a good whipping and then shown to the town line. The opening line evokes two parallels with the Jesus tradition, intimating that the governor is a victim of the mob and likening the fate of Paul to that of Jesus. Thecla will be immolated. Dramatic compression is at work. The judgment against Paul would have been rendered by officials of the colony. Governors could probably expel someone from a province, but not officially from a self-governing city. Provincial governors did, however, execute Christians in public spectacles enlivened with both such tortures as ingenuity might contrive and as part of *tableaux vivants* of mythological adventures. For examples, see the *Acts of the Martyrs of Lyons*. For a person of Thecla's social standing such an execution was less likely, but not unheard of. In book 10 of Apuleius' *Metamorphoses* a woman of at least moderate rank is condemned by the governor to a most shameful death in the arena.

Theaters served such municipal purposes well, and, in accordance with the canons of light fiction, the event took place immediately, governor and mob (i.e., citizenry) moving directly from outdoor court to theatrical spectacle. Thecla has left the world of romance. She is now looking for a shepherd rather than a lover. The heroines of romantic novels, Thecla's social peers, are routinely threatened with death (and worse), but never exhibited naked in the theater. (See the Notes.)

The narrator's eye abruptly shifts to Thecla, who continues to look for Paul. The simile of a lamb in the wild seeking its shepherd alludes to Mark 6:34 and thus reinforces the parallel between Paul and Christ. In this episode Paul is the absent shepherd who looks out for his sheep. It would be unfair to ask how she was going to see Paul, since she presumably knew that he would spend no more time in the vicinity than was required to give him a flogging and hustle him out of town. Whoever does raise such a question will be sharply reprimanded, for Thecla, now in the theater, sees him, so she thinks. In fact, it is Jesus who has come to deputize for his apostle.

In the more or less orthodox tradition it was accepted that the glorified Lord could assume different forms. Cf. Luke 24:13–35; Ps.-Mark 16:12; Irenaeus, *Adv. Haer.* 2.22; Origen, *Commentary on Matthew* 36. Ancient theologians viewed this as condescension to human need. In what would become characterized as the non-orthodox tradition the earthly Christ could assume various forms. The ApocActs utilize this trait, most famously in the *Acts of Thomas* 11. Since the apostle is Jesus' twin brother, exchanges are interesting. For other examples, see Cartlidge, "Transformations." Polymorphy was congruent with Modalistic Monarchianism.

Thecla's comment constitutes her first reported spoken words. These should not be taken as a reproach, since the epiphany is the answer to her prayer. As she has constantly done, the prospective martyr keeps her eyes upon her savior as long as possible. Mission accomplished, the Lord returns to his abode. Thence a miracle will be worked. (This vignette conflicts with the next scene, in which Thecla is brought into the theater.)

§22. Members of the groups attracted to Paul's message participate in the execution, representing the community that has been defiled. As in public stonings, the populace must take a hand in eradicating the impurity. Nudity was not the preferred attire for immolations (although Polycarp is said to have stripped himself, *Mart. Polycarp* 13.2). Highly combustible clothing, such as cloths saturated with a flammable substance, was normal. These outfits probably increased the pain, although they may have hastened the process. See Barnes, *Hagiography*, 9, who cites Seneca, *Epistle* 14.5. For those exposed to the beasts nudity may have served some function, but degradation was primary. This did not always work. Perpetua and Felicity were set against a heifer, female vs. females (quite unlike Thecla, chap. 4): "So they were stripped naked, placed in nets and thus brought out into the arena. Even the crowd was horrified when they saw that one was a delicate young girl and the other was a woman fresh from childbirth" (*Acts of Perpetua and Felicitas* 20.2; trans. Musurillo, 129). They were taken back and clothed in tunics. The Iconians were rather less sensitive, since Thecla was ever so much younger and more delicate than Perpetua, a married mother. Thecla is nude here to establish a parallel with chap. 4. There she will find many sympathizers, human and animal. In Iconium her sole known sympathizer is the governor.

The experts now construct a proper pyre and have Thecla get on it. Her courage and self-possession are remarkable. Most would have to be hauled onto the pyre and held in place. Polycarp, no craven creature, refused to be nailed to the wood, although he was tied (*Mart. Polycarp* 13.3—14.1).

The fire is ignited, and . . . The narrator will not keep us in suspense. Thecla was unharmed. It would have been sufficient to say: "God sent a heavy shower." The language magnifies the epiphanic features. The details may stem from a source, for the narrator has purloined an item from Zeus' wallet: "On sundry occasions Zeus by means of a timely rain extinguished a pyre and saved the life of a victim." With those words Cook introduces the section on "Pyre-Extinguishing rain" in his monumental study (*Zeus*, 3:506–24). The borrowing was made less difficult because the God of Israel was often described in the language associated with storm gods. The Egyptian gods could utilize the Nile for this purpose. In *An Ephesian Tale* 4.2.7–10, the hero Habrocomes is rescued from the blazing pyre to which he has been condemned by an eruption of the Nile. Finally, with this incident, the author has prepared the way for a fine parallel with the story of Paul (9.25). The storm served both as a judgment upon the wicked people and as a means for Thecla's rescue. The conclusion is left to the reader. That such a storm was viewed as a divine intervention and vindication may be taken for granted, but no sequel is provided. Thecla, last seen drenched and naked on an extinguished pyre, presumably covered with soot, will next appear shopping in the market (§23). The Syriac (Wright, 128) gives a longer, more circumstantial, and orthodox account, but offers the same abrupt ending.

Excursus: *APl* 22 and the Martyrdom of Polycarp

An intertextual relationship between this passage and *Mart. Polycarp* 15–16 exists. Italicized words in the following citation represent identical or nearly identical words:

> 15.1 . . . [T]he men in charge of the fire *lit* it. And as *a mighty flame blazed up*, we saw a miracle . . . 2. For the fire, taking the shape of an arch, like the sail of a ship filled by the wind, completely surrounded the body of the martyr [*producing a fine*

> *aroma*...] 16.1 When the lawless men eventually realized that his body could not be consumed by the fire, they ordered an executioner to go up to him and stab him with a dagger. And when he did this, there came out a dove and a large quantity of blood, so that it *extinguished the fire*. (trans. M. Holmes, 323–25)
>
> Both texts relate a remarkable phenomenon in response to the fire, which is extinguished by an unexpected means. Although traditional dating would suggest that *APl* imitates the *Martyrdom* (which is located in Smyrna), the present form of this text may be later and utilize *APl*. Based upon this episode alone, *APl* 23 would appear to be the source of the *Martyrdom here*. Note Moss, "Dating," who proposes that the present form of the *Martyrdom* stems from the third century.

Notes

Strongly moved. The phrase is difficult and best seen as evocative of Matt 27:19. Castellius is in the position, and takes the option, of Pilate. See Vouaux's evidently incomplete note 2*, p. 185.

Flogged. On the grounds of the Coptic, Barrier (122) wishes to read *mastigoun* and thereby remove the link to Mark 15:15//Matt 27:26. The infinitive yields no sense. Greek loan-words in Coptic translation do not always show the underlying Greek. The participle *phragellōsas* is rare and thus intended to evoke the Gospels (Hills, "Acts," 36). The expulsion echoes Acts 13:50.

Violent spectacle. Anankē can refer to painful or violent action, suffering under duress. Textual variations indicate that the term was readily misunderstood.

Lamb. Cf. 9:23, where another Pauline convert—a lion—acts like a lamb.

Seated there. Cf. Acts 7:55. This reinforces the comparison of Paul to Jesus.

Naked. The word *gymnos* has a range of meanings. Here it evidently means stark naked. As stated in the comment, this humiliation would not befall the heroine of a romantic novel. Callirhoe is admired in the bath by other slaves (*Callirhoe* 2.2.2). The word "naked" does not appear. She is admired when undressed (*apodysamenē*); what is "inside (her clothes)" is astonishing. Such euphemism could satisfy the strictures of the Victorians. (The text of *Callirhoe* is damaged here, perhaps due to censorship.) This is part of the punishment used in vicious capital executions, such as crucifixion. In addition to the examples cited above, see the *Acts of Carpus et al.* 6.4, where Agathonice was sentenced to death: "And when she was led to the spot, she removed her clothing and gave it to the servants. But when the crowd saw how beautiful she was, they grieved in mourning for her" (trans. Musurillo, *Christian*, 35).

Force. One might expect to read that the governor was amazed by her beauty, as in the preceding example. Some witnesses change "force" to "beauty," or the like, while others expanded the passage to include patience and constancy. The governor has, it would seem, heard enough of Paul's message to focus upon inner rather than outer beauty. Note the *Acts of Perpetua and Felicitas* 9.1, where the prison superintendent apprehends his charges' great power (*magna virtus*).

Young boys and girls. Variants make them all girls or public slave girls, missing and thus proving the point.

Mounted. Barrier (125) characterizes this as a virginity test of Thecla. That it is not.

Cross. Latin witnesses specify different forms: "on her forehead," the earliest reported manner of this Christian gesture. Another is "with outstretched hands," forming a cruciform shape with her body. Cf. the story of Blandina, exposed to the beasts on a stake and become a type of Christ to her fellow believers (*Martyrs of Lyons* 41).

Touch her. A pun in Greek, as one touches off a fire.

Subterranean rumble. The subterranean rumble intimates an earthquake, a standard sign of God's presence. See Pervo, *Acts*, 123. The verb "overshadow" appears in Matt 17:5 (the Transfiguration). Cf. also Luke 1:35; Acts 5:15.

Discharged: the picture is not clear, as variants indicate. Perhaps one should envision the theater as a bowl that contained water. How would Thecla escape the flood? The safest solution is to envision the killed and injured as victims of hail, as in chap. 9. The Syriac (Wright, 128) attributes the action and the noise to God's Spirit.

Bibliography

Barnes, Timothy D. *Early Christian Hagiography and Roman History.* Tübingen: Mohr/Siebeck, 2010.

Cartlidge, David R. "Transfigurations of Metamorphosis Traditions in the Acts of John, Thomas, and Peter." *Semeia* 38 (1986) 53–66.
Cook, Arthur B., *Zeus. A Study in Ancient Religion*. Vol. 3. Cambridge: Cambridge University Press, 1940.
Moss, Candida, R. "On the Dating of Polycarp: Rethinking the Place of the Martyrdom of Polycarp in the History of Christianity." *Early Christianity* 1 (2010) 539–74.
Musurillo, Herbert, ed. *The Acts of the Christian Martyrs*. Oxford: Clarendon, 1972.

3.23–26. Reunion

23. Meanwhile, Paul and the Onesiphorus family were fasting in an unsealed tomb on the road *outside of* Iconium. As day after day passed foodless, the children said to Paul: "We're hungry." They lacked the wherewithal to purchase food as Onesiphorus had abandoned worldly affairs and followed Paul with his entire family. Paul took off his coat and said, "Go, my child, buy a substantial amount of bread and bring it here." While the son was shopping, he saw, to his astonishment, his neighbor Thecla. "Thecla, where are you going?" he asked.

"Since my delivery from the fire I've been looking for Paul."

"Come, I'll take you to him. He has been distraught with worry about you, praying and fasting for six days now."

24. At the tomb she came upon Paul praying on bended knee, "Father of Christ, let not the fire touch Thecla, but be with her, for she is yours."

Standing behind him, she exclaimed, "Father, the maker of heaven and earth, the father of your beloved son Jesus Christ, I praise you because you have delivered me from fire so that I might see Paul."

Paul arose, saw her and prayed, "God, to whom all hearts are open, the father of our lord Jesus Christ, I praise because you heard me and hastened [to do] what I asked."

25. Love abounded in the tomb. Paul rejoiced, as did Onesiphorus and everyone else. They had five loaves, vegetables, and water and were celebrating the holy deeds of Christ, when Thecla said to Paul: "I shall cut off my hair and follow you wherever you go."

He replied, "The times are so ugly and you are so pretty. Another trial, worse than the first, may overtake you, a trial that you will not be able to withstand but be conquered by fear."

"Just give me the seal in Christ," she countered, "and no adversity will touch me."

"Be patient, Thecla. You will receive the water."

26. Paul sent the Onesiphorus family back to Iconium.

Comment

§23–26. Thecla successfully reunites with Paul but is frustrated in her desire to receive baptism. The scene opens naturally enough—for an apocryphal acts—with Paul and the Onesiphorus engaged in a fast. They are dwelling in a tomb outside of Iconium, from which city Paul has been expelled. At the surface level their living arrangements reflect the homelessness of itinerants (Luke 9:58, a saying about to be invoked). They are worse off than animals. Symbolism may also be suspected. If it was good enough for Jesus . . . (see the Notes). A more probable symbolic reference is that the dwelling signifies that they have died to the world.

Readers may suspect that the faithful family has suffered confiscation of their property or expulsion, if not both, because of harboring the horrid evangelist, but their action was entirely voluntary (in a hierarchical context). The fast was not entirely voluntary, and, in due course the children complained to Paul—not to their father. The boys command our sympathy, and probably that of early readers. Embedded in this episode is an edifying example. The ideal is that itinerants summon people to abandon all and follow. That is what Jesus did (Mark 1:16–20, e.g.). While engaged on that mission the itinerants were dependent upon a network of support, i.e., people who had *not* given up all and followed. See the instructions for itinerants in Mark 6:6–13; Luke 10:1–12. Although the ideal was that all renounced everything, it was not simply not possible, it was not desirable. The result was a compromise, one with many parallels in the history of religions. This scene shows what happens when the householder becomes an itinerant: nobody eats. In the end Paul will tell Onesiphorus, in effect, to take back what he has renounced, return home, and stop following him. See Pervo, "The Hospitality of Onesiphorus."

To remedy the immediate situation Paul offers his cloak for sale. The author probably has 2 Timothy 4:13 in mind, but it is also true that the true ascetic philosopher did not require such fripperies. The apostle requires no sacrifice of others that he is unwilling to make for himself. The bread he is casting upon the waters (readers must exert themselves to determine that the youth will sell the cloak and use the funds to purchase bread) will return abundant reward. This is a well-crafted piece of plotting. Needing food, Paul dispatches a likely agent who, as a neighbor, would recognize Thecla. Her answer more or less explains her action: she is on the way out of town in pursuit of Paul. It does not explain how she came to be released or why she is left unmolested by the citizens who had been howling for her blood. Her program has not changed. She wants to see Paul. That Simmias or Zeno can bring about. It transpires that Paul has devoted six days of fasting and prayer to Thecla's plight. The author is fond of revealing data in this manner, rather than opening with a statement that Paul was distraught about his protégé. This technique does not explain the failure to narrate how she escaped, nor, for that matter, does one possible indicator of a lost episode.

MacDonald and Scrimgeour prepared a brief study of a homily attributed to John Chrysostom ("Pseudo-Chrysostom's *Panegyric to Thecla*") that initially appears to fill the gap:

> After she had been freed from judgment, she pursued the chase for Paul, and guided by heavenly voices she took courage on the roads that led to Paul. The devil, however, was watching the maiden, and when [he] saw her travel down the road he marched in the suitor against the girl, like a thief of virginity in the desert. As the noble woman continued on her way, the suitor, with the lewdness of a horse, lying in wait behind her, shouted for joy at the thought of seizing her. There was no exit anywhere. The attacker was strong, the attacked was frail. Where in a desert was there refuge for shelter? But turning toward heaven, the virgin shouted with a loud wailing to the one who stands by all anywhere who call, "O Lord, my God, I have hoped on you. Save me from all who pursue me, and rescue me, lest at any time he should seize my soul as a lion, while there is none to ransom, nor to save" (Ps 7:12). The maiden's help was quick; immediately she became invisible and the suitor went away having won only one thing, a horserace of licentiousness. (Ps.-Chrysostom, *Panegyric to Thecla*; trans. MacDonald and Scrimgeour, 156. For the text, see Aubineau, "Le panégyrique")

The setting seems appropriate to the situation after her deliverance. The story may be a Christian version of Apollo's pursuit of Daphne (Nauerth and Warns, *Thekla*), possibly comparable with the mythological background of her rescue from the pyre. On the other hand, the story is set in a mythical place (the desert) and employs a mythical character not otherwise found in these chapters (the Devil). Johnson locates this among the later stories about Thecla as a heroine of the desert saints (*Life*, 232–33; see also Davis, *Cult*, 87–94). The homily does not preserve a missing episode from the cycle. The narrator does not describe the aftermath of Thecla's survival of the fire because she has but a single function in the narrative up to this point: to focus on Paul as the font of discipleship. Like John the Baptizer, she can only point to the apostle and will not consider the possibility that he might decrease. This is, to reiterate, the viewpoint of the author, who wants to portray Thecla as utterly, albeit chastely and piously, enthralled with Paul.

§24 is an edifying reunion in A-B-A structure. Thecla reaches the tomb at the very moment when Paul is praying for her. In theory he was doing so at every moment, but it is no less pleasant for that. His prayer represents a timeless request. One should not criticize him for making this petition six days after the scheduled immolation. His prayer includes a negative petition, followed by a positive request with a motive. Her thanksgiving is at once an answer to his prayer and an announcement of her presence. She offers a standard type of thanksgiving, beginning with creedal ascriptions before giving the specific reason for thanksgiving. All praise and gratitude is grounded in the gifts of creation and redemption. (Later theology would add sanctification. On the titles, see the Notes.) Why was Thecla saved and why was she grateful? So that she might see Paul. The narrator is not going to make it easy to overlook this point. These words of devotion to Paul are the first she has spoken in the narrative.

§25 begins with a description of what might be called the after-miracle party. Love transformed their simple fare into a real banquet. *APl* promote an austere lifestyle that need yield nothing to early Egyptian monasticism, but the text is redolent with the joy that characterizes Christian existence. Five loaves, provided by a boy, evoke the feeding stories (Mark 6:30–44) and all that they imply. (See Pervo, "*Panta Koina*.") The specific focus of the celebration is, of course, the wondrous deliverance of Thecla.

In this context did Thecla offer her services to Paul, which he did brusquely refuse. Her proposal derives from a type of apophthegm or pronouncement story (see Berger, *Formgeschichte*, 80–93; Dormeyer, *New Testament*, 174–81) dealing with vocations, on which Jesus summons one or more persons to follow him, leading to a response and comment or dialogue. See Crossan, *In Fragments*, 227–44. The dialogue has four parts, each addressing two subjects.

Associated with vocation stories are conditions for entrance into the sphere of God's reign. The first clause of her statement is like: "I shall give

The Acts of Paul

all that I have to the poor and follow you." It is a positive response to an unstated call. The second clause is based upon the Q saying in Luke 9:57. She would follow Paul as others followed Jesus. Modern readers are less likely to be so intrigued by the equation of Paul with Jesus (cf. 3.21) as with her promise.

The proposal to cut off her hair will make it possible for Thecla to pass as a man and not attract notice. This would be prudent for a woman itinerant, as chap. 4 will show. Few attribute this offer to simple prudence, however, and with good reason. The act represents less a denial of sexuality than a transcendence of sexual differentiation, viewed as a decline from the original human unity. See MacDonald, *There is No Male and Female*; Meyer, "Making"; and Patterson, *Thomas*, 154–55. For examples of women who adapted masculine appearances, see 4.15 below. On wearing men's clothes and cutting hair: *An Ephesian Tale* 5.1.7; *Acts of Thomas* 114; and *Acts of Philip* 4.6. Note Castelli, "Virginity." Gal 3:28c ("no longer male and female") is a creedal basis for bobbed hair. *Gospel of Thomas* 22.5, ". . . and that you might make the male and the female be one and the same, so that the male might not be male nor the female be female" (trans. Layton, *The Gnostic Scriptures*, 384), illustrates its function. Celibacy was a means for acting out this transcendence (and rejecting the procreation of additional inadequate creatures), cross-dressing a symbolic expression of it. (See the note.)

The apostle's response poses obstacles rather than a direct rejection. The implication is that life with Paul means arrest and condemnation. Torture is always a possibility. Just because a miracle got her out of the fire last time is no guarantee that you have a lifetime get out of jail free card. Martyrdom happens. He doubts that she has the strength for it. Readers of nearly every generation who have witnessed her firmness on the pyre (as the dramatic Paul did not) will incline toward disagreement with the apostle on this point.

Thecla's response will only increase the frustration. She asks for initiation on the sound theological grounds that sacramental grace will give her the strength to burn, if need be, or to marry. The audience may know that Paul has baptized a lion on demand. (See the comments on chap. 1.) In chap. 9 he will baptize two women in prison, as he might well have done for Thecla. (See, however, the comment on that chapter.) The narrator's problem is that Thecla will undergo a martyr's baptism. Rather than ignore the subject, he flaunts it to raise tension and suspense. It will transpire, to no one's surprise, that Thecla can resist temptation without the benefit of the sacrament. Paul ends with a pious comment about the need for patience. The dialogue may address controversies about the time of preparation for baptism, which often lasted for years. In the result, the only effect of this dialogue is that Thecla does not change her appearance, for she does accompany Paul, at his own initiative. On the ironies of this section, not all of which are intentional, see Lipsett, *Desiring*, 74.

The chapter ends with the return of Onesiphorus and family to their home, as it began. Readers will conclude that their property and resources were recoverable.

Notes

Meanwhile. Some Latin copyists could not tolerate the abrupt transition. One (Lb) adds "while these things were happening." Lbc reads "Thecla left that place."

Outside of. The Greek text states that they were traveling on the road from Iconium to Daphne. The best known place with that name is a suburb of Syrian Antioch. The term is omitted by some Latin mss., the Syriac, and the Armenian (Coptic is missing here). This is a secondary addition. The text rendered is hypothetically restored in light of the Syriac (Wright, 129). The Armenian editor, possibly scandalized by residence in a tomb, offers the house of a young man with a suitably placed door (so that they could see Thecla?, Conybeare, 73–74).

Unsealed tomb. The term means "openable," i.e., not cemented or the like. The mss. offer many variants. These include "new," enhancing the Gospel parallel (John 19:41, where "empty" is an alternative). Fluctuation between "new" and "empty" in the witnesses is stimulated by their nearly identical sounds in Greek. Other witnesses resolve the issue by omission of the adjective. Latin alternatives include "closed" and "hidden." On people who squatted in tombs, see Beard, *Pompeii*, 105. This offended ancient sensibilities. The NT example, Mark 5:3, finds such living arrangements appropriate for the demon-possessed. Here *APl* displays a trace of the "Cynic" quality of the itinerant tradition: fearless disdain for social conventions.

Worldly affairs. Cf. 1 Cor 7:33–34; Luke 14:33; Matt 4:20.

Saw. A Latin witness assures the reader that he saw Thecla in the street.

Delivery. A Greek witness (F) omits this phrase, probably because it has not been narrated.

Looking. One could say "been in hot pursuit of." *Diōkō* implies vigorous and determined action.

Father of Christ, etc. Some of the variants identify or equate Father and Son. The original language may well have been tinged with Monarchian sentiment.

Maker. This is a common creedal statement, found in Acts (4:24; 14:15), with many antecedents in the LXX. See Barrier, 131n11.

Praise. On the language, see, e.g., Luke 1:64; 2:28; 24:53; *Mart. Poly.* 14.2; Jos. *Ant.* 7.380.

Open. Lit., "God who knows the heart." This phrase, although common in the second and third centuries, derives from Acts (1:24; 15:8). See Hills, "Acts," 45–46; and Pervo, *Dating Acts,* 272.

Asked. Syriac expands, providing symmetry, a broader audience, and a bit of pious edification: ". . . and has granted me to see Thecla, me and these persons who are with me; and in Thy hands it is an easy thing to deliver from all distress one who praises Thy name for ever" (Wright, 130).

Holy Deeds. This (cf. 3.20) refers to miracles, presumably including Thecla's rescue as well as those of the historical Jesus.

Cut off. The verb does not evoke trimming or cutting short, but shaving. Cf. 1 Cor 11:2–16, Acts 18:18, and the description of Paul in *APl* 3.3. Iconography tends to depict her with short hair. See Cartlidge and Elliott, *Art,* 160.

Ugly . . . pretty. The Greek words are succinct and euphonious.

Trial. The term *peirasmos* enjoys a range of meanings, with particular reference to the great eschatological test.

Fear. This rare verb is taken from 2 Macc 8:13, where it characterizes those who do not fight the invading Syrians.

Seal. This was a common term for Christian initiation, particularly during the second century. It stresses identity (seals marked the owner of items) and protection (e.g., water-tight seal). Those sealed belong to God through Christ and were guarded from evil powers.

Water. Witnesses expand this term to stress its function.

Years. The *Apostolic Tradition* 17.1 specifies three years as the period of the catechumenate, i.e., preparation for baptism. How old and general that practice was is uncertain.

Bibliography

Aubineau, Michel. "Le panégyrique de Thècle, attribué à Jean Chrysostome (BHG 1720): la fin retrouvée d'un texte motile." *Analecta Bollandiana* 93 (1975) 349–62, 351–52.
Beard, Mary. *The Fires of Vesuvius: Pompeii Lost and Found*. Cambridge, MA: Harvard University Press, 2010.
Berger, Klaus. *Formgeschichte des Neuen Testaments*. Heidelberg: Quelle & Meyer, 1984, 80–93.
Cartlidge, David R., and J. Keith Elliott. *Art and the Christian Apocrypha*. London: Routledge, 2001, 160.
Castelli, Elizabeth, "Virginity and its Meaning for Women's Sexuality in Early Christianity." *Journal of Feminist Studies in Religion* 2 (1986) 61–88.
Crossan, John D. *In Fragments: the Aphorisms of Jesus*. New York: Harper & Row, 1983.
Davis, Stephen J. *The Cult of Saint Thecla: A Tradition of Women's Piety in Late Antiquity*. Oxford Early Christian Studies. New York: Oxford University Press, 2001.
Dormeyer, Detlev, *The New Testament among the Writings of Antiquity*. Translated by R. Kossov. Sheffield: Sheffield Academic, 1998, 174–81.
Hills, Julian V. "The Acts of the Apostles in the *Acts of Paul*." *SBLSP* 33 (1994) 24–54.
Johnson, Scott F. *The Life and Miracles of Thekla: A Literary Study*. Washington, DC: Center for Hellenic Studies, 2006.
MacDonald, Dennis R. *There is No Male and Female. The Fate of a Dominical Saying in pox and Gnosticism*. HDR 20. Philadelphia: Fortress, 1987.
MacDonald, Dennis R., and Andrew D. Scrimgeour. "Pseudo-Chrysostom's *Panegyric to Thecla*: The Heroine of the *Acts of Paul* in Homily and Art." *Semeia* 38 (1986) 151–59.
Meyer, Marvin W. "Making Mary Male: The Categories 'Male' and 'Female' in the Gospel of Thomas." *NTS* 31 (1985) 554–70.
Nauerth, Claudia, and Rudiger Warns. *Thekla, Ihre Bilder in der fruchristliche Kunst*. Göttinger Orientforschungen II. Studien zur spätantiken und frühchristlichen Kunst 3. Wiesbaden: Otto Harrrassowitz, 1981, 72–81.
Patterson, Stephen J., *The Gospel of Thomas and Jesus*. Sonoma, CA: Polebridge, 1993.
Pervo, Richard I. "The Hospitality of Onesiphorus: Missionary Styles and Support in the Acts of Paul." In *The Rise and Expansion of Christianity in the First Three Centuries of the Common Era*, edited by Clare K. Rothschild and Jens Schroter, 341–51. Tübingen: Mohr/Siebeck, 2013.
———. "PANTA KOINA: The Feeding Stories in the Light of Economic Data and Social Practice." In *Religious Propaganda and Missionary Competition in the New Testament World*, edited by L. Bormann et al., 164–94. Festschrift for Dieter Georgi, Suppl NovT. Leiden: Brill, 1994.

Chapter 4: Antioch

The division between the Iconium and Antioch episodes is marked in the translation of Rordorf and will become standard. The traditional division into forty-three sections derives from the separate existence of the story of Thecla. The general practice of modern editors is to assign an entire chapter to each missionary station with a substantial narrative. The Heidelberg papyrus (Schmidt, *Acta*, 14*) marks the change with dividing marks used elsewhere. The division between chaps. 3 and 4 takes place in the midst of 3.26. The hitherto conventional numbers will be placed in parentheses.

Chapter 4 follows the same pattern as 3: Thecla is arrested, condemned, delivered from death, and eventually reunited with Paul and other members of her family and the community in Iconium. See Esch-Wermeling (151). After the motivating conflict with Alexander the narrative follows the pattern A-B-C-A-B:

> A. 1. Thecla and the Proconsul. Condemnation. (Women protest.)
>
> B. 2–7. Thecla under Tryphaena's protection. (Women protest twice at procession.)
>
> C. 8–11. Thecla in the Arena. (Women take action; crisis in 11, as Tryphaena believed dead)
>
> A. 12–13. Thecla and the Proconsul. Vindication. (Women approve.)
>
> B. 14. Thecla under Tryphaena's protection.

Within this framework are many differences. The plot is richer and more circumstantial than that of chap. 3. Thecla is not alone; Paul is absent. As in Iconium, the governor is sympathetic. In addition she has a patron/maternal support figure, Tryphaena, a member of a royal family (of client kings, like the Herods). Whereas the entire public of Iconium appeared to oppose Thecla, at Antioch she has strong female support from both humans and animals. Hansen, ed., *Anthology*, 53: "Within this apostolic vacuum the whole feminine gender coalesces across the species to show its support for Thecla." The docile, silent Thecla of chap. 3 is replaced by a firm, determined, active, and eloquent defender of her faith and rights. Not until she has been delivered from death, at her own initiative, and vindicated does Thecla suddenly and unaccountably renew her longing for Paul.

The reason for this longing does not take long to discover. It is due to the editorial work of the author, who integrated a preexisting and most probably written story of Thecla into his story of Paul. Thecla was great—and she was a disciple of Paul. His action implies that association with the virgin of Iconium enhanced Paul's status, i.e., Thecla did not gain by entering the Pauline circle but Paul gained through recruiting this remarkable disciple. The author determined to send her off, like Barnabas in Acts 15:39, and get back to his main story. This did not succeed. Thecla had her own cult and would develop a shrine far more famous than any site devoted to Paul in Antiquity and the early Middle Ages. In due course these chapters would be detached from the *APl* and given a new ending of suitable length and quality to dovetail with the shrine of St. Thecla, whose fame would extend throughout the Mediterranean world. See Davis, *Cult*; and contrast Eastman, *Paul the Martyr*).

Thanks to her, these chapters of *APl* are well attested in abundant mss. and versions.

4.1–2 Thecla Confronts Alexander

1 (26b). Taking Thecla, Paul traveled to Antioch. Just as they were entering the city the head of the Syrian chapter of the Empire League named Alexander saw Thecla and became passionately enamored of her. He plied Paul with offers of money and gifts, but Paul said, "I do not know the woman about whom you speak; she is definitely not mine." Alexander, with his considerable strength, embraced her in the middle of the street. She would not put up with this but kept on looking for Paul. She cried out, sharply, "Don't assault a visitor; don't assault God's slave. I am a prominent citizen of Iconium, from which I was expelled because I was unwilling to marry Thamyris."

She grabbed Alexander, tore his cloak, knocked the crown from his head and turned him into an object of derision.

2 (27). Both desiring her and ashamed at what had happened to him, Alexander arraigned Thecla before the governor. When she admitted what she had done he condemned her to the beasts, since Alexander was going to provide games. This astonished the women, who shouted, in the presence of the court: "Wicked judgment! Impious judgment!" Thecla asked the governor that she might remain a virgin until her encounter with the beasts. So a

wealthy woman of royal lineage named Tryphaena, whose daughter had died, took her into protective custody, viewing Thecla as a consolation.

Comment

Although Paul has apparently declined Thecla's offer to follow him, she does go with him to *Antioch*. At that moment he had also expressed fear that a great trial might come upon her. His fear is about to be realized, and Thecla will have to face it without his help. That she can do. Hypothesizing an underlying scene in which Thecla arrived in Antioch as an itinerant missionary is not difficult. Granting that the narrator who has inserted Paul into the picture must get him off stage, the means for removing him are troubling. The late Sir William Ramsay, who believed that the story "contains much that is fine . . . but it also contains much rubbish, much that is glaringly incongruous with the finest parts" (*Church*, 378), would evidently include among the latter "the detestable incident of Paul's denial and desertion of Thekla, when she was exposed to the insults of Alexander" (395). Paul was, of course, a gentleman, and no gentleman would so conduct himself. Based upon the assumptions that the author of the *APl* is responsible for this material—it would be quite intelligible if the product of someone who wished to make Paul look treacherous and craven—the critic must seek a positive understanding (which is not identical to giving a positive "spin" to an unpleasant episode).

The most probable narrative hypothesis is that Alexander, predatory elitist oaf that he was, did not feel free to make advances to any woman. Thecla, evidently unveiled but not otherwise immodestly appareled, in public with a male companion, was taken for a prostitute, most likely as a slave of her owner. To that owner Alexander makes a commercial proposal, probably for outright purchase of Thecla, with whom he has, after the fashion of romantic villains, fallen in love/lust at first sight.

Alexander's action is intelligible; Paul's rejoinder is less than heroic. From the narrowly legal perspective it is clever. He does not know such a woman, nor does he own this one. Alexander is in no mood for cleverness. Since the man claims no authority, he will seize the woman. The quest for possible inspiration brings to mind Gen 20:1–18 (Abraham and Sarah; cf. the parallel in 26:6–11). This is well developed by Snyder, "Remembering," 153–55. Barrier's proposal (140) that this is a convention of the romantic novel is not germane. Romantic principals lie quite often, but they do not knowingly throw their partners to the wolves. There is an important

Translation, Commentary, and Notes : Chapter

difference from the Genesis story: Abraham lied to save his own skin; Sarah's fate was inevitable. Paul did not need to protect himself. The result of this encounter is to vindicate Paul's statement that Thecla is too good looking for this occupation (3.25). Women should be hesitant about serving as itinerant missionaries. Thecla will take precautions, including male clothing and a large entourage the next time she takes the road (§15). The narrator wishes to have Paul say "I told you so" and leave the heroine to face the consequences. Being as innocent as a pigeon and shrewd as a snake (cf. Matt 10:16) wins no medals. This is also a reminder that the tactics of the powerless may require unpleasant choices. Modern, middle class readers who belong to egalitarian cultures will require time to forget Paul's treachery. That time they will receive.

As Thecla's crush on Paul was an example of pure and proper love at first sight, so Alexander typifies improper, i.e., sexual, love at first sight. Such love, when rebuffed, often transforms itself into rage. The theme is a staple of romantic novels (e.g., *An Ethiopian Story* 7.25.2; 8.5.10–6.2; *An Ephesian Tale* 2.5–6), the plots of which it usefully serves. Note *Leucippe* 6.19, which discusses the transformation.

With the lack of subtlety that is one of his enduring characteristics, the irresistible Alexander tries to take possession of his prize. This should not be regarded as acceptable *public* behavior for males, particularly for those wearing the regalia of imperial authority. These advances she would never have tolerated. Her first reported reaction, doubtless a contribution of the author, was a frantic visual search for Paul. To the audience this amounts to a signal that the apostle has elected the better part of valor. His absence liberates Thecla. She gives three reasons why he may not rape her:

1. She is a "visitor" (*xenē*), protected by the requirements of hospitality.

2. She is the "*slave* of God." To mistreat the "slave" (a word that could have a number of meanings) of a god is to dishonor that god.

3. She is a citizen of high status at Iconium.

To these excellent qualifications Thecla adds the statement that she was expelled from Iconium for refusing a marriage. Although this may support, by analogy, her disinclination to engage in public sex, it also raises questions about her standing at Iconium. The narrative has not stated that Thecla was expelled. This may be a residue of the source, which described her decision for celibacy at Iconium and subsequent expulsion. It is also true that her status is of no help in the future. In the source she may have defended herself by the solitary claim to be a servant of God, or with action. (See below.) At

149

any rate, Alexander will now have the opportunity to consider her claims, offer a provisional apology, and make such amends as he deemed sufficient.

That opportunity he does not receive. Instead, she counter-attacks. This precipitate action leads to the hypothesis that the source moved directly from his assault to her physical defense. The great Alexander had been beaten up by a girl. Difficult as it may be to believe, Roman males of high status were dishonored by losing a fight to a girl. In so doing she had done something even worse: she had assaulted the imperial house. Price (*Rituals and Power*, 170) states: "This scene from the Acts of Saints Paul and Thecla . . . vividly illuminates not only the social context of the imperial cult, but also the privileged position of the imperial image." These crowns displayed up to fifteen busts of the current emperor, his family, and his predecessors. For illustrations, see plates 1a and 2f (*Rituals and Power*, 198–99). The milieu, as Esch-Wermeling aptly notes (*Thekla*, 122), belongs to the thought world of the *Acts of the Alexandrians*, where insults to authorities are often coupled with assertions of high status. This is to say that, unlike most of the Christian martyr Acts, *APl* 4 is overtly hostile to imperial authority. The political stance in chap. 14 does not arrive without foreshadowing.

In §2 Thecla readily confesses to the unspecified crime when brought to the governor's bench by the angry and disappointed Alexander. Neither accuser nor defendant nor judge nor narrator waste time on the trial. Thecla is condemned to the beasts. The severity of the punishment, not customary for a person of her status, arouses the ire of "the women," a claque that pops up without preparation. On the other hand Thecla's request for protection from molestation led to her placement in the care of a woman of very high status. Censorship of the Greek text (which removes the assault upon imperial majesty) may puzzle readers. What has Thecla done to merit *damnatio ad bestias* (execution by wild animals for the entertainment and edification of the public)?

Romans—and probably Greeks and others—were reluctant to execute virgins, more likely a matter of age more than sexual status. Tacitus, *Annals* 5.9, reports that a daughter of Sejanus was raped by the executioner to avoid this impropriety. That could account for Thecla's fear, although guards were doubtless able to engage in various abuses. See, e.g., the *Martyrdom of Potamiaena and Basilides*, 3; and Jensen, *Töchter*, 185–95. That the governor was willing to consider Thecla's petition is an effect of her evident status. She may have committed a ghastly crime, but she is entitled to the considerations that befit her rank.

Tryphaena, who will provide protection, is an historical character making an appearance in a work of fiction. She was an ideal subject for this role, minor enough to be living in (widowed?) retirement, but still a royal of substantial prestige. The account is very terse. The narrative could well state that the governor had inquiries made and learned that Tryphaena was willing to be responsible for the girl, who was transferred to her custody in a form of house arrest. The Syriac is smoother. See the Notes. The final line may be the product of a person responsible for contributing §28–29, since it stresses Tryphaena's status as a grieving mother more than her social power.

Tryphaena bursts onto the scene as abruptly as Alexander, and not by accident. Scholars debate whether she should be viewed as a surrogate mother or as a patron. Misset-van de Weg, "A Wealthy Woman," shows that, formally, adoption of a daughter by a woman is juridically vague, whereas the social category of benefactor is better defined and quite apt here, but, as the introduction of Tryphaena immediately indicates, maternal sentiments are also important. See Lipsett, *Desiring*, 77–78. Tryphaena is the antagonist of Alexander. He is a civic patron whose benefactions include the delectation of having a young woman publicly shredded by animals. As a lover he represents rapacious sexual desire, untrammeled by such factors as interest or consent. Tryphaena, by contrast, represents familial love, expressed in affectionate care. As a patron she is a model of care for the needy (MacDonald, *Legend*, 51). In the middle stands Thecla, like a daughter to Tryphaena and as a fighter against the beasts.

Notes

(26). Numbers in parentheses represent the former system of treating the material about Thecla as a single chapter.

Taking. Syriac has him holding her hand, "and those persons who were with him" (Wright, 130). The translator has left Paul holding too many hands. Once again, the object is not to leave the apostle alone with a woman.

Antioch. The text does not specify which city named Antioch is in view. Two cities of that name (among many) are associated with Paul: the capital of Syria, Antioch on the Orontes, and Antioch in Pisidia. The itinerary of *APl* moves from Antioch (chap. 2) to Iconium (3) to Antioch (4). The former of these is evidently envisioned as Syrian Antioch (Despite the use of Acts 13:50–51, which belongs to Pisidian Antioch). Does chap. 4 intend to report a repeat visit? The next station reported is Myra, distant from both Antiochs, but more accessible (by sea) from Syrian Antioch. The *Acts of Titus* 4 evidently speaks of a second visit to Antioch, which is not clear. Nicetas of Paphlagonia would seem to favor Syrian Antioch.

The Acts of Paul

Two facts may be posited. The author and/or subsequent editors of *APl* confounded the two cities. The plot does not give much weight to one over another. Wherever the narrative travels a Roman governor is close to hand. The second fact is a product of the editorial theory. Which site did the independent story about Thecla have in mind? One hypothesis is that the underlying story featured Syrian Antioch, but that incorporation into the *APl* distorted this. Unfortunately the argument is quite reversible. Many (Dunn, "Acts of Paul," 20–21; Rordorf, 1137; Esch-Wermeling, 93–96, quite ambivalently) incline toward Pisidian Antioch. Those who posit a historical core to the Thecla story also argue for Pisidia. See Ramsay, *Church,* 381; and Jensen, *Thekla.*

Tilting the scale, in my judgment, is the data about Alexander. Although most editors (e.g., Vouaux, Rordorf) characterize him as a "Syrian" (*Syros*), one important Greek ms. (C) reads "Syriarch," which can be glossed as "head of the provincial council" (and possibly high priest of the Imperial Cult). This is read by Lipsius and Esch-Wermeling, 319 (Barrier prints *syriarchēs* but renders "Syrian," and seems, 138n1, to prefer the latter). It is unlikely that someone characterized as Syrian in origin would gain high status in Pisidian Antioch, geographically, culturally, and ethnically different from Syria. Alteration of "Syriarch" to "Syrian" is more probable than the opposite, particularly since he was evidently wearing a crown with the imperial imagery. The original setting of this story was at Syrian Antioch.

Entering. It is characteristic of popular writing that the narrator does not let Paul and Thecla roam the streets for a few days (doing . . . ?), but has Alexander ready and waiting at the city gates. The timing also attests to her beauty: Thecla need no more than enter a town to excite interest.

Empire League. See the note on Antioch. The Syriarch was head of the provincial council, the major purpose of which was maintenance of loyalty to Rome. The Imperial Cult was a major function of this council. See Kraemer, *Unreliable Witnesses,* 138n78. "Empire League" expresses its function in modern terms (e.g., "Union League," formed to support the United States against secession). Other Greek mss. read "a leading citizen of the Antiochenes." F and G add "Active in many ways in that city with his authority."

Do not know. Perhaps more resonantly for modern than for ancient readers, this statement recalls Peter's denial of Jesus. Cf. Mark 14:17 (and 3.12). Coptic alters to "know this woman as a woman" (Schmidt, Acta, 14*). This makes the denial an affirmation of "no male and female." Paul rejects sexual differentiation.

Not mine. A Latin witness (lcc) adds: "and he left her."

Considerable strength. Primarily physical power is meant, but it could also imply that Alexander could act with impunity because of his political power.

Slave of god. This represents a known cultic status. See Esch-Wermeling, *Thekla*, 275n539, for relevant examples, the best known of which are the Vestal Virgins. Those devoted to a god were also under the god's protection. An apt example is Anthia, heroine of *An Ephesian Tale*, who, although a slave, fended off a suitor by stating that she was devoted to the goddess Isis until she reached the age of marriage (3.11).

Derision. The Greek word *thriambos* can also mean "triumph" and becomes, in the light of subsequent events, ironic. Syriac has a good claim to be more original: "And she laid hold of Alexander, and tore his garments, and pulled off from him the golden crown of figures [two mss.: the figure of Caesar], which was placed on his head, and dashed it to the ground, and left Alexander standing naked" (Wright, 131).

The Armenian is also worthy of note: "[A]nd because I would not be wife to Thamyris my husband, they cast me out of the city. And straightway she attacked Alexander and rent his raiment, and tore off the golden crown of the figure of Caesar, which he had on his head, and dashed it to the ground, and left him naked, destitute and full of shame" (Conybeare, 76–77). On his vestment and crown, see Esch-Wermeling, under *provide games*, below. The most remarkable feature of this version is that Thecla was viewed as married and denying conjugal rights to her husband. An argument for its originality would fail on the grounds of her virginity. His dishabille would make the later exhibition of Thecla nude a bit of poetic justice.

Desiring. The Greek verb is *phileō*, often used for familial love, but not always. See Esch-Wermeling, 276. This feeling may best be understood as the rage of a frustrated lover. Thamyris had similar feelings, 3.10. See also Barrier, 144n1. The variants show that ancients recognized that the text has him act only in response to his injured shame. The Armenian makes a contrast: "Now Alexander loved her at sight, but . . ." (Conybeare, 77).

Governor. Latin (Lb) states that she was charged "as a profaner" (*ut sacrilegam*). This relieves any suspense. Armenian is more circumstantial: "[Alexander] gave information to the judge, to the effect that Thekla did thus and thus to me, and she denies not that which she did; but do thou judge her and order that she be thrown to the wild beasts" (Conybeare, 77).

The Women. Some Latin witnesses and Syriac make the body inclusive: "The entire city." Cf. the post-martyrdom judgment of the spectators in the *Martyrdom of Carpus, Papylus, and Agathonice* 4.5.

Provide games. This phrase is restored from the versions: Latin, Syriac, Coptic, and Armenian. On his role as agonothete, giver of the games, an individual who, often in conjunction with an office, provided games at his own expense, see Esch-Wermeling, 123–30, who has a wealth of information and argument. She argues that the role of agonothete is primary. For a high priest in charge of games, see *Mart. Polyc.* 12.2.

Tryphaena. Antonia Tryphaena was linked by descent, marriage, and parentage to a number of client kings, ruled Thrace, and was a descendant of Mark Antony and evidently a distant cousin of Claudius. Despite her role here, Tryphaena most likely lived in retirement at Cyzicus, of which she was a substantial benefactor, following her departure from Thrace at the behest of Emperor Gaius in 38. Her brother Polemon (II) was a husband of Julia Berenice, the brother of Agrippa (II) (Acts 25:13–26:32) and beloved mistress of the future Emperor Titus. See Bremmer, "Magic," 52. Davis (*Cult*, 17) relates Tryphaena to the order of widows. Her wealth and generosity make her a model in some ways, but few male church leaders would be happy with a widow who possessed as much power as Tryphaena. To this extent she is a female fantasy of the head of a body of widows.

The Syriac follows Thecla's request with a response from the governor: "Go whither thou please, and be in safe keeping." Then comes the information about Tryphaena (Wright, 132). This is probably an invention of the translator. One Latin witness (lcd) states that she was a widow. Lc begins with the phrase: "and while the proconsul was investigating who might properly take care of her." These variants show that some early readers found the text deficient.

Bibliography

Bremmer, Jan N. "Magic, martyrdom and women's liberation in the Acts of Paul and Thecla." In *The Apocryphal Acts of Paul and Thecla*, edited by Jan N. Bremmer, 36–59. Kampen: Kok Pharos, 1996.

Davis, Stephen J. *The Cult of St Thecla: A Tradition of Women's Piety in Late Antiquity.* New York: Oxford, 2001.

Dunn, Peter W. "The *Acts of Paul* and the Pauline Legacy in the Second Century." PhD diss., Queens College, Cambridge University, 1996.

Eastman, David L. *Paul the Martyr: The Cult of the Apostle Paul the Martyr in the Latin West.* WGRWS 4. Atlanta: SBL, 2011.

Hansen, William, ed. *Anthology of Ancient Greek Popular Literature*. Bloomington: Indiana University Press, 1998.
Jensen, Anne. *Gottes selbstbewusste Töchter. Frauenemanzipation im frühen Christentum?* Freiburg: Herder, 1992.
———. *Thekla—Die Apostolin: Ein apokrypher Text neu entdeckt*. KT 172. Basel: Herder, 1995.
Kraemer, Ross S. *Unreliable Witnesses. Religion, Gender, and History in the Greco-Roman Mediterranean*. New York: Oxford University Press, 2011.
Lipsett, B. Diane. *Desiring Conversion: Hermas, Thecla, Aseneth*. New York: Oxford University Press, 2011.
Misset-van de Weg, Magda. "A Wealthy Woman named Tryphaena: Patroness of Thecla of Iconium." In *The Apocryphal Acts of Paul and Thecla*, edited by Jan N. Bremmer, 16–35. Kampen: Kok Pharos, 1996.
Musurillo, Herbert. *The Acts of the Pagan Martyrs*. Oxford: Clarendon, 1954.
Price, Simon R. F. *Rituals and Power: The Roman Imperial Cult in Asia Minor*. Cambridge: Cambridge University Press, 1984.
Ramsay, William M. *The Church in the Roman Empire*. London: Hodder and Stoughton, 1897.
Snyder, Glenn E. "Remembering the *Acts of Paul*." PhD diss., Harvard University, 2010.

4.3–4. Thecla Paraded in Public

[(3) 28. For the opening parade of the animals Thecla was bound to a fierce lioness. *Queen Tryphaena followed her. The lioness kept licking the feet of Thecla who was seated atop her. The crowd marveled at this.* The charge inscribed on a sign was, "Thecla, the sacrilegious violator of the gods, who dashed the imperial crown from the head of Alexander." In contrast, the women and children began to shout once more: "O God, an impious judgment is being carried out in this city!"

[[*Tryphaena then took her back home after the procession, for her late daughter Falconilla had told her in a dream, "Mother, take this abandoned stranger Thecla in place of me, so that she may pray for me and I may be translated to the place of the righteous."*]]

(4) 29. When Tryphaena took Thecla back to her home after the procession, she felt grief because of the next day's combat with the animals and deep affection for her like that for her daughter Falconilla, asking her, "My second child Thecla, please pray for my child, so that she might live forever. For I saw this in my dreams."

Thecla immediately raised her voice: "Heavenly God, son of the most high, give her what she wants: that her daughter Falconilla live for ever."

The Acts of Paul

> *After these words Tryphaena grieved as she considered that such beauty was going to be tossed to beasts.]*

Comment

§3–5 appear to be a secondary addition to the text. §6 follows §2 quite aptly, but the argument from improved transition can be risky. Within this larger proposed interpolation is an interpolation (marked with [[ ]] in the text). This sentence is repetitious and disruptive. The interpolation is marked by the characteristic repetition of a phrase (lit., "Tryphaena took her from/after the procession"). See Esch-Wermeling, 164. The proposed larger interpolation adds a new and attractive feature: a parade of the animals on the day preceding the events, much like the circus parades that once marked the arrival of the circus in town and constituted its major advertising. This passage also foreshadows—perhaps overly so—the lion's attitude toward Thecla and provides yet another—possibly excessive—opportunity for women (and children) to express disapproval. These are, or seemed to be, good things, but the primary reason for expanding the text was to inject an atmosphere very much like—and possibly dependent upon—the story of Perpetua. (See the Notes.) The theological issue is the efficacy of the prayers of faithful believers, particularly those who have achieved the status of confessors (confessors were those arrested as Christians, but, through no known fault of their own, not executed) upon the fate of those who died outside the faith. The medium is revelation through dreams. Confessors, of whom Thecla is an example, may be able to "pray people out of Hell." See below. That achievement would make Thecla a reciprocal client, offering services and benefactions in return for others. Dream revelations and concern for redemption of dead family members do not arise elsewhere in these two chapters. Textual support for the view that §3–5 are later additions can be seen from the different arrangement of the Syrian and Armenian translations. The Syriac moves from Tryphaena's reception of Thecla to her removal to the theater, stripping, and exposure to the lioness, who licked her feet, popular reaction, the *titulus* (placard identifying the offense), the loosing of other animals, who did not attack, and Tryphaena's eventual removal of Thecla from the theater. After suitable prayers for the dead daughter, Alexander appears the next dawn, but is refused by Tryphaena. Two different groups of agents must be sent by the governor before Thecla is once again naked in the arena (Wright, 132–35). This version is a combination of two or three different editions, the shorter/est of which moved directly from Tryphaena's acceptance of Thecla

Translation, Commentary, and Notes : Chapter

to her exposure in the theater. Were the Syriac coherent, one could argue for the Greek as an abridged text.

§3. A full-scale celebration might often include the honoring of participants, a procession, sacrifice, accompanied by prayer(s) and a choral offering, perhaps composed for the occasion, a banquet, the games, and oratory. The initial procession, the narrator's sole interest here, often took place on the day of the games. See Apuleius, *Metamorphoses* 10.29, with a description of the show, mainly mythological reenactments, 29–34. For Paul's parallel experience, see 9.22 (also on the day of the contest).

The narrative may portray Thecla as Cybele, riding upon a lion. For the reader this is ironic, like the depiction of Jesus as a king during his trial and execution. Thecla has taken over the role of "mistress of the animals," an ancient goddess (Esch-Wermeling, 224–28, 300; and Vermaseren, *Cybele*). That she is bound to the animal is coherent with the symbolism of binding, if difficult to envision. To the astonishment of the crowd, rather than display antagonism toward his alleged victim, the lioness licked her like a grateful and affectionate kitten. Alexander's plan is not working. The narrator then turns to two opposing views: that of officialdom, portraying Thecla as a religio-political criminal, and the innocents: the standard grouping of women and children. The narrator depicts these people as bewailing the judgment as the procession makes its way toward the theater. Cf. Luke 23:27–31.

What the governor views as the self-evident righteous judgment of a self-confessed criminal these opponents, excluded by sex and age from formal participation in civic decisions, call unrighteous. (On these cries, see Esch-Wermeling, 161–63.) A contemporary analogy to the patriotic component would be assaulting the color-bearer at a Memorial Day parade and then burning the flag. (Memorial Day is a patriotic American holiday honoring those who died in combat.) For the religious dimension one should imagine assaulting a bishop during a Corpus Christi procession, after pulling off his miter and cope and trampling upon them. Thecla has done both and is arraigned, as it were, before a devout judge of Italian heritage who is a member of the American Legion.

The presumably added sentence at the close of §3 reduces the abruptness of the introduction of the subject in §4. Although the language is terse (see Notes), the narrator does not intend to say that Tryphaena could yank Thecla off of the lion and out of the procession. Her relationship to Thecla has changed as she has become a recipient of revelatory dreams. That message appears to take the form of the classic *quid pro quo* of ancient religion: if Tryphaena accepts Thecla as a surrogate daughter, Thecla will reciprocate by praying to have her daughter translated to the abode of the blessed. The

157

text assumes that this lies within Thecla's power and that it is appropriate. See the long note 1* of Vouaux, 204.

§4 serves the present text as retardation and reiteration. The reported feelings are rather otiose. See the Notes. The narrator wishes to emphasize that Tryphaena has come to view Thecla as a second daughter. This generates pathos, as she has already lost a daughter, Falconilla. Comfort is to be found in hope for the afterlife. Thecla's prayer is addressed to Christ as God. It appears to be a modification of a more Monarchian earlier form. (A more orthodox prayer would be addressed to God the creator, as variants show.) The prayer for eternal life better fits the view that the dead have no existence. Tryphaena's lament is not quite suitable. It forms an *inclusio*, but the reference to beauty does not seem germane. See §9, where the governor shares the sentiment.

Notes

Perpetua. Examples of visions are the *Acts of Perpetua* 4, 7, 8, 10, 11, and 14. 7 and 8 are important, for they discuss her dead brother, Dinocrates, and her vision of his redemption.

Lion. Although Cybele, a fertility goddess from Asia Minor, identified by Greeks with other "mother goddesses," is most often portrayed as driving a lion-drawn chariot, she is also depicted as riding a lion. See the plates in Vermaseren, *Cybele,* 145–76, and drawings, *passim*. In Lucian's *Dialogues of the Gods* 20 (12), Eros (Cupid) boasts that he rides lions, who let them put a hand in their mouths and lick it. This shows the power of love. Lions are a common symbol of power and majesty. The lioness was herself sometimes identified as a goddess and associated with leading goddesses (Puech, "Lioness"). Both Paul and Thecla form strong bonds with lions, who respond by rejecting violence. This symbolizes their power and the arrival of the eschatological/utopian era in which the conflicts among species disappear. The lion is a unifying image in *APl*, providing the most obvious of the Thecla/Paul parallels.

Bound. Latin lb has her put in a cage atop the lion. This is more practicable. It would eliminate the mythological parallel identified in the previous note.

Queen. The text is difficult. See Esch-Wermeling, 333n6.

Imperial Crown. This comes from the Armenian (Conybeare, 78), deleting the clause that Alexander wished to treat her impurely. Christian theologians in the Chalcedonian tradition remained sensitive to assaults upon imperial dignity. By imperial standards the Syrians and Armenians were heretics—Nestorians and Monophysites. The latter labeled Chalcedonian orthodoxy (referring to the definition of the two natures at Chalcedon, 451, and the condemnation of Nestorius at Ephesus, 431) as "Melkite," i.e., "imperial." By adjusting the charge to *hierosylos*, "sacrilege," "defiler of the sacred," the Greek tradition transformed it into a general assault upon polytheism. The parallel with Jesus (Mark 15:26) is patent. On the crime of insulting imperial images, see Leontius of Neapolis (seventh century), who equates this with an insult to the emperor in person (*Sermo contra Iudaeos*; PG 93:1604C).

Children. Some witnesses eliminate the children. Children were not usually admitted to such spectacles (nor were women in many places).

Procession. Some Latin witnesses expand this phrase to show Tryphaena taking Thecla home and caring for her needs, indicating its abrupt character. Bremmer, "Magic," 53; and Price, *Rituals*, 110n66.

Abandoned stranger. The phrase evidently seemed too harsh and led to numerous emendations in the manuscript tradition.

Translate. The verb is used of the movement of Enoch from earth to heaven, as it were: Heb 11:5; *1 Clem* 9:3. *Topos* (place) is used of one's destiny. See Pervo, *Dating Acts*, 289.

Deep affection. This term disturbed editors and translators, who introduced abbreviations and alternatives.

Bibliography

Bremmer, Jan N. "Magic, martyrdom and women's liberation in the Acts of Paul and Thecla." In *The Apocryphal Acts of Paul and Thecla*, edited by Jan N. Bremmer, 36–59. Kampen: Kok Pharos, 1996.
Coleman, K. M. "Fatal Charades: Roman Executions Staged as Mythological Enactments." *JRS* 80 (1990) 44–73.
Price, Simon R. F. *Rituals and Power: The Roman Imperial Cult in Asia Minor*. Cambridge: Cambridge University Press, 1984.
Puech, Emile. "Lioness." *DDD*, 524–25.
Riemer, Ulrike. "Miracle Stories and Their Narrative Intent in the Context of the Ruler Cult of Classical Antiquity." In *Wonders Never Cease: The Purpose of Narrating Miracle Stories in the New Testament and Its Religious Environment*, edited by Michael Labahn and Bertjan L. Peerbolte, 32–47. Library of New Testament Studies 288. London: T. & T. Clark.

The Acts of Paul

Spittler, Janet, E. *Animals in the Apocryphal Acts of the Apostles*. WUNT 247. Tübingen: Mohr/Siebeck, 2008.

Vermaseren, Maarten J. *Cybele and Attis. The Myth and the Cult*. Translated by A. Leemers. London: Thames and Hudson, 1977.

4.5–6 Thecla to the Arena

5 (30). In the morning Alexander (who was the sponsor of the hunt) arrived to take Thecla, announcing, "The governor has taken his seat and the crowd is growing restive at our failure to get the show on the road. Give me the one condemned to the beasts so that I might take her away."

But Tryphaena routed him, shouting, "My household is experiencing fresh mourning for my Falconilla, and there is no one to help, not a child—she is dead, nor any relative. I am a widow! God of Thecla, my child, help her."

6 (31). The governor dispatched soldiers to convey Thecla, but Tryphaena did not leave her, but personally took her by the hand and escorted her, with these words: "I escorted my daughter Falconilla to the grave; you, Thecla, I am escorting into battle with wild beasts."

Thecla wept with bitter groans to the Lord: "Lord God, in whom I believe, to whom I have fled for refuge, who delivered me from fire, reward Tryphaena, who has taken pity upon your slave, because she kept me chaste."

Comment

§5, the final part of the addition, provides additional retardation and gives Tryphaena an opportunity to match Thecla in Alexander-bashing. Alexander has no authority over the prisoner. He cites two reasons for expediting transportation of the prisoner, whom, some will suspect, he may wish to molest on the way to the stadium. Outside of that quickly obliterated hypothesis, the scene is comic. How can Thecla be so insensitive as to keep not only the public but even the provincial governor waiting?

Tryphaena chases him off by taking the melodramatic role of the poor little defenseless widow who is devoid of relatives and whose home is in mourning for her only child. The part is utterly improbable for a woman so powerful that she can convulse a city by fainting. The author of the PE would view her as the kind of widow who can make strong bishops faint, the uppity widow of their nightmares. See Pervo, "Aseneth and her Sisters." This section ends, like the previous, in a prayer. Just as Thecla prayed for the daughter, whose name is now revealed, so Tryphaena prays for Thecla.

Such comic relief as this material has provided ends with §6, which takes place as if the foregoing material had not existed. According to the editorial history here proposed, it did not originally exist. The narrative picks up from §2 (Barrier, 154, errs in stating that Alexander now sends reinforcements). Dignified pathos characterizes the scene. Tryphaena continues her protective role. Her comment offers a nicely balanced parallel between her final act on behalf of her natural daughter and that performed for her fictive child.

Thecla's intensely emotional prayer compliments Tryphaena's statement. This is her Gethsemane. She addresses God as the object of her faith, her guardian, and preserver. Her petition is not explicitly for herself, but for Tryphaena. The verb "reward" (*apodos*) corresponds to Alexander's demand for Thecla (*dos*, §5). Tryphaena deserves to be "given" Thecla. The major motive is that Tryphaena kept her chaste, forming, as Lipsett notes (*Desiring*, 78), an *inclusio* around this ministry. Repetition of "slave" reinforces the close of this unit.

Notes

Morning. Cf. Luke 24:1. This will be the day of Thecla's new birth

Leader. This may be a reminder for the audience or floating information. If the latter, it should be deleted.

Condemned. From Alexander's viewpoint this is the meaning of *thēriomachos*. For the readers it means "beast fighter." This is one of the "Johannine ironies" of Thecla's passion.

Restive. The colloquial language expresses the notion that the crowd is applying pressure upon Alexander.

Take. Witnesses expand the phrase, in character, but it is effective as it is.

My child. Witnesses revise these statements in directions evidently viewed as realistic. "My child" seems inappropriate on the lips of a person who has just claimed to be bereft of children, but the two sentences belong to different viewpoints.

Convey. Witnesses seek to improve the abrupt transition and add suitable details.

Refuge . . . delivered. Cf. Ps 143:9. The prayer evokes the soliloquies of Aseneth. "Refuge" occurs more than fifteen times there. See, e.g., 13:12. "Deliver" is also common, e.g., 27:10.

Bibliography

Lipsett, B. Diane. *Desiring Conversion: Hermas, Thecla, Aseneth.* New York: Oxford University Press, 2011.

Pervo, Richard I. "Aseneth and her Sisters: Women in Jewish Narrative and in the Greek Novels." In *"Women like This": New Perspectives on Jewish Women in the Greco-Roman World,* edited by Amy-Jill Levine, 145–60. SBLEJL 1. Atlanta: Scholars, 1991.

4.7–10 Baptism

7 (32). *When they arrived* the place was in an uproar, with bellowing creatures and competing calls for action from the People and the women. The latter sat together. The former shouted, "Bring in the defiler of the sacred," while the women rejoined: "Down with the city for this lawlessness. Kill us all, governor! A wretched spectacle! A wicked judgment!"

8 (33). Thecla was taken from Tryphaena, stripped [given a sash], and thrust into the arena. Lions and bears were set upon her. A savage lioness ran up and up but lay down at her feet. The crowd of women let loose a loud shout. A bear dashed up against her, but the lion ran toward the bear, encountered it, and ripped it to shreds. Now another lion, one that had been provided by Alexander and had been schooled to attack people, rushed toward her. Lioness grappled with lion. Both died. The women redoubled their laments now that the lioness that had helped Thecla was no more.

Translation, Commentary, and Notes : Chapter

(9) 34. While Thecla stood praying with outstretched arms, they launched numerous beasts at her. Her prayer finished, she turned and saw a large pit filled with water. "This is my opportunity to wash," [*throwing herself into the water with these words: "In the name of Jesus Christ I am baptized on my last day."*]

The women spectators—as well as the whole crowd—shouted, "Don't jump into the water!" Even the governor was reduced to tears at the thought that such beauty would become a meal for seals. She threw herself into the water in the name of Jesus Christ. The seals floated dead upon it after seeing a flash of fiery lightning. A fiery cloud surrounded her, preventing the beasts from touching her and shielding her nudity from sight.

(10) 35. When additional, more fearful beasts were loosed, the women raised a piercing lament. Some threw flower petals, others nard, others cassia, still others amomum. The resultant abundance of aromas reduced all of the attacking animals to unconsciousness. They did not touch her.

Whereupon Alexander said to the governor, "I have some very scary bulls. Let's tie the condemned to them."

The governor gave his unhappy consent: "Do what you want."

So they tied her by the feet between two bulls and applied red-hot irons to their genitals so that, greatly provoked, they would kill her. The bulls were galvanized, but the scorching flame had burnt through the ropes, leaving Thecla effectively unbound.

Comment

Thecla, whose opponents will soon seek to tear her apart, has torn Antioch apart. The narrator succinctly and aptly portrays a bedlam of human and animal sounds. The residents are divided, like ancient sports factions, but in this case, evidently, one faction is composed of the *demos*, the male citizenry, the other of women (presumably female citizens), sitting together, rather than with the male relatives who have responsibility for and authority over them. See Esch-Wermeling, 155. "Evidently" concedes that the textual history is complicated. From the Syriac and its Armenian derivative versions it seems quite possible that the Greek represents an abbreviated tradition.

The Acts of Paul

No Hollywood version of a Roman spectacle lacks a presiding official to say, "Let the games begin!" Neglect of that necessity here is repaired by several Latin witnesses. The account in §8 and 9 may be abbreviated. See the Notes. Description of the attack begins with a summary ("lions and bears") followed by details. Martyr acts presumed to be historical often note the finicky behavior of creatures. See Ignatius, *Rom* 5:2; *Martyrs of Lyons* 42; *Perpetua* 19; 21.1. Ignatius feared that the lions would shirk their duty. Animals were said to discriminate in favor of women (Spittler, *Animals,* 172–76).

The sequence is dramatic. The narrator does not draw things out. The first antagonist is a most frightening lioness, who defies expectations by sitting at Thecla's feet like a domestic cat. The women roar. One for our side. Next comes a bear. The lioness shifts from friendship to defense. Scratch one bear. Alexander puts a man-killing lion into the fray. The ensuing struggle leaves both creatures dead. Thecla's protector has died in her behalf.

With §9 comes a wholesale barrage of beasts. Thecla, who was at prayer, overlooked them. When the opportunity presented itself, she saw a pool. The readers view this from Thecla's perspective and do not realize that it contains aquatic creatures. The dramatic audience sees the seals and is alarmed. Among those is the governor, whose sentiment exactly matches that of Tryphaena (§4). Their focus on appearance (in contrast to celestial values and reality) shows that they are sympathizers rather than converts.

Seals are not particularly frightening beasts, but ancients classified them among the more carnivorous and it is reported that they fought polar bears (Calpurnius Siculus, *Eclogues* 7.64–66—presumably not imports from the arctic). Nomenclature varied; people used inexact terminology. Superstition held that lightning did not touch seals (Pliny, *Natural History* 2.146). This provided the narrator with a fine irony. See Schneider, "Thekla"; and Spittler, *Animals,* 138n57 and 181, as well as the references in Barrier, 162n11. In the dramatic context the seals would have been intended for a subsequent hunt. Their wholesale electrocution would have been a great disappointment to the public and no small financial loss to Alexander.

Thecla's baptism generates a number of questions. Among these is whether it should be characterized as autobaptism or as a martyr's baptism. In the edited text Thecla's quest for Christian initiation has been central and §9 is a dénouement. This was not the case in the free-standing story behind the current chap. 4. The author is most probably responsible for expanding the incident into a proper sacrament in Augustine's definition: "Accedit verbum ad elementum et fit sacramentum" ("The word intersects the [material] element and a sacrament results" [*In Johannis evangelium tractatus* 80.3]). Nevertheless, however diminished in importance, the incident is presented as a baptism. Thecla was not simply having a swim. The action is endorsed by epiphany: lightning and cloud are two characteristic signs of divine presence (e.g., Exod 19:16. In the background are the marks of the epiphany of a storm god). According to Justin, *Dialogue* 88.3, fire appeared at the baptism of Jesus. These manifestations here were not merely decorative. The lightning took care of the seals, contrary to convention, while the cloud clothed her. This is a paradoxical event, a clear sign of divine aid, as lightning has appeared out of nowhere to kill the lightning-proof creatures but leave Thecla uninjured. The localized cloud is equally "unnatural."

In general this act should be viewed as an extraordinary baptism under emergency circumstances. Thecla may well, so to speak, have preferred to be baptized by the bishop at the Easter Vigil, but that was not possible. She was evidently moments away from death. No one was present to serve as a minister of baptism. She therefore immersed herself. If the verb is taken as passive, the text avoids technical autobaptism (*Baptizomai* can be construed either as passive, "I am baptized [by God]," or as middle, "*I baptize myself*"). Note 9.21, where Artemilla immerses herself (after Paul lays a hand upon her).

Martyrs' baptism or "the baptism of blood" affirms that none who die because of their faith are to be viewed as incomplete Christians. Texts invoked in discussion of whether martyrs are literally baptized in their own blood include Tertullian, *On Baptism* 16; and *Perpetua* 21. Extant ancient writers did not dispute the validity of Thecla's baptism and routinely described her as "protomartyr," the pioneer (woman) martyr. See Esch-Wermeling, 87–88.

Most tyrants would have been able to read these signs of the times. Not Alexander. His solution was to raise the ante: more and fiercer beasts. (The cloud has been allowed to evaporate from the narrative, as it were.) Thecla's women supporters will now seek alleviation through aroma therapy. (See the note on drugs.) The Syriac once more represents an arguably unabbreviated text:

> And when the women, who were sitting in the theatre, saw that other beasts were being let in at Thecla, which were worse than the former, they broke out into wailing and say: "Thy help (we implore), O God! What do we see in this city?" And then these women came and cast perfumes upon Thecla; there were some who cast spikenard, and some sweet-marjoram (*amaracus*), and some *tarphuse*; and they were throwing perfume into the midst of the theatre upon Thecla. And the beasts, which they had let loose at her, came up to her, and sat down around her, behind

her and in front of her, and lay down and slept; and not one of them harmed Thecla. (Wright, 137–38)

This account is more reasonable in that the women do not fill the entire (outdoor) theater with scents but douse Thecla with them. They provide her with a postbaptismal anointing (so also Barrier, 163). From the possibly abbreviated Greek text it is reasonable to conclude that these materials had a narcotic effect upon the animals. The longer Syriac text is amenable to view of Thecla as mistress of the animals, who brings the peace (and the aroma) of paradise to that place. The putative Greek redactor would have lessened the prestige and power of Thecla by shifting the argument in a "natural," albeit improbable direction, since sleep-inducing drugs would also have affected spectators.

As mistress of the beasts Thecla evokes a range of images and roles. The ancient Anatolian mountain goddess was depicted in many places. Famous examples come from Greece and Crete, where she has the wasp waist and bell skirt that were long fashionable in the area. An eight-thousand-year-old depiction survives in a terracotta from Çatal Hüyük, in Turkey, where a figure of fertility goddess proportions is seated with a lion on either side. See Vermaseren, *Cybele*, figs. 1–5, pp. 12–15, and the photographs following p. 144. As noted above, this pre-Indo-European goddess continued to be worshipped under various names, especially Cybele, into the common era. Asia Minor remained the center of her worship. Thecla is competing with the goddess on her home field. See Esch-Wermeling, 171, 224–28, and 300.

Mastery over animal life is a common feature of the charismatically endowed person. In addition to Pythagoras and Apollonius of Tyana are a number of apostles, all well described and analyzed by Spittler, *Animals*. See also Bieler, *Theios Anēr*, 1:104–10. The giver of these games at which she was to be sacrificed was also a priest of the imperial cult. The divine character of the Emperor Titus produced just that exemplary concord among species also achieved by Thecla:

> As the startled hind fled the swift Molossians [*dogs*] and with various cunning spun lingering delays, suppliant and like to one begging she halted at Caesar's *feet; and the hounds did not touch their prey* [lacuna] ... Such was the boon she won from knowing her prince. Caesar has divine power ... (Martial, *De Spectaculis* 33 [29; 30] 1–7; translated by D. R. Shackleton Bailey, LCL, 37; emphasis added)

Lions play no small role in these anecdotes from the theater (Riemer, "Miracle Stories," 35). For all of the learned contempt exhibited by learned Greeks toward the theriomorphic gods of Egypt, Hellenic gods also took the form of animals. Otherwise stated, various animals could serve as attributes, associates, or agents of particular gods. Among the creatures associated with Zeus are the eagle (a symbol that, much demythologized, endures in the iconography of the United States and other nations) and the bull (on which see Cook, *Zeus* 3/1:605-55). This symbol of authority and virility, a not particularly subtle multiple stand-in for Alexander, will lead to the climactic attempt to execute Thecla. One difficulty of the Greek text is that the incidents are presented without link or transition. The Syriac is less abrupt:

> And again Alexander ran (and) came and said to the hēgemōn: "I have two bulls, which are very strong and savage; let us bring them and bind between them this (woman who is) doomed to be devoured by beasts, so that perchance they may become furious and destroy her." And the hēgemōn said to Alexander: "Go and do whatever seems good unto thee." And he sent and had the bulls fetched; *and they brought Thecla from among the beasts, and took hold of her, and threw Thecla upon her face, and took hold of her feet* and bound her between the two bulls. And they brought spits and put them in the fire, and made the spits hot with fire, and laid them upon the thighs of the bulls, that they might become furious and in their anger destroy the captive. And the bulls, because of the pain they suffered, sprang up suddenly; but a flash of fire ran and consumed the ropes which were fastened to the feet of Thecla, *and Thecla sprang up and stood beside the bulls, as if she had no pain and as if she had not been bound.* [And when the hēgemōn and the whole city saw the great marvels which God had wrought with Thecla, they praised God for what they had seen.] (Wright, 138-39)

Fulsome detail is often a sign of textual expansion. This is possible here, as always, but a comparison of the two strongly suggests that the Greek text is abbreviated. The governor is clearly taking the role of Pontius Pilate (cf. Matt 27:24-26; Luke 23:25) while the imperial high priest is taking the role of the Jewish high priest. The narrative does not suggest that Alexander is proposing a mythical reenactment, such as that of Dirce (e.g., Spittler, *Animals*, 188), for it is presented as a spontaneous suggestion. One temptation is to view this as specifically sexualized: the bulls will tear her in two by the legs, ending her virginity with her life. See Davies, *Widows*, 106, strongly endorsed by Barrier, 167. Esch-Wermeling, 282-87, has many interesting comments. A difficulty with this interpretation is that Thecla's upper body would have to be secured and the bulls persuaded to gallop in opposite directions. The simplest reading is that the bulls would trample her. See Spittler, *Animals*, 178. The danger is to perform what amounts to an historical

The Acts of Paul

reconstruction. In a work of fiction the critic can seek to discover what the author intended but not what historical facts were misrepresented, etc.

Thecla is to be executed by the actions of savage representatives of hypermasculinity, whose literally inflamed sexual organs represent the sexual passion and rage of Alexander, who has now become her prosecutor and judge. Thecla's innocence has been vindicated. Alexander is guilty of tyrannical *hybris*. Part of his punishment will be that he must come crawling on his knees to beg for her release.

Notes

Arrived. The italicized clause is supplied to provide transition.

Uproar. Cf. Mart. Poly. 8.3.

Factions. The racing teams in large cities were named for their colors, not unlike some venerable American baseball teams. Their fans constituted well organized claques, whose services are unison shouters could be utilized for other purposes, such as politics.

Sash. This phrase should probably be deleted. Although the word *gymnos* has a varied range, the context presumes that Thecla was stark naked. The verb is an active construction (lit., "received") amidst others in the passive voice (i.e., "she was given a sash" would fit). See also Kraemer, *Unreliable*, 138n79. The versions indicate recognition of the difficulty. A Latin witness (Lca) says that she was given a "sentence," perhaps a placard indicating the crime. Coptic says that she was tied. Thecla is depicted wearing this sash in the famous limestone at Kansas City. See Cartlidge and Elliott, *Art*, 155 (Fig. 5.10). The Syriac tradition reveals the difficulty:

> [*The young men*] led her into the theater to throw her to the beasts. And they brought (her) and made her stand in the midst of the theater, and stripped (her), and took away her clothes, and put a cloth round her loins, and she was standing naked, and said: "My Lord and my God, the Father of our Lord Jesus the Messiah, you are the helper of the persecuted, and you are the companion of the poor; and behold your handmaid, for the shame of women is uncovered in me, and I stand in the midst of all this people. My Lord and my God, remember your handmaid in this hour." (Wright, 135–36, alt.)

The translation postdates the putative addition of the covering, here a loin-cloth put on her by men. Yet the phrase "the shame of women is

Translation, Commentary, and Notes : Chapter

uncovered" almost certainly refers to the genitals, for which "shame" is a trope. The Armenian is similar (Conybeare, 81). Once again it seems probable that the Greek text has been abbreviated through the excision of a speech

Lioness. The sentence antedated the added description of the procession. Some Latin witnesses make the link explicit.

Antagonist. Syriac follows the bear with a leopard.

Large pit. Various Latin witnesses note here that the pit contained dangerous creatures.

Throwing herself. The text reports that Thecla twice threw herself (*ebalen heautēn*) into the pool. The text of §9 reports (1) that she threw herself in, reciting a baptismal formula; (2) that the women, together with the other spectators, called upon her not to jump; (3) that this moved the governor to tears; and (4) that she threw herself into the water, citing a formula but not stating that Thecla spoke. The first of the two plunges is an interpolation. (Why the reviser did not just change the second reference is difficult to fathom, but critics are grateful.) For Thecla the pool presented an opportunity to "wash," a term for baptism (Lampe, 813, *s.v. louō*). When reporting to Paul in §15 she will speak of "bath" and "bathing." The second reference does not mention the intention (be baptized) or the use of a spoken formula. The addition rectifies these shortcomings. See Esch-Wermeling, 86–87. In its earlier form chap. 4 did not make Thecla's baptism the basis for narrative tension and suspense. Ms. E and Syriac resolve the problem by preserving the second leap into the water and the initial formula (Wright, 137).

Last day. This is probably not eschatological in the sense of "for the end," but a reference to this as the last day of her life. Some Latin witnesses provide the full Trinitarian formula. On baptism in the name of Jesus, see, e.g., Vouaux, 213.

Unnatural. Defining miracle as "exception to laws of nature" or the like is inappropriate. The behavior of the lioness is no less miraculous. See Parsons and Pervo, *Rethinking*, 92–96.

Scents. Nard is oil derived from the spikenard plant. Cassia is related to cinnamon, and amomum evidently to cardamom; cf. Theophrastus, *De Odoribus* 32. On cassia, see Theophrastus, *Hist. Plant.* 9.5; Pliny, *H. N.* 12.41–45; Ancients were attentive to the medicinal and magical properties of various aromatic substances. See Faure, *Magie der Düfte*. Amomum is difficult to identify. All were very expensive, indicating both the extravagance and wealth of Thecla's supporters. Cf. Mark 14:3–9. See Esch-Wermeling, 227–28; and Spittler, *Animals*, 177. The latter favors understanding the chemicals as soporific. Davis, *Cult*, 9, associates these scents with burial. They indicate that the women have concluded that Thecla is about to die. Coleman, "Charades," 52, notes that machines could spray an audience with perfumes during games. This parallel speaks against the practicality of what the Greek text describes. Mind-altering substances (wine mixed with incense) are used for the opposite purpose, to stimulate elephants to trample the proposed Jewish victims of a pogrom in 3 *Maccabees* 5:1–12. In so far as this is a martyrdom, the scents could evoke the "odor of sanctity," as in *Mart. Polyc.* 15, following his death.

Whole city. The bracketed sentence is omitted by a Syriac ms. See Wright 139n.a. It is probably secondary.

Ropes. Armenian reads "But the flame of the fire caught the bonds" (Conybeare, 83), while otherwise agreeing with the Syriac. This is probably best understood as a "natural event," but the matter is disputable and the Greek text is uncertain. See Vouaux, 215n3* (who regards the narrator as overly fond of miracles); Barrier, 167n14; and Spittler, *Animals*, 178. The apparatus of Lipsius, 262, indicates varied perceptions.

Condemned. Literally, and doubly ironically, the term is "beast-fighter." See Spittler, *Animals*, 179. The term was applied to Heracles, as in Lucian, *Lex.* 19. See chap. 9. On women in the arena, see Schäfer, "Frauen in der Arena," 243–68. The existence of women beastfighters increases the subtlety of applying the term to Thecla, who overcomes actual animals through trust and defeats moral "beasts" by virtue.

Bibliography

Bieler, Ludwig. ΘΕΙΟΣ ΑΝΗΡ: *Das Bild des "Göttlichen Menschen" in Spätantike und Frühchristentum.* 2 vols. 1935–1936. Reprint, Darmstadt: Wissenschaftliche Buchgesellschaft, 1967.

Cartlidge, David R., and J. Keith Elliott. *Art and the Christian Apocrypha.* London: Routledge, 2001.

Coleman, Kathleen M. "Fatal Charades: Roman Executions Staged as Mythological Enactments." *JRS* 80 (1990) 44–73.

Cook, Arthur B. *Zeus. A Study in Ancient Religion.* Vol. 3. Cambridge: Cambridge University Press, 1940.

Davies, Stevan L. *The Revolt of the Widows: The Social World of the Apocryphal Acts.* Carbondale: University of Southern Illinois Press, 1980.

Davis, Stephen J. *The Cult of St Thecla: A Tradition of Women's Piety in Late Antiquity.* New York: Oxford, 2001.

Esch, Elisabeth. "Thekla und die Tiere, oder: Die Zähmung der Widerspenstigen." In *Aus Liebe zu Paulus? Die Akte Thekla neu aufgerollt,* edited by Martin Ebner, 159–79. SBS 206. Stuttgart: Katholisches Bibelwerk, 2005.

Faure, Paul. *Magie der Düfte. Eine Kulturgeschichte der Wohlgerüche. Von den Pharaonen zu den Römern.* Munich: Taschen, 1990.

Kraemer, Ross S. *Unreliable Witnesses. Religion, Gender, and History in the Greco-Roman Mediterranean.* New York: Oxford University Press, 2011.

Parsons, Mikeal C., and Richard I. Pervo. *Rethinking the Unity of Luke and Acts.* Minneapolis: Fortress, 1993.

Riemer, Ulrike. "Miracle Stories and Their Narrative Intent in the Context of the Ruler Cult of Classical Antiquity." In *Wonders Never Cease: The Purpose of Narrating Miracle Stories in the New Testament and Its Religious Environment,* edited by Michael Labahn and Bertjan L. Peerbolte, 32–47. Library of New Testament Studies 288. London: T. & T. Clark.

Schäfer, Dorothea. "Frauen in der Arena." In *Fünfzig Jahre Forschungen zur Antiken Sklaverei an der Mainzer Akademie, 1950-2000,* edited by Heinz Bellen and Heinz Heinen, 243–68. Stuttgart: Steiner, 2001.

Schneider, Horst. "Thekla und die Robben." *VC* 55 (2001) 45–57.

Spittler, Janet, E. *Animals in the Apocryphal Acts of the Apostles.* WUNT 247. Tübingen: Mohr/Siebeck, 2008.

Vermaseren, Maarten J. *Cybele and Attis. The Myth and the Cult.* Translated by A. Leemers. London: Thames and Hudson, 1977.

The Acts of Paul

4.11–14 Vindication

11 (36). At this Tryphaena, who was standing near the field, by the facing around the gate, collapsed, leading her servants to cry: "Queen Tryphaena is dead!"

The governor called a halt to the games; the whole town was in a tizzy. Alexander prostrated himself before the governor and said: "Have mercy on me and upon the city. Release the condemned woman, so that the city will not perish as well. If the Emperor learns about this he may well destroy the city along with us, since Queen Tryphaena, his relative, died at the gate."

12 (37). The governor summoned Thecla from the menagerie and asked: "Who are you? What powers are associated with you that not a single animal touched you?"

"I am a slave of the living God. As for my powers, I have come to believe in God's son, in whom God is well pleased, because of whom none of the animals touched me. He is the sole definition of salvation and the basis of immortal existence, a refuge for the storm-tossed, relief for the oppressed, a haven for the desperate, and, in sum, any who do not believe in God's son will not live but die forever."

13 (38). At this the governor directed that clothing be brought and told her: "Put on these clothes."

"The one who clothed me while I was naked among the beasts will clothe me with salvation on the day of judgment," she rejoined. Thecla then took the clothes and put them on. The governor thereupon issued a decree: "I release to you Thecla, the reverent slave of God." All the women shouted unison praise to God loud enough to make the whole city shake: "There is one God, who saved Thecla."

14 (39). When she had been apprised of the welcome decision, Tryphaena met Thecla with a large entourage, embraced her, and exclaimed: "Now I believe that the dead arise! Now I believe that my child lives! Come in; I shall convey all of my property over to you." So Thecla went with her into her house, where she rested for eight days, instructing her in the word of God, with the result that most of her female staff also became believers. Joy abounded in her household.

Comment

The passage begins awkwardly, implying that Tryphaena collapsed because of Thecla's deliverance. Even more awkward is the narrator's failure to state that Tryphaena was not dead and describe her revival. Abbreviation appears to be the culprit. See the comment on §14. Be that as it well may, Tryphaena has performed a swoon more effective swoon than that of any Victorian belle of the ball in novel, drama, cinema, or reality. Technically this is called *Scheintod*, apparent death; it was among the more hackneyed devices of ancient light fiction (see Pervo, *Profit*, 148n42). For all the reader knows Alexander may have pulled some predatory birds out of his pocket, or killer bees; against Thecla the proconsul will begrudge him a free hand, but Tryphaena is sacrosanct. Now the reader understands why Thecla's protector had to be a woman of more than ordinary municipal or even metropolitan prestige. She had to be a woman so important that a stubbed toe would give officials the vapors.

Tryphaena was that important. The report of her death, unverified (as is customary in popular narrative), prostrated Alexander as a suppliant before the governor. His request bristles with altruism: have mercy on me and the city. The narrator is evidently playing with such passages as John 11:48; Mark 12:8. In this case it is better that one condemned prisoner live than that the whole city perish.

Rather than, as before, yield to this request, or seek precise information about Tryphaena's condition, the possible cause of her death, the governor summons Thecla for a fuller interrogation. (The preceding trial was not unjust in that Thecla readily confessed.) Her speech in §12 is one section of chap. 4 that can be assigned in large part to the author. This is a Paul-Thecla parallel that is unusual in that, rather than fashioning an incident to show that what Thecla could do Paul could also do, Thecla's speech resembles the apologetic style that characterizes Paul's rhetoric and to some of its concepts. (See, however, Leinhäupl-Wilke, "Einfluss," 157–58). Paul will offer similar words elsewhere, e.g., chap. 9.

The Acts of Paul

Table 4.1

Structure/ Features	Paul *APl* 3.17	Thecla *APl* 4.12
Summons Questions: Who? What?	... the governor summoned Paul to the bench and said: "**Who are you** and what is it that you are teaching? These are grave charges."	The governor summoned Thecla from the menagerie and asked: "**Who are you?** What powers are associated with you that not a single animal touched you?"
Response: What (Paul) Who (Thecla) Who (Paul) What (Paul)	17. Paul spoke loudly, "If, proconsul, I am being examined today regarding my teaching, listen. The **living God**, the avenging God, the jealous God, the God who requires nothing yet needs that humanity be saved has *sent me* to draw them away from corruption, impurity, every pleasure, and death, so that they may cease erring. Therefore God sent his **son**, who *alone has compassion for a world gone astray*, whom I proclaim and in whom I teach that people should hold their hope, so that they may not be subject to condemnation but rather have confidence in and reverence for God, as well as intimacy with majesty and passion for truth. So if I teach matters revealed to me by God, what law am I breaking, Proconsul?"	"I am a *slave* of the **living God**. As for my powers, I have come to believe in **God's son**, in whom God is well pleased, because of whom none of the animals touched me." He is the *sole definition of salvation* and the basis of immortal existence, a refuge for the storm-tossed, relief for the oppressed, a haven for the desperate, and, in sum, any who do not believe in God's son will not live but die forever."
Disposition	The governor then ordered that Paul be secured and held in custody until he might have the opportunity for a more thorough hearing.	(13) 38. At this the governor directed that clothing be brought and told her: "Put on these clothes."

Each speech follows a common, albeit quite conventional, outline, with a focus upon Christology and soteriology, which motivate and justify the mission. Each uses a rhetorical list or catalogue. Paul includes a list of four divine attributes and provides several virtues deriving from hope. His speech is bracketed with the theme of teaching, Thecla's with the implicit theme of immortality. See **Table 4.1**. The failure of the animals to kill her is a sign of the faith that brings life everlasting. In a narrative the speeches are cumulative, i.e., the implied readers of this address have the contents of Paul's earlier address in mind. The parallel has another function. Thecla is fully capable of preaching the apostolic message. See Barrier, 173.

At present Paul's whereabouts are unknown. The governor's question suggests that Thecla is hedged about with divinity, although magic cannot be eliminated. He is not, however, looking for another capital charge against her. See the Note on *powers*. Her response is an "I am" statement that says what rather than who she is. In Bultmann's classification (*Das Evangelium des Johannes,* 167n2) this is a qualification type of "I am" statement. "Slave" hearkens back to her statement to Alexander in 4.1. Slaves of a god merited protection. The term is not self-deprecatory. As Paul's usage (e.g., Rom 1:1) indicates, to be a slave was to be entirely under the owner's authority, but also to enjoy some of the owner's power and prestige. Her answer evokes Acts 16:17, but the content is inspired by Acts 4:8–12 (Peter's speech to the Sanhedrin). She also alludes to the divine announcement following Jesus' baptism in Mark 1:11, appropriately, as she has just received baptism.

The images of refuge, relief, and haven could read like a summary of Acts 27:1—28:6, understood as a symbol for deliverance from the storms of life. See Pervo, *Acts*, 639–75. In any case, this is a vivid set of rhetorical images (Leinhäupl-Wilke, "Einfluss," 154–55). The speech closes with a negative form of the promise of John 11:25–26. Cf. also Ps.-Mark 16:16. The governor appears, improbably, to accept this reply. His next action indicates her vindication. Thecla, who was stripped as part of the humiliation of punishment, will dress to show that the charge has been canceled. He has unwittingly tripped over the rite and symbolism of baptism. Candidates remove all their clothes to symbolize renunciation of the old life, enter the water, come up wearing the outfit of the new born, and are dressed to symbolize putting on Christ. See the *Apostolic Tradition* 21. Thecla's rejoinder treats the shielding cloud as the postbaptismal clothing and shows her confidence in the ultimate apparel. 1 Cor 15:53 is the source. The proffered outfit is mere clothing. That understood, she will and does get dressed.

The proconsul framed the acquittal as a formal decree. Thecla, characterized without irony as the devout slave of God, was released to the people. This generated an acclamation from the women, who have been Thecla's consistent supporters, in praise of Thecla's god. The story has moved from condemnation to release. Alexander and his charges have disappeared from the narrative. The acclamation is not necessarily monotheistic. It means something like "He's the one!" in English. Thecla's god is the one god who gets the job done. The shaking up of the city is an *inclusio* with the statement that word of Tryphaena's death convulsed the place. The verbs are different, but the comparison is clear.

Abbreviation may once again be suspected. None of the texts report Tryphaena's revival. It would have meant a shift of scenes, better, a messenger to announce that she had only fainted. C, and the versions such as the Syriac cited in the Notes, improve the announcement to Tryphaena. Whatever events preceded, the two women reunite. Tryphaena makes a double affirmation, that the dead are raised and that her daughter (Falconilla, presumably) lives. Both are grounded in the power displayed in Thecla's delivery. Since God so prizes Thecla, her statements about that god must be true. Thecla has also symbolically experienced resurrection in her deliverance from death (and her baptism). This brings to a close the discussion about resurrection raised in 3.11–14. See also Barrier, 176n3. Conveyance of property speaks of a relationship like adoption. The action is the proper response to an invitation to discipleship. Cf. Mark 10:28. For the present, however, Tryphaena remains in control of her own property.

Thecla demonstrates her "apostolic" vocation. She engages in a household mission, another rounding off of the story that began in chap. 3 with the mission based in the home of Onesiphorus. This house-based mission is like those described in Acts (Matson, *Household*), with one important difference. All of Thecla's converts are women. This is a matter of choice rather than restriction. When men appear in her entourage, in the following paragraph, their presence is probably due to the author. The result is "joy," another *inclusio* (3.5). This story is complete. Thecla is a competent, successful missionary who has acquired a patron of means.

Notes

Facing. *Abax* is of uncertain meaning here. "Scoreboard" fits the context. Cf. "abacus." Another possibility is "marble wall slab"—Syriac takes it to mean "by the entrance door." The second usage is plural. *Arena* does not mean "arena" here, but the sand-covered field. Tryphaena remains at ground level, probably near where she entered. The witnesses show great variety, improving the narrative transition. A number omit the location. Syriac is clear: she fainted "because she thought that Thecla was dead" (Wright, 139).

Queen. As often, some Latin witnesses omit "Queen." It is dramatically effective here.

Collapsed. This verb (*ekpsychō*) means "expire," "dies" in the NT (Acts 5:5, 10; 12:23), but "black out" is well attested.

City. A Latin witness (lbc) has the entire city join in the petition.

Condemned. This is the third use of the term that literally means "(female) beast fighter." Cf. §5 and 10. The term is not elsewhere found with the feminine article. Her combat involves victory without the use of violence. Van den Hoek and Herrmann, "Thecla," assign a piece of pottery from North Africa to this theme. It depicts a half-naked woman with arms raised in the orans position with lions at her feet. The inscription *domina victoria* may be rendered: "Lady, victory is yours." (Other translations are possible. See also Spittler, *Animals*, 179–80.)

Powers. The vague neuter plural *tina* could be rendered "things" or "divine beings." Some Latin witnesses read (magical) art or incantations. See the discussion of Barrier, 170–71. Bovon, "Vie," 154, understands the concept as a protective barrier. This should not be understood as the shielding cloud, which vanished, as it were, before the bulls were introduced.

Definition. The Greek mss. are divided between *hodos* ("way") and *horos* ("definition," "boundary"). The former is probably an assimilation to the familiar expression, as in Acts 16:17, alluded to above. Another possible reading is *oros* ("mountain"). *Horos* receives support from Syriac and by the Latin *salutis terminus* ("definition of salvation"). *Horos* became associated with Valentinian thought, another motive for alteration. See also Bovon, "Vie," 154n56; and Barrier, 171n7.

Thecla's Speech is quite different in Syriac: The proconsul asked who was beside her. She said:

> I am the handmaiden of the living God, and He who was beside me is the Son of the living God in whom I have believed, by reason of whom not one of those beasts came night unto me; and He is the limit of life; for He is a companion to all the persecuted, and to those who have no hope, He is hope and life. I tell thee then, hēgemōn, and these men who, lo, are standing before thee, that he who does not believe in God—for, lo, ye have seen the great things of God, what He hath done to His handmaiden—he who does not believe in Him shall die for ever. (Wright, 140)

This probably represents a revision of the Greek speech rather than an earlier edition. It is a bit more appropriate and has more circumstantial details.

Oppressed. Cf. 2 Thess 1:7.

The Acts of Paul

Clothes. Syriac (Wright, 140) includes the direction that Thecla first remove the loincloth and the statement that she did so. This is additional data, logical and indicative of the secondary character of this garment. On the symbolism of nudity and spiritual clothing, see the *Gospel of Philip* 21.

Released to the people. The verb *apolyō* (release) is used of Pilate's release of Barabbas.

God. Syriac reads:

> And the hēgemōn made criers proclaim to the whole people: "Thecla, who is God's, and Thecla, who is righteous, I have released and given unto you." And the women . . . said: "God is One, and the God of Thecla is One, who has preserved her alive, and brought her forth from the midst of all these beasts." And with the voice of the women who shouted the whole city trembled. And straightway they ran (and) announced it to queen Tryphaena. (trans. Wright, 140)

This version sends out public criers, a nice touch. In place of the "slave of God" title is a statement of Thecla's innocence. It is probably secondary, although the improved transition may come from an earlier Greek edition.

Welcome decision seeks to capture two senses of *euangelizō*: "good news" and "official message."

Entourage. The phrase is anarthrous; otherwise one would refer it to the crowd from the theater.

Come in. The more difficult reading.

Eight days. The number varies. On instruction, see Gal 6:6; Acts 18:11.

Her. C E read "all in the household." Latin lcd speaks of crowds of maidens and matrons. Note that the text says "most," rather than "all." This enhances realism. "Female staff" is probably the best translation.

Bibliography

Bovon, François. "La vie des apotres. Traditions bibliques et narrations apocryphes." In *Les Actes apocryphes des Apôtres: christianisme et monde païen*, edited by François Bovon et al., 141–58. Publications de la Faculté de Théologie de l'Université de Genève 4. Geneva: Labor et Fides, 1981.

Bultmann, Rudolph. *Das Evangelium des Johannes.* 10th ed. KEK. Göttingen: Vandenhoeck & Ruprecht, 1964.

van den Hoek, Annewies, and John J. Herrmann, Jr. "Thecla the Beast Fighter: A Female Emblem of Deliverance in early Christian Popular Art." *Studia Philonica Annual* 13 (2001) 212–49.

Pervo, Richard I. *Profit with Delight: The Literary Genre of the Acts of the Apostles.* Philadelphia: Fortress, 1987.

Spittler, Janet, E. *Animals in the Apocryphal Acts of the Apostles.* WUNT 247. Tübingen: Mohr/Siebeck, 2008.

Lalleman, Pieter J. "The Resurrection in the Acts of Paul." In *The Apocryphal Acts of Paul and Thecla*, edited by Jan N. Bremmer, 126–41. Kampen: Kok Pharos, 1996.

Leinhäupl-Wilke, Andreas. "Vom Einfluss des lebendigen Gottes: Zwei Bekenntnisreden gegen den Strich gelesen." In *Aus Liebe zu Paulus? Die Akte Thekla neu aufgerollt*, edited by Martin Ebner, 139–58. Stuttgart: Katholisches Bibelwerk, 2005.

Matson, David L. *Household Conversion Narratives in Acts: Pattern and Interpretation.* JSNTSup 123. Sheffield: Sheffield Academic, 1996.

4.15–16 Reunion with Paul

15 (40). Thecla continued to long for Paul and kept trying to find him. She sent out inquiries in every direction and was advised that he was in Myra. Collecting some young people of both sexes, and belting herself into a coat that she had sewn into a man-styled garment, she set out for Myra, where she found Paul engaged in proclaiming God's message. When she approached him he was amazed to see her—and her entourage. When she perceived that he thought that some new trial had come upon her, she said: "I have received the bath, Paul. For the one who has worked with you for the gospel has also worked with me for the washing."

16 (41) Taking Thecla by the hand Paul led her to Hermias' house, where she told him everything. He was quite amazed, while the other auditors found their faith strengthened and offered prayers for Tryphaena. Thecla arose and announced to Paul: "I shall go to Iconium."

"Go and teach God's message," he replied.

Tryphaena sent her a large amount of clothing and gold. She left these things to Paul for the care of the poor.

Comment

The contents of §13–14, which round off the story, suggest that the author has had a hand in their shaping. Much of §15–18 stem from the author. Intriguing questions arise. Was the author responsible for Thecla's use of mannish clothing? Or did he take up the notion and domesticate it? Thecla had not enjoyed success in her previous stint on the road. How did Thecla's story end in the source? That text may have reported her continued itinerancy until she reached Seleucia. The reunion with Paul is brief but warm. Rather than reiterate her desire to remain always with Paul, Thecla announces her departure for Iconium on a mission that receives Paul's blessing. The return to her native city provides opportunity to wrap up, by one means or another, any unfinished business. Thecla's story is a "there and back" tale. In this sense it is like the romantic novels, which end with a homecoming (*nostos*) and a happy life thereafter, and unlike the various Acts. A line will suffice to dispatch Thecla to Seleucia, where she will one day enjoy a cult site and a large following.

In §15 Thecla's old longing for Paul suddenly reemerges. He has not been mentioned since his less than creditable disappearance at the beginning of the chapter. Thecla did not, as in 3.21, look for him as a means of support. Now that she has beat the charge of sacrilege and converted the household of Tryphaena, her old feelings returned to the surface. In reality, of course, the author has intervened to place her in proper relationship to the apostle. The reader is to infer that she could send out Tryphaena's slaves on missions of inquiry. By this means, through establishing contact with believers who would initiate their own inquiries, word arrived that Paul was in Myra.

Thecla takes an entourage. The implication is that she has converted some young men. This is a contribution of the author; the core of chapter 4 exhibits no interest in support from males of any species. Strictly construed, the narrative does not say that she put on a man's clothes but that she tailored her outer garment in a mannish fashion. Three non-exclusive reasons can be advanced for this appearance. First, ease of travel: women's clothes were not well suited for outdoor work. A second is prudence: disguised as a man Thecla would be safe from the Alexanders of this world. Her companions would also help in that capacity. A third reason would be to act out Gal 3:26–28, an expression of the transcendence of gender. See the comment on 3.25. (Latin lcd states that Thecla cut her hair.) In the present context the third explanation seems unlikely, as the habit is worn on the road, and not otherwise mentioned. This restriction may well be due to the author. On the subject, see the bibliography in Bremmer, "Magic," 55n68; and Davis, *Cult*,

32–34. Transvestite female saints are well represented in Byzantine hagiography. Maximilla regularly dresses as a man in the *Acts of Andrew* (19, 28, and 46). No one within the narrative remarks on her dress, and readers are left to guess whether she continued to wear it.

As in Acts, overland travel (presuming that is in mind here) receives no attention. One left point A and got to point B. In truth it was slow, arduous, and dangerous. The narrator is equally unconcerned about how Thecla located Paul. Perhaps he should be envisioned as preaching in public, as he leads her to a house. That she discovered him while he was engaged in preaching (cf. Acts 13:5) is perfectly apt; this also provides the author with a link to the next chapter, which opens with Paul preaching in Myra.

Just why the sight of her and her entourage makes Paul suspicious is far from transparent. What is clear is that this is a replay of 3.25, in which Paul firmly but ineffectively denied Thecla's request to follow him. The comparison and contrast is evident. Readers may wonder why Paul continues to be suspicious of Thecla. The answer to that may be that the suspicion applies to her sex. Women may evidently play important roles in the mission, but they should be carefully tested and supervised. In that view the author would agree with the Pastor (e.g., 1 Tim 5:22). Charisma and institution clash here. (In truth it would be difficult to list many organizations of any era that would let a person of about fourteen operate as an independent representative, not least in a culture where few women have public roles.)

The response is an intelligible parallel. Whereas in 3.25 she begged for the seal, Thecla announces that she has received it. She, with the help of the narrator, has read Paul's mind. The image of bathing conforms to §9. Her explanation borrows from Gal 2:8. The evident meaning is that, just as Christ commanded Paul to be a missionary to gentiles, so too her baptism was in response to a divine command. That is how the Syriac views it. See the note.

§16 begins with the same participle as 3.25 (*labomenos*, "taking"). This forms an inclusion marking her separation from and reunion with the apostle. Paul's base is in the home of Hermias (a name that varies in the witnesses). At this point the Syriac offers a fuller account:

> And straightway Paul arose, and took her and all the people who were with her, and led her to the house of Hermaeus. And Paul and Thecla, and the people who were with them, sat down; and she narrated to them everything that they had done with her; and Paul marveled greatly at the power which was given to Thecla; and all who were standing there and hearing what God had done with her, were greatly confirmed and established. And straightway they all arose, and praised God, who works great

things in everyone who believes in Him and does His commandments. And they prayed and besought of God for queen Tryphaena, and said, "Our Lord and our God, the Father of the Most High, reward queen Tryphaena, who has had compassion upon Thy handmaiden and kept her in purity." (Wright, 142–43)

The Armenian (Conybeare, 86–87) is longer than the Greek, but does not quote the prayer for Tryphaena. Other witnesses also exhibit some expansions. The most prudent course is to view the Syriac form as an expansion, both pedantic and intelligent. Like the D-Text in Acts, the Syriac often exposes problems in the Greek tradition.

Thecla's subsequent declaration reveals a substantial shift. Whereas in 3.25 she had promised to follow Paul wherever and forever, now she declares her own itinerary. Paul agrees, delivering a missionary commission (cf. Matt 28:16–20). Thecla has come of age. She did not need Paul's authorization in that she had already converted many in the household of Tryphaena (and she will not, in fact, engage in a mission at Iconium), but the author wishes to show that Paul had given his blessing to Thecla's evangelistic activities.

She then became Paul's patron, transferring some or most (the witnesses vary) of Tryphaena's largesse to Paul.

Notes

Long for. Some witnesses omit this verb, probably because of its erotic connotation.

Myra was an important city on the coast of Lycia in what is now Southwest Turkey, with its port about five kilometers away. Mentioned as transfer point in Acts 27:5–6 and later famous as the home of St. Nicholas. The name varies in the witnesses. Vouaux, 223n2*; and Barrier, 178n7, state that this is additional evidence for locating this Antioch in Pisidia. The text is so succinct that one could imagine that Myra were an adjacent town. The summary could cover a sea voyage from Syrian Antioch as well as the difficult overland journey from Pisidia. At the end Thecla sets off for Iconium as if that were close to hand. The narrator does not have a firm grasp on the geography of the hinterland.

Young People. See the note on 3.9. It could be young men and slave girls. Witnesses vary. F states that the group was large; G omits it.

Trial. Peirasmos. See the note on 3.25. E, C, and some Latin and Syriac witnesses read "him." F, G, and some Latin witnesses omit the phrase. One difficulty is that a great trial *had* come upon Thecla.

Baptism. Wright (142) renders the Syriac: "I have received baptism; for He who commanded thee to preach, commanded me too to wash myself." Autobaptism it may have been, but Christ commanded it. Conybeare's translation of the Armenian reads: "I have received baptism, for he who commanded thee to preach, the same commanded me also to baptize" (86). This makes for a more symmetrical statement, but it is probably erroneous or secondary, since the subject is Thecla's baptism.

Bibliography

Bremmer, Jan N. "Magic, martyrdom and women's liberation in the Acts of Paul and Thecla." In *The Apocryphal Acts of Paul and Thecla*, edited by Jan N. Bremmer, 36–59. Kampen: Kok Pharos, 1996.

Davis, Stephen J., *The Cult of Saint Thecla. A Tradition of Women's Piety in Late Antiquity.* Oxford Early Christian Studies. Oxford: Oxford University Press, 2001.

4.17–18 Wrapping up Thecla

17 (42) Thecla went on to Iconium, entered Onesiphorus' house and knelt down on the floor where Paul had sat teaching the oracles of God. In tears she exclaimed:

"My God, and God of this house, where the light illumined me, | Jesus Christ, the son of God,

   my deliverance in prison,

   my deliverance with governors,

   my deliverance from the fire,

   my deliverance from wild animals,

   you indeed are God.

   To you be glory for ever. Amen."

(18) 43. She learned that Thamyris was dead, but her mother still alive. Summoning the latter, she said: "Theocleia, mother dear. Can you believe that the Lord lives in heaven? If you desire possessions, the Lord will give them to you, on my behalf. If a child, look: here I am!"

The Acts of Paul

Following this exhortation she went to Seleucia, where, after enlightening many with God's word, she enjoyed a noble death.

Comment

§17–18 provide a satisfying wrap up. Thecla's return has nothing of triumph. This passage does show that her crush on Paul is a thing of the past. One could gather that an adult is returning to her childhood home. Developmentally, this is true, but the elapsed time has amounted to, including travel, no more than a few months. Thecla is evidently alone (!); nothing is said about her manner of dress.

First on the agenda is a sentimental visit to Onesiphorus' home, from, but not in, which she had first heard the message. In contrast to 3.20, where she was fixated on Paul, her current focus is on the message. The prayer functions as a soliloquy summarizing her adventures. Cf. the soliloquies of Aseneth, as in the end of her psalm (*Aseneth* 21:21), and Anthia's catalogue of adventures (*Ephesian Tale* 5.14.1–2). The second person is appropriate for hymns of praise, e.g., the *Te Deum*: "You are God; we praise you." Except for the phrase "son of God," the prayer looks quite Monarchian. The Syriac version is thoroughly orthodox but less affecting. Barrier speculates that the community was meeting in a proximate workspace (185–86). He has yielded to the temptation to treat the narrative as realistic, if not historical. The house is vacant because the narrator has no concern for the presence or absence of other people; in any case, the community did not meet without ceasing.

With the by now customary indifference to transition (supplied awkwardly by the Syriac, smoothly by Latin lcd), Thecla learns that the narrator has helpfully killed off Thamyris; her mother presents a different case. The narrator evidently does not wish to abandon the conflict without seeking a reconciliation of sorts. Rather than visit Theocleia, Thecla summons her (to Onesiphorus'?). She will show who is boss. The speech is difficult, a request/demand for faith coupled with two potential bonuses: wealth and a child. The Syriac (Wright, 144) is more ample and omits the reference to a child. This promise of worldly benefits strongly contrasts with everything in *APl*. Some witnesses modify this offer. Three Greek witnesses alter "possessions" (*chrēmata*) into "words" (*rhēmata*), allowing for "words of eternal life." Perhaps the narrator intends to show that no blandishments could bring Theocleia into the fold. Most intelligently, the narrator leaves the result open. Having made her testimony, Thecla set out for Seleucia. There her life as an itinerant, such as it was, ended. At Seleucia Thecla "enlightened" many. The term is ambiguous in that it can refer to Christian initiation, but the use of "word" suggests a teaching mission. The *APl* has illustrated two interesting phenomena. Onesiphorus exemplifies the problems that can arise when a householder abandons all and follows. Thecla is an example of an itinerant missionary who settled in a single place as a residential missionary. Both examples are clear but fictitious.

It does not seem likely that the author omitted additional information about Thecla. Perhaps a legend of her work in Seleucia already existed. Another possibility is that this reference was the source of the later traditions. On those, see Dagron, *Vie*; Fitzgerald, *Life*, 227–30; Davis, *Cult*; and Appendix II. The author wished to finish the story of Thecla as quickly as possible. One thing this author understood was terse narration. After two chapters dominated by a subordinate character, the narrator returns Paul to center stage.

Notes

Floor. Cf. Acts 22:7. Her conversion is likened to the call of Paul. Cf. the reference to light at the beginning of her prayer.

Exhortation. Some witnesses expand the text.

Character. Giving the spotlight to another character is not unusual in the Acts. Cf. Philip in Acts 8 and Maximilla in the *Acts of Andrew*.

Bibliography

Dagron, Gilbert, ed. *Vie et miracles de Sainte Thècle: Texte grec, traduction, et commentaire*. Subsidia Hagiographica 62. Brussels: Société des Bollandistes, 1978.
Davis, Stephen J. *The Cult of Saint Thecla. A Tradition of Women's Piety in Late Antiquity*. Oxford Early Christian Studies. Oxford: Oxford University Press, 2001.
Johnson, Scott Fitzgerald. *The Life and Miracles of Thekla: A Literary Study*. Cambridge, MA: Center for Hellenic Studies, 2006.
Talbot, Alice-Mary, and Scott F. Johnson. *Miracle Tales from Byzantium*. Cambridge, MA: Harvard University Press, 2012.

The Acts of Paul

Chapter 5: Myra

Primary sources: P.Heid 28-35/38-49. Secondary sources: *Cena Cypriani*, Nicetas of Paphlygonia 84.

This chapter offers good evidence for the existence of a unified *APl*, i.e., a text that embedded the material about Thecla within the story of Paul. Evidence from fifth-century Italy (*Cena Cypriani*), sixth-century Egypt (P.Heid.), and tenth-century Byzantium (Nicetas) testifies to this sequence. About two-thirds of the chapter survives, including both the beginning and the final words. The author established a link with the previous section. In 4.15, he resumed the theme of Thecla's quest for Paul: "She heard that he was in Myra, where she found him proclaiming the word of God." Chapter 5 opens with similar words. It is characteristic of the author to neglect even the vaguest transitions, such as "meanwhile, Paul was teaching...," let alone, "After Thecla had departed with his blessing, Paul..." At 4.15 Paul's base seems to be in the house of Hermias. That name does not reappear. The Coptic superscript (below) states that Paul had "left" Antioch. That is a necessary assumption, but the text of chap. 4 does not state that Paul left. He simply vanished from the narrative. Presuming that this chapter does not contain local tradition, one may ask why Myra was selected. One possibility is to fill in a blank, since Acts 27:4 reports a stop there, and Paul did visit Myra at 21:5, according to the D-Text. The latter would supply a more probable motivation, as the author may well have known a form of the D-Text.

The setting is like that of chaps. 2 and 3. In contrast to the story of Thecla, which reported no healing miracles, this chapter contains three. The focus is upon a family, here the household of Hermocrates and Nympha, who have two sons, Dion and Hermippus. The canonical Acts does not speak of conflict within families (despite Luke 12:49–53). The *APl* and other ApocActs assign such conflict a central place. This may be a dim reflection of Christian history where divided families (a problem already noted in 1 Cor 7:12–16; 1 Pet 3:1–6, e.g.) became a source of tension and a cause of criminal procedures. For comparison, see the story of the Roman woman in Justin Martyr's *Second Apology*, as it is called.

Greed rather than sex generated the conflict at Myra. Paul's healing of Hermocrates grieved his older son, Hermippus, who was looking forward to his inheritance. This is a nice inversion of the plot of chap. 3: here the parents convert and a son is hostile. For balance, the other son, Dion, is receptive to Paul. Hermippus brings about, evidently through poison, Dion's death. He was presently revived, but his death evidently motivated Hermippus to organize a mob to attack Paul. This generates a parallel to the assault

Translation, Commentary, and Notes : Chapter

by Thamyris (3.15) and the Passion of Jesus. In the course of this attack Hermippus is immediately struck blind and becomes a penitent. The rest of the chapter is devoted to his ultimate recovery and acceptance into his household and the household of faith.

5.1 Hermippus Healed

When He Had Left Antioch and Was Teaching in Myra

(p. 38) 1. While Paul [*was proclaiming*] the word of God at Myra, a man named Hermocrates, who suffered from edema, stood in the presence of all and said to Paul: "Nothing is impossible for God, especially for the god whom you proclaim. Ever since the arrival of the one whom you serve, many have been healed. Now we cast ourselves at your feet, I, my wife, and my children. (p. 39) [*Have mercy on me*] so that I also may believe, as you have come to believe, in the living God."

[*Paul*] said to him, "I shall give you [...] without charge, but [*by the name*] of Jesus the Messiah you will be [*healed in*] the presence of all these persons." [...] As he pressed his hand downward [...], a huge amount of water gushed [*out of him* ...], he collapsed like [...] so that some said, "It would have been better for him to have died rather than suffer so." But when Paul had quieted the crowd, he [*took*] Hermocrates by the hand, lifted him, and asked, "Hermocrates, [*what*] do you want?"

"I want to eat."

Paul took some bread and gave it to him to eat. Hermocrates was healed at that moment. Together with his wife he received the grace of the seal in the Lord.

Comments

With an absolute minimum of setting, not unlike some gospel stories, Paul heals Hermocrates of dropsy. Hermocrates' comment aptly notes that many healings had taken place, making this act an example of the apostle's ministry rather than a singular event. This has features of a typical healing: the patient, with symptoms identified, in the presence of a crowd, petitions Paul for relief and demonstrates his faith. Healing is accomplished both through the use of a formula and by touch. A demonstration proves the efficacy of the healing. The abundance of liquid indicates the gravity of the malady. No acclamation is recorded. On the form of healing stories, see Bultmann, *History*, 209–15; and Theissen, *Miracle Stories*, 90–94.

This is a novella, which may be understood as a developed and circumstantial account of an event. Of the NT healings, Mark 10:14–27 is the most comparable. Hermocrates makes a short speech. The instant and copious discharge of liquid (through his anus) causes him to faint. His apparent discomfort generates hostility from the crowd rather than praise. Unperturbed, Paul waited for the crowd to settle down, then raised the patient (a symbol of healing and resurrection; cf. Mark 1:31), and enquires into his desires. The wish to eat was a proof not only that Hermocrates lived (cf. Mark 5:43) but that his symptoms had been relieved. The climax is the baptism of husband and wife, but not of the children.

Hermocrates' speech begins with flattery, not of Paul (this tactic is called *captatio benevolentiae*, a bid for approval), but of Paul's god. The presence of his family indicates the number of his dependents. He pleads for mercy and claims that healing will bring him to faith. By this means the narrator distinguishes between faith in the god's power and that belief that will lead him into the community of Christ.

Paul's initial response seems gratuitous, as Hermocrates has not offered money. Its evident purpose is to affirm that grace is free. Cf. Acts 3:6; 8:20. The healing, like baptism, is accomplished by invoking the name of Jesus. That is normal in the ApocActs. See Achtemeier, "Miracle Workers," 170. The recovery appears to have begun gradually, turning the crowd against Paul. This is a test of his faith, and he meets it well. The account reports the parents' baptisms. The reason for excluding one of the children will emerge in the next episode.

Notes

Edema. This is a non-technical term for the accumulation of water in the body. Causes are varied. "Dropsy" is an older English term for the condition.

Gushed. Cf. *Cena Cypriani* 20.12b: *Ventrem aperuit Hermocrates*. (Hermocrates opened his stomach); and 26.16: *Effudit Hermocrates* (Hermocrates poured).

Seal. The author returns to his preferred terminology. See chap. 3.

Impossible. Ancients regarded a number of actions as impossible, for example: the moon could not descend to earth. These notions were more common sense than science. Miracle workers and magicians took exception to these restrictions. Those objections stimulated the development of the view that God could make exceptions to the "laws of nature." See Grant, *Miracle*, 127–34. Mention of this principle often amounts to a signal that a miracle is about to occur. For the principle, see Philo, *Spec. leg.* 1.282; *Moses* 1.174; *Migr. Abr.* 112; Mark 10:27; Luke 1:37; *1 Clem* 27:2; Ps.-Lucian, *Halcyon* 3.

Living God. See p. 173. The expression appears about ten times in *APl.*

5.2–3 The Wrath of Hermippus

2. His son Hermippus, however, was angry with Paul and was alert for the opportunity to spring into action with his peers (p. 40) to do away with Paul. He had not wanted his father to be restored, but to die so that he could quickly get control of his estate. The younger son, Dion, on the other hand, heard Paul gladly.

So those allied with Dion's brother plotted to [*start a fight*] with Paul, with the intention that [*Hermippus*] [...] and try to kill him. He fell and ... Hermippus gave Dion to drink [...] Hermocrates [*loved*] Dion more. [He was] seated at Paul's feet [...] unaware that Dion was dead.

3. At the death of Dion his mother Nympha tore her dress and went to Paul. She took a place next to her husband and Paul. Concerned at her arrival, Paul said, "What is it, Nympha?"

"Dion is dead." The whole crowd wept at the sight of her. Paul looked at the distraught crowd and dispatched some youths, with these words: "Go and bring him here to me." They set out, but Hermippus [seized] the body en route and shouted, "[...]

(A leaf is missing, with two pages of text. Paul revived the dead Dion.)

The Acts of Paul

Comments

§2–3 set out the conflict. Hermippus is the older son, but Hermocrates is more fond of the younger child, Dion. This did not endear him to Hermippus, who had frankly hoped that his father would soon die, making him head of the household. Paul had thwarted that prospect. To make matters worse, Dion is fond of Paul's message. Hermippus, with his friends and peers, is plotting to kill Paul. Unlike other rivals, he does not seek official action. While awaiting his opportunity Hermippus evidently eliminated his brother, probably by poisoning him. The story of Dion's death and resuscitation is an internal parallel with the story of Patroclus in chap. 14. See the Note.

This news reached his mother, Nympha, first, as her husband was engaged in listening to Paul. She went to the apostle, who sensed that something was wrong. Upon learning of the problem he sent some youths to fetch the corpse. See (ironically?) Acts 5:1–11. Both the dramatic and the literary audiences know what to expect: the corpse will be brought in and revived by Paul. Hermippus must have been aware of resurrections, for, presumably with his thugs, he kidnapped the dead body. At this alarming moment, the text has a gap. A complication of this nature is not typical of the ApocActs, both with regard to the missing text and the missing corpse.

From the subsequent story one may gather that, some means or another, the body was recovered and Dion revived. Resurrections are the prevalent type of healing story in the ApocActs. This is less because of their sensational character, important as that is, than because revivals of the dead symbolize rebirth to new life in Christ. See Pervo, "Johannine Trajectories."

Notes

Peers. One might imagine these to comprise his buddies from the gymnasium.

Gladly. See the Note on 3.20.

But God. The French translation closes the quotation with "body" (Rordorf, 1144). This may be a typo. In any case it is better to view the quotation as continuing. (So Schmidt, Acta, 54.) The form is more coherent: a warning followed by a promise.

Dion. The parallel with Patroclus (and Acts 20:7–12) is even closer if one follows the restoration of Schmidt, who renders: "*Dion fell and died*" (54, translating the German, with restorations italicized.). Without an attempt at restoration it is not clear who fell. It is possible that Dion fell and injured himself and was given the *coup de grâce* by Hermippus.

5.4 Paul's Arrest and Miraculous Vindication. The Punishment of Hermippus.

4. (p. 43) [...] he [...] the word to [him].

Now a messenger of the Lord had said to him that night, "Paul, [...] this day there will be a great assault against your body, but God, [the father of] his son Jesus, the Messiah, [...]" When Paul awoke he went to the believers, but remained downstairs (?) while asking, "What is this [*vision*]?" While he was so occupied he saw Hermippus approaching with a sword in his hand, accompanied by young men armed with clubs. Paul [*said to them*] "I am [*not*]a robber; no murderer am I. The God of the universe, [the father] of Christ, will turn aside your arms, put your sword back in its sheath, and transform your strength into weakness. For I am a slave of God, alone and a stranger, small and meaningless among the polytheists. But you, O God, look down upon their plots and do not let them annihilate me."

(p. 44) [...] Hermippus [...] his sword [...] upon Paul [...] [but] he became [*blind*], and [*cried out*] "[ ] [*my*] friends do not forget [...] Hermippus! I have [*pursued*] Paul; I have persecuted [*innocent*] blood. Learn, you people, whether you are dull or perceptive: the world is nothing. Money is nothing. All possessions are nothing. I once overindulged myself with all manner of goods; now I am a beggar. I implore all of you: Hear me out, my friends and all residents of Myra. I mocked a man [*who has*] [*healed*] my father, I have [*reviled*] [...] a man who revived my brother [...] a man who did me no injury. But, ask him! The one who saved my father and revived my [*brother*] will have the power to save me also." Paul stood weeping, mindful of God, since God had heard him so quickly, mindful also of the people, because pride had been corrected. He turned and went (p. 45) [*to Hermocrates' house?*]

The Acts of Paul

Comments

As §4 opens, following the gap, Paul was evidently sharing the message with someone, or possibly speaking of his coming suffering. The narrator then shifts to report a nocturnal revelation to Paul. An angel delivered a warning, evidently coupled with a promise of protection. The revelation resembles those in Acts 18:9–10; 23:11; 27:23–24. It is an Oracle of Assurance. See Aune, *Prophecy*, 266–68. The sequel appears to borrow from Acts 10:17–18. Paul seeks the wisdom of fellow believers to interpret the oracle, although its meaning does not seem obscure. The author wishes to stress the process. Even the great apostle reflected with others about the significance of a revelation. Their ruminations were interrupted by the attack of Hermippus and his merry men. Once again (see chap. 3) Paul shares the fate of Jesus. The description of his attackers comes from Mark 14:43; "robber" evokes Mark 14:48. His command to Hermippus to sheath his sword is reminiscent of Matt 26:52 and even more evocative of John 18:11.

Because this is a criminal assault, it cannot lead to a trial at which Paul will take a brave stance and deliver a bold speech. It does, however, offer the opportunity for miraculous vindication. In his subsequent address Paul denied that he was a criminal and stated that the ruler of heaven, a title evidently selected for its intelligibility to non-believers, quickly glossed (originally?) with a statement about Christ, would thwart their aspirations. Reminding God, as is customary, of his lack of protection, he appeals for divine assistance.

That he will receive. Apparently undeterred by Paul's prediction, Hermippus pressed his attack, with what may safely be called crippling results. Blinding was the most common type of punitive miracle. See Pervo, *Acts*, 242n73. Blindness possesses obvious but powerful symbolic value. Conversion can be described as illumination, the passage from darkness to light, or the gift of sight to the spiritually blind. Unstated in the extant text but essential to understanding is that Hermippus is fully alienated from his family. Otherwise he would presumably have turned to them for assistance.

Blind Hermippus made a full and frank confession of his errors. His actions remind one of Paul's in Acts 9. The speech has some elements of the diatribe and resembles philosophic rejections of wealth. This criticism of worldly goods, a frequent theme in *APl*, is bracketed by two statements about his persecution of Paul, the first general, the second specific. Hermippus has fallen from the top of the ladder of status and consumption to the bottom; he is now a beggar. Blind beggars are known from the gospels (e.g., Mark 8:22; 10:46). Few other occupations were left open to them. In his desire to gain controls of his family's possessions Hermippus has lost everything. From his catalogue of Paul's mighty works he is able to draw one conclusion. Paul can save him also.

He is right, but that healing will not take place immediately. Paul wept tears of uncertain meaning, grateful not only that God had acted so promptly in his behalf, but also because the entire affair had provided a good moral lesson, instruction that will benefit from time in which to season. Even the blinded Saul was given time to reflect upon his sins (Acts 9).

Notes

Slave of God. See 4.1; 4.6; 4.12; 4.13; (of Thecla); 9.27; 12.3; 12.5 (of Paul, once "slave of Christ").

House. From the close of §4 it appears that Paul had left the house to confront Hermippus.

5.5–6. The Family Is Restored and the Mission Concludes.

5. [...] And the sons [...] feet. They carried Hermippus [...] to the place where Paul [...] They left him at the door of [...] the house. When they were [...], a large crowd was proceeding [...], another [crowd] to see the blinded [Hermippus]. For his part he would entreat everyone who entered to intercede for him. Now [when those who entered saw Hermocrates and] Nympha rejoicing [at] the revival of Dion and bringing in food for his wellbeing and money for the widows, they saw their son Hermippus, looking like the second [...] He touched the feet of all, including those of his parents, and implored them, like a stranger, for healing. His parents were astonished by this and lamented to all who entered. [Some of the latter], however, asked, "Why are they weeping?" [...]

Hermocrates (p. 46) set out [and] blessed the goods; he then took them and distributed them. Thereafter [...] Hermocrates was upset [...], primarily because they had eaten their fill, "[...] and so let's leave the [food] [...], and let us attend to [...] Hermocrates [...] Nympha [...] much [...] upset [...] he has [...] because [...] Hermocrates [...] to the [...] so that [...] Hermippus may

The Acts of Paul

see and stop [...] and fighting against Christ and [...] But they, with Paul, have [sinned] against God. "

Once he had regained his sight Hermippus turned to his mother and said, "Paul came and laid a hand on my hand while I was weeping. From that moment I could see everything clearly." Nympha took him by the hand and led him inside into the presence of the widows and of Paul. As Paul wept bitterly, Hermippus [...] said, "Whoever [believes] ... "

6. (p. 49) [...] a word [...] in the manner [...] [for the church], in [the peace of God] Amen. [Paul, together with] the believers who [were with him in] Myra, left for [Sidon].

Comments

The text of §5 suffers gaps. The course of the narrative is clear. Some persons carried Hermippus to the house where Paul was conducting his mission and left him at the door. Two crowds appear, one to see the vanquished Hermippus, the other to assemble with the believers. In this segment the community at Myra is shown to be much larger than a single family unit. Among the faithful is a number of widows who can be described as a body. For widows in *APl*, see 9.7. Literature includes Thurston, *Widows*; and Price, *Widow Traditions*. An *agapē* is in process, a nourishing meal with some religious ceremony. See the directions for observing an *agapē* in Apostolic Tradition 29c (Bradshaw, Johnson, and Philips, eds., *Apostolic Tradition*, 156–60). Note also instructions for a widows' supper, *Apostolic Tradition* 30a. Hermippus' behavior is that of a classic penitent in the description of Tertullian, who says that the penitential state

> requires ... that you sigh and weep and groan day and night to the Lord your God, that you prostrate yourself at the feet of the priests and kneel before the beloved of God, making all the believers commissioned ambassadors of your prayer for pardon. (Tertullian, *On Penitence* 9.4; trans. Le Saint, 32)

See the note on *Penance*. The setting is thus exemplary: the faithful are taking care of the needy while the sinner does public penance. Hermocrates and Nympha, possibly the hosts, are celebrating the revival of their son Dion and receiving contributions of food and money from the faithful. Hermocrates presides over this action, taking, blessing, and distributing the gifts.

The narrator ignores the crowds other than those gathering for worship. Hermippus begs all to intercede in his behalf, including his parents. Their reaction is not easily understood. Grief for the condition of the older son is quite intelligible. They take no action (such as pleading with Paul) to help him. Evidently they regarded his sins as unforgiveable. The ensuing events are very difficult to grasp. Hermocrates was quite upset, perhaps lamenting that people were eating while Hermippus suffered. Nympha also became upset. Schmidt's reconstruction of this material (57–58) is more intelligible than that of Cherix (Rordorf 1145), but not more probable. Hermocrates' statement continues to view Hermippus as an enemy of God (*theomachos*), like the Saul (Paul) of Acts prior to his "conversion" in Acts 9.

Meanwhile—not enough of the text is missing to allow for it to have contained a detailed report—Paul has visited and healed Hermippus in a manner like Ananias' restoration of Paul's sight (Acts 9:17). His mother went out to visit him and learned this. She then took him inside where Paul and the widows were assembled. Nothing is said of Hermocrates. Paul's weeping makes no sense. One solution is to regard Paul's visit as taking place in a vision. Cf. Acts 9:12; and Klauck, *Apocryphal Acts*, 46. If, to add further speculation, his sight was destroyed by Christ who appeared with some traits of the apostle, the result would be a fine parallel with 3.21. This is the view of James, *Apocryphal New Testament*, 283n1. The text provides limited warrant for such interpretation, but it may have been explained in the missing material. Hermippus responds by making what appears to be a general promise, to the effect of "Whoever believes in me will have eternal life."

Two pages are missing. Paul's work with the family of Hermocrates has provided a wide range of wonders: healing of a dread illness, restoration of life to one killed, and the return of sight to a person punished by blinding. Much of the residue, following reconciliation of Hermippus with the family, his baptism (probably), and, possibly, further explanation of his healing, was probably given over to a farewell address by Paul.

Notes

Sons. The Coptic word *shēre* can mean young persons (e.g., for *neaniskoi*; Crum, 584). Schmidt renders it thus (56). One might then propose that the youths sent to retrieve the body of Dion had guided blind Hermippus' feet.

Second. Schmidt proposed "second suffering," with the Greek loan word *pathos*, but this is both obscure in meaning and unlikely (57, 24*).

The Acts of Paul

Penance. See also 10.5; Tertullian, *On Purity* 3.5; 13.7; Vouaux's note, 242n2; and Le Saint's introduction, 3–13.

With the believers. This reconstruction prepares for the list of fellow travelers at the beginning of chap. 6. It cannot be taken to mean all of Paul's converts at Myra. Schmidt's reconstruction (58, 25*) differs somewhat from that followed here.

Bibliography

Achtemeier, Paul J. "Jesus and the Disciples as Miracle Workers in the Apocryphal New Testament." In *Aspects of Religious Propaganda*, edited by Elisabeth Schüssler Fiorenza, 149–86. South Bend, IN: University of Notre Dame Press, 1976.

Aune, David E. *Prophecy in Early Christianity*. Grand Rapids: Eerdmans, 1983.

Bradshaw, Paul F., Maxwell E. Johnson, L. Edward Phillips. *The Apostolic Tradition*. Hermeneia. Minneapolis: Fortress, 2002.

Bultmann, Rudolf. *The History of the Synoptic Tradition*. Trans. John Marsh. Rev. ed. New York: Harper & Row, 1968.

Grant, Robert M. *Miracle and Natural Law in Graeco-Roman and Early Christian Thought*. Amsterdam: North-Holland, 1952.

Le Saint, William P. *Tertullian: Treatises on Penance*. Westminster, MD: Newman, 1959.

Pervo, Richard I. "Johannine Trajectories in the *Acts of John*." *Apocrypha* 3 (1992) 47–68.

Price, Robert M. *The Widow Traditions in Luke-Acts: A Feminist-Critical Scrutiny*. SBLDS 155. Atlanta: Scholars, 1997.

Theissen, Gerd. *The Miracle Stories of the Early Christian Tradition*. Translated by Francis McDonagh. Philadelphia: Fortress, 1983.

Thurston, Bonnie Bowman. *The Widows: A Women's Ministry in the Early Church*. Minneapolis: Fortress, 1989.

Chapter 6: Sidon (?)

Primary source: P.Heid; pp. 35–39/49–61; secondary sources: Ephrem Syrus (probably), the *Acts of Titus* (see the note), and possibly the *Acts of Barnabas*. (See the note on the latter.)

Rigsby ("Missing Places") has proposed that the original setting of this story was Side, in Pamphylia, where Apollo was a major deity, unlike the situation in Sidon. This is logical, but it would have belonged to an independent story, since the subsequent destination is Tyre, which is close to Sidon, and this destination is reached by ship. Local or localized traditions and legends are in theory normally possible; this story is so complex that it is almost certainly literary, i.e., written rather than the summary of an oral legend. Sidon was an ancient Phoenician city routinely paired with Tyre in the prophetic tradition (e.g., Luke 10:14).

The itinerary is, in any case, quite difficult. The most reasonable means for journeying from Myra to Sidon is by water, but the text gives no suggestion of a voyage, as food is taken beneath a tree. On the other hand, it could be argued that the apostle contemplates leaving (Cilicia and) Pamphylia, making a more distant destination feasible. Paul has an entourage consisting of two couples from Perga (where, according to Acts 14:25, he had preached). How and when they joined his company is not clarified. In any case they seem to have bankrolled his travels, like the women in Luke 8:1–3 who supported Jesus. This is quite certainly Paul's first missionary visit to the city, which lacks a Christian community, although it has had believers. The focus of this poorly preserved chapter is the conflict with polytheist religion. The major inspiration appears to come from Acts 16, the mission to Philippi.

In §1–3 a debate about the new religion develops, motivated by the group's lunching in the vicinity of a sacred spot. This soon becomes public. Paul warns against the possible consequences of mistreatment. The result is that the three men are cast into the Temple of Apollo (§5) and richly fed. As a result of Paul's prayer much of the temple, including the god's statue, collapsed, leading to a trial in the theater. The ending is unknown, but successful, as Paul boards a ship for Tyre.

The Acts of Paul

Chapter 6: Sidon

After leaving Myra, [Paul Goes to Sidon]

1. [Paul], after[leaving Myra] went to[Sidon]. Great distress beset the believers in [Cilicia] and Pamphylia, because they longed for his message and his holy Christ-given grace. Some couples from Perga [followed] Paul: Thrasymmachus and Aline, as well as Cleon and Chrysa. In the course of the journey they fed Paul. While they were sharing bread [beneath] a tree, as they were about to say "amen," there came (p. 50) [...] the believers [...] to partake of it, were [...] on them [...] images [...] [eternal] become [...] [the] table of demons [...] for that reason s/he dies. [But whoever] [...] believes in Jesus Christ[the one who has cleansed us from] all stains, [from] all impurities[and from] all wicked [thoughts] shall eat[of it] [...] they have approached [the table] in an impure state [...] images [...] stand upright [...] tutelary [images].

2. An elderly man [...] stood up among them and [said] to them "Men, [wait] a little while to see what happens to the priest who approaches our god. Now when our fellow citizen Charinos had listened to this and attacked the gods, he died, along with his [...]. Thereafter Xanthos also died, as did Chrysa and [...] died of dropsy, [with] his wife

3. [...] (p. 55) like a stranger [...]

4. [unknown speaker] "Why do you presume to undertake actions that are unacceptable? Have you—yes, you—really not heard what happened when God wrought [judgment] upon Sodom and Gomorra, because [they had] seized [others], including (?) strangers and women [...] God [had no pity on them], but cast them down into the underworld. Now, however, we are not people of the [sort] that you say or think; we are proclaimers of the living God and his [well-beloved.] [And] never be able to [accomplish] evil. For this matter, [...] those who bear witness for [him] ... "

5. They did not listen to him, but they [were seized] and cast into the [temple of] Apollo to be secured until [...], so that the [whole] city might gather. They were given large amounts of expensive food, but Paul, fasting for the third day, was exhausted after

Translation, Commentary, and Notes : Chapter

preaching all night. Falling prostrate, he prayed, "God, take note of their threats, do not let us stumble and permit not our enemies to lay us low *(p. 56)*, but deliver us and bring down your justice quickly upon us." Just after Paul, with the believers Thrasymmachus and Cleon, had thrown himself to the ground, the temple collapsed. He [...] so that the guards [*informed*] the magistrates, who were [...] some others among them in [...] fell on the ground [...] fell to the ground [...] turned [...] in the midst of the two [parts] [...]. They [*entered*] [*to see what had*] happened [*and*] marveled [that] [...] in their [...] and that they [...][were] rejoicing [at the collapse] [...]. They cried out: "Truly the [...] people of a mighty god!" They left and proclaimed throughout the city: "Apollo, the god of the Sidonians, has fallen, together with half of his temple." All the residents dashed toward the temple and saw Paul and his colleagues weeping at this trial, which would make them a spectacle for all. The mob shouted, "Bring them to the theater." The magistrates came to fetch them. And they groaned bitterly in their hearts. [...]

6. *(p. 61)* [...] from my hand. Remember [...] Do not ask [...] They cannot do such things [...] The behavior of Christ [...] not in faith [...] and that you [...] as for you [...] long-suffering [...] of the Egyptians [...] of the hail [...] the crowd [...] followed Paul [saying] "Blessed be the god [...] who has sent Paul [...] so that we are not [...] [of] death." Theudes [...] begged Paul [...] he grasped his feet [...] for the seal in the lord. [...] *[He]* commanded them to go to Tyre. [...], Before they [...] [*They*] put Paul [*aboard a ship*] with [*them*].

Comment

Paul's entourage resembles that of John in the *Acts of John* 59. These two (presumably celibate) married couples have evidently liquidated their property and become itinerants. It is not clear whether one or both couples remain in Sidon or continue to travel with him. §1 seems to address the need for being in a worthy state to receive communion, or, conversely, that food sacrificed to idols cannot harm the pure and true believer. The latter seems less likely. The underlying theological basis is 1 Cor 8:1–10:21 ("table of

199

The Acts of Paul

demons" is cited) and 11:30 ("For this reason many of you are weak and ill, and some have died") plays a prominent role. The blessing before their meal was interrupted by a person (apparently) who may have noted, perhaps with hostility, that the site was sacred. A roadside altar, grove, or shrine seems to have been overlooked or ignored by the Christians. The subsequent speech (presumably by Paul), evidently in a public, judicial setting, focused upon the danger of contamination by polytheism. This represents the view of "the weak" in 1 Corinthians 8–10 rather than that of Paul, who regarded these fears mainly as superstitions that should only be honored to avoid giving offense. This passage indicates how thoroughly the historical Paul had lost that argument. Followers of Christ did not eat food that had been sacrificed to idols. See Pervo, *Acts*, 376–78.

A ceremony appears to be in the offing, possibly a contest between the followers of Paul's god and those of the civic god (Apollo). A senior citizen who did not need to read 1 Cor 11:30 and who appears to be following the time-honored path of Gamaliel (Acts 5) urged delay. The story would be more intelligible if the "priest who approaches our god" is Paul, but that is quite uncertain. The speaker recites a catalogue of those who had been mortally punished for hostility to the gods grounded upon the Christian message. The outcome of this is unknown, but it did not end the dispute, for, after a gap of two pages, Paul is attacking the civic leaders for their action. That action would appear to be kidnapping. Paul, Thrasymmachus, and Cleon have been taken captive as slaves, victims, or offerings to Apollo. (The Greeks were not as innocent of human sacrifice as we might wish. See Cook, *Zeus*, 3/2:1279, under "human sacrifice.") The reference to Sodom and Gomorra (see Note) raises the suspicion of sexual misconduct, but the major issue in Genesis 19 is the treatment of strangers.

Paul and co. were not viewed as strangers deserving fine hospitality, but as miscreants of some sort, perhaps magicians who had brought about the deaths of their clients. Paul, it will transpire, had been engaged in preaching all night. Objections notwithstanding, the three were secured as prisoners to await the proper occasion, perhaps a festival of the god, which need not be later than the subsequent day. The situation is reminiscent of the *Acts of Andrew and Matthias among the Cannibals*, in which strangers were seized, blinded, and fattened up for the table, but the parallel is misleading. The rich food offered is probably the condemned person's last meal. See *Perpetua* 17.

The adventure fits generally into the category of "Liberation Miracles" (on which, see Weaver, *Plots*; and Pervo, *Acts*, 409–15), in particular that of Acts 16:25–39, in which Paul does not take the opportunity to flee. As in Acts 16:25 Paul is praying. Here the contents are specific: five petitions arranged in chiastic (A B C B A) fashion, the first of which appears inspired by

Translation, Commentary, and Notes : Chapter

Acts 4:29 (where an earthquake follows the prayer), while the central command, "permit not our enemies to lay us low" (C) conveys a delicious irony, as Apollo is about to be laid low. The trio does not seem to be manacled. Prostrating themselves for prayer was both pious and prudent, as the temple immediately collapsed.

Czachesz ("Acts of Paul") notes the intersection of the D-Text, Ephrem Syrus' commentary on Acts, and this portion of the *APl*. His proposal that Ephrem made use of the *APl* and/or an earlier form of the D-Text is quite interesting. At the least the data make it quite probable that the *APl* knew the D-Text form of Acts 16. See the note on the D-Text. His data are of minimal use in reconstructing the text of *APl*.

Earthquakes were not rare in Asia Minor. Everyone knew that gods caused them (Cook, *Zeus* 3.2.1274, under "Earthquakes"; and, in the biblical world, *DBI* 224–25). An important question could be which god or gods had caused the quake and why. We look for fault lines; ancients look for gods. The evidence here is difficult to refute. Half of the temple collapsed, including the statue of the god, whereas the part occupied by Paul and his companions was not destroyed. Comparison with Sodom and Gomorra is apt, for a substantial number of the citizens remained unmoved.

Gaps make the immediate aftermath unclear. Some persons, possibly the magistrates, more likely their agents, entered to inspect the damage. Some persons were rejoicing. These were not the prisoners, who are described as weeping within a few lines. The celebrants may have represented a civic faction that supported the Christians, if for no other reason than that their municipal rivals opposed them. Cf. Acts 14:1–5. These persons acclaim the power of the believers and rush out to spread the news of Apollo's downfall.

The mob, which was the ruling force in Sidon, was not about to be confused by the facts (strictly speaking, by an interpretation of facts). They demanded that the condemned be brought to the theater. Paul and his colleagues were not going to be asked to stage a scene from Euripides. Does this mean that the narrator envisioned a change of venue for the ceremony, since the temple was no longer in service, or had the theater been their eventual destination all along? If so, why had they been held in the temple of Apollo? Or were they there only for the sacred banquet? It is not clear that these questions could be answered if the text had survived in full, as the narrator is not, by the criteria of demanding readers, particularly conscientious. What is clear is that the collapse of Apollo's sanctuary, thrilling as it was, did not bring relief to the detainees.

The absence of relief is quite apparent: the three are weeping at this trial (*peirasmos*, a term used for eschatological and other "temptations"). The

The Acts of Paul

author ventured a pun, preserved in Coptic's use of Greek loan words. The crowd is eager to get the victims to the theater (*theatron*), a suitable place for executions, as seen in chaps. 3–4 and will be seen again in Ephesus (chap. 9). By metonymy (here substitution of effect for cause) the term was used, as it still is, for what took place in theaters, a spectacle. 1 Cor 4:9 is probably in mind. For the philosophical use of the concept, see Conzelmann, *First Corinthians*, 88). The apostle thinks: "We get to star in this terrible show," and the crowd shouts: "Off to the show." The magistrates (*stratēgoi*) cooperate, perhaps without enthusiasm.

At this point a large gap intervenes. The one certainty is the single issue about which no attentive reader who knew how many chapters remained could have any doubt: Paul was vindicated. When the text resumes, he is addressing a large audience. He may be explaining that Christians do not seek or take vengeance. The reference to hail could refer to the means by which Paul was delivered. In its favor is its occurrence at two other points of the narrative (3.22: Thecla; 9.25: Paul). Against this reconstruction is its occurrence in two other places. Twice is a parallel; three times begins to look like a cliché. Another possibility is that the hail was a reference to the seventh plague against Egypt (Exod 9:13–35).

Whatever the almost certainly miraculous means the ever fickle crowd has gone over to support of Paul and begun to chant his praise, possibly because he has delivered them from immediate death or because his message has ended the fear of death. One fresh adherent, Theudes (or Theudas) begged, like Thecla (3.25), for baptism. Paul does not assent to this request. (For humans, at least, baptism is not administered suddenly.) He rather directs an uncertain group to go to Tyre, for which place he also embarks.

Notes

Acts of Titus. At the end of sec. 3 the text reads: "He healed Aphphia, the wife of Chrysippus, who had been possessed by a demon. After a fast of seven days he cast down the idol of Apollo. Then he went to Jerusalem and in turn ["*or again*"] to Caesarea." (The name "Aphphia" is variously spelled.) By accident or otherwise, this text inverts the order of Sidon and Tyre (chaps. 6 and 7), neither city being named. The current text does not speak of a seven days' fast. This may be an exaggeration.

The *Acts of Barnabas* (on which, see Pervo, *Making*, 169–71) reports in section 19 that, after the apostle rebuked *something* because of an athletic competition featuring naked men and women in a race (At Sparta and in some other locations girls and women might race naked, as men always did, but not in mixed settings), there was a fateful collapse (of something), causing the survivors to flee to the temple of Apollo. Shortly thereafter Barnabas and Co. find themselves under a tree. The author may have used *APl* 6, but this incident provides no help in its reconstruction.

Pamphylia. According to the far from trustworthy *Life of Polycarp* 2, Paul encountered at Smyrna a disciple of his named Strataeas, whom he had converted in Pamphylia, a brother, according to the author of Timothy. See the introduction, p. 51, and the comments on chap. 8.

Matter. This may be a reference to the Christian "way," or to the charge laid against them, or to something else.

Sodom and Gomorra. Cf. Rom 9:29; *Ascension of Isaiah* 3.10; 5 Ezra 2.8; the *Apocalypse of Paul* 39. The two cities serve as a symbol for those who oppose God's intentions and of the consequent judgment. See "Sodom and Gomorrah," *DBI*, 802–4.

The D-Text/Ephrem and Acts. Czachesz ("Acts of Paul," 112) notes that, in describing the separation of Paul and Barnabas Ephrem refers to the separation of Abraham and Lot, with the latter going to teach among the people of Sodom (*Commentary*, p. 428). *APl* 6 may have put the theme in his mind. The text of Acts 16:35–36, with D-Text in bold reads: "The next morning the chief magistrates **assembled together in the city center. Reflecting upon the earthquake that had occurred, they were filled with awe, and** . . . sent their police escort with the message, 'Let those people **of whom you took custody yesterday** go.' 36 The jailer *went in* and gave Paul the word: 'The chief magistrates have sent orders . . .'" (cited from Pervo, *Acts*, 398). Ephrem reads: "The astaritae the optimates of the city were appalled and terrified by the earthquake, and learning the truth knew that this earthquake was actually because of them, but they would not admit it. They sent secretly to liberate them [*Paul and Silas*]" (*Commentary*, 430). As in the *APl* these two witnesses (who may be two witnesses of a single tradition) wish to stress the public character of the calamity, whereas the conventional text of Acts treats it as a private matter between Paul and the jailer.

Stratēgoi. In Acts 16 this term (lit., "general"), used twice in this chapter and not otherwise in *APl*, occurs four times for the *duoviri*, chief magistrates of the Roman colony of Philippi.

Bibliography

Conzelmann, Hans. *First Corinthians.* Trans. J. W. Leitch. Hermeneia. Philadelphia: Fortress, 1975.

Cook, Arthur B. *Zeus. A Study in Ancient Religion.* Vol. 3. Cambridge: Cambridge University Press, 1940.

Czachesz, István. "The Acts of Paul and the Western Text of Luke's Acts: Paul between Canon and Apocrypha." In *The Apocryphal Acts of Paul and Thecla,* edited by Jan N. Bremmer, 107–25. Kampen: Kok Pharos, 1996.

Ephrem Syrus. *Commentary on Acts.* Quoted in *The Beginnings of Christianity,* edited by Frederick J. Foakes Jackson, and Kirsopp Lake, 3:373–453. New York: Macmillan, 1920–1933.

Pervo, Richard I. "The 'Acts of Titus': A Preliminary Translation with an Introduction, Notes, and Appendices." In SBLSP 35:455–82. Atlanta: Scholars, 1996.

Rigsby, Kent J. "Missing Places." *Classical Philology* 91 (1996) 254–60.

Weaver, John B. *Plots of Epiphany: Prison Escape in Acts of the Apostles.* BZNW 131. Berlin: de Gruyter, 2004.

Translation, Commentary, and Notes : Chapter

Chapter 7: Tyre

Primary source: P. Heid, p. 40/62; secondary: The *Acts of Titus* 3.

Tyre is about forty kilometers south of Sidon, with which it is often paired in the biblical tradition. The itinerary, for once, presents no puzzles. The narrator has Paul traveling south. This chapter is almost too fragmentary to present puzzles. Tyre (and Sidon) had followers of Jesus from an early period, judging from Mark 3:8; 7:24, 31. This section may be inspired by Paul's journey in Acts 15 (cf. 15:3), as Jerusalem seems to be the goal, but the journey described in Acts 18:22–23; 19:1 is another possibility. Sidon featured polytheist opponents. In Tyre Jews engage Paul, but the extant material reports no conflict. Paul's gifts duly impress the crowd, which assigns the credit to God. The extant material consists of a spectacular exorcism and a healing (prospectively).

After leaving Sidon, Paul resolved to set out for Tyre

7.1 Arrival and Exorcism.

1. *(p. 62)* Following [the arrival] of Paul [at Tyre, a] crowd of Jews [approached] him. The latter [...] and they heard the [...] The [...] were astonished [...] that Amphion [...] [saying] "Chrysippus [...] demons with [*him*] [...] numerous [wonders] [...]" As Paul [...], saying, [...] God. And no one [...] with Amphion. They have [...] through the demon [...] So no one has [...], saying to him: "Save [me] [...] of the dead." While the crowd [...] the demon also appeared [...] in the [...] and immediately the demons [...] So the crowd [...] of God, they glorified the one who had [...] for the benefit of Paul. One person had a [son] who had never had the ability to speak.

Comment

The narrator, as usual, wastes no time on details. Paul is, to all intents and purposes, met at the dock by a crowd of Jews (see the Note) who appear to have been seeking signs (1 Cor 1:22), more fairly, relief for their loved ones. From *Acts of Titus* 3: "He healed Aphphia, the wife of Chrysippus, who had been possessed by a demon," she alone was exorcised. ("*Amphion*" is a diminutive form on the name.) Other victims of possession may also have been

205

helped. On the formal features of exorcisms (which should be distinguished from healings, although the texts may mingle them), see Bultmann, *History*, 209–10, 231–32. If the narrative began with a recital of wonders worked through Paul's agency and then proceeded to relate an exorcism and a healing, it would be a mirror image of Mark 1:21–34, which narrates an exorcism, a healing, and then offers a summary. The effect is the same. These incidents are examples of what God can do—in the theological world of *APl*—(and, by implication, at least, exorcisms and healings are symbols and synecdoches of God's rule and intentions for the human race).

The exorcism began with a petition from the patient, probably Apphia, although not certainly. S/he effectively dwells in the realm of the dead, i.e., her symptoms have separated her from human society. This condition is presented literally in Mark 5:3. The result is sensational, with a visible manifestation of the demons' presence. Cf. Mark 5:13. The crowd reacts with acclamation. These "choral endings" have two notable functions: they serve as proof of the "reality" of the event, which took place in the presence of a number of witnesses. Secondly, they allow the audience hearing the story to join in; crowds have room for everyone.

The sequel begins with a parent who has a speech-impaired son. See Luke 11:14 (Q) and Mark 7:31–37. To this person will come the gift of free and easy speech. The episode may have contained no conflict or antagonism, for Paul is now bound for Jerusalem and the narrator may well have wished him to arrive with fresh laurels but no fresh scars or bleeding wounds from his opponents.

Notes

Jews in Tyre. Tyre contained a substantial Jewish community. See, e.g., Josephus, *Antiquities* 14.306–22, on rights Josephus claims were upheld by Roman rulers. For its existence in the late third century CE, see Smallwood, *Jews*, 537–38.

Amphion. The form Aphphia (*v. l.* Amphia) found in the *Acts of Titus* 3 is a known variant of this name. See Pervo, "*Acts of Titus*," 462–63.

Bibliography

Bultmann, Rudolf. *The History of the Synoptic Tradition*. Trans. John Marsh. Rev. ed. New York: Harper & Row, 1968.

Pervo, Richard I. "*The Acts of Titus*: A Preliminary Translation, with an Introduction and Notes." In *SBLSP*, 455–82. Atlanta: Scholars: 1996.

Smallwood, E. Mary, *The Jews under Roman Rule*. SJLA 20. Leiden: Brill, 1981.

Translation, Commentary, and Notes : Chapter

Chapter 8: Jerusalem (to Smyrna)

Primary sources: P Heid, pp. 67–82 (Cherix); secondary: *Acts of Titus*; Nicetas of Paphlagonia, *Life of Polycarp* (?)

The end of chap. 7 is lost. At the beginning of what is now designated as chap. 9, Paul went from Smyrna to Ephesus, a relatively short coastal journey. According to the *Acts of Titus* 3, following the healing of Apphia, Paul "went to Jerusalem and in turn/again to Caesarea." Caesarea Maritima was the probable point of departure for Smyrna. The issue is apparently complicated by the encomium of Nicetas (83r), which has Paul directed by the Spirit to visit Jerusalem so that he might interview Peter, whom he had never met. The language imitates Galatians 1:18. The role of the Spirit might well derive from Gal 2:1. Nicetas merges visits and issues that are distinct in Galatians 1–2. That encomiast also reports a conflict with Peter (83_v–84_r), the result of which was the total abolition of the Torah. In short Nicetas tends to follow Galatians (which alone admits of a quarrel between Peter and Paul) while confusing its chronology and supplying a clear conclusion: Paul triumphed. The historical evidence rather suggests that Paul lost that argument, as he broke with Antioch thereafter. Acts reports a victory for Peter, who uses Pauline theology. James endorses Peter's view. (See, e.g., Pervo, *Acts*, 364–84.) Nicetas' view of the encounter between Peter and Paul is at variance with the general patristic tradition (Wiles, *Divine Apostle*). Since it disagrees with Acts and with Galatians, Nicetas may have derived his information from the *APl*. This understanding would clarify much of chap. 8, less through dovetailing with it than through superimposing a structure upon it. Details aside, this appears to be *APl*'s equivalent to the Galatians 2/Acts 15 visit. It is possible that the Jewish audience at Tyre in chap. 7 raised questions about Torah observance. At no prior point in the extant text of *APl* has this issue been raised. It nonetheless seems to be present in these fragments. The author of a book about Paul might reasonably have presumed that this question should be addressed, as it was central to Paul's career. The allusions to Galatians 1–2 and the discussion of Paul's relation to Peter and other members of the Twelve support this understanding.

Although the *APl* may have reported more than one visit to Jerusalem, the visit described in these fragments is the central visit, that reported in Galatians 2 and Acts 15. Rordorf and Cherix include here various fragments of the Coptic P Heid, numbered by them as pp. 67–82, some of which may have once belonged to other sections of *APl*. By comparison, chaps. 3–4 comprised pp. 6–28. This is a sensible editorial decision, so long as it is understood to be both provisional and arbitrary. None of this material is unsuitable to an intra-Christian conversation.

The Acts of Paul

The value of the *Life of Polycarp* (Lightfoot, *Apostolic Fathers* 2/3: 433–34) is uncertain. According to that text Paul arrived in Smyrna from Galatia, in need of rest. He stopped with Strataeas, apparently the brother of Timothy, with whom he shares mother and grandmother (cf. 2 Tim 1:5). Paul had known Strataeas in Pamphylia. Galatia and Smyrna would *precede* Jerusalem as destinations, according to this text.

Chapter 8

1. (*p. 67*) [...] to my house [...] in the [...] of Cilicia [...] so that [...] to them, so you say [...] to proclaim the savior [...] the son of God [...] look [...]

2. (*p. 68*) [...] in [...] he who is [...] who is [...] be [...] numerous [...] large [...] these [...] of Cilicia [...] in order to place [...] for which I run [...] Moses [...] with me [...] move forward [...] move forward [...]after [*he*] [...]

3. (*p. 69*) [...] For what we are saying has already been realized [...] look, we shall bring you to this place [...] so that [...] for you, for hearing [...] your [holy] thoughts [...] fulfilled [...] outside of...

4. (*p. 70*) [...] to God whose will has been fulfilled [...] by him. [*In this*] manner [...] the father [...] Jesus the [Christ] [...] outside of [...]

5. (*p. 73*) [...] You are face to face with Jerusalem [...]. As for me, I trust in the Lord [...] in truth [...] so that you [e.g., *turn*]. to him, to him who has [...]

6. (*p. 74*) [...] [He who was crucified,] on whom the [blame] [...] afflicted [...] chosen because [...] he who has [...] our flesh [...]

7. (*p. 75*) [...] outside of [...] Paul [...] Paul [...] of the person [...] Cleanthes [...] the law [...] that which is called [...] way, haven't we followed him [*in*] all the cities? And after they [...] he turned to [...] to this [...] ancestors. And he [...] exists [...] nothing [...] words of this type, nor does he preach [...] as you preach [...] O Paul, so that you won't [...]

Translation, Commentary, and Notes : Chapter

8. *(p. 76)* [...] Christ [...] hidden [...] who has [...] [but] [...] that I may go [...] who have [...] with [...] by him. But were water [...] being thirsty [...] so that they might not be [...] among the wild beasts [...] out of the ground, but so that they may not be burned by the fire. They have begotten these works for the age which [...] The one who was a persecutor.

9. I *(p. 77)* [...] [...] to him [...] great glory [...] to you [...] what I have taught [...] nor [...] he will come [...] [...] in [...] Israel [...] necessity [...] he has not [...] [...] much [...] [...] outside of [...] But he [...] a freedom [...] and, having placed [...] with the yoke [...] all flesh [...] [...] those who [...] of whoever confesses [...] he is the Christ who is the glory of the father [...]

10. *(p. 78)* [...] [...] we [...] in Syria [...] in Cyrenaica [...] to ruin them [...] in [...] in [...] you [...] because [...] [...] Moses [...] [...] I die [...] an abomination [...] Again, I tell you [...] I am the one who does [...] me [...] [...] because the person will be justified [...] but because he will be justified [... the] deeds of righteousness and he [...]

11. *(p. 81)* [...] [*the*] Christ. [...] all of you. The [...] to them. This [...] exists for him [...] Paul, he who has [...] while they take [...]. The day when [...] to persecute/pursue the apostles who are with me outside of Jerusalem. I have [...] I have comfort and we [...] They are content [...] The message according [...] I have fallen [...] in numerous troubles [...] [I have submitted] to the Torah, as [...] you. Now [...] night and day in my [struggles] [...] Christ. While I [...] a lamb [...] of his [...] He opposes the [...] He abuses [...] *(p. 82)* Paul ... shepherds [...] concerning/over [...] by Paul [...] because of the search [...] concerning Peter [...]. He cried out "[...] God is one, there is no [other god] than He. Christ is also one [...] his son [as] we have [...], he whom you have [...] proclaimed [...] he whom we have crucified, he whom the [...] views with great [...] Now you yourselves say [that] [...] he is God. And the [...] he the judge [of] the living and [the dead] [...], king of [...], while you [...] of his [...], the person [...] about [...] thus as I say [...] in the manner that [...]

The Acts of Paul

Comment

The setting is probably a speech delivered to fellow Christians by Paul, in which he reviews his own history. §1 may refer to a house of Paul in Cilicia. A logical setting for this would be in the gap between Acts 9:30 and 11:25, in which the narrator had parked Paul in Tarsus, which is in Cilicia, without a hint of any missionary activity on his part (cf. Gal 1:21.), but this activity does not readily fit into the structure of *APl*, unless it is placed in chap. 3. §2 may suggest that Paul had converted many (cf. Acts 11:26). That the Pauline gentile mission is under discussion is suggested by "run," an allusion to Gal 2:2, the reference to Moses, a metonymy for Torah, "progress," an allusion to Gal 1:14. (The Coptic borrows the Greek *prokoptein*.) The context of §3 and 4 is uncertain. §3 is quite possibly addressed to Paul by the Jerusalem leaders, who request a consultation. §5–9 follow a three-page gap. Perhaps Peter is speaking to Paul. §5–6 are christological.

The subsequent section evidently contains a debate about Torah. An individual named Cleanthes enters the discussion. "All the cities" is reminiscent of Acts 15:21. Cleanthes evidently proclaims the obligation of Torah for followers of Jesus. The next section (§8) appears to begin with a disclosure formula based upon the contrast "Once hidden now revealed." See Dahl, *Jesus*, 30–36. For comparisons, see Col 1:26; Eph 3:5. The subsequent imagery is not atypical of the sermons in *APl*. The plight of the unredeemed is likened to the fate of those in dry uninhabited lands patrolled by wild beasts. See 13.5.

The section ends with a reference to a persecutor. That is Paul, who so describes himself in Gal 1:13, 23. It is likely that Paul is the speaker, describing his own past and making use of the antitheses favored by the author. See the note to 60 l.5, in Schmidt, Acta; p. 68. § 9 is also redolent of Galatians. "Necessity" (*anankē*) has several meanings. Here it may well contrast to "freedom," the theme of Galatians, in the sense of Torah as compulsion vs. freedom. "Yoke" is also an ambiguous symbol for Torah (see, e.g., Pervo, *Acts*, 374), found in Gal 5:1 (and Acts 15:10).

Persons in Syria and Cyrene (present day Libya) are appealed to in some capacity. Syria, i.e., Antioch, was a major cradle of early Christianity, and Cyrene, which had at one time a large Jewish population and had Greek cities, is often mentioned: Mark 15:21 (Simon), Acts 2:10 (Pentecost visitors); 6:9 (synagogue in Jerusalem) and 11:20; 13:1 (Lucius of Cyrene, an early leader in Antioch). The subject is justification. "Righteous deeds" are required. The situation is Deutero-Pauline, reflecting a period when the Pauline sense of "works" in connection with Torah-observance looked like an invitation to lawlessness (antinomianism). See Pervo, *Dating Acts*, 266–68.

Translation, Commentary, and Notes : Chapter

The final portion, which begins after a gap of three pages, is particularly tantalizing. Peter is a likely speaker as the fragment opens. This may envision Peter and the others lying low beyond the city borders during a persecution led by the authorities. Could this encompass Acts 8:1? It scarcely fits Acts 12:1–3. Peter, the presumed speaker says to (presumably) Paul that both have submitted to Torah. "Night and day in my struggles" is probably to be attributed to Paul. See the note. Peter may still be speaking, however. According to Nicetas (83r-v) Peter sought to explain his behavior by saying that the Jews were so menacing that he separated from the gentiles. This was labeled as hypocrisy. Gal 2:11–14 is in view. Paul argued, according to Nicetas, that the incident proved the ineffectiveness of law for justifying anyone.

The subsequent fragments utilize the image of lamb and shepherd, familiar in the early discussions about pastoral responsibility. See Pervo, *Dating Acts*, 204–8. Thecla is a lamb to Paul's implicit shepherd, 3.21. The final speaker may be a converted enemy, who now confesses that Jesus is the Messiah and God's son. The claim that "We have crucified Jesus" is best placed on the lips of a leader, such as the high priest or a member of the Sanhedrin, but it may, according to the viewpoint of Acts (e.g., 3:12–26) be applied to any resident of Jerusalem. The relationship between this confession of faith and Torah observance is unknown.

Although these fragments are so small and vague that they might be amenable to a number of reconstructions and interpretations, the frequency of allusions to Galatians 1–2 and Acts 15 make it highly probable that they related a visit to Jerusalem and an argument between Paul and Peter that discussed events that had taken place *after* the visit described in Galatians 2. Since the author of the *APl* had little interest in depicting full and perfect harmony and consensus among the apostles, it is quite possible that he portrayed Paul as triumphant in this argument. Granting these fragile hypotheses, the *APl* would follow Acts (chap. 15) in placing this theological controversy in the middle of the book. Since the end of the chapter is lost, the sequel is not clear.

Notes

Struggles. See Spicq, *Lexicon*, 2:322–29. Passages include 1 Thess 2:9; 1 Cor 4:12. From the Deutero-Pauline orbit are Acts 20:31, 35; 1 Tim 4:10.

Shepherds. Before this Rordorf and Cherix restore "twelve." That is possible, but not certain.

Bibliography

Dahl, Nils. *Jesus in the Memory of the Early Church.* Minneapolis: Augsburg, 1976.
Lightfoot, Joseph Barber. *The Apostolic Fathers.* 5 vols. in 2 parts. New York: Macmillan, 1889–1890.
Spicq, Ceslas. *Theological Lexicon of the New Testament.* Translated and edited by J. D. Ernest. 3 vols. Peabody, MA: Hendrickson, 1994.
Wiles, Maurice F. *The Divine Apostle: The Interpretation of St. Paul's Epistles in the Early Church.* Cambridge: Cambridge University Press, 1967.

Chapter 9: Ephesus

Primary sources: P Hamb (Greek); P Bod (Coptic); secondary sources: "Hippolytus," *Commentary on Daniel*; *Acts of Titus*; Commodian, *Carmen Apologeticum*; Jerome; Nicephoras Callistus; the *Letter of Pelagia*.

The story of Paul's Ephesian mission is the first largely complete chapter since chap. 4 and the first full chapter in which Paul is the central figure throughout. For the work as a whole the chapter is important for a number of reasons: it demonstrates that the author was not without compositional skill and that he elaborated a unified work with at least one flashback, created parallels between characters (Paul and Thecla, most notably), made use of both the canonical Acts and Paul's letters, and therefore sought to produce an independent view of Paul's ministry. Each of these points has been disputed.

For early and Medieval Christians this story raised interesting questions about literal and symbolic interpretation, e.g. "fighting with beasts at Ephesus" (1 Cor 15:32), parallels between the testaments (Daniel and Paul in conflict with lions) and the completeness of Scripture. Did the author of Acts say all there was to say or were some incidents not reported there? Does the *APl* have any standing beside the canonical Acts? Divergent answers were and are given to these questions.

The author was addressing matters that have long challenged historians of Christian origins. The provenance of the "imprisonment epistles" (Philippians and Philemon among the undisputed letters of Paul, to which are added Colossians, Ephesians, 2 Timothy, *3 Cor*, and the Correspondence between Paul and Seneca) is a vexing question. Difficulties with placing these letters in Caesarea (cf. Acts 23:33–26:32) or at Rome (cf. Acts 28) led to the hypothesis that Paul was incarcerated at Ephesus. Pertinent passages include 2 Cor 1:8–11; 6:5; 11:23; Phil 1:12–26; as well as the famous 1 Cor 15:32. See Pervo, *Acts*, 465n16. More than a little support for this hypothesis comes from the gaps and complexities of Acts 19 (the account of the mission in Ephesus). Nearly half of that tumultuous chapter is occupied with a riot (vv. 23–40) in which, according to the narrator, Paul was not involved, but after which he left town. When Paul returns, he does not stop at Ephesus but requires the leaders of that community to come to Miletus to hear what he has to say by way of farewell (20:17–35). One may ask why he did not speak to them before leaving Ephesus and, more pointedly, why he required that the elders travel to see him.

The author of *APl* posits, like many modern scholars, that Paul got into great difficulty at Ephesus. The difference is that he narrated the difficulty rather than construct a hypothesis. His account is much more interesting than those of the scholars and is utterly suspect, but it serves the same end: explanation of difficulties in Acts and in the epistles. This is to say that the author was not utterly indifferent to historical questions and problems. Even historical novelists may engage questions of fact. This chapter "replaces"/is an alternate to Acts 19.

The story has a number of scenes:

I. 1–10. Paul's pastoral missionary work in Ephesus: Arrival, Angelic epiphany, Speech about events after his affiliation with the followers of Jesus.

11. Transition. The success of the mission. Procla as an example.

II. 12–15. Arrest, hearing in the theater, condemnation.

III. 16–21. Subplot: Eubula and Artemilla.

IV. 22–26. Judgment in the theater. Departure.

V. 27–28. Resolution of plot and subplot, with a happy ending. Epiphany.

I. 1–10. Pastoral and Missionary Activity in Ephesus.

1. When he had finished speaking, Paul left Smyrna for Ephesus. He went into the house of Aquila and Priscilla, where he was happy to see the believers whom he most happily loved. They also rejoiced that they had been deemed worthy for Paul to set foot within their house. Joy and gladness abounded.

2. They devoted the night to a prayer vigil, seeking, with gladness and unanimity, discernment in complete assurance. The angel of the lord came into Aquila's house and stood in the sight of everyone. The angel spoke with Paul to the discomfiture of all, for, although he was seen by everyone, they could not hear what he was saying to Paul.

3. After the angel had ceased speaking with Paul in tongues, the onlookers, filled with fear and trembling, kept silent. Paul looked at the believers and said: "Brothers and sisters, the angel of the lord has come to me, visible to all of you, and said: 'A great fire will descend on you during Eastertide [...] but take [*courage*], because many distresses are coming from the Evil One. [*But*] trust in the

God Jesus Christ and hand over everything to him. Give him all (your) anxiety and your every deed and he will sustain you.'"

4. But Paul could not be unhappy, on account of Eastertide, as it is a festival for those who have come to believe in Christ, catechumens no less than (full) believers. Great joy and abundant love prevailed, accompanied by songs and praises addressed to Christ, all of which strengthened those who heard.

5. Paul said: "My brothers and sisters, listen to what happened to me, when I was in Damascus, when I persecuted the faith in God, when mercy struck me, mercy from the father who proclaimed the message of his son to me, so that I might live in him, having no other life but that in Christ. I entered into a large assembly with the support of blessed Jude, the brother of the lord, who gave me from the beginning the sublime love bestowed by faith.

6. "I conducted myself then in grace, with the support of the blessed prophet and through the revelation of Christ *who was begotten before all the ages*. As he was being proclaimed I rejoiced in the lord, nourished by his words. But when I was able to be worthy of the Word, I spoke to the believers—Jude encouraged me, and I became dear to those who heard me.

7. "When evening arrived I left the agapē prepared by the widow Lemma and her daughter Ammia. I intended to reach Jericho in Phoenicia by this night hike. We covered a lot of ground, so that when dawn came I perceived that Lemma and Ammia, who had provided the agapē, had been following me all along, for they were so enamored of me that they wished to be close to me. Then a huge and famished lion came out of the valley of the field of bones. As for us, we were praying fervently; Lemma and Ammia *fell before the beast in prayer*. When I had finished praying, the beast was crouched at my feet. Filled with the spirit, I looked at it and said, 'Lion, what do you want?'"

"'I want to be baptized.'

8. "I praised God who had given speech to the beast and safety to God's servants. That spot featured a large stream; I went down into it, the creature following. As pigeons gravely threatened by eagles seek protection in a house, so Lemma and Ammia, who

were clinging to me would not let me go until I blessed and praised God. I was also seized by ordinary fear, wondering how I was going to drag the lion and toss it into the water. I stood on the bank of the river, sisters and brothers, and cried out, 'You who dwell in the heights and take notice of the downtrodden, You who give respite to the oppressed, You who stopped the jaws of the lions set against Daniel, You who have sent me our lord Jesus Christ, grant us also a means for escaping from the beast and accomplish the established divine plan!'

9. "Following this prayer I grabbed it by the mane and immersed it three times in the name of Jesus Christ. When he had come up out of the water he shook out his mane and said to me, 'Grace be with you.'

"'And also with you,' I replied.

"When the lion dashed off into the country, rejoicing—this was revealed to me in my heart—a lioness encountered him, but he would not even look at her but turned away and headed for the forest.

10. "So you also, Aquila and Priscilla, who have come to faith in the living God [...] That which you have received proclaim like me."

Comment

I. This "scene" has several sub-sections. §1–3 get Paul to Ephesus, provide a happy beginning, and display an encounter between Paul and an angel. This and the closing angelophany constitute two of the three angelic revelations in the book, although the incident reported in 5.2 may have been solely verbal. Paul tells the faithful that a trial is coming and exhorts them to trust.

The chapter begins quite abruptly. Within a few words Paul has ended a sermon or speech, journeyed from Smyrna to Ephesus, and lodged with Prisca and Aquila, where he receives an exalted welcome. His presence is a blessing. This attitude reflects the status of the apostle among second-century admirers. Once more the *APl* represents joy as the characteristic Christian emotion. Cf. 3.5 and 4.14, e.g.

The arrival of an apostle does not mean getting all the answers; it stimulates a night-long prayer vigil in quest of discernment. The resultant event is dramatic, mysterious, and suspense-building. "The angel of the Lord," a biblical figure (Rad, *angelos, TDNT* 1:77–78), is manifestly visible, but not audible. This last item is a reminiscence of Acts 22:9.

§3 adds a new element. The angel spoke with Paul in tongues. This reflects the view that glossolalia is angelic language, the *lingua franca* of heaven, as evidently hypothesized in 1 Cor 13:1. That view is reflected in the *Testament of Job*. Job's daughters receive magic belts that convey the gift of ecstatic speech, identified as angelic: *T. Job* 48.3 (cf. 49.2; 50.2). The reaction of the onlookers confirms that an epiphany has taken place. Paul, exemplifying the instructions given in 1 Cor 14:26–28, provides an interpretation. A fire, in the figurative sense (BDAG, 898c), is about to befall the community. Fire can destroy, but it may also purify. Readers, like the dramatic audience, do not know what form this fire will take. Persecution is never a bad guess. One reason for the metaphor is the association of fire with Pentecost, the "tongues of fire" of Acts 2:3, but "Pentecost" in this chapter does not refer to a single day but to what are called the Great Fifty Days, or Eastertide, the festival time between Easter and Pentecost Sundays. Paul follows this warning with a series of exhortations and promises. The "God Jesus Christ" is a trace of the Monarchian theology that was pervasive in the earliest editions of *APl*.

§4 is an odd transition, apparently aimed more at inculcating piety than in advancing the plot. From §3 it would seem that Eastertide lay in the future. These comments do not prepare for the subsequent speech. §5 follows §3 better than this section, which may be an interpolation. At any rate, it is an edifying digression.

Paul's speech in §5–10 serves the present context in that it is an example of courage in the face of adversity. Rescue from a ravenous lion symbolizes divine power to deliver the afflicted (Ps 22:21). In the general context it prepares the audience for what is to come. Acts 9, 22, and 26 present three stories of Paul's "conversion," the second and third of which are in the first-person singular. The pressing question is the shape of the encounter with the lion in *APl* 1. Is Paul providing more detail here? Less? Essentially the same, with minor differences? Many of the dramatic audience may be hearing the story for the first time.

One detectable omission is the life-changing epiphany itself and the call, fragments of which can be found in (material assigned to) chap. 1. It is possible, if unlikely, that the narrator did not tell the story of the encounter with the lion at that time. See the comments on chap. 1. A third theme that will be of value in the coming scenes is celibacy, of which the lion is an inspiring example. The text utilizes both Galatians 1–2 and Acts 9. The former of which is predominant. As in Galatians, but not in Acts 9, Paul is not punished for his persecutions. He is illuminated by mercy rather than blinded by power. The event takes place in Damascus, as one could gather from Galatians, whereas in Acts 9 it takes place outside of Damascus. "[T]he father who proclaimed . . . me" alludes to Gal 1:16. The phrases that follow are indebted to Gal 2:18–20.

This account implies that Paul's host in Damascus, Judas (Acts 9:11), was none other than the brother of Jesus. Early Christians tended to subscribe to a law of conservation of names. The promotion of this unknown to membership in the holy family did nothing to damage Paul's status. Hearty approval by this sibling aligned Paul closely with the family and followers of Jesus. See the note. This Judas is not called an apostle, possibly in keeping with Galatians 1, where Paul disavows contact with earlier apostles.

Insofar as one can tell from §6, Paul's period of instruction lasted less than a day. He attributes his learning both to the message heard, i.e., tradition, and through revelation. The latter conforms to Gal 1:11–12. In due time he was proclaiming the message, supported by the Lord's brother.

§7–9 relate the most famous, i.e., notorious, story in *APl*: the talking, baptized lion. Antiquity knew many tales about lions. See Spittler, *Animals*, passim. Lions that talked were not common, as Spittler notes (185–86.) Talking animals are, however, attested in the biblical tradition, including Balaam's famous donkey (Num 22:28–30). Revelation knows of an aquiline creature that speaks (6:7), as well as an actual speaking eagle (8:13), not to mention an inanimate speaking object (an altar: 9:13.) The serpent in Genesis 3 talks, although that was before the fall—and that's the point. Commodian's *Apologetic Poem* (probably from Africa in last third of the third century) affirms (623–24) that, if so desired, God can give animals speech. As proof he offers Balaam's donkey, Simon the magician's dog (*Acts of Peter* 11–12), the articulate lion, and the infant of *Acts of Peter* 15 (ll. 625–30). Matthews, "Articulate Animals," provides a good review of the subject. Animals talk in fables and fairy tales. Ancients learned Aesop's fables in school (217–18). When a lion drops by for a chat, one knows that a fable is probably under way.

Talking with lions is one thing; baptizing them is another. Schneemelcher focused upon this fact in his fine study "Der Getaufte Löwe." The uniqueness of this situation has been mitigated by the appearance of animals saddened because they are not deemed worthy to receive communion in the *Acts of Philip* 12. (See the discussion of this episode in Matthews, "Articulate Animals," 225–31.) If the appearance of a talking animal signals a fable that will convey a moral message or present a moral example, the baptism of a lion is a declaration that the episode is symbolic. Too many interpreters who were taught to despise non-concrete interpretation have projected their dogma upon early Christians. The inspiration for this episode is the parallel between the lives of Jesus and Paul, specifically Mark 1:9-13, which links an etiological story (the baptism of Jesus) to a wilderness "trial" and the restoration of harmony among warring species. See Pervo, "Christ Figure," and Table 1.2, p. 65.

The story opens with compact narration. Insofar as the audience might know, on the evening of the very day of his change of allegiance, Paul sets out, presumably for Jerusalem. Solitary travelers rarely moved by night, if not compelled to do so. The apostle ambles off as if on an after-dinner stroll to aid his digestion. His goal is Jericho, about 185 kilometers from Damascus, a journey of six hard days. Chapter 1 may have provided more details, filling in stops between Damascus and the locale of Lemma and Ammia. Jericho was famous for its palms (Greek *phoinix*) The city is not in "Phoenicia." As it stands, the journey takes place in never-never land, which is just the proper place.

Thecla was not the only woman who did not wish to let Paul out of her sight. His hostesses, Lemma and Ammia, possibly deserting their guests (and the washing up), followed him throughout the night. Following is the role of disciples. Their particular role in this story is to provide normal human reactions to a large, hungry, and menacing lion. They could serve as witnesses of the remarkable event, but the narrator does not assign them that role. After displaying adequate terror—a means of showing the audience how horrifying things were—they vanish from the narrative. (See the note on "we.")

In a transition that is abrupt even by the standards of *APl*, the lion bursts upon the scene, from the valley of dry bones, here characterized in the language of Ezek 37:1-9 LXX (see the note). This is not a geographical aid to mark Paul's location on the map. The lion is making the baptismal passage from death to life, from darkness to light. See Drijvers, "Der getaufte Löwe." Paul and Co. were not thinking of initiation-seeking lions just then. He was praying. The women may have attempted to call attention to their visitor, which Paul found crouched before him when he opened his eyes. Paul's question is a natural response to a suppliant. That he asks it shows that the Spirit has revealed that the lion will talk. The answer is simple and direct. It is the normal introduction to the catechumenate, a period of preparation that can last for several years. That will not happen here, because this is not a typical baptism.

The theme of §8 is the proper disposition toward God's grace. Paul begins by recognizing two "miracles": the speaking lion and the uneaten humans. When baptism is the subject water will not be far off. Cf. Acts 8:26–40. Paul resorts to a simile in his description of the clinging women, who like pigeons fluttering about in a building in which they have sought refuge, are as liable to injure themselves as to find deliverance. The apostle has another problem: how is he going to get this presumably hydrophobic feline into the river? ("Living," i.e., fresh, running water was preferred for baptisms [e.g., *Didache* 7.1], but not always available [e.g., *Didache* 7.2.])

His subsequent prayer has five ascriptions, two of which are historical instances, followed by a two-fold petition. The evocation of Daniel's rescue foreshadows his later encounter with the lion. The "divine plan" is an important concept here. Its primary application is not to the delivery of Paul and the women. Early Christians did not subscribe to the modern American, individualistic notion that "God has a plan for your life." The divine plan (the word here, *oikonomia*, is borrowed from Greek) encompasses the universe.

Kurfess noted long ago ("Hamburger Papyrus") that the theme was the universality of God's providence and grace, which extended to nature, pointing to Romans 8:19–23. Animals are not outside of God's plan for the world. Schneemelcher ("Getaufte Löwe") agreed in general, but would not concede that much theological sophistication to *APl*. In that he erred, for *APl* is not quite so devoid of theology as he then thought, and the use of Pauline correspondence is no longer disputed. One of the eschatological goals for the world is the termination of conflict among species, the establishment of the "peaceable kingdom," in which lions and lambs happily frolic together. See Isa 11:6–9; 65:25; Hos 2:18; *2 Baruch* 73:6. This was the original state of affairs in Eden, prior to the Fall.

Baptism could be described as entry into Paradise (see, e.g., Origen, *Sel in Gen*, 2:13; Cyril of Jerusalem, *Catechetical Lectures* 19.9; Gregory of Nyssa, *Bapt. Diff.* [PG 46:420C-D]. This is symbolized by the administration at first communion of milk and honey, according to *Apostolic Tradition* 21.33). The idea can be inferred from Mark 1:13. (The argument is not that these interpretations reflect the intent of Mark, but that they are possible.) Both Matthew and Luke delete the phrase: "Jesus was in the wilderness forty days, tempted by Satan; and he was with the wild beasts (*meta tōn thēriōn*); and the angels waited on him." The item that does not fit here is the temptation by Satan. (The oft-cited *T. Naph.* 8.4 does not speak of satanic temptation but of the flight of the devil from the virtuous.) To associate with wild creatures and to be waited upon by angels evoke the experience of Israel in the wilderness as a foreshadowing of and model for celestial life.

A relatively minor point of this narrative is to demonstrate Paul's charismatic power, which includes mastery over the animal kingdom. On this theme, see Bieler, ΘΕΙΟΣ ΑΝΗΡ 1:103–10, and the note below. Baptism was performed by a triple immersion "in the name of Jesus Christ." The formula is that used by Thecla (4.9), while the threefold immersion suggests the name of the Trinity (e.g., *Apostolic Tradition* 21.14–18). Following the rite the two exchange a greeting of peace. For his departure the narrator borrows a resonant and appropriate line from Acts 8:39.

There is a postscript. In consequence of his initiation the lion confirmed the legitimacy and suitability of the administration of the sacrament by thwarting the lubricious advances of a libidinous lioness. Paul, the internal narrator, explains his omniscience by appeal to a revelation. The lion is a model of postbaptismal existence. Its value for that purpose loses nothing because lions enjoyed a reputation for advanced sexual potency and enthusiasm (Adamik, "Baptized Lion," 67; with a reference to Pliny, *Natural History* 8.42). The implicit argument is, "If Christian initiation empowers virile creatures to embrace chastity, how much more . . ." The author associates death/darkness/the uninitiated life with sexuality, and initiation with celibacy, true humanity, light, and life. This episode is quite complex and multivalent, a rich theological resource with enough material for several sermons.

Paul concludes with a charge to his hosts. Aquila and Priscilla are to preach this message. The content of the message emphasizes postbaptismal celibacy. The sermon itself closes with an example of the process of tradition: what they, in effect a third generation, are to pass on from what they have received from Paul. Cf., e.g., 1 Cor 15:3.

Notes

Aquila and Priscilla. The form of these names comes from Acts, as Paul does not use the diminutive "Priscilla." The immediate source is, however, 1 Cor 16:19. The couple sponsors a house church in Ephesus. See Trebilco, *Early Christians*, 110–24.

Pentecost. Lampe, *Lexicon* 1060, gives "the festival period of fifty days after Easter" as the former of two Christian meanings of *pentekostē*. "Eastertide" is a bit quaint, but more economical than "the Great Fifty Days," the current terminology. The earliest citation for "Day of Pentecost" as the definition of the word is from Athanasius. The chronology coordinates somewhat with the *Life of Polycarp* 1–2, which has Paul in Smyrna around Passover. That text is Quartodeciman, named for a liturgical practice, widely observed in Asia Minor, of observing the Paschal Events on 14 Nissan, according to the Jewish calendar, the beginning of Passover. *APl* may have followed the Quartodeciman calendar. On the practice of not kneeling during this period, Lampe, 321, under *gony*, "knee," shows that Eusebius traced the custom back to Irenaeus.

Jude/ah/as. Five men in the NT share this name. "Thomas" is not a proper name. With the full name Judas Didymos Thomas that figure could be identified as the twin brother of Jesus and obtain, in addition to the book of *Thomas the Athlete* and the *Gospel of Thomas*, his own, essentially complete Apocryphal Acts.

Begotten. This phrase is probably a contribution from a fourth-century editor of anti-Arian sentiment.

Agapē. See 5.5 and the comments there.

We. The word is anticipatory in that Paul does not yet know that he is not alone, unless it is editorial. See below under "in prayer."

Ezekiel 37. Since the era of the sacramentaries (service books that first appeared in the early Middle Ages) this passage was a normal reading in the baptismal vigil of Easter Even in the West. Early Christian authors associated this passage with the resurrection: e.g., Justin Martyr, *1 Apol.* 52.5; Irenaeus, *A. H.* 5.15.1; Tertullian, *On the Resurrection* 30-32.

In Prayer. The restoration is far from certain. See Kasser and Luisier, 321n9. The "we" may be editorial. Paul, praying with closed eyes, did not sense the beast, while the women displayed the ordinary human reaction. §8 portrays them as still holding on to Paul for dear life.

Filled with the Spirit. This is typical of (Luke and) Acts: e.g., Acts 2:4; 4:8; 7:55; 13:9; 11:24, especially at moments of trial. The D-text sometimes adds the phrase, e.g., Acts 26:1.

Downtrodden. Kasser and Luiser, 323n10, observe that one could treat the construction as parallel and render the second member as "depths."

Pigeons. One image associated with doves or pigeons is the ability to hide: Song 2:14; Jer 48:28; Ezek 7:16, but their lack of sense is probably primary.

Mastery of the Animal World. Additional Jewish and Christian examples include *T. Napht.* 8:4 (noted above) and the *Vita Pachomii* 21 (which follows a temptation scene). Control of animals exhibits the unity of all nature. This mastery manifests thorough knowledge of the laws of nature. See Georgi, *Opponents*, 52-53.

Translation, Commentary, and Notes : Chapter

I. 11 Transition

11. In response to Paul's message a large crowd was added to the community of faith, resulting in jealousy and opposition to Paul *from leaders throughout Asia*, who wanted to put him to death.

A woman in the city named Procla did many good works for the Ephesians. Paul baptized her together with her entire household. The renown of grace, with abundant praise, spread abroad between [...] and Eastertide. The crown of Christ grew by large numbers, so that jealousy arose [*giving impetus*] to a widespread rumor in the city: "This stranger has destroyed the gods, saying, 'you will see them consumed by fire.'"

Comment

§11 provides a transition from Paul's internal to his external mission. The text is uncertain (Kasser and Luisier, 325n12), but the point is clear: Paul's success arouses jealousy from the leadership. The author has borrowed from Acts 19, utilizing 19:10 on the general dissemination of the message and 19:26 (all Asia). In distinction from Acts, jealousy is not attributed to "the Jews," and opposition begins from the top, rather than among artisans. The italics give one possible sense of the passage. Another is that it is an anticipatory summary, a view supported by the forthcoming reference to jealousy and the eventual enmity of the leadership.

The example is Procla, evidently a woman of means and the effective head of her household, all of whom were initiated by Paul (cf. 1 Cor 1:13–17). Since celibacy is ignored, it appears that she is not married. The subsequent text has gaps. Evidently Easter approaches. Has a year elapsed since the initial prophecy (9.3)? The implication is that Paul is to be killed for encouraging benefaction. Rumor, on the other hand—the text is once more defective—identifies Paul as an enemy of the civic gods. The allegation that the apostle claims that fire will consume the images is not slander. Paul repeats this prediction in 9.13 and 17. Chap. 14 is not the only apocalyptic patch in the book. Contrast the speeches in Acts 14 and 17 (at Lystra and Athens). Opposition arises, as in Acts 19, because of Paul's critique of the idols, but there is no economic factor.

The Acts of Paul

II. A. 9.12 Arrest.

12. As Paul was setting out for a place in the country, the citizens, together with magistrates, seized him, hauled him to the theater, and urged the governor to come. When he arrived he questioned Paul: "Why do you offer these [*ideas*] and teach what monarchs have condemned and the world has rejected? Nor have we been taught these things. We are given to understand that you exalt your god and have destroyed [*our gods*], those of the Romans and of this people here. Say now what you proclaim when you would persuade the public."

II. Apprehension and Condemnation

Introduction

The chapter has been building toward persecution, i.e., an attack upon Paul. Taken into custody, Paul is hastened to the theater, where the urban mob is, of course, assembled and waiting, while the proconsul comes at their beckoning. Given the opportunity to defend himself, Paul offers an entrée of apologetic polemic against polytheism and its concomitant morality, seasoned with a bit of apocalyptic threat, and capped off with an invitation to repent. The governor, typically (cf. 3.17), takes the role of Pontius Pilate. The circumstances are less than ideal for reflecting upon the judicious words of an oratorically adept philosopher. He then abandons judgment to the very audience that made the setting unpropitious. The results are predictable. While awaiting death, Paul experiences the awesome sounds of a predacious lion.

A (§12) begins with an apparently unmotivated journey by Paul to a rural location. See Kasser and Luisier, 324n17. If this reconstruction is correct—in any case Paul is evidently leaving the city—the motif is that of the *Martyrdom of Polycarp* 5.1, where the bishop took refuge in a country house. The theme is best attested in the controversy over Cyprian's rustication during the persecution under Decius: should the bishop immediately accept martyrdom or, in some cases, withdraw to care for the flock in its travail? Among the ApocActs, the prime example is the famous *Quo Vadis* episode (*APet. Mart.* 6). Here, if the relation is intertextual, *M. Poly.* must have priority, as the actions are well motivated there and nearly random here. The only function of the journey here is to provide an occasion for arrest. That action is executed by a band of citizens, headed, in this case by public officials (on whom, see the note). Rather than proceed to the municipal courts, as it were, they go to the theater and summon the governor, who asks Paul why he opposes the traditional gods, noting the widespread rejection of his views. This is altogether just, polite, and intellectually oriented.

Whether opposition to Roman and civic gods in general constitutes a capital offense is not debatable. The text does not accuse Paul of a crime against Caesar. The "Roman gods" is rather vague. The chief local deity is Artemis, whose cult collided with Paul in Acts 19. At this point the Greek text of P.Hamb becomes available. The two mss. are not in perfect harmony. The Greek ends the governor's words with: "Tell us, what are the attributes of the god whom you proclaim?" This is probably earlier than the Coptic, which is a request for a missionary sermon. (See the note.)

9.13 II. B. Defense Speech

13. Paul said [to him], "Proconsul, do as you will, for your authority extends only to my body, which you can destroy, but you have no power to kill my soul. Listen now how you can be saved. Take all that I say to heart. This is the one who created the sky and the land. This is the one who created the sun, the moon, the stars, authorities, dominions, and the world with its adornment, and fashioned all the good things that are in the world for the sake and use of humankind. God has not rejected his creature, i.e., humankind. But (*people reject God*) when they have been led astray through moral inversion and aberration, captured by their lust for gold, silver, precious stones, sexual misconduct, the drunken revels that are congenial to the pursuit of pleasure, and the life of darkness that leads to evil. People have obtained all that we have mentioned and are dead. Now, however, because of the deceit resident in the world, the Lord wills us to live in God and not die in sins; he saves us through those who preach the unalloyed Word, so that you might repent and come to believe that Jesus is the Messiah and that there is no other (god). Your gods are worthless, bronze, stone, and wooden objects, which cannot eat, see, hear, or stand erect. Make the right choice and be saved, lest God become angry

The Acts of Paul

and burn you with inextinguishable fire and the very memory of you be eradicated."

9.14. II. C. Judgment; Reaction of the faithful

14. When the governor, as well as the crowd in the theater, had heard this, he said, "Gentlemen of Ephesus, We know that this man speaks well, but this is not the proper occasion for learning such matters. We are well aware of the unsuitable character of this (setting). Judge for yourselves what should be done."

"Burn him in front of the temple," shouted some.

But the goldsmiths countered with the unison shout: "To the beasts!" In the midst of a substantial uproar Hieronymos judged that Paul should be whipped and thrown to the beasts. For their part the believers, since this took place during Eastertide, did not weep, nor did they kneel, but they rejoiced, praying with [...]

9.15 II. D. The Lion

15. Six days later Hieronymos provided an exhibition of animals to impress all the spectators with the size of the animals. Although he had been placed in custody... Paul did not avert his eyes [*e.g., from the spectacle*], but he drew as close as he could, heard the hiss of the wagons [*and the racket of those*] transporting the animals. When [*a lion*] ... entered through the side gate of the stadium in which Paul was incarcerated, it roared loudly, and [everyone] hollered, "The lion!" It roared so harshly and seve[*rely that even Paul*] was frightened enough to interrupt his prayers.

Comments

Paul's response (B) is a personal appeal to the proconsul, in effect an appeal for conversion. The body is framed by an *inclusio*: "Be saved." The speech has many apologetic features, as the Notes indicate, but it opens with a challenge to the governor's authority and ends with a threat. The words would be suited for a hostile tyrant; the governor's not unfriendly response is a bit surprising.

After the initial exhortation, the argument begins with an affirmation of the unity of the divine and God's role as creator. The primary purpose of this standard opening is to reject the gods, including the emperor. The reassurance that God has not rejected the human race precedes the enumeration of human failures, "gospel" preceding "law," as it were. The essence of human failure, as described in the following catalogue of vices (see the note), is the failure to control desire. Desire is manifested in two principal ways: longing for riches and sexual lust. The closing phrase "life of darkness" is evocative of the development of catalogues of vices and virtues in the catechetical tradition of the "two ways," a widespread phenomenon. Among the most relevant are the ways that lead to life or death in *Didache* 1–6 and 1QS 3.18–4.26 (the Community Rule of Qumran), with ways of darkness and light. See the note. These texts and traditions would be evoked for the actual audience. For the implied dramatic audience the denunciation would not have been especially alien to the realm of popular moral philosophy. The conclusion suits the model of the enthymeme: people have wanted wealth and sexual satiety, have got them, and are now dead. In brief: these things do not lead to life. The critique of the desire for material goods is reiterated in §17.

Through use of the passive voice and indirect expressions Paul avoids attributing evil to a personal agent, such as the Devil. In so far as this brief account permits analysis, salvation is through faith. Salvation is God's will and begins with repentance. The agents of the divine will are proclaimers. Cf. Rom 10:14 and the note. The Coptic text is Monarchian in appearance. The Greek appears to be a correction. Through a brief closing the polemic against idols is summarized. (This critique is both traditional and erroneous.) The closing exhortation follows, coupled with a threat. This has been no more of a defense than any other martyrological sermon. Paul has been asked to state his views and has done so.

Comparison with Paul's last speech to a proconsul in 3.17 shows that the author, like his model, the author of Acts, utilizes both repetition and variation. Variation averts boredom, gives scope for displays of literary and oratorical skill, and, most importantly, allows for the addition of new material in a familiar context. 3.17 was not polemical. Both addresses come as invitations to Paul to summarize his teachings in the face of accusation. Themes recur: God's love of the human race, which led to the sending of the Son to deliver those led astray by sin, in particular. The earlier speech had

The Acts of Paul

no direct missionary function. Both governors found merit. The sentences differ.

II. C begins promisingly enough, as the governor both acknowledges Paul's rhetorical gifts and the unsuitability of the occasion for hearing a lecture on philosophical theology. (See the Notes on the text.) He then rather surprisingly borrows a tactic from Pontius Pilate (Mark 15:6–14) and invites the mob to render judgment. The result is implicit agreement on execution but disagreement about which unpleasant means to employ. (This chapter does not treat Paul as a *Roman citizen*. That status will come into play, by implication, in the last chapter.) The proconsul chooses *damnatio ad bestias* (execution by wild animals) for reasons that will soon become apparent. This will be preceded by a whipping, as in Mark 15:15 and many public executions, e.g., *Mart. Justin* 5. The governor has unwittingly launched one of the strongest internal parallels in *APl*: both Thecla and Paul were condemned to the beasts.

Some call for Paul to be burned in front of the temple, evidently the Temple of Artemis. (See the note.) This would be eminently suitable, as Paul has attacked the gods and threatened the listeners with destruction by fire. Moreover, it would establish a nice parallel between the fates of Thecla and her master, as she was condemned to be burned in chap. 3. Another group, evidently organized as a claque and prepared to exhaust any opposition by interminable unison shouts, was composed of goldsmiths.

The introduction of metalsmiths is a clear sign of the creative use of Acts 19. Their role here is well-motivated, for Paul has attacked the value of gold in general and manufactured gods in particular. The metalsmiths prevail (although readers will soon learn that the governor, whose name, Hieronymos, suddenly transpires, has personal motives for his choice). Judgment emerged in time to prevent matters from getting out of hand.

The reaction of the believers, characterized by joy, presents a strong contrast to the cruel bloodlust of the polytheists. Cf. Acts 4:23–31. The reference to Eastertide as a time when kneeling was forbidden and fasting seems gratuitous. It does not mark an apt inclusion with §4. It is tempting to see these references as propaganda in a controversy about the Great Fifty Days. Following the initial line of §15, four pages of the Coptic P. Bod are missing.

§15 appears to open the narration of Paul's condemnation to the beasts. Suspense rises with the introduction of a fierce lion. Then will come a substantial retardation, as the text relates the conversion of Eubula and Artemilla. All three specific converts in this chapter are women. The analysis will, however, argue that § 16–21 are a later addition. Apart from that material the parallels to Thecla in chap. 4 are close. Hieronymos (Jerome in English) is, like Alexander, the sponsor of the games. Prior to the actual games a procession of animals, featuring a lion, occurred in both cases. Since chap. 4 is attributed to a source, the author evidently created the parallels in chap. 9. They show that the *APl* exhibits a literary plan. Such symmetry demonstrates that both Thecla and Paul were divinely authorized and protected agents. Readers may choose whether they show that Thecla was equal to Paul or vice-versa. The author skillfully narrates the story from Paul's perspective, emphasizing the congeries of sounds and the confusion of sights poorly glimpsed through narrow slits. The lion's roars were sufficiently terrifying even to distract Paul from his prayers. Contrast §7.

Notes

Magistrates. The Greek term, *prytaneis*, is used (spelled *pyrtanis*).

Proclaim. Cf. Acts 19:13.

Do as You Will. This is a staple of martyr literature (e.g., *M. Polyc.* 11.2) and of light fiction (e.g., *An Ephesian Tale*, 2.4.3).On the limits of officials' authority, see Matt 10:28; John 19:11–12; *AThom* 140; 152; 163.

How . . . saved. Lit. "must," in sense of "only by this means." Cf. Acts 4:12.

Creation. See the speeches in Acts 14 and 17; the *Mart. of Justin* 5.

Authorities, Dominions. These words, derived from Eph 1:21; 3:10; 6:12; Col 1:16; 2:10, 15; 1 Cor 15:24; Rom 8:38, appear only in the Greek.

Sake. The apologetic tradition affirmed that the universe was created for the sake and use of humankind: e.g., *Diog.* 4.1; 5.1; 6.1–3, 10.2. Aristides, *Apol.* 1.3; 5.4.

Catalogue of Vices. On these lists (which often include a corresponding "catalogue of virtues"), see Betz, *Galatians*, 281–83. This list is not typical, despite similarities to Rom 13:13; Gal 5:20–21; *1 Clem* 30.1, since most catalogues emphasize mental and emotional qualities more than does this.

Two Ways. See Niederwimmer, *The Didache*, 59–63.

The Acts of Paul

Led astray. See 1 Cor 12:2 (a discussion of "pagan" backrounds); *Diognetus* 9.1. "Error" (*planē*) and "deceit" (*apatē*) are widely used in moral and religious literature. Although congenial to dualistic modes of thought, they need not have been so viewed.

Unalloyed Word. The Greek text of P Hamb (p. 1 l.16) reads "through the holy men who proclaim . . ." This is probably secondary.

Messiah. The Greek (p. 1 ll.17–18) reads, after a brief gap, "and one Jesus Christ (Messiah Jesus)." As Schmidt, *Praxeis* 25, concludes—witness his restoration "God is one"—the Greek avoids Monarchian statements. The Coptic is more original here.

The idols. This polemic built upon a venerable Jewish tradition. It is erroneous in that the idols were viewed as representatives of gods, not the gods themselves. See Rev 9:20; *Diognetus* 2.2; *Mart. Apollonius* 16, e.g.

Choice. The word *prohairesis* is important in philosophical ethics. Cf. *Acts of John* 44.

Pilate. Cf. Mark 15:6–14. Both accounts use the same (not particularly rare) Greek verb: *thelō*.

Text. The Greek reads "I know," probably secondary to the "we" of authority in the Coptic. A pedantic corrector evidently distinguished the governor's evaluation from that of some of the audience.

Occasion. Coptic has two statements about the suitability of the occasion; Greek none. The Coptic text may be an accidental repetition. If original, it is emphatic. See Kasser and Luisier, 329n27.

Theater. On links between the theater and the cult of Artemis, see Pervo, *Acts*, 495n89.

Claque. See Pervo, *Acts*, 494.

Goldsmiths. Acts 19:23–40 speaks of silversmiths who produce devotional souvenirs for the cult of Artemis. The change may be an elevation in status. Although the text of Acts exhibits some difficulties, most of which are related to the production of temple models in silver (Pervo, *Acts*, 491n54), "goldsmiths" is not a variant. Ephrem identified Demetrius as a "goldsmith" in his commentary (trans. Conybeare, 3:384, 440). Ephrem evidently took this datum from *APl*. See, e.g., Czachesz, "Acts of Paul," 114. In a fragment from a Greek catena (collection of excerpts) of commentators, Ephrem stated,

Translation, Commentary, and Notes : Chapter

"For it was about this that he wrote to the Corinthians" (Conybeare, 441). 1 Cor 15:32; 2 Cor 1:8–9 are in mind. Acts 19 does not narrate a persecution that bought Paul into mortal danger. The *APl* does.

Uproar. Schmidt and Schubart restore this word (*thorybos*), *Praxeis,* 24n28. That would evoke Acts 20:1. An alternative, *tarachos* ("disturbance"), evokes Acts 19:23. For the former see *APl* 4.7.

In the midst . . . This sentence is missing from the Coptic because of a sight error. (When two lines in close proximity have a similar ending—homoioteleuton—the eye can leap over intervening lines.) See Kasser and Luisier, 329n29.

Six Days. Cf. Mark 9:2. There is no warrant for presuming symbolism, but it is always possible.

Exhibition. The text says that Hieronymos provided a hunt. The translation attempts to indicate the implicit idea of a preliminary parade.

Roman Citizen. The canonical Acts proposes that Paul was a Roman citizen, but this status functions as a literary device and is open to question. The epistles provide no solid grounds for this status. See Pervo, *Acts,* 554–56.

III. 16–21. Subplot: Eubula and Artemilla.

16. The wife of Diophantes, a freedman of Hieronymos, was a disciple of Paul and attached herself to him day and night. This made Diophantes jealous and eager to expedite the animal fight. Now Artemilla, the wife of Hieronymos, wanted to hear Paul at prayer. She said to Eubula (Diophantes' wife) "[*I wish*] to hear (the) prayer [and message] of the beast-fighter."

Eubula wen[t] and reported this to Paul. Filled with joy he said: "Brin[*g h*]er." After changing into rather somber clothes, Artemilla went with Eubula to see Paul.

17. When he saw her, he groaned and said, "Madam, ruler of this world, mistress of much gold, citizen possessing abundant luxury, you who boast about your wardrobe, sit down on the floor and forget your wealth and beauty and adornments, for none of these will help you, unless you implore God, who views what is

The Acts of Paul

considered great in this realm dung but bestows what is marvelous in that realm. Gold perishes, wealth is consumed, clothing wears out, beauty fades, great cities fall, and fire destroys the world because of human lawlessness. God alone abides, and the adoption bestowed through him, the only path to salvation. Now then, Artemilla, hope in God who will deliver you, hope in Christ who will give you forgiveness of sins and bestow upon you the crown of freedom, so that you will cease worshiping images and with offerings but (worship) the living God and father of Christ to whom be glory forever and ever. Amen." In response Artemilla (with Eubula) begged Paul that he would baptize her immediately. (The beast fight was scheduled for the next morning.)

18. Diophantes advised Hieronymos that their wives were seated next to Paul night and day. Hieronymos was infuriated with Artemilla and the freedwoman Eubula. He retired early from the table in order to speed up the show. The women asked Paul: "Do you want us to bring a blacksmith so that you can get free and wash us in the sea?"

"No. For I have confidence in God, who has rescued the whole world from chains."

19. It was Sabbath and the Lord's day was approaching, the day on which Paul was to be thrown to the beasts. He cried out "My God, Christ Jesus, who has delivered me from so many perils, grant that these shackles may be shattered and fall from my hands, in the presence of Artemilla and Eubula." While Paul was vigorously entreating for this, a very attractive youth came in, released Paul's shackles, and promptly left, smiling. Because of this celestial manifestation that he had received and the exceptional miracle of the shackles, Paul's grief about the beast-fight evaporated and he leapt in joy as if in Paradise.

20. Taking Artemilla (by the hand) he exited the cramped a[nd gloo]my [place in which the in]carcerated were held. When, after eluding the guards, they were outside and safe, Paul solemnly invoked his God: "The d[oors opened] [...] to praise your providence [...] so that Artemilla might be initiated with the seal of the lord..." [...] the outer [g]ates flew open immediately at the n[a]

Translation, Commentary, and Notes : Chapter

me of God [...] the guards were held in a deep sleep. The mistress left first, followed by the blessed Paul, with [Eubula] into the [thick] darkness. A yout[h physically resembling] Paul preceded them to the [seashore], illuminating (the path) not with a lamp but by the brightness of his body.

21. At that point the illuminator came to a stop. After praying, Paul laid a hand upon Artemilla, descended into the water [*e.g., with her and, after she confessed her faith, baptized her*] in the name of Christ Jesus. [*e.g., When they had come up*], the water glowed, which so terrified Artemilla that she nearly fainted. Anxious, Paul prayed, "You who illuminate and reveal, help, lest the gentiles say that the prisoner Paul escaped after killing Artemilla." Just as the youth smiled again, the matron revived and set out for home. Dawn was breaking. When Paul went back indoors the guards were still asleep. He broke bread, offered water, and after quenching her thirst for the word, sent Artemilla to her husband Hieronymos. Paul then returned to his prayers.

Comment

III. The retardation (§16–21) does not merely raise tensions. This account of the initiation of Eubula and Artemilla shows that baptism is genuine liberation from the bonds of wickedness (see Poupon, "Le baptême d'Artémylla"; and the Note). This is a prison escape story (see p. 234), like that in Acts 12 in that Paschal symbolism is central, while a heavenly being effects release through a number of barriers, and similar to that in Acts 16 in the association with baptism. See Pervo, *Acts.* 299–315; 397–415. The social dimension is also interesting. The first devotee of Paul noted is Diophantes' wife, whose proper name, Eubula, emerges a few lines later. Like her husband, she was a former slave. This story illustrates how missionary movements could move up the social ladder through slaves who share their faith with an owner. The earliest biblical example is the story of Naaman in 2 Kings 5. Her mistress had the fortunate name of Artemilla, a name that honors the patron god of Ephesus. Despite the estrangement of wives from husbands, the subject of celibacy does not appear. See the Note.

The creator of this scene was more skilled in the broad outline than in details. The passage moves from prison and home to the shore and back to prison and home, A-B-A. The last is a good example of the problem with details. Artemilla sets out for home but goes first back to the prison. The character of Eubula falls out of the story. The administration of the sacraments receives no clear narration. The sources of these glitches are uncertain. These include abbreviation, damage to the text, censorship, and authorial incompetence. Most of these possibilities would have antedated both the extant Coptic and the Greek mss.

Excursus: Eubula and Artemilla: An Addition to the Acts of Paul?

Suspicions about the episodes in §16–21 thus arise. Its content is reminiscent of other (and later) Acts, such as the *AJn* and the *AThom*, in which an account of an initiation of women in an exotic setting, accompanied by epiphanic features, would be at home, literarily and theologically. A cogent parallel is *AThom* 118–22, where the apostle slips out of prison, accompanied by a great light, to baptize Mygdonia. Following this is a eucharist with bread and water. A heavenly voice so frightens her nurse Marcia that she also requests and receives initiation. Thomas returns to the prison to find the doors open and the guards asleep. Baptism is presented and characterized as liberation (Klijn, *Acts of Thomas*, 205). The initiation of two women, one of whom serves the other, by an apostle who escapes prison through divinely opened gates, supports the hypothesis that *APl* 9.16–21 imitates this very episode.

Doors likewise open at apostolic in command in *AJn* 73, at a tomb where Christ also appears as a beautiful youth. (See the note on *Puer Speciosus*.) Christ takes the form of a handsome young man in connection with a baptism in *APet* 5. The youthful Christ appears in the ApocActs in association with prison escapes, an evident heritage of the Dionysiac tradition, and in association with initiation and resurrection, where he aptly presents the image of the newly (re)born. That image alone does not demonstrate dependence upon other acts. Christ is also polymorphous in the *APl* (as is Paul, 3.3), where he takes on the appearance of Paul (3.21).

The best evidence for the originality of §16–21 to *APl* is the denunciation of worldly goods in §17, which closely conforms to Paul's speech in §13 and the language of *APl* elsewhere, e.g., "living God" (3.17; 4.12; 5.1; 6.4; 9.10; 13.6; 14.4, 5). However, criticism of wealth is not rare in the ApocActs. For proximate examples, see *AThom* 37, 117, and 88. The last is cited below. Chap. 117 occurs just prior to the episode cited. One could hypothesize a competent imitator of the text as the fashioner of this speech. One difficulty is reconciling that person with the author of §18. Dependence upon *AThom* would mitigate the difficulty.

The strongest literary clue that §16–21 could be later is the extremely awkward opening of §18: "Diophantes advised Hieronymos that their wives were seated next to Paul night and day," followed by, "The women asked Paul: 'Do you want us to bring a blacksmith . . . ?'" The first sentence is a repetition, with appropriate, albeit inept, doubling of the characters, of §16. This material intends to link the subplot with the main plot. It stands out as an insertion, with no marks of interlacement (a narrative technique for raising suspense by moving between (sub)plots, as in the venerable "meanwhile, back at the ranch . . ."). One faint possibility is that this is an abbreviation of a longer (and more competent) paragraph, but it is more likely that this is an interpolation.

In favor, then, of viewing §16–21 as a later addition are (1) a religious character like that of later ApocActs; in particular, (2) a close resemblance to *AThom* 119–22; (3) the awkward and intrusive character of the opening of §18; and (4) some atypical language, such as the reference to "Sabbath" (= Saturday), "The Lord's Day," "adoption," and "gentiles," none of which are found elsewhere in the text, as well as infelicitous repetitions. (For other examples, see the detailed Comments and Notes.) If this is due to an interpolator, that scribe has understood and enhanced the parallels between Paul and Thecla, as the notes and comments indicate. The speech in §17 occupies an intermediate point: it is characteristic of the *APl*, but, on the other hand, repeats a message delivered a few short paragraphs earlier. On the other side, one can again point to strong parallels in *AThom*, including 37 and 88. Note the speech to Mygdonia in 88:

> Rise up from the ground and remove your adornments. For this ornament which you have on will not help you at all, nor the beauty of your body, nor your garments . . . For the exhibition of jewelry is destroyed, and the body ages and changes, and garments wear out, and power and dominion pass away . . . Jesus alone remains for ever and they who hope in him." (trans. Elliott, 481)

This speech is arguably the major source of §17. Note the themes of clothing and jewelry, the decay of nations, and the statement that Jesus (God) alone remains forever and is the source of hope. See the note for another comparison. After formulating the hypothesis of dependence upon *AThom*, I discovered that Peterson, writing before any of the P Bod text had

The Acts of Paul

> become available, had made the same proposal, with regard *AThom* 88, a good half-century ago ("Bemerkungen," 185–87, 200–201). He concluded that *APl* imitates *AThom* here. Peterson did not reflect upon the possibility that the passage was a later addition to *APl*. (Snyder, "Remembering," 194–96, also views this story as a later insertion. He offers no theory about its origin.) Dependence upon *AThom* here obviates the requirement to make the hypothetical interpolator both competent and clumsy. It also strengthens the notion that the entire episode borrows from *AThom*.
>
> If this episode is a subsequent addition to the text, the last paragraph of §22 and sections §27–28 must likewise be later, for the women, Artemilla and Eubula, appear only in §21–26. The last two sections present no difficulties for the interpolation. They are set after Paul's departure from Ephesus. This is quite uncharacteristic. Reports normally end when Paul leaves town. Its use of divine beings in active roles is also congruent with §21–26. See the Comments.
>
> The likelihood that this is a later addition probably inspired by *AThom* is strong, but not certain. If it is original, the opening of §18 has been corrupted. Because of strong doubts about its presence in the original narrative, this scene should not constitute a basis for theological or other proposals about *APl*.

Eubula was no less devoted to Paul than had been Thecla. Her husband, Diophantes, was, for some reason, jealous that she was spending 24/7 with another man. He couldn't wait for the beast fight, which would eliminate his rival. That fact is a reminder of how unnecessary the opposition of these two men is for the plot, since Paul is already under an imminent sentence of death. The other shoe promptly drops: Artemilla (Mme. Hieronymos) wanted to hear Paul at prayer. *APl* assumes that Paul prays incessantly (cf. 1 Thess 5:17), not least while incarcerated (Acts 16:25). Why does Artemilla wish to hear Paul praying? Does she hope to acquire potent magical formulae? The narrative summary is followed by the same matter in direct speech. However cumbersome its expression, the proposal pleases Paul, who, like Thecla, is called "beastfighter" (*thēriomachos*; 4.5, 10, 11).

Artemilla's attempt to dress in something close to mourning was evidently unsuccessful, for she is told that her life as a clothes horse has come to an end. As discussed in the excursus, this speech supplies the best data for attributing the episode to the early *APl*. The rhetoric is of good quality, and the theme of destruction by fire, as well as the general tenor, correspond to §14. A detailed statement of the transitory nature of worldly goods and

Translation, Commentary, and Notes : Chapter

institutions precedes an invitation to transfer her allegiance to God and Christ. However, as pointed out in the excursus, this speech also has general and specific parallels to *AThom*, in particular *AThom* 88. The transition and narrative sequel are inept and abrupt. Paul did not, like Peter in Acts 2:38, close with an exhortation to baptism, but Eubula nevertheless requested the sacrament on this her first encounter with the Christian message. Since Paul will perish tomorrow, urgency is required, but it could be better expressed. The last line is quite similar to 4.5 (Thecla).

§18 is the literary nadir of the *APl*. The alternatives considered are (1) this is the work of an interpolator who by these three short sentences related this story to the overall plot; and (2) that its quality is due to incompetent abbreviation. The former is more cogent. See the excursus. After an abrupt lack of transition, it falls to Diophantes (whose name, "[the one who] shows Zeus/the high god," is quite ironic), to advise Hieronymos as to his wife's whereabouts. This evidently took place at dinner. The language of unremitting attendance comes from §16; the narrator overlooks that Artemilla is just then paying her first visit to Paul. Hieronymos left early to attend to his duties. Without a moment of transition, the narrator snaps the heads of the audience back to the prison, where the baptismal candidates offer to get a smith to remove Paul's fetters. It is preferable not to ask how they expect the authorities to allow this to take place. Why the ocean is necessary is also unclear. It is certainly "living" (fresh, flowing) water, but the incarcerated were accustomed to baptisms in less dramatic circumstances. Cf. Acts 16:33 and *Acts of Perpetua* 5. The question does provide the apostle with opportunity for a cogent reply: redemption, appropriated through baptism, is liberation.

Unlike the various apostles in Acts, Paul prays that his shackles be miraculously removed in the presence of witnesses, who doubtless will both be edified and share the word. The time is noted, as is proper in passion stories. Cf. Mark 14:1. The prayer was not literally answered, but Christ, who was addressed, arrived in the form of a *puer speciosus* (see note) and removed the chains. The account in §19–20 is like Peter's delivery in Acts 12:1–10: prayer, the arrival of a celestial visitant, light, removal of shackles, guidance through gates. See above. Paul has it somewhat better in that his guide does not abandon him at the moment of greatest peril. For now, however, he departs. The same verb (*anachōreō*) is ironically used of both Hieronymos and the Christ figure. The miracle encouraged Paul mightily. This is a message. Even mighty apostles need the strength that comes from sensing the presence of Christ. Poupon ("Le baptême," 90) remarks on the juxtaposition of "paradise" with an animal fight, since the species are at peace in paradise.

§20 relates the escape proper. The Coptic text is once more available, as Paul's prayer begins, but both the Greek and Coptic mss. are damaged. The general meaning is clear. The narrator first summarizes the action. One might gather that the three simply evaded the guards. Paul's subsequent prayer supplies additional, miraculous details. Status consciousness is strong, somewhat atypically of *APl*. The initiation (see Note) of Artemilla is the center of God's attention. Perhaps the readers are to assume that Eubula has already been baptized. The narrator would have done well to verify this hypothesis. The prayer juxtaposes the opening of doors and initiation. On the theme of the unredeemed life as imprisonment, see, e.g., *Odes of Solomon* 17.8; and the comments of Lattke, *Odes*, 90. Darkness is emphasized, both because prisons were dark and as a contrast with the coming light. Thereafter follows a routine, if you would, prison miracle, with the gates opening of their own accord while the guards snoozed, as in Acts 12. The difference is that Paul, presumably, commanded these actions by invoking the name of God. The modern notion of a boundary between "religion" and "magic" has effectively evaporated. Cf. Poupon, "Le baptême," 80.

Now, rather than be led by Paul, Artemilla assumes the lead, followed by the apostle and, apparently, her companion for their journey in pitch darkness. Darkness yields to light as a heavenly visitant appears as a luminous beacon. Cf. *AThom* 118. The symbolism is straightforward: Christ illumines the path of those who follow him out of the realm of sin and death. The imagery is uncertain. The Greek text, followed here, is more amenable to a youth who resembled Paul. Following "a youth like" (both requiring restoration) and a gap of a good five letters are, quite probably *ma*, followed by *paulou*. Schmidt and Schubart (*Praxeis*, 34) propose *sō-*, yielding *sōma paulou*, "a youth like ... body of Paul." The nouns are not in the right case to be construed readily as "similar to Paul in appearance." The Coptic, on the other hand, is best taken along the lines of "like the one who had appeared earlier" (Kasser and Luiser, 333 and n35). §21, which refers to the youth smiling again, presumes identity of this figure with the earlier individual. The Greek is thus more difficult. The parallel with 3.21 comes to mind, but that would yield two Pauls. The Coptic is more likely to be a correction, although one must keep in mind that neither is undamaged. Taken as a double of Paul, the figure is the apostle as the illuminator who brings the light of Christ to those who dwell in darkness. See the *Acts of Xanthippe and Polyxena* 7. Paul, like Christ, is transfigured. See 3.3 and the note on *brightness*.

§21 completes and rounds off the episode. The text is quite difficult. The extant material does not narrate the baptism of Artemilla. A conventional description would include the candidate undressing, entering the water, and receiving the sacrament. In this circumstance Paul would have to enter the water with the candidate, who would have to go out far enough to be immersed. The text is defective. If this is a later addition based upon *AThom*, the interpolator may have abbreviated the account, as *AThom* would have been, especially by Western standards, heretical. In *AThom* emphasis lies upon the unction. Water is, by comparison, given little attention. See *AThom* 121. Initiation may also begin with an imposition of hands, as in *AThom* 49, where the laying on of hands is described, without mention of anointing or immersion. The proposed interpolator could have abbreviated the source. An alternative is that the text was censored. Whatever the cause, the current text stems from a common Greek ancestor of both the extant Greek and Coptic texts. Nicephorus Callistus summarizes the story in his own less than fully reliable manner:

> But Eubula and Artemilla, wives of eminent men among the Ephesians, being his attached disciples, and visiting him by night, desired the grace of the divine washing. And by God's power, with angels to escort them and enlighten the gloom of night with the excess of the brightness that was in them, Paul, loosed from his iron fetters, went to the sea-shore and initiated them into holy baptism, and returning to his bonds without any of those in care of the prison perceiving it, was reserved as a prey for the lions. (*Ecclesiastical History* 2.25, trans. James)

Nicephorus advances the status of Eubula and her husband and twins the women, both of whom are baptized. The handsome young men are angels. From these data it is not possible to ascertain what his source read, but the requested baptism is assumed to have taken place. The glowing youth stops to mark the place for initiation. For baptism administered in the ocean, see *APet* 5; and *Clementine Homily* 9.19. The seashore is a major boundary and thus an ideal marker of liminality, a term historians of religion use to denote those in the process of undergoing a rite of transition. The shore is also a potent narrative symbol. See Doody, *True Story*, 320–27. The teller of this story has absolutely no interest in exploiting or developing the potential of the setting, or even, evidently, of helping the audience grasp the ritual of a seaside baptism. (The narrator is not concerned whether one can move from central Ephesus to a convenient beach.)

The focus of the current text is upon the aftermath. (This may be an effective means of distracting the audience from attending to the narrator's failure to describe the baptism.) The baptism is marked by an epiphany of light in the *water*. Something similar is reported of Thecla's baptism (4.9), and of the baptism of Jesus: Justin, *Dialogue* 88.3; the *Gospel of the Ebionites*, according to Epiphanius, *Panarion* 30.13.7–8. The basis for this symbolism is the understanding of baptism as illumination (e.g., Justin, *1 Apol.* 61.2). The narrator does not present Artemilla as an aficionado of symbolism just then. She collapsed. Has baptism killed her? So Paul fears. (Only the Coptic text records his anxiety.) He informs God that her death will do his reputation no good (nor, by implication, God's). The term "gentiles" for non-believers is found only here in the extant *APl*. The motif of apparent death is a most popular suspense propellant in ancient popular literature (for examples, see Pervo, *Profit*, 148n2). This may be intended as a vulgar and exciting representation of baptism as death with Christ (Rom 6:3–11; cf. Poupon, "Le baptême," 92). The obvious parallel is to Tryphaena, 4.11.

The narrator does not exploit the potential, relying, as usual, upon immediate gratification of many readers' wishes. Readers interested in other forms of gratification have to cope with another surprise. The youth smiled once more; Artemilla revived. The smile is a symbol of divine favor and beneficence; Artemilla did not have to see the smile; its healing effect required no participation from her. All well and good. The difficulty is that the text apparently assumes that the youth has been with them all along, despite discontinuities. The narrator evidently assumes that readers will understand that this figure is the polymorphous Christ. (Another matter for concern is the disappearance of Eubula.)

Having survived her initiation and what was, by any standards, a night to remember, Artemilla set out for home. This action is quite reasonable, but she did not go there, yet. The narrator has once again, probably unintentionally, confused the reader. The terseness of the narrative is remarkable. A storyteller could spend ten minutes on the swoon without exhausting its possibilities. "Dawn was breaking." This provides a link with §22, but the narrator has other interests than synchrony. Dawn is the time of the discovery of Jesus' resurrection (Luke 24:1) and, for that reason, the time of baptism (*Apostolic Tradition* 21.1). More generally, and not unrelatedly, dawn is a time of transition, from darkness to light, death to life. Paul (Greek, "he"; Coptic, "they") returned to prison without difficulty, as the guards remained asleep. (Although this motif suits prison escapes, it is also evocative of the greatest escape of all, Jesus' exit from the grave, Matt 28:4, and thus another Easter symbol.) Few would cast a rock of blame at Paul had he chosen not to return to custody and provide breakfast for a famished lion, but rather to take flight. This is, like Acts 16, apologetic in thrust. The apostle does not use his supernatural gifts to evade the course of the law, wicked as it may be. Poupon ("Le baptême," 91) points to the parallel story about Apollonius

Translation, Commentary, and Notes : Chapter

(*Apollonius of Tyana* 7.38), who could loosen his fetters but would not use them as a get out of jail free card.

A reasonable understanding of the sequel is that Paul celebrated a baptismal eucharist, after which the women left. *AThom* 122 is a good model. A literal rendition of the Greek text is: "[H]e broke bread and offered water; he watered with speech; he sent back to her husband Hieronymos." The last two verbs lack connectives. Asyndeton ("I came; I saw; I conquered") can be effective, but the first two verbs are joined by "and." The second, asyndetic pair also lacks an object. Just as the narrative did not describe the baptism, so it also passes over her reception of communion. One option is to presume that the text (Coptic is deficient here) is corrupt and assume that, through abbreviation and error, a narrative of offered bread and water, sanctified by prayer ("with speech"; see note) and delivered to the newly baptized should be restored. A more conservative, although not necessarily more probable, option is to take the verb "water" metaphorically, as in this translation. Cf. 1 Cor 3:6.

Our law-abiding, socially conservative apostle then sent Artemilla back to her husband. She does not renounce him to follow Paul, and not a word is said about sex. The apostle then returned to his ceaseless prayer (omitted by Coptic, perhaps as gratuitous.) The story has come full circle: Artemilla at home and Paul at prayer. The narrator of this tale apparently knows how to tie a fine ribbon around this package, but less about how to wrap it, and still less about fashioning the contents. It may well have been mutilated in transmission. As it is, 9.16–21 is the most incompetent piece of narrative in the book. As an interlude, interpolation or not, it is effective both as a retardation and as a symbolic story within a story, an insert that shows what real liberation is—Christian freedom embraced in baptism. The episode as a whole will show what this freedom means: a world in which lions need not act like lions nor, by implication, sinful human beings like sinners.

Notes

AThom 88. P. 2, l.22 of P.Hamb (Schmidt and Schubart, *Praxeis*, 28) reads *ouden gar se tauta ōphelēsei*; the Greek of *AThom* 88 (p. 203, 10, Lipsius-Bonnet) has: *ouden gar se ōphelēsei*. Verbal identity of this nature urges an intertextual approach.

Artemilla. Her name is convenient. Verisimilitude requires that she came with her husband from Rome. The author did not worry about such niceties.

The Acts of Paul

Change of clothes. See *Aseneth* 10. See also Peterson, "Bemerkungen," 183–84.

Two women initiates. See Peterson, "Bemerkungen," 183n2.

Celibacy. If §16–21 is a later addition based upon *AThom*, there would be no need for noting that baptism required celibacy thereafter. If this story is integral to *APl*, the need for celibacy may well have been censored, for instance in the now defective §18. See the excursus.

Denunciation of worldly goods. See *Clementine Homilies* 8.21, and, for other references, Peterson, "Bemerkungen," 184n5.

Destruction through fire. Compare Tatian, *Oration* 17. If, as seems likely, this is a later contribution, the interpolator differed from *AThom* on the theme.

Liberation. On baptism as liberation, see, e.g., Rom 6:1–23; The *Excerpta ex Theodoto* 78.2. For a theological exposition, see Heinrich Schlier, *eleutheros*, *TDNT* 2:487–502, esp. 499–502. See also Klijn, *Acts of Thomas*, 205.

Puer Speciosus (beautiful youth). The association of youth and beauty is more or less ubiquitous. The notion of divine beings as beautiful creatures entered Christianity from the Greek world. The figure of the beautiful young god is characteristic of the cult of Dionysus. See, e.g., *Homeric Hymn 7, to Dionysus*, 14–15, where bonds fell away from the smiling god. Smiling is also associated with Aphrodite (*Hom. Hymn* 10.3). The underlying assumption is that Christ is polymorphous, can assume any form, size, or appearance desired. A notable example of this quality can be seen in *AJn* 88–89. See Peterson, "Bemerkungen," 199; and Poupon, "Le baptême," 88–89. For artistic portrayals of Christ as a youth, see Mathews, *Clash*, 115–41.

Day and night. This phrase, "constantly," was applied to Thecla in 3.8. See also 9.18; cf. 1 Thess 2:9; Acts 26:7.

Message. This is awkward. Schmidt and Schubart delete it as a gloss (*Praxeis* 29, 14), followed by Rordorf, 1156.

Only path to salvation. Cf. Acts 4:12 and Table 4.1, p. 174.

Offerings. An alternative is "worship images and offerings." The verb takes the dative. "Offerings" is lit. "fats" or "odors," i.e., incense. The trope is a jibe against animal sacrifices. Cf. *Diognetus* 2.8; 3.5.

By the hand is supplied.

Paul solemnly invoked. The phrase is odd. The verb *diamartyreō* is not customary for introducing prayers. "Paul bore witness to his own god" is the literal meaning. "His own" (*idios*) would work best in an address to unbelievers. Cf. *AJn* 39. The sense is "our god (as opposed to the god[s] of others)," as in Josephus *Ant.* 8.280.

Providence. Oikonomia. See p. 74.

Initiate. The verb *myeō* (whence "mystery") is not commonly used of Christian baptism before c. 200.

Eubula. The Greek reads "mistress" (*matrōn*, borrowed from Latin), while the Coptic identifies Artemilla by name. "Eubula" is a logical restoration (Schmidt and Schurbart, 35). The preposition *syn* implies accompaniment (i.e., with a person rather than "with anger" or "with a headache," etc.). Coptic omits, perhaps because it seems undignified.

Blessed Paul. This is a mark of a later hand, appropriate for the interpolator of this episode; otherwise it is a subsequent addition to the text.

Brightness. Lit., "holiness." Divine beings manifest the light of heaven. The conventional representation of this is the halo that marks saints.

Water. Schmidt and Schubart (*Praxeis,* 34, regarding ms. p. 3 l.33) propose that the water became agitated. This is possible, but a light epiphany is much more probable. See the Comments; and Peterson, "Bemerkungen," 198. Kasser and Luisier propose to restore the Coptic to read that the water became fiery (332n38).

With water. Eph 5:26 is an interesting possible parallel. The expression *en rhēmati* could refer to the baptismal formula. By analogy the meaning here might refer to the Eucharistic Prayer. BDAG 856 cites this passage from *APl* as an example of metaphorical usage. Cf. 1 Cor 3:2. See also Spicq, *Lexicon* 3:145–48.

9.22–26 IV. Judgment in the Arena.

22. At dawn the citizens began to cry, "Let's go to the spectacle. Let us go and see the one who 'possesses God' fighting with beasts." Hieronymos was present in person, driven both by suspicion of his wife and determination that Paul not escape. He directed

The Acts of Paul

Diophantes and the other slaves to bring Paul into the stadium. As he was being dragged about he said nothing but kept his head bowed down and groaned because he was being led in triumph by the city. After being paraded, he was tossed directly into the field. His dignity exacerbated the multitude.

Because Artemilla, not to mention Eubula, had fallen ill to the point of mortal danger because of the ruin of Paul, Hieronymos was very unhappy. On top of this was the widely circulated story that she was no longer in harmony with him.

23. When Hieronymos had taken his place, he commanded that a very fierce lion, recently taken, be let loose upon Paul, leading the entire crowd to shout: "Let the rapacious lion devour the one who 'possesses god!'"

So when the cage was opened and the lion came forth, Paul set out to meet it as a suppliant, praying to the lord Jesus Christ. The attendants who urged the lion to attack were astonished at the size and ferocity of the creature. Meanwhile, Paul paid no attention but continued with his responsibility of prayer and witness. The lion, puffed up to full size, looked around the stadium, then came at Paul on the run, reclining by his legs, like a trained lamb ... When Paul had finished praying, the lion got up on its paws and said to Paul, in a human voice, [*"Grace be with you!"*] Unperturbed, Paul replied, "Grace be with you, lion," and put his hand on its head. At this the crowd hollered in unison: "Get rid of this sorcerer, get rid of this magician!"

24. Paul and the lion looked at one another, Paul reckoned that this was the lion that had come [*and been baptized*]. Supported by his faith, Paul greeted the lion [*with a kiss*] and said, "Are you the one that I baptized?"

"Y[es]."

Paul spoke again: "How were you captured?"

"Just like you, Paul" replied the lion [...]

25. Hieronymos sent many wild animals to kill Paul and archers to dispatch the lion. Despite the clear sky a huge and voluminous rain of hail plummeted down from the sky, so dense that it killed many and sent the rest fleeing for shelter. Both Paul and the lion

were unharmed, but the other animals perished from the volume of hail. Hieronymos' ear was hit and sliced, and the fleeing crowd kept shouting: "Save us, O God! Save us, God of the one who fights the beasts!"

26. Paul then said farewell to the now silent lion, left the stadium, went down to the harbor, and boarded a ship bound for Macedonia. Many were sailing away, supposing that the city was about to fall, so Paul went aboard in the guise of a refugee. For his part, the lion set out for his accustomed haunts in the hills.

Comments

IV. §22–26 bring about the climax of Paul's work in Ephesus, in which he eludes the cruel death prepared for him. The parallels to the story of Thecla in chaps. 3 and 4 have been noted. These parallels constitute sufficient proof that the individual primarily responsible for the extant *APl* should be characterized as an "author," a person who could fashion and execute a literary plan independent of (although influenced by) those found in the canonical gospels and Acts. This author evades inerrancy. Attribution of section III (§16–21) to a later editor requires regarding subsequent references to its distinctive characters as the work of the same hand. One or more of these may have appeared earlier in the original narrative. An example is Diophantes, not introduced in §22, but identified as a slave, rather than a former slave, as in §16. He may, hypothetically, have been introduced here as a chief slave of Hieronymos, and been promoted by the interpolator.

In chap. 4 the lioness supported and died for Thecla as a symbol of female solidarity and power (as well as her role as "mistress of the beasts"). The lion in chap. 9 unites Paul's story with Thecla's and pulls together his entire ministry, from the moment of his conversion to the present in Ephesus. The symbolism of the lion is much more complex (or more cloudy, if you prefer) than in chap. 4. It is also a more appealing story, a sentimental tale that is made most attractive because of its back story (re-)related at the beginning of the chapter. This lion, like Paul, makes a successful escape. Here, as in chap. 4, the antagonist is not deterred by leonine failure. Reserves are brought in from the menagerie. Rescue must come from above. The close is rather typical of the canonical Acts: Paul was not compelled to leave because of persecution, but leave he did. Cf. Acts 16:38–40; 18:12–18; 20:1.

The Acts of Paul

Dawn signals, for Christians, the beginning of new life. For the crowd, presented as Paul's implacable foes, it is the occasion for a new death. So eager are they that they jump out of bed and say, "[O]n with the show!" (see also 4.5. On "let's go," see 3.1 and; for "spectacle," 3.21). The epithet that Paul "possesses god" (rather than being possessed by a god) is intended as an insult. It is ironic in that, while possessed by God, Paul also "possesses" Christ. "*Beastfighter*" is doubtless intended ironically. The term is also used of Thecla (4.5, 10, 11).

The other opponent is the governor, who takes personal charge of the display. (The motive of suspicion of his wife is presumably a later addition.) Like Thecla (4.3), Paul was part of a triumphal procession. Like Jesus (Mark 14:61), Paul did not speak; he did exhibit shame at public humiliation. Like Thecla (4.8) he was unceremoniously dumped onto the field at the end of the procession. As on an earlier occasion (3.17) his dignity was impressive. These are common martyrological motifs. The ball is in play.

The last two sentences are an awkward insertion from the source of §16–21. The narrator has not given them much time for their romantic malaise, since they could have scarcely beaten the dawn home, by which time the crowd was screaming for blood. How the governor learned of the women's illness is not revealed, although rumor worked rapidly in Ephesus, since their reputed lack of harmony has been gestating for about twelve hours. The narrator does not wish to hint at the root cause, which is typically withdrawal from the conjugal bed. Because of the sub-plot, Hieronymos needs two reasons for animosity to Paul.

As §23 opens the governor is finally in place. He directs that the Christian be thrown to a lion ("fierce," as was Thecla's lioness, 4.8). Reference to the presumed arrival of this creature in §15 is lacking. The crowd demands that the lion add god to its diet. Suspense mounts. Paul does not try to bluff or face down the creature. He petitions for peace, praying to Christ. Suspense does not diminish. The keepers, experienced with a wide range of predatory animals, can't believe how frightening this creature is. As for Paul, he had other matters on his mind. The lion put on his feline swell, checked out the crowd, and sprinted toward Paul. Excellent drama, but one must ask who is teasing whom? The lion Paul? The narrator the audience? Neither is very commendable. The narrator makes up for this cheap trick with a splendid simile: the lion acts like a lamb, thus evoking the peaceable kingdom.

Action must, of course, await the close of Paul's prayer, which was not disrupted by the mere charge of a lion. The translation follows the reconstructed Coptic (Kasser and Luisier, 336). Schmidt and Schubart (38) reconstruct the Greek to state that the lion arose as if from sleep. A (reconstructed) greeting follows, but recognition is not yet achieved. The crowd and the apostle react in distinctly different ways. After Paul fearlessly laid a hand on the creature's head and returned the greeting, the crowd demands his extermination, identifying him as a practitioner of magic, by which means he made the lion both behave and appear to speak. This is not the first time that such a charge has been raised. The crowd in Iconium called Paul a *magos* because he had bewitched Thecla and other girls and women; the crowd there made the same demand for death, without reference to magic, regarding Jesus (Luke 23:18) and Paul (Acts 21:36; 22:22).

Recognition comes through sight. The scene is simple and affecting. Paul now bestows the Christian greeting of a kiss upon the fellow-creature. ("Supported by his faith" is absent from the Coptic, the kiss is conjectural, and the rest of §24 after the question is omitted from Coptic through a visual error; see Kasser and Luisier, 339n55.) The apostle initiates a friendly conversation: What's a nice lion like you doing in a place like this? The simple answer evokes in a few words their common fate, with a slap at the cruelty of capturing wild animals. They are both creatures, both captives.

Paul's encounter with a lion is less dramatic than Thecla's but it is more appealing. This is because of the "back story," their previous encounter. Since Metzger's 1945 article, "St. Paul and the Baptized Lion," scholarship has generally accepted that this is a Christianized form of the story of Androcles and the lion, which exists in a number of accounts, ranging from a graffito (Shear, "Excavations"—which may not refer to Androcles), to fable (Perry, ed., *Babrius and Phaedrus*, Appendix, no. 563, p. 526), to "scientific" and miscellaneous literature (Aelian, *The nature of Animals* 7.48; Aulus Gellius, *Attic Nights* 5.14). The last identifies as his source the Egyptian Apion, who, he stated, claimed to have witnessed the event at Rome. (Apion was an antagonist of the Jews and the target of Josephus' apology, *Against Apion*.) The latter two relate a similar story. (Italics represent shared themes.)

Androcles, an escaped slave, fled to the Libyan desert and took refuge in a cave, the regular tenant of which returned, injured. Androcles helped the *lion* and shared his cave for three years, eventually leaving, only to be captured by Roman officials and *condemned to the beasts*. The lion assigned that task, *also captured by the Romans*, was none other than his old cavemate. He recognized his victim, fawned on him and *lay at his feet. Androcles recognized the lion; they hugged*. According to Aelian this generated the suspicion that Androcles was a *magician* (*goēs*; not used in *APl* 9), leading to the dispatch of a leopard, which the lion kills. The last incident is very like *APl* 4.8. If the author knew the story familiar to Aelian, he may have borrowed this slice to embellish the adventures of Thecla. Androcles and the lion are both freed at the demands of crowd.

The Acts of Paul

Many tales were told then (and later) of animals who befriended and refused to devour humans (examples in Spittler, *Animals*, 173–76; note also Riemer, "Miracle Stories"; a particularly interesting example is the story of a pet snake in Aelian, *Varia Historia* 13.46); similarity in detail indicates that the author of *APl* made use of a literary account. The fable of *The Lion and the Shepherd* (see the reference to Perry above) has two interesting features. Like Paul, the shepherd was unjustly condemned. (Androcles was a fugitive slave.) Also, the lion talks. Talking animals are more or less required in fables, but this is a form of the story that includes a vocal lion. The benefaction is different. The narrator could have taken up the story neat and had Paul heal an inarticulate animal that later reciprocated his friendship. That different choices were made establishes the symbolic thrust: the removal of divisions brought about by human sin, including the division between the sexes and the wars among species.

The governor's interests at that time did not include symbolism. Where one beast failed, many might succeed. Cf. Thecla, 4.9. As for the lion, arrows were in order. God then takes a direct hand. Out of a clear sky, as the saying has it, burst a lethal hail storm that did not touch either Paul or the lion but killed all the other animals. The parallel with the storm that saved Thecla in 3.22 is as clear as day, if you would. One hailstone gashed the governor's ear. Cf. Mark 14:47; John 18:26 (i.e., this is a parallel with the passion of Jesus). This event is not in the Coptic, which is evidently corrupt here. The crowd, last heard (§22–23) mocking the beastfighter and his god have experienced a change of heart, calling now for that god to rescue them. This forms a nice inclusio for the adventure in the arena.

That is, it's all over but the shouting. In the face of a populace begging for deliverance, an entire city eager to convert, Paul decides to leave rather than continue his mission. A ship is about to sail to Macedonia. In light fiction characters do not need to wait about for the next departure. It happens when they get there. In this instance the probability is greater because of a general exodus caused by the hailstorm. Paul is leaving Ephesus in accordance with Acts 20:1. The lion headed for the familiar hills, which, in this case, were far from his native haunts. His part in the story has ended.

Notes

Led in triumph (*Ethriambeueto*). The clear sense of this passage is that Paul is a captive, the victim rather than a triumphant leader. This deserves citation in discussions of 2 Cor 2:14.

Puffed up. This attempts to understand the text as referring to the feline tactic of assuming the largest possible size.

Beastfighter. This epithet, applied to both Paul and Thecla, was an important moral image in the Greco-Roman world. Heracles was extolled as a beastfighter in the moral writers because his legendary exploits were viewed as allegories of the war against *hēdonē* ("pleasure"), the central vice of *APl*. See Malherbe, *Paul*, 82–85, who understands Paul's language of "fighting with beasts" as metaphorical.

Lamb. Schmidt and Schubart (38) propose a second simile: "like a slave." This would be anticlimactic. The Coptic is defective here. "Hippolytus" (*Commentary on Daniel* 3.29.3–4) says that the lion licked Paul, but he said the same of the lions in Daniel. Thecla is also a lamb in Paul's flock (3.21).

Hand. This clause is missing from Coptic. See Kasser and Luisier, 339n51. This would amount to a handshake.

Just like you. The Greek text says, "with one voice." This would be appropriate for a crowd shouting in unison, but makes no sense here. Schmidt and Schubart (41n4) take note of Commodian (*Carmen Apologeticum* 628): *Leonem populo fecit loqui voce divina* (He made the lion speak with a divine voice), and reconstruct this process of corruption: *theiai* (divine) *thiai* (a normal spelling change) *mia*. "Divine voice" is possible, but it makes limited sense here ("divine" does not refer to quality—sounding like a god—but to the source—God).

Plummeted. The rain came down, in a flight of poetic justice, like arrows, as the verb *akontizō* intimates.

9.27–28. V. Resolution of the Subplot.

27. Artemilla and Eubula were dreadfully upset and occupied themselves with fasting and [*weeping*] in their anxiety over what had happened with Paul [*and the lion*]. That night [*the handsome youth*] appeared manifestly in the bedroom where the women were comforting one another and Hieronymos lay with a suppurating ear. Artemilla had not gone to tend to him because of her grief. The youth said to them, "Don't be upset or ill, but be secure in the name of Christ Jesus and in his might. For Paul, the slave

of Christ, the prisoner, has left. He has gone to Macedonia to accomplish the lord's plans entrusted to him. But you ... the father's grace ... will encourage." This news left them beside themselves with amazement.

Hieronymos, brought to his senses by a night of agony, cried out: "God who came to the help of the beast-fighter, save me through the youth who appeared in the closed bedroom via a vision."

28. When the youth saw the attendants [fleeing] in terror, he called back the physicians and cried loudly: "Through the will of Christ Jesus heal his ear!" It became well. The youth then directed him, "Treat it with honey."

Comments

V. This anticlimactic unit was necessitated by the insertion of the story of Artemilla and Eubula (§16–21). Their distress about Paul (§22) continues. While the two women comfort one another in the master bedroom, neglecting the suffering governor, a divine being (identified as an angel in the Coptic, perhaps secondarily, as it was probably the handsome lad of the earlier episode) appeared, with a typical bit of opening assurance, to bring them (just Artemilla in the Coptic) up to date, borrowing from Acts 19:21. Their reaction, borrowed from Mark 5:42, indicates that they thought Paul dead.

The camera then shifts, awkwardly, to poor Hieronymos. His suffering has been salutary, for it drove him to take the view of the crowd and pray to Paul's God. (The text is damaged; the translation mainly follows the Greek.) The governor appealed to the handsome youth, who is, in fact, the god of the beastfighter. Although neglected by his wife, Hieronymos was not alone. He was surrounded by aides, including physicians. The reader must assume that they were unable to treat a wounded ear. The youth demands that the physicians return, presumably to serve as witnesses. Luke 22:51 has inspired the healing of an opponent's ear. The (evidently) loud voice is part of the treatment, although it is characteristic of exorcisms (Mark 1:26; 5:7). The final direction is for after-treatment. Honey had medicinal uses (Theophrastus, *History of Plants* 9.11.3; 18.8. Cf. Prov 16:24.) It would protect the skin. An alternative, based upon the poor state of the text would treat the honey as material to be applied before and as a material supplement to miraculous healing. Cf. John 5:1–7; and the note.

Why has the putative interpolator elected to end the episode on this anticlimactic and prosaic note? To be sure, someone who has felt obliged to supply an anticlimactic epilogue might not blush at an anticlimactic closing. A critic of today would find it apt, if not brilliant. The day after you have been healed is the first day of the rest of your life. Even those miraculously healed must take care of themselves. At the prosaic level the practice may relate to ceremonies for healing in which honey, rather than or in addition to oil, was applied to the affected tissue.

Notes

Honey. For use of honey as a magical healing substance, see Dittenberger, *Sylloge*³ 1173.15–18.

After the final line, the Coptic has a line of marks indicating a division (]]]]]]] . . .) followed by the Greek title, in two lines: *praxis paulou*. The first word could be read either as *praxeis*, "acts," or singular, "act." The latter is more likely. Behind this text stands an edition of a single chapter.

Bibliography

Adamik, Tamás. "The Baptized Lion in the Acts of Paul." In *The Apocryphal Acts of Paul and Thecla*, edited by Jan N. Bremmer, 60–74. Kampen: Kok Pharos, 1996.
Betz, Hans Dieter. *Galatians*. Hermeneia. Philadelphia: Fortress, 1979.
Bieler, Ludwig. ΘΕΙΟΣ ΑΝΗΡ: *Das Bild des "Göttlichen Menschen" in Spätantike und Frühchristentum*. 2 vols. 1935–1936. Reprint, Darmstadt: Wissenschaftliche Buchgesellschaft, 1967.
Conybeare, Frederick C. "Commentary of Ephrem on Acts." In *The Beginnings of Christianity*, edited by F. J. Foakes-Jackson and K. Lake, 3:373–453. London: Macmillan, 1926.
Czachesz, István. "The Acts of Paul and the Western Text of Luke's Acts: Paul between Canon and Apocrypha." In *The Apocryphal Acts of Paul and Thecla*, edited by Jan N. Bremmer, 107–25. Kampen: Kok Pharos, 1996.
Doody, Margaret Anne. *The True Story of the Novel*. New Brunswick, NJ: Rutgers University Press, 1996.
Drijvers, Han J. W. "Der getaufte Löwe und die Theologie der Acta Pauli." In *Carl-Schmidt-Kolloquium an der Martin-Luther Universität 1998*, edited by P. Nagel, 181–89. Wissenschaftliche Beiträge 9. Halle: Salle, 1990.
Georgi, Dieter. *The Opponents of Paul in Second Corinthians*. Philadelphia: Fortress, 1986.
Kasser, Rodolphe. "Acta Pauli 1959." *RHPR* 40 (1960) 45–57.
Kasser, Rodolphe, and Philippe Luisier. "Le Papyrus Bodmer XLI en Édition Princeps l'Épisode d'Èphèse des *Acta Pauli* en Copte et en Traduction." *Le Muséon* 117 (2004) 281–384.

The Acts of Paul

Klijn, Albertus F. J. *The Acts of Thomas: Introduction, Text, and Commentary*. 2nd ed. NovTSup 108. Leiden: Brill, 2003.

Kurfess, Alfons. "Zu dem Hamburger Papyrus der *Praxeis Paulou*." *ZNW* 38 (1939) 164–70.

Lattke, Michael. *The Odes of Solomon*. Translated by Marianne Ehrhardt. Hermeneia. Minneapolis: Fortress, 2009.

MacDonald, Dennis R. "A Conjectural Emendation of 1 Cor 15:31–32: Or the Case of the Misplaced Lion Fight." *HTR* 73 (1980) 265–78.

———. *The Legend and the Apostle*. Philadelphia: Westminster, 1983.

Malherbe, Abraham. *Paul and the Popular Philosophers*. Minneapolis: Fortress, 1989.

Mathews, Thomas F. *The Clash of Gods. A Reinterpretation of Early Christian Art*. 2nd ed. Princeton: Princeton University Press, 2003.

Matthews, Christopher R. "Articulate Animals: A Multivalent Motif in the Apocryphal Acts of the Apostles." In *The Apocryphal Acts of the Apostles*, edited by François Bovon, Ann G. Brock, and C. R. Matthews, 205–32. Cambridge, MA: Harvard University Press, 1999.

Metzger, Bruce M. "St. Paul and the Baptized Lion." *Princeton Seminary Bulletin* 39 (1945) 11–21.

Niederwimmer, Kurt. *The Didache*. Trans. Linda M. Maloney. Hermeneia. Minneapolis: Fortress, 1998.

Pervo, Richard I. "A Hard Act to Follow: The *Acts of Paul* and the Canonical Acts." *Journal of Higher Criticism* 2, no. 2 (1995) 3–32.

———. "Shepherd of the Lamb: Paul as a Christ-Figure in the *Acts of Paul*." In *Portraits of Jesus: Studies in Christology*, edited by Susan E. Myers, 355–69. WUNT 321. Tübingen: Mohr/Siebeck, 2012.

Peterson, Erik. "Einige Bermerkungen zum Hamburger Papyrus-Fragment der Acta, Pauli." In *Frühkirche, Judentum und Gnosis*, 183–208. Freiburg: Herder.

Poupon, Gérard. "Excursus: 'Le baptême d'Artémylla ou la vraie libération,' to 'L'accusation de magie dans les Actes Apocryphes.'" In *Les Actes apocryphes des Apôtres: christianisme et monde païen*, edited by François Bovon et al., 86–93. Publications de la Faculté de Théologie de l'Université de Genève 4. Geneva: Labor et Fides, 1981.

Riemer, Ulrike. "Miracle Stories and Their Narrative Intent in the Context of the Ruler Cult of Classical Antiquity." In *Wonders Never Cease: The Purpose of Narrating Miracle Stories in the New Testament and Its Religious Environment*, edited by Michael Labahn and Bertjan L. Peerbolte, 32–47. Library of New Testament Studies 288. London: T. & T. Clark.

Rordorf, Willy. "Quelques jalons pour une interpretation symbolique des Actes de Paul." *Early Christian Voices: In Texts, Traditions, and Symbols*. FS F. Bovon. BIS 66. Leiden: Brill, 2003, 251–65.

Schneemelcher, Wilhelm. "Der Getaufte Löwe." *Gesammelte Aufsätze zum Neuen Testament und zur Patristik*, 223–29. Analecta Vlatadon 22. Thessaloniki: Patriarchal Institute for Patristic Studies, 1974.

Shear, Theodore L. "Excavations in Corinth in 1926." *AJA* 30 (1926) 446–63.

Snyder, Glenn E. "Remembering the *Acts of Paul*." PhD diss., Harvard University, 2010.

Spittler, Janet, E. *Animals in the Apocryphal Acts of the Apostles*. WUNT 247. Tübingen: Mohr/Siebeck, 2008

Trebilco, Paul. *The Early Christians in Ephesus from Paul to Ignatius*. WUNT 166. Tübingen: Mohr/Siebeck, 2004.

Translation, Commentary, and Notes : Chapter

Chapter 10: Philippi

Primary sources: P.Heid 45–50, 41–42; 44a; P.Bodmer 10. Secondary sources: cf. Nicetas of Paphlagonia.

3 Corinthians has a rich textual history, including, in addition to the Greek and Coptic, Latin, Syriac, and Armenian. *3 Cor* was included, after 1–2 Corinthians, in many Armenian bibles as late as the nineteenth century. Ephrem Syrus commented upon the epistle, which he regarded as genuine. (See Johnston and Poirier, "Nouvelles citations." On the attribution, see Bundy, "Pseudo-Ephremian.") Five Latin mss. include *3 Cor* (often with *Laodiceans*) at the close of the Pauline correspondence or of the New Testament, once with the specific stipulation that it is not authentic. See Hovhanessian, *Third Corinthians*, 3–16. Testuz, *Papyrus Bodmer X–XII*, 23–24, notes that *3 Cor* remained in favor in the (proudly independent) diocese of Milan until as late as the thirteenth century. On the textual tradition, see Dunn, "Legacy," 102–4, with a provisional stemma on 104; and Snyder, "Remembering," 68–73.

Excursus: 3 Corinthians

3 Corinthians, a designation for a complex of two letters, one from the believers at Corinth (II), the other from the apostle (IV), as well as two narratives (I, III). Only P.Heid has all four sections. P.Bod, some Latin mss., and some Armenian mss. contain only the letters. This material was not an original component of *APl*. The most probable explanation is that an author composed this pair of letters toward the end of the second century. A subsequent editor wrote the narrative links (I, III) and inserted the material into *APl*. The alternative is to attribute introduction of *3 Cor* to the author of *APl*. Dunn ("Legacy") makes a detailed argument that the insertion was the work of the author. The basis of his case is his perception of theological agreement between *3 Cor* and *APl*. That would accomplish no more than show that *3 Cor* was not objectionable to the author. The chief, and, in my view, decisive, reason for assigning the interpolation to a later editor is that the contents of the narrative cannot be reconciled with the subsequent visit to Corinth (chap. 12).

The author of the correspondence anticipates a modern objection to the practice of reconstructing the views of Paul's rivals from his own refutations, which no one can pretend to be comprehensive, and objective accounts of those opposing views. The letter presents the opponents' position in six short, sharp, and clear propositions, a manner that readers will regard as objective. This material also satisfies the desire to read something that Corinthian believers wrote to Paul (cf. 1 Cor 7:1). Dramatically, the contrasting letters work like a rhetorical duel in which two sides offer opposing speeches. (See Pervo, *Acts,* 594–95.) This little collection reveals an author not lacking dramatic sense, as well as the impetus for pseudepigraphic letter collections to take on the features of epistolary novels. See Pervo, *Making,* 96–104; and Glaser, *Briefroman.*

The apostle confronts these suspect teachings with a specific, more or less point-by-point refutation, embellished with apt illustrations. What heretics are in view? Despite Rordorf's learned and informative attempt to associate the opposition with a specific heresy, that of Saturninus ("Hérésie," 35–44), it is likely that the author wished to produce a text that would serve as a weapon against Marcion and a number of "Gnostic" groups. (See Luttikhuizen, "Apocryphal Correspondence," 91; Hovhanessian, *Third Corinthians,* 126–31; and Snyder, "Rembering," 67–113.) Rordorf does show that the views represented by the opponents are more suitable to the gnostic systems proper than to the school of Valentinus, or to Marcion, for example. The principal concern of *3 Cor* is to assert the importance of the flesh as the vehicle for incarnation and resurrection. *Docetism* was the major problem.

Evidence that *3 Cor* was not a part of the original *APl* is clear and uncontestable. Only P.Heid includes *3 Cor* in the *APl*. P.Hamb did not contain this text. The narrative sections I and III are sometimes absent. No ancient authority, including Ephrem, who utilized *APl* and commented upon *3 Cor,* links this text to the Acts. The major justification for including the text in this commentary is as a demonstration of an unsuccessful attempt to make a substantial interpolation into *APl*. The interpolation shows that *APl* was considered defective on the question of refuting heresies and that it was important enough to be supplemented on this matter.

APl presents a view of church order that is more "primitive" than the canonical book. House-based communities are led by the heads of the household. In *3 Cor* the Corinthian community is headed by a bishop, with his council of presbyters and some assisting deacons. Two of the latter are named. This was the normal arrangement in Asia Minor by the middle of the second century, but it does not jibe with the rest of *APl*. A second egregious inconsistency emerges in the personnel. The names of the itinerant teachers were not drawn out of a hat. The church historian Eusebius claims (*Ecclesiastical History* 4.22.4–6) that Hegesippus, who was active in the third quarter of the second century, placed Simon (identified with the Magus) and Cleobius at the head of his list of false teachers. (See also the *Apostolic*

Constitutions 6.8;16). The author of 3 *Cor* probably took these names from tradition. This lends historical verisimilitude. An infelicitous result of this tactic is that one of the believers in Corinth also bears the name Cleobius (12.3). Persons of that name also appear in the *Acts of John* (e.g., 18) and the *Acts of Peter* 3; it is not extremely rare, but, presuming that the Cleobius of *APl* 12 also derived from tradition, which is quite unlikely, the author would have been obliged to supply a note distinguishing him from the itinerant false teacher, as in John 14:22. For an interpolator to overlook this conflict is intelligible; it is difficult to imagine an author, or an author as interpolator, doing so. Cleobius is but a symbol of the lack of agreement. To the category of names belongs the list of officers that headed up the letter; none of them appear in chap. 12. When Paul arrives in Corinth, there is not so much as a word about the difficulties previously unleashed by the nefarious Simon and Cleobius. The Corinthians who had so forgotten the teachings of their apostle have also forgotten that they had forgotten, and so had the apostle. Paul's letter (III) says nothing of a forthcoming visit to Corinth. As the text stands, this is a surprise. The excess of narrative glitches suffice to show that 3 *Cor* did not enter the *APl* through the work of its author.

A final point relates to characterization. Otherwise in *APl* the apostle is a kind of superman who can accomplish what Jesus had done. Remarkable miracles and astounding sermons suffice to win over unbelievers, vanquish rivals, and stifle opposition. Here is the hard-working apostle oppressed by his difficulties familiar to readers of the canonical letters. On the other hand, like the Paul of Acts, he is subordinate to the followers of Jesus who were apostles before him (see the commentary on IV.4). It is interesting that the Corinthians salute Paul as "brother" (II.1), rather than as "teacher" or "apostle."

The interpolator chose the location wisely. It could scarcely follow quickly after the visit to Corinth and would in any case be quite anticlimactic there. Philippi was an apt choice. At the close of chap. 9 Paul sailed for Macedonia, where Philippi would be among the first stops. Cf. Acts 16:11–12. The name of the city must be restored, but sec. I states that Paul was in Macedonia, while chap. 11 takes place in Philippi, from which Paul goes to Corinth. Nicetas offers this sequence: Ephesus, Philippi, *Thessalonica, Athens, Beroea*, and Corinth (87r). The italicized names correspond to Acts (inverting Athens and Beroea), but, in Acts, Troas is the point of departure.

The overall effect of the interpolation is to raise suspense through retardation. Matters in Philippi intimate a potential crisis, but attention shifts to Corinth, where the community is dismayed by false teachers. Not until Paul has quashed the opposition via a letter does attention return to his difficulties in Macedonia. The additions also contribute. The opening anxiety about Paul's death in sec. I raises the danger of battling false teachers after the apostle's departure.

The narrative account of what the two itinerants were teaching differs from the Corinthians' epistle. These differences indicate that the narrative and epistolary materials come from different authors. They probably expose different emphases. Both distance God from the world and reject the importance of Christ's bodily existence. (Denial that Christ was born of Mary is not to suggest that he had another mother, but to reject the significance of Jesus' humanity. A similar judgment applies to the crucifixion.) Both descriptions protect the highest god from entanglement in the world and its evils.

Table 10.1: Two Lists of the Rival Teaching

Simon and Cleobius according to I	Simon and Cleobius according to II
Resurrection *of spirit not flesh.*	Reject *Old Testament.*
Human *body not divine creation.*	God *not almighty.*
God *neither knows nor created world.*	No *resurrection of flesh.*
Christ *not crucified.*	Humans *not divine creation.*
Appeared *human but not born of Mary nor of Davidic descent.*	Christ *not true human nor born of Mary.*
	Angels, *not God, created world.*

I is distinctive in that it applies less to the teaching of *Marcion* than does II. Marcion is noteworthy for his non-use of Jewish Scripture. Despite his docetic orientation, Marcion did affirm that the savior was crucified and suffered. The narrative was subsequently altered to correspond with modifications of the two letters (Hovhanessian, 52). As Snyder ("Remembering," 82–83) proposes, these statements do not outline a heresy so much as offer antitheses to the recommended views. The importance of these matters for emerging Christian orthodoxy is apparent when they are read against the Apostles' Creed, which almost appears to have been composed to refute them. See Table 10.2, p. 257.

Table 10.2: Baptismal Interrogatories

Apostolic Tradition 21.13–17	Simon and Cleobius according to 3 Cor
Do you believe in God the Father Almighty?	God not almighty (II)
Do you believe in Christ Jesus, the Son of God, who was born by the Holy Spirit from the Virgin Mary	Christ not human, nor born of Mary (I & II)
and crucified under Pontius Pilate, and died and was buried	Christ not crucified (I)
and rose on the third day alive from the dead . . .	
Do you believe in the Holy Spirit and the holy church and the resurrection of the flesh?	No resurrection of the flesh (I & II)

These questions were posed to baptismal candidates as they stood naked in the water. After a positive response to each, they were immersed. See Bradshaw et al., *The Apostolic Tradition*, 114–16. For a standard account of the development of the so-called Apostles' Creed, see Kelly, *Early Christian Creeds*, esp. 368–434. On the "rules of faith," which were similar in content, see Snyder, "Remembering," 93.

In summary: the letters contained in 3 *Cor* were composed late in the second century to show Paul directly and indisputably refuting rival teachers of that era, at least some of whom made use of his correspondence in formulating and expounding their systems. At a later date this material, with narrative supplements, was clumsily inserted into *APl*. Reasons for this interpolation could include the desire to display Paul as a letter-writer, and, more clearly, to place him firmly within the orthodox fold.

One motive for this addition could have been a desire to give the *Acts* a more catholic flavor, since questions had been raised about its orthodoxy, most notably by Tertullian, *De baptismo* 17.5. See the discussion by Hilhorst, "Tertullian on the Acts of Paul." Since he is more concerned with practice than with doctrine, and little was said in criticism of *APl* on theological grounds, this objection is not persuasive, but, with the inclusion of 3 *Cor*, the *APl* was a more up-to-date weapon in the arsenal of orthodoxy.

Theologically 3 *Cor* is not distant from Irenaeus, relating creation to redemption, stressing the Incarnation, and emphasizing the physical human body ("flesh"). Use of Irenaeus' *Against the Heresies*, is possible. The relation of the incarnation to creation and redemption that is the focus of Paul's letter is quite similar to the emphases of Irenaeus. In line with other

The Acts of Paul

later Pauline writings 3 *Cor* does not take up such subjects as the cross, law, sin, and justification. See Hovanessian, 103.

A more direct influence is the Pastoral Epistles (PE, Pastorals). One avoids rather than argues with opponents. Like the PE, 3 *Cor* offers a set of clear propositions as items to be accepted rather than debated. Specific allusions are present, many indicated in the following notes, as are other allusions to the Pauline corpus. See Penny, "Pseudo-Pauline Letters," 292–94; and Snyder, "Remembering," 93. 3 *Cor* says what the author imagines, what the author of the PE would have said had he written fifty years later. 3 *Cor* imitates the PE in style and narrative atmosphere. One notable difference is that, whereas in the PE Paul is the only apostle, in 3 *Cor* he has taken a place beneath Peter and the others.

Chapter 10

When he had departed from [...] and went [*to Philippi*]

1. Now when Paul came to Philippi [...] he went [*into the house of* ...] great joy abounded [*among the believers*] and to all [...] the lawless one [...] the reward. They [...] in [...] single prayer [...] All and each [...] Paul to comfort [...] [*Philippi*]

3 Corinthians

I ... The Corinthians were gravely concerned about Paul because he was going to leave the world before the proper time. Simon and Cleobius had come to Corinth with this message: "There is no resurrection of the flesh but [only] of the spirit, and the human body is not a divine creation, and, with regard to the world, God neither created it nor knows it, nor has Jesus Christ been crucified— he was mere appearance, he was neither born of Mary nor was he of Davidic descent." In sum, they taught many things in Corinth, deceiving themselves and many others. When therefore the Corinthians heard ... they sent [a letter to Paul] in Macedonia [by the hand of the deacons] Threptus and Eutychus. The letter read:

Translation, Commentary, and Notes : Chapter

[The Corinthians to the apostle Paul]

(2) II. 1. Stephanas and his fellow-presbyters Daphnus, Eubulus, Theophilus, and Zeno to Paul, who is in Christ: greetings. 2. Two individuals have come to Corinth, Simon and Cleobius; they overthrew the faith of some with corrupt words. 3. These you will examine, 4. for we never heard such things either from you or from the others. 5. But we maintain what we have received from you and from them. 6. As the Lord has shown us mercy, we should hear this from you again while you are still in the flesh. 7. Either come to us or write to us, (8.) for we believe, as it was revealed to Theonoe, that the Lord has delivered you from the hand of the lawless one. 9. They say and teach as follows: 10. The prophets are not to be utilized; (11) God is not almighty; (12) there is no resurrection of flesh; (13) God did not fashion the human race; (14) The Lord neither came in the flesh nor was he born of Mary; (15) the world is not of God but of angels. 16. Therefore, brother, please hasten here, so that the Corinthian church may continue without stumbling and the foolishness of these men may be exposed. Farewell in the Lord.

(3) III 1. The deacons, Threptus and Eutychus, took the letter to Philippi. (2) When Paul received it, although he was in prison because of Stratonike, the wife of Apollophanes, he became quite upset, (3) and exclaimed "It would have been better had I died and were with the Lord than to remain in the flesh and to hear words that heap sorrow upon sorrow. 4 How dreadful it is to be in prison while Satan's wiles flourish!" 5. And in considerable affliction Paul wrote this reply to the letter.

Comment

Cherix (in Rordorf, 1161) begins with the page numbered 45 by Schmidt and 109 by him. Schmidt is followed here for the opening. The opening words are marked as a section heading in P. Heid. The opening fragments present a conventional beginning. The apostle arrives in a city and lodges with a certain person. The faithful rejoice at his appearance. Love (*agapē*) is mentioned. All offer prayer. The message is pastoral. Paul speaks of a reward and mentions the evil one ("lawless," found in II also). A bit of interlacement follows, as the scene shifts to Corinth and trouble there. The gap may have reported a decision by those at Corinth to communicate with Paul in Philippi.

The Acts of Paul

Corinthian anxiety about Paul's death is a red herring, based upon sec. 8 of II. The situation in Ephesus may have been in mind. The narrative summary in I is not in perfect harmony with the letter, as noted in the Introduction. This summary reports that Simon and Cleobius enjoyed considerable success. This circumstance is reminiscent of the opening chapters of the *Acts of Peter*. Nevertheless, the entire community is responsible for the letter, which is not said to be written by Stephanas or any other leader. Cf. *1 Clement*. Deacons are typically used as agents. Cf. Burrhus (not identified as a deacon, Ignatius *Phil.* 11.2). These agents would have supplemented the written message.

The *title* (from P.Bod.) is fashioned after those in collections of Paul's letters. The epistolary features resemble the letters of the Apostolic Fathers. Like the letters of Ignatius (e.g., *Romans*, *Polycarp*) the greeting is the standard *chairein* (lit., "rejoice"). Paul played upon this in his use of "grace [*charis*] and peace." The closing of II also follows the Greek convention of "farewell": *errōso/sthe*. Cf. Acts 15:29; Ign. *Rom.* 10; *Smyrn.* 13. As indicated in the note *fellow-presbyters* the author essentially copies the prescript of Polycarp, *Philippians*. One might expect "greetings in Christ," but the phrase is applied to Paul. The general conventions of wishes for good health and statements of prayer for the recipients are absent. The letter gets right down to business. A Latin ms. (L) labels this letter as a petition, i.e., an example of deliberative rhetoric. Verse 2 begins with a narrative summary, followed by a request for Paul to examine the opponents' claims, assurance that the community has remained steadfast, and a renewal of the petition in vv. 6b–8, with a rationale: Paul remains alive. Verse 7 is the thesis. Verses 9–15 narrate the opposing doctrine, in propositional (creedal) form, followed in v. 16 by a concluding repetition of the request. The general principle is that believers should adhere to what is presented as the teaching of the apostles, whose number includes Paul. That will be accomplished with apostolic words. The letter states that Simon and Cleobius have met with some success. The use of proper names for opponents is generally avoided (see Pervo, *Acts*, 371n23). *3 Cor* follows the practice of the Pastoral Epistles in this, and other, matters. See Dunn, "Legacy." Nothing is said about attempts on the part of the leadership to refute the heretical duo. Paul will take care of that.

The testimony that the Corinthians have not heard "such things" from Paul or "the others" is noteworthy. For variants, see the note. Close readers of 1 Corinthians will take it to include Peter (Cephas) and Apollos (e.g., 1 Cor 3:22). In his response Paul will speak of those who were apostles before him (IV.4). Verses 6–8 introduce a bit of pathos and drama. They want more from Paul before he dies. Anxiety was relieved by a revelation to a woman, Theone. The intermediate agents of his death would have been public

Translation, Commentary, and Notes : Chapter

officials, behind whom stood the *lawless one*. This datum aligns 3 *Cor* with both emergent orthodoxy and apparent support of the New Prophecy (commonly called Montanism). A number of persons of indisputable orthodoxy, including Irenaeus, did not condemn the prophetic movement. This is one of the points *APl* and 3 *Cor* have in common.

Verse 10 implies that Jewish scripture, viewed as promise/prophecy, was not a basis for faith and morals. No reasons are provided. Possibilities include the view that these writings derive from an inferior deity and mislead the faithful or that they are not relevant to salvation. The latter view is often associated with Marcion.

Verse 11 is to be taken in the sense that God the creator, the first person of the Trinity, so to speak, is *pantokratōr*, ruler of all, i.e., against the view of many called gnostics that the creator (demiurge) was an inferior god who was quite probably unaware of the existence of higher entities.

With v. 12 comes the vital issue: resurrection of the flesh. Establishing this doctrine created a number of difficulties for the *proto-orthodox*. One is the question of why the notion assumed such great importance. A second is that Paul did not espouse it, if one appeals to the plain surface meaning of 1 Cor 15:50. (One can—and Paul did—speak of a resurrection body that was not composed of flesh but of some eternal substance. Cf. 1 Cor 15:44.) Resurrection of the flesh constituted a full affirmation that God through Christ had redeemed human beings in totality, not just their spirits or souls. See Snyder's discussion, "Remembering," 96–103.

Verses 13 and 15 are related, the former anthropological, the latter cosmological. These propositions correspond to gnostic systems, such as that of Saturninus (Irenaeus, *Against Heresies* 1.24.1–2). The object of such systems was to provide an explanation for the origin of evil. A classic problem of theodicy in monotheistic systems is to explain how an omnipotent and benevolent deity could allow the existence of evil. Gnostic systems typically begin with absolute perfection and show how it went wrong, then describe the cosmic battle to restore perfection. Irenaeus took up the scheme with a moral focus. Failure is a necessary prerequisite to growth.

Verse 14 affirms the doctrine of the Incarnation: the savior was a true human being, born of a mortal woman. Nothing is said here of the virgin birth, emphasis upon which can be seen in the roughly contemporary *Protevangelium of James*. The petition closes with a call for haste, identifying two goals: preservation of the purity and integrity of the Corinthian community and revelation of the nature of Simon and Cleobius' teaching. The latter is to prevent them from doing more damage elsewhere. The presence of Paul called for by the Corinthian leaders will be in the form of a letter. This is correct. Paul wrote, at least in theory, when and because an immediate visit was not possible. In the second century the absent Paul was only "present" through his letters, but that mode of presence sufficed. See Pervo, *The Making of Paul*.

III. This narrative insert is not included in P.Bod. It is a normal component of the Armenian tradition, which does not include I. Scholars would like to know whether the data about Paul in v. 2 derives from a lost portion of chap. 12 or if the author simply made it up. It does not derive from Acts 16, which reports different reasons for jailing Paul, who did not spend an entire night in prison. In favor of invention is that the situation, which even a casual reader of ApocActs will readily reconstruct. Paul converted Stratonike, a woman of high standing. Her consequent absence from the marital bed disappointed her husband, Apollophanes. He, probably a magistrate, had the missionary incarcerated. Such episodes are not much less frequent than sunrises in most ApocActs, but these scenes are not that characteristic of *APl*. This may be the result of ecclesiastical censorship, for, although Medieval Christian authorities approved of converting unmarried women like Thecla, they did not wish to portray apostles breaking up lawful marriages. The remains of chap. 11 do, in fact, suggest a kindred situation, but none of the names recur. These data therefore cannot serve to reconstruct an episode of *APl*.

Pathos dominates vv. 2b–5. In the Deuteropauline world such pathos is manipulative, seeking to evoke the reader's sympathy (and guilt). The "wish I were dead" line evokes (and exaggerates) Phil 1:23. Paul writes the Corinthians amidst many tears (cf. 2 Cor 2:4). The resultant portrait is classically Deuteropauline: the imprisoned apostle continues his pastoral care. The author of this short piece is thoroughly immersed in the Deuteropauline tradition and *modus operandi*.

Notes

Saturninus. An early teacher. Irenaeus locates him at Antioch and attributes to him a classic gnostic system (*Against Heresies* 1.24.1–2). This system included a distant original principle, which created a number of spiritual beings. Seven angels fashioned the universe, and an unsuccessful Adam, who was vivified by a spark of true light. The first parent sent the Messiah to deliver those possessing the divine spark and to destroy the evil powers, among whom is the God of Israel. He rejected marriage and eating meat (as does *APl*). The Hebrew bible is a mixed product; some texts derive from the angels that fashioned the universe, others from wicked angels.

Docetism. In a general sense this term refers to the view that the humanity of Jesus is irrelevant to salvation. Sharply formulated docetic Christology holds that Jesus was a phantom who condescended to appear in human form but was not a true being of flesh and blood. In that sense it was compatible with Greco-Roman religions, which generally held that gods could appear in any form they wished. The view that Christ was polymorphous is common in the ApocActs and a number of the treatises from Nag Hammadi, for example. Docetism protects a high Christology; it survives in an attenuated sense in the reluctance of many believers to acknowledge that Jesus had human feelings or engaged in normal human activity.

Marcion. Although possibly influenced by some gnostic theologians, Marcion developed his own understanding of Christianity. He distinguished the genuine god revealed by Jesus from the creator, set aside Jewish scriptures, and promulgated a Christian scripture of Gospel and Apostle (corresponding to Law and Prophets). Paul, the only true apostle, occupied the center of Marcion's theology. Peter and the rest were "Judaizers." After splitting from the Roman community, Marcion, a brilliant organizer, established a large and enduring church.

Joy. Joy is the characteristic quality of Christian life, regularly noted on the occasion of Paul's arrival. See 1; 3.5; 4.14; 9.1, 4; 12.1; 13.1; 14.1.

Appearance. This represents the Coptic word reconstructed as C[MA]T. This term has many meanings. See Crum, 340–42, *s.v.* CMOT). Note the discussion of Luttikhuizen, "The Apocryphal Correspondence," 83n16.

Letter to Paul. Bracketed [ ] material supplied from III.

Title. The short title derives from P.Bod X. For others, see Hovhanessian, 139.

Stephanas. Variant: "Stephanus." The versions obscure the difference between "Stephanas" (1 Cor 1:16, etc.) and "Stephen." The question is whether "Stephanas" is a correction to bring the narrative into the orbit of 1 Corinthians. Since the text displays other efforts to coordinate with the authentic Corinthian correspondence, "Stephanas" has a strong claim to originality.

fellow-presbyters, lit. "the presbyters with him." This probably implies that S. was the bishop. See the essentially identical wording of the prescript of Polycarp, *Philippians*. Lampe, 1290, *s.v. sympresbyteros*.

Daphnus, etc. For variants in the list of names, see Hovhanessian, 139.

The Acts of Paul

Petition. Petitions include a statement of the background generating the request and the request itself, placed within opening and closing. On official petitions, see White, *Petition,* esp. 1–19. White briefly discusses private letters of request, 2–3n2.

Overthrew. Cf. 2 Tim 2:18.

These you will examine. This refers to the words, not the persons.

Others. Many variants are specific: "apostles."

Theone. The Armenian (mss. and Ephraem) make her a man: Theonas, Etheonas. In part of the Latin tradition she is Atheona(e). For similar changes of a woman to a man, see the variants for "Junia" in Rom 16:7 and "Nympha" at Col 4:15.

Lawless one. This word, of Jewish origin, served as a title for God's ultimate enemy. Cf. 2 Thess 2:8 (possibly); Irenaeus, *Against Heresies* 3.7.2. Paul would not have selected this word, which gives the Torah a central place in soteriology, as a designation for the Devil.

Hasten. Cf. 2 Tim 4:9.

Satan's wiles. Cf. Phil 2:27; Eph 6:11.

Proto-orthodox. Historians conscious of anachronism have struggled to develop terminology for characterizing Christian writers and communities whose organization, views, and practices foreshadow what would later be regarded as sound in structure and belief. One may draw a line from 1 *Clement* to Irenaeus of Lyons, for example, but this line will intersect others that share some characteristics but not others. In the second century the most important features of what is characterized as "proto-orthodoxy" are: a rule of faith affirming the unity of the godhead and the identity of creator and redeemer, well-organized communities led by a single bishop (eventually) assisted by presbyters and deacons, and a strict, generally conventional morality. The notion of orthodoxy implies attempts to identify and exclude rejected beliefs and their proponents. Otherwise stated: the chicken of "heresy" had to precede the egg of "orthodoxy." The presence of the general features listed above does not alter the presumption that, had other views triumphed, they would have been labeled orthodox.

Translation, Commentary, and Notes : Chapter

IV. The Letter of Paul

Paul to the Corinthians

Concerning the Flesh

(4) IV. 1. Paul, the prisoner of Jesus Christ, to the believers at Corinth: greetings. 2. Since I am undergoing numerous misfortunes, I am not surprised that the teachings of the evil one are experiencing rapid success. 3. The Lord Christ will quickly come, since he is rejected by those who falsify his teaching. 4. For I delivered to you first of all what I received from the apostles before me who were always with Jesus Christ, (5) that our Lord Christ Jesus was of Davidic descent, born of Mary, into whom the Father sent the spirit from heaven (6) that he might come into this world and liberate all flesh by his own flesh, and that he might raise us in the flesh from the dead as he has shown us by example. 7. Humanity was created by his Father (8) and was thus sought by God when lost, so that it might become alive by adoption.

9. For the almighty God of the universe, maker of heaven and earth, sent the prophets first to the Jews to deliver them from their sins, (10) as he desired to save the house of Israel; therefore he distributed some of the spirit of Christ and apportioned it to the prophets who proclaimed the true worship of God over a long period.

11. Yet the [evil] prince wished to be god himself and laid his hands on them and bound all human flesh to lust. 12. But the almighty God, who is just, did not wish to nullify his own creation (13) and sent Spirit through fire into Mary the Galilean, [v. 14: see below] (15) that the evil one might be conquered by the same flesh by which he ruled and be convinced that he is not god. 16. For by his own body Jesus Christ saved all flesh, (17) so that he might exhibit a temple of righteousness in his own body (18) by which we are liberated. 19. Those who impede the providence of God by denying that heaven and earth and all that is in them are works of the Father are children of wrath, not of righteousness. 20. They possess the accursed faith of the serpent. 21. Avoid them and keep your distance from their teaching. [vv. 22–23: see below]

(5) 24. For those who tell you that there is no resurrection of the flesh there will be no resurrection—(25) Those who do not believe the one who thus [*in the flesh*] rose. 26. For they do not know, Corinthians, about the sowing of wheat or other seeds that one casts naked upon the ground and dies, then

The Acts of Paul

rises by God's will, in a body and clothed. 27. God not only raises the sown body but also bestows upon it abundant blessings.

28. If we cannot develop a parable from seeds, (29) you know of Jonah, the son of Amathios who, when he refused to preach to the Ninevites, was swallowed up by a sea-monster. 30. After three days and three nights God heard the prayer of Jonah from the depths of Hades. No part of him was corrupted, not even a hair or an eyelid. 31. How much more, you of limited faith, will he raise those who have believed in Christ Jesus, as he himself was raised up? 32. When some Israelites threw a corpse on the bones of the prophet Elisha, the person's body was raised. So also will you, upon whom the body, bones, and Spirit of Christ have been thrown, will be raised on that day with a whole body.

(6) 34. If, however, you receive any different teaching, do not trouble me, (35) for I have shackles on my hands so that I may gain Christ and marks on my body so that I may attain to the resurrection of the dead. 36. Whoever abides by the rule which we have received through the blessed prophets and the holy gospel, shall receive a reward, (37) but whoever transgresses these, and those who did so earlier will receive fire, (38) since they are godless persons, a generation of vipers. 39. Rebuff them by the power of Christ. 40. Peace be with you.

Comments

IV. Paul's letter was subject to frequent expansion to achieve more precise delineation of doctrinal positions. This, like II, exhibits the influence of deliberative rhetoric (Luttikhuizen, "Apocryphal Correspondence," 86–91).

1. 2–3 Introduction. The source and origin of Pauline theology.
2. 4–8 Narrative, with thesis: God would restore the human race to its primordial state.
3. 9–21; 24–32. Proof, closing with admonition to avoid the rivals.
4. 32–34. Supplementary thesis: God will deliver humanity by raising the body.
5. 34–39. Epilogue in pathetic style, complimenting v. 2.

Verses 36–37 are a "judgment saying," combining a promise and a threat. Verses 19–24 and 37–39 are parallel. Proofs (vv. 9–21) include those called "inartistic," accepted data, here a salvation-historical creed. Other types of proof are analogies from nature (vv. 26–29) and, in vv. 29–32, historical examples. The second set involves an analogy from nature (vv. 26–29), followed by two historical examples in vv. 29–33, later expanded. (See the note on v. 34.) The letter is a lesson in bodily resurrection. One begins with the creed, which reputes to report what believers have always affirmed, followed by natural and scriptural argumentation. The framing *inclusion* in vv. 2 and 34 involves pathos, an effort to gain the audience's sympathy. This document is not a careless pastiche of citations from Paul's letters, but an organized exposition. The body constitutes a refutation of the opposing theses in II.9–15. For a content-based outline, see Hovhanessian, 99–100.

The opening (v. 1) is more Pauline than the community's letter, imitating Phlm 1, although the Greek *chairein* replaces "grace and peace." Verse 2 seems to base the opposition's success upon his own misfortune. It is more likely to mean: "things are bad all over." The background of v. 3 is the notion that the appearance of false teachers is an indication that the end is near (e.g., 1 John 2:18). This particular formulation of that view leaves much to be desired.

The Narrative. Verse 4 utilizes a Pauline formula for the transmission of tradition ("I handed on what I received;" cf. 1 Cor 15:3) and a Pauline phrase from Gal 1:17 in a new and unpauline manner. The apostle happily concedes here that he was instructed by those who preceded him in the apostolate. See Penny, "Pseudo-Pauline Letters," 303–5. Conflict is eliminated by yielding the essential point. What Paul teaches is what Peter, Andrew, John, and the others also teach. Paul is one apostle among the college.

The theme of Davidic descent (v. 5) does not emphasize messianic claims, although it does imply fulfillment of a promise. The similar claim in a variant at 3.1 probably derives from harmonization of the text. See the comments there. Rom 1:3 is a Pauline source of this view. P.Bod and the Coptic P.Heid do not affirm the virginity of Mary. The versions do; Armenian A and Latin L refer to the Annunciation, blunting the implication that Mary was impregnated by the Spirit. Ephrem's formulation is the fullest: "Mary, and not passed through her, and from the lineage of David, and not a heavenly body, and according to the annunciation of the Holy Spirit sent to her from heaven, and not through Joseph's approach to her" (Hovhanessian, 141). (See the note *Passed through*.)

Verse 6 states the purpose of Jesus' human birth: to "liberate all flesh" by his flesh and to raise believers in the flesh. This intimates the soteriology set out in vv. 15–18. Prior to that the author grounds the soteriology in cosmology, with particular emphasis upon anthropology. This is well-integrated theology. The affirmation that humanity was sought by its parent when lost (8) links creation and redemption. Because God is father/parent, God loves the human race and will not forsake it. Rival systems would agree that the highest god sought lost particles of divinity, but lack the simple image and link between creation and redemption. The v. does not take up the fall but merely affirms that God sought to overcome its consequences. See v. 11.

Adoption (v. 8) is a Pauline concept (Gal 4:5; Rom 8:15, 23; cf. Eph 1:5), used in reference to baptism. In the background is the understanding that God chose and called Israel to be God's own. See Rom 9:4. The presumption is that humans were not by nature the offspring of God. For another view, see Acts 17:22–31. The concept is also found in the *APl* at 9.17 (probably an interpolation).

With v. 9 the author begins to elaborate the thesis. After reaffirming God's role as creator of all, the narrative turns toward the continuity of salvation history, an important concept for arguing with Christians who reject Israelite scripture. The "Spirit Christology" serves admirably to unite the eras of salvation history. Although insufficiently sophisticated to survive the complexities of a later period, the theme is found in *APl* 13.5 and other texts of roughly the second century (see the note.)

The explanation of the Fall is far from clear. The context allows the event(s) in question to occur after the prophets. The origin of the evil one receives no explanation. Wishing to usurp the place of God this entity introduced *hēdonē* (lust, desire) as the governing principle of human existence. Lust is the essence of sin for this author. See Snyder, 100. This remains valid even if one renders the final phrase as "to serve his pleasure." The understanding of the ethical life as combat with pleasure was a familiar theme in Greco-Roman popular philosophy. See p. 249. The context suggests that the evil one succeeded by attacking the prophets, an understanding expanded in the versions. The basic thought is that sin corrupts the flesh. Rather than discard the corrupted material, God decided to rescue it. Why is this called "fair"? If Marcion viewed the contrast between old and new as the opposition of justice to love, this author unites the two.

Redemption involved fighting fire with fire, utilizing the incarnate flesh of Jesus to defeat the evil one. Construing Christ as a union of spirit and flesh was familiar at that time. See, e.g., *2 Clem* 9; *Hermas* 59. The understanding of redemption as the liberation of the flesh from bondage to the devil is developed by Irenaeus, *Against Heresies* 5.21.2–3. The association of spirit with fire for the conception of Christ is surprising. The source may have been a description of the conception of Jesus. Fire is often associated with epiphanies (e.g., Acts 2:3), while the link between "spirit"/"wind" appears in the message of John the Baptizer (e.g., Luke 3:16). The fire here may have been regarded as the element that purified Mary's womb. See Klijn, "The Apocryphal Correspondence," 16n27.

Versions may include a v.14: "Who believed with all her heart and conceived by the Holy Spirit that Jesus could come into the world." This focuses upon Mary's willing assent to her vocation. Verses 16–18 reiterate the foregoing, closing the circle by equating flesh with body, an identification at variance with Paul's thought. The next verse introduces the image of the body as a temple, well known from 1 Cor 3:16–17; 6:19. For Paul the body of Christ, the community, is the temple. Christ's body was an example of proper conduct. *3 Cor* does not diminish the soteriological role of Christ's physical (fleshly) body, but it does reflect and/or encourage an individualistic view of the temple imagery. Each believer is a temple. Cf. *APl* 3.5, which characterizes the celibate as "a temple of God."

Verses 19–21 wrap up this section of the proof by denouncing those who separate creation from redemption. "Providence" here refers to the integration of the universe in the economy of redemption. See Rordorf, "Hérésie," 38–39. The author offers denunciation rather than refutation. "The accursed faith of the serpent" presumably refers to Genesis 3. The order to avoid false teachers is an abandonment of any attempt at dialogue or persuasion. This is characteristic of the Deuteropauline world, especially the Pastorals, e.g., 2 Tim 3:5.

The second part of Paul's *probatio* (vv. 24–32) takes its basis, quite intentionally, from 1 Corinthians 15:

3 Corinthians	1 Corinthians
4.24–25	15:12
4.26	15:36–38
4.31	15:20

See Hovhanessian, *Third Corinthians*, 122–24, who points to Paul's detailed analogy from *planting*. *3 Cor* 4.26–27 has a succinct analogy from *nature*. Planting, however, is a human activity. *1 Clem* 24–26 utilizes natural arguments for resurrection. (See the note *Natural theology*.) This "seed parable" conforms to that understanding. Seeds "die" by metonymy (i.e., are buried, substituting result, burial, for cause, death) before "rising." Cf. John 12:24. The resultant growth is "clothed," i.e. enfleshed. Since "seed" was a technical term in various gnostic systems (for examples, see Hovhanessian, 124) and in Stoicism (*logoi spermatikoi*), the author could deflect two birds with one homely stone.

3 Cor does not appeal to 1 Cor 15:50–57, and with good reason. Tertullian will argue vehemently against efforts (by wily heretics) to interpret 1 Cor 15:50 literally. As Penny states: *3 Cor* uses data based upon those of Paul in his argument in 1 Corinthians 15 against people who opposed his understanding of the resurrection of the dead, but uses those data to refute those who deny resurrection of the flesh. Where Paul saw great discontinuity between present and future existence, *3 Cor* looks for continuity (Penny, "Letters," 301–2; see the note on *Flesh*). The opposing view, that resurrection is a "spiritual" phenomenon, can also be called a misinterpretation of Paul, although the arguments remain admirable for their theological depth and sophistication.

Verses 24–25 receive elaboration, particularly in the Armenian: "Those, however, who say that there is no resurrection of the flesh, will themselves not rise to eternal life but to damnation. They will be raised up to judgment with their unbelieving bodies. There will be no resurrection for those who say there is no resurrection of the body [!]. For such people will be denied from resurrection" (Hovhanessian, 143–44). "Heretical" writers of the second century constructed sustained and able arguments in support of resurrection as a "spiritual" phenomenon. See the note on *Spiritual Resurrection*. Verse 27 rounds off the section with a promise that the resurrection flesh will be an improvement upon the worldly model.

The author shifts to historical examples in vv. 28–32. Examples were (and for that matter remain) potent tools for persuasion. The example of Jonah was one of the most common themes in early Christian art (for examples, see du Bourguet, *Early Christian Art*, 39, 106–10) and appeared in no less scholarly a work than Tertullian, *de Res.* 32. Jonah is viewed as one fully dead, in Hades (based upon the psalm in Jonah 2). In short, he is not a type of resurrection but an instance of it. Verse 31, in diatribe fashion, challenges the audience to see this as a lesser instance of what is to come. The Elijah-Elisha cycle (2 Kings 13:21) supplies the second instance. That material influenced the developing gospel tradition and was further developed in Luke and Acts. For some examples see Pervo, *Dating Acts*, 30–34, 48.

Armenian (and Ephrem) improves the rough imagery of v. 32: "If the bones of Elisha the prophet, falling upon the dead, revived the dead, by how much more shall you, who are supported by the body and the blood and the Spirit of Christ, arise again on that day, with a restored body?" Armenian and Latin M supply a second example, based upon 1 Kings 17:17–24 (v. 33). The latter reads: "Also Elijah the prophet: he raised up the widow's son from death: how much more shall the Lord Jesus raise you up from death at the sound of the trumpet, in the twinkling of an eye? For he has shown us an example in his own body" (Latin; see Hovhanessian, 144–45).

The closing (vv. 34–39) lacks some of the normal features, most notably greetings, travel plans, and a final blessing. Even the closing "good-bye" is a later addition. Its most direct models are the end of Galatians and Philippians 3, which has some of the features of a testament. The pathos, like that of the opening, is frankly manipulative, and the tone does not cohere with the circumstances. The apostle is not writing a rebellious or apostate community, but one whose leaders remain loyal and have sought his help. The basis of v. 34 is Gal 6:17, upon which v. 35 builds. Paul has shackles that he wears (e.g., Phil 1:7) and marks on his body (Gal 6:17). For Paul the shackles may have been metaphorical. The two are developed into a parallel sentence, with goals of gaining Christ (Phil 3:8) and attaining the resurrection (Phil 3:11). These look like rewards earned by suffering, a notion confirmed by v. 36. Verses 36–37 form a kind of inclusion with vv. 3–4. They promise beatitude to right believers and punishment to those who err. (See *Rule*.) The fate of the latter is amplified. Judgment is retroactive. The author adds a motive clause: they deserve "fire" because they refuse divine direction. Reference to their serpentine parentage evokes vv. 19–20 (and Matt 12:33–37; see *Generation*).

Verse 39 approaches the spirit, although not the words, of Paul. The gift of salvation empowers believers to resist evil. The extremely curt closing is expanded in in Armenian and Latin M (Hovhanessian, 145).

The conclusion is uncertain, as both P.Heid and P.Hamb are defective—the former at the end, the latter at the beginning. It is likely that the interpolator added a third narrative unit, describing the sending of the letter and its reception in Corinth. In matters like this early Christian texts do not intentionally leave readers in suspense.

Notes

Title. P. Bod adds the subtitle. One strand of the Latin tradition (Hovhanessian, 141) reads, "The third epistle to the Corinthians, which is not authentic."

Always. Cf. Acts 1:22. Constant presence with Jesus implies that, in addition to the other benefits of his company, the apostles missed no secret teaching by their master.

Passed through. Ephrem is refuting a docetism most fully developed in the sophisticated gnosis of the Valentinians. Hippolytus credits the Italic school of Valentinus with this view:

> Some say that [*the demiurge*] brought forth Christ, his own son, but only as psychic, and spoke about him through the prophets. This however was the one who passed through Mary just as water flows through a pipe, and upon him the savior formed from

the Pleroma of all [the eons] descended at the baptism of Jesus in the form of a dove. (Ref. 6.24)

The view that Mary retained her virginity in giving painless birth is a kind of "naïve Docetism" that is attested in Syria: Ignatius, *Eph.* 19; *Odes of Sol.* 19, but see also the *Acts of Peter* 24, which evidently stems from Asia Minor. This view is maintained with considerable crudity in the *Protevanglium of James* 19–20.

Come into the world. Cf. 1 Tim 1:15.

Spirit Christology. In so far as a Christology identifies Christ with the Spirit it is binitarian. This model is in some ways similar to systems that attributed prophetic inspiration to the pre-incarnate Logos (Word). See Grillmeier, *Christ,* 197–200. Early texts used to support a Spirit Christology include 1 Peter 1:10–12; Ignatius, *Magn.* 8; Justin, *1 Apol* 32–39; Irenaeus, *Adv. H.* 4.20.4; 4.33.9; Tertullian, *Prescription of Heretics* 13.

By which. The relative could refer to "Christ," "temple," or "body." The last is most proximate and therefore preferable.

Verses 22–23 are subsequent additions. Latin M and the Armenian read: "22. For you are not children of disobedience but of the beloved church. 23. Therefore is the time of the resurrection preached to all." This provides an upbeat ending to the section.

Natural theology. In addition to the arguments of *1 Clem.* 24–25, see also Theophilus, *Ad Autolycum* 1.13; Tertullian, *De res.* 12. These arguments were developed by Stoics: Grant, *Miracle and Natural Law,* 235–45.

Flesh, as the substance of the post-mortem body, is assumed by a range of texts: e.g., *2 Clem.* 2:9, Justin, *Dial.* 80.4; Irenaeus, *A.H.* 1.22.4; 1.27.3.

Flesh by flesh. See, e.g., *1 Clem* 49:1; *2 Clem.* 9:4; *Barn* 5:6.

Spiritual resurrection. See Hovhanessian, 116–19. Two Nag Hammadi texts, The *Treatise on the Resurrection* (1.4) and the *Gospel of Philip* (2.3) are fine examples. The former utilizes a number of Pauline epistles, while *Gos. Phil.* (which probably dates from c. 250) takes up the question of whether the risen are clothed (56.27–57.9), on which cf. *3 Cor.* 4.26. See also Dunderberg, "Valentinus," 87–88.

Rule. The term *kanōn* (from a semitic stem meaning "reed"; cf. "cane") appears in Gal 6:17, where its sense is uncertain. "Standard" or "criterion" are

Translation, Commentary, and Notes : Chapter

possibilities. By the late second century, however, the term was used for the "rule of faith," creedal tests. ("Canon" in the sense of Scripture and law are still later.)

Generation. Verses 37–38 are defective in Greek. Snyder ("Remembering," 85–86) proposes that the nonsense *teknēmata* be emended to *technēmata*, "artificial products." This is attractive. The customary emendation to *gennēmata* is preferable because of the biblical parallel.

Bibliography

Bradshaw, Paul F., Maxwell E. Johnson, L. Edward Phillips. *The Apostolic Tradition*. Hermeneia. Minneapolis: Fortress, 2002.

Bourguet, Pierre du. *Early Christian Art*. Translated by Thomas Burton. New York: William Morrow, 1971.

Bundy, David. "The Pseudo-Ephremian *Commentary on Third Corinthians*: A Study in Exegesis and Anti-Bardaisanite Polemic." In *After Bardaisan: Studies on Continuity and Change in Syriac Christianity in Honour of Professor Han J. W. Drijvers*, edited by Gerrit J. Reinink and Alexander Cornelis Klugkist, 51–63. Orientalia Lovaniensia Analecta 89. Louvain: Peeters, 1999.

Calhoun, Robert Matthew. "The Resurrection of the Flesh in Third Corinthians." In *Christian Body, Christian Self: Concepts of Early Christian Personhood*, edited by Clare K. Rothschild and Trevor W. Thompson, 235–57. WUNT 284. Tübingen: Mohr/Siebeck, 2011.

Callahan, Allen Dwight. "Dead Paul: The Apostle as Martyr in Philippi." In *Philippi at the Time of Paul and after His Death*, edited by Charlambos Bakirtiz and Helmut Koester, 67–84. Harrisburg, PA: Trinity, 1998.

D'Anna, Alberto. *Terza lettera ai Corinzi. La risurrezione*. Letture cristiane del primo millennio 44. Milan: Paoline, 2009.

Dunderburg, Ismo. "The School of Valentinus." In *A Companion to Second-Century Christian "Heretics,"* edited by Antti Marjanen and Petri Luomanen, 64–99. Leiden: Brill, 2008.

Dunn, Peter W. "The *Acts of Paul* and the Pauline Legacy in the Second Century." PhD diss., Queens College, Cambridge University, 1996, 101–26.

Glaser, Timo. *Paulus als Briefroman erzählt*. SUNT 76. Göttingen: Vandenhoeck & Reprecht, 2009.

Grant, Robert M. *Miracle and Natural Law in Greco-Roman and Early Christian Thought*. Amsterdam: North-Holland, 1952.

Grillmeier, Aloys. *Christ in Christian Tradition*. Vol. 1. Translated by John Bowden. Atlanta: Knox, 1975.

Hilhorst, A. "Tertullian on the Acts of Paul." In *The Apocryphal Acts of Paul and Thecla*, edited by Jan N. Bremmer, 150–63. Kampen: Kok Pharos, 1996.

Hovhanessian, Vahan. *Third Corinthians: Reclaiming Paul for Christian Orthodoxy*. Studies in Biblical Literature 18. New York: Lang, 2000.

Johnston, Steve, and Paul-Hubert Poirier. "Nouvelles citations chez Éphrem et Aphraate de la correspondance entre Paul et les Corinthiens." *Apocrypha* 16 (2005) 137–45.

The Acts of Paul

Kelly, J. N. D. *Early Christian Creeds*. London: Longmans, 1960.

Klijn, A. F. J. "The Apocryphal Correspondence between Paul and the Corinthians." *VC* 17 (1963) 2–23.

Luttikhuizen, Gerard. "The Apocryphal Correspondence with the Corinthians and the Acts of Paul." In *The Apocryphal Acts of Paul and Thecla*, edited by Jan Bremmer, 75–91. Kampen: Kok Pharos, 1996.

Penny, Donald N. "The Pseudo-Pauline Letters of the First Two Centuries. PhD diss., Emory University, 1979, 288–319.

Pervo, Richard I. *Acts: A Commentary*. Hermeneia. Minneapolis: Fortress, 2009.

———. *Dating Acts. Between the Evangelists and the Apologists*. Santa Rosa, CA: Polebridge, 2006.

———. *The Making of Paul: Constructions of the Apostle in Early Christianity*. Minneapolis: Fortress, 2010.

Rordorf, Willy. "Hérésie et Orthodoxie selon la Correspondance apocryphe entre les Corinthiens et l'apôtre Paul." In *Lex Orandi, Lex Credendi: Gesammelte Aufsätze zum 60. Geburtstag*, 380–431. Paradosis 36. Freiburg: Universtitätsverlag Freiburg, 1993.

Snyder, Glenn E., "Remembering the *Acts of Paul*." PhD diss., Harvard University, 2010, 67–113.

Testuz, M. *Papyrus Bodmer X–XII*. Geneva: Bibliotheque Bodmer, 1959, 9–45.

White, B. L, "Reclaiming Paul? Reconfiguration as Reclamation in 3 *Corinthians*." *JECS* 17 (2009) 497–523.

White, John L. *The Form and Structure of The Official Petition*. SBLDS 5. Missoula, MT: Scholars, 1972.

Chapter 11: Philippi

Sources: P.Heid 41–42/117–19. Nicetas of Paphlagonia. Secondary: *Acts of Titus*

Introduction. Specific reasons for locating this material at Philippi are the data from manuscripts. The title of P.Hamb. 6 is "From Phi[li]ppi to Corinth." The close of P.Heid. 44 reads, centered between lines: "*When he had departed from [. . .] and went [to Philippi]*." The restoration is made certain from the appearance of the place name two lines below. While at Corinth (chap. 12) Paul narrates what he had suffered "in Philippi in the workhouse (?)" (For discussion of the difficulties in interpreting this sentence, see the Comments in the next chapter.) *3 Cor* also indicates that an episode at Philippi occurred between Ephesus and Corinth. The narrative components in *3 Cor*, the summary in chap. 12, and the remarks in P.Heid all state that Paul was confined to hard labor, perhaps in the mines. This would have been the result of a criminal conviction.

The author of *APl* evidently wished to focus upon a single station in Macedonia, omitting Thessalonica and Berea. This is also true of some other provinces. Chapters 3 and 4, which tell the story of Thecla, are the exception to this principle, a principle that goes back to Acts, indeed, to Paul (e.g., Rom 15:26). The operative principle is synecdoche: some converts in a city equals conversion of the city, which equals conversion of the province. The grounds for this chapter come from Acts 16:11–40 and 1 Thess 2:2.

Another issue is the absence of this episode from P.Hamb. If *3 Cor* alone were absent, the case that this piece was added by the Greek archetype of P.Heid but not by the archetype of P.Hamb would be stronger. P.Hamb, however, reveals both that the previous narrative had evidently described adventures in Philippi and that they were omitted. Either the editor of P.Hamb or a predecessor excised the Philippi episode. One explanation is abbreviation: the entire episode was omitted to produce a shorter text. This is possible, although shortening of several or all episodes would be more likely. Another possibility is intentional omission for cause. Schmidt (*Praxeis*, 98) attributed omission to the presence of *3 Cor*, which had by that time been rejected in the Greek-speaking Christian world. In effect, *3 Cor* was in danger of contaminating *APl* and was thus removed, together with Paul's adventures in Philippi, which constituted its wrapper. Irony exists, for one sound explanation for the earlier addition of *3 Cor* was to enhance the orthodox cachet of *APl*. See the comments on chap. 10. In short: one editor added *3 Cor* to make *APl* more orthodox, and another editor removed it to make *APl* more respectable. This hypothesis has strengths; on the debit side

The Acts of Paul

is the general indifference of those who transmitted *APl* to such categories as canonicity. The state of the text does suggest that *3 Cor* was excised from rather than absent from the text represented by P.Hamb. Another possible cause for deletion is that the chapter portrayed Paul condemned to hard labor, a circumstance viewed as too demeaning. For a highly speculative theory of suppression, see Callahan, "Dead Paul," 78–81. His stimulating claims abound in sweeping judgments and lack firm foundation in evidence.

The P.Heid fragments probably derive from the climactic episode of the mission to Philippi. Paul has been given a harsh sentence of hard labor. Such sentences were expected to end with the death of the convict. Not much more than a generation after the appearance of *APl*, Callistus, a Roman bishop, was condemned to the mines, but later freed by a grant of clemency (Hippolytus, *Refutation* 9.12.9). This sentence is far harsher than any of the incarcerations mentioned in Acts. Whereas Luke wishes to portray Paul's confinements as relatively mild, reflecting his status and the admiration felt for him by various officials, *APl* exhibits no apologetic interest of this sort (although officials may admire his views, as in chaps. 3 and 9).

Other named characters are Longinus and Firmilla, a married couple, with their daughter Frontina, who is, apparently, dead. Latin names are appropriate for a Roman colony. One will not greatly err by suspecting that Frontina had been persuaded by Paul's message. The cause of her death is uncertain. This would not be the first time that Paul has been accused of bringing about the death of a convert. See 9.21. Whether by accident, illness, or legal action, she is dead. Thecla had also received a capital sentence, while Paul was expelled (3.21). Presuming that Frontina was already dead, the rude disposal of her body was a mark of disgrace. Readers may reasonably imagine that condemned persons were hurled naked from a cliff onto underlying rocks. If they were fortunate, they died upon impact. If not killed immediately, they would die from injuries and neglect. Burial was not permitted. So also, if Longinus had his way, was Paul to die. An alternative reconstruction is that Frontina was still alive, but carried to her death on a bier. If a parallel from the Coptic *Act of Peter* (preserved in Codex Berlin. 8502.4, 128–32, 135–41) is followed, one could imagine that Frontina was paralyzed, perhaps as a means of preserving her chastity. Nowhere, however, does *APl* display such blatant misogyny. The simplest and thus most preferable reconstruction is that Frontina had cheated execution by dying, but was not to be permitted a proper burial. In addition to the shame experienced by her family, lack of a proper burial could mean misery for the surviving shade. On Roman burial practices, see Toynbee, *Death and Burial*, 61–64; for Greek practice, see Garland, *Greek Way*, 21–47. On those not properly buried, see Garland, *Greek Way*, 101–4, 165–66.

Translation, Commentary, and Notes : Chapter

At this point in the narrative a gap intervenes. A miracle has probably forestalled the plans of Paul's adversaries. Miracles are not rare in *APl*. By some means both the apostle and the young woman were prevented from being heaved onto the rocks. Paul, moved by the mother Firmilla's grief, resuscitated Frontina, causing the immediate onlookers to flee in fear of a zombie and the citizenry in general to acclaim God. At the house of his former enemy, Longinus, Paul offered the eucharist.

Chapter 11

1. [...] Longinus [...] Longinus [...] Paul [...] "Since [...] the mine [...] Nothing good has happened for my house." He determined that, as Frontina, his daughter, was going to be thrown [*from a cliff*] that Paul also should be thrown with her, alive. Paul was aware of this, but he continued to toil with the other convicts [*and fast*], in great good cheer, for two days.

2. They [...] on the third day [*brought forth*] Frontina. The [*whole city*] followed. Firmilla, Longinus and [*the*] soldiers [*lamented*]. The prisoners carried the bier. When Paul saw the elaborate mourning spectacle, with the young woman and eight [...] (*gap of several lines*)

3. and without [...] heart [...] Paul alive with the young woman. When Paul had taken the young woman in his arms, he sighed to the lord Jesus Christ because of Firmilla's grief. He threw himself to the ground on his knees [...] praying for both mother and daughter. At that very moment Frontina arose. The onlookers fled in terror. Paul took her by the hand [*and led her*] through town to the house of Longinus. The crowd cried out in unison: "There is one God, the creator of heaven and earth, who has given life to [this young woman through the agency] of Paul. [...]"

4. [a loaf] He blessed it [...] so that they might bless [...] without [...] then [...] Paul [...]

Comments

The story opens with a comment about Longinus, who is evidently a person with juridical authority. He observes that since the condemnation of Paul to the *mine*, his family has suffered nothing but misfortune. Presumably the (apparent) death of his daughter is an example of these setbacks. His solution is to have Paul undergo the same fate, alive. The application of the adjective to him is one piece of evidence that the woman is dead. By some means (revelation?) the plan became known to Paul, who was, of course, quite unfazed by the prospect of imminent death, other than to manifest joy. "Fasting" is a reasonable conjecture. Cf. 6.5. This continues for two days. What will the third bring? The symbolism is a bit obvious but none the worse for that.

The narrative scarcely leaves room for explanation of why disposal of the corpse was delayed for three days, nor is any space wasted on a description of Paul's transport to the place of execution. The entire populace is present. Prisoners serve as pall-bearers. Ancients evidently loved a scene in which someone arrived on a bier and walked home. Luke 7:11–17 comes to mind. The story of how the physician Asclepiades prevented the immolation of a still living person was quite popular (Pliny, *Natural History* 7.37; 26.8; Celsus, *On Medicine* 2.6; Apuleius, *Florida* 19. Cf. also Philostratus, *On Apollonius* 4.45. See also *Acts of Peter* 27–28.) The scene is well and typically set for some kind of resuscitation.

What form the miracle took is unknown, because of a gap in the ms. It does not exceed five lines. One hint comes from one of the most thrilling tricks in the bag of the expert magician: the ability to fly. On the biblical side is Ps 91:11–12: "For he will give his angels charge of you to guard you in all your ways. On their hands they will bear you up, lest you dash your foot against a stone." The devil cited this passage to Jesus while inviting him to attempt to fly (Matt 4:5–7). By so doing Jesus would "tempt" God by using supernatural power for his own benefit and by assuming divine protection in any and all circumstances. The present case would, on the contrary, exemplify "white magic," divine power to alleviate human need. Paul does not, like Simon in the famous story found in *Acts of Peter* 31–32 (= *Passion* 1–2), seek personal honor and gain. See the note on *Flying*.

Paul is moved by compassion for the mother, Firmilla. The resuscitation is indebted to the story of Eutychus (Acts 20:7–12). See Pervo, *Acts*, 510–14; and the comments on chap. 14.1, below. It would be inappropriate for Paul to lie upon the young woman (which is not to defend his lying prostrate upon the young man). He thus kneels with Frontina in his arms.

He prays for both persons. The goal of this prayer is that the miracle "work" properly, bringing about a change of the mother's heart. See the note on *sigh*.

The revival terrified the onlookers (whose identity is uncertain). At the formal level they are reacting to the appearance of a ghost or revenant. Symbolically the action evokes the reaction of those at Jesus' tomb (Mark 16:8; cf. *APl* 16.7) and thus to the meaning of new life for all. Paul guides the newly risen Frontina through the city (cf. Acts 20:12), accompanied by an acclamation (see p. 206). Rather than hail the "god of Paul," the crowd identifies the source of the wonder as the creator and Paul as his agent. This is quite orthodox, possibly due to later revision. The story ends with an offering of the eucharist, as in Acts 20:11. Readers will assume that the converts had gathered at the home of their former enemy, Longinus. Technically speaking, Paul is in custody. As often, the narrative silently assumes that his wondrous delivery constitutes vindication.

The residue may have related the baptism of Firmilla and Longinus, included farewell words from Paul, and his departure to Corinth.

Notes

Section numbers are mine, not Rordorf's.

Mine. The word *metallon* is fairly certain. Although this Greek loan word can have several meanings, "mine" seems most appropriate here. On "workhouse," see *Acts of Titus* 4, Appendix 3.

Flying. Magical parallels include *PGM* 4.2506–7; Lucian, *Philopseudes* 13. Cf. the role of Zephyr in Apuleius, *Metamorphoses* 4.35–5.27. On Simon, see also the Ps.-Clementine *Recognitions* 4.37.

Sigh. Although interpreted as an expression of emotional sympathy, this term may seek to represent sounds uttered by healers and exorcists. See Bonner, "Technique."

Bibliography

Bonner, Campbell. "Traces of Thaumatugic Technique in the Gospels." *HTR* 20 (1927) 171–81.
Callahan, Allen Dwight. "Dead Paul: The Apostle as Martyr in Philippi." In *Philippi at the Time of Paul and after His Death*, edited by Charlambos Bakirtiz and Helmut Koester, 67–84. Harrisburg, PA: Trinity, 1998.
Garland, Robert. *The Greek Way of Death*. Ithaca, NY: Cornell University Press, 1985.

The Acts of Paul

Rordorf, Willy. "Was wissen wir über Plan und Absicht der Paulusakten?" In *Oecumenica et Patristica: Festschrift für Wilhelm Schneemelcher zum 75. Geburtstag*, edited by Damaskinos Papandreou, Wolfgang Bienert, and A. Schäferdiek, 485–96. Stuttgart: Kohlhammer, 1989, 71–82.

Toynbee, Jocelyn M. C. *Death and Burial in the Roman World*. Ithaca, NY: Cornell University Press, 1971.

Translation, Commentary, and Notes : Chapter

The Passion of Paul: *APl* 12-14.

Chapter 12: Corinth

Sources: P.Hamb pp. 6-7; P.Heid pp. 51, 52, 71

Introduction. The Hamburg Greek papyrus is once more available, supplemented by a few lines of Coptic. Although the beginning of the visit is marked with a typical geographical formula, "From Philippi to Corinth," the ms. has no indicator of a break between what scholars now designate as chaps. 12 and 13. Until the end of the ms. no chapter dividing marks survive. The absence of a title like "From Corinth to Rome" could be indicative of the structure. The author (or a subsequent editor) did not view Corinth as simply another station. The narrative supports this hypothesis. (See also Snyder, "Remembering," 207-10, who offers similar views with a different motivation.) Corinth is the beginning of what might be called "the Pauline passion narrative." The episode is inspired by Acts 20:17-21:14, Paul's final journey to Jerusalem. See Pervo, "Hard Act," 16-17. This is both obscured by and underlines a basic contrast between Acts and *APl*: in *APl* the apostle travels to Rome as a free person. In keeping with the tone of a "passion," the only miracle performed by Paul is a resurrection (14.2; cf. Acts 20:7-12, the only miracle of the unit.)

Foreshadowing is an important component of this passage. Like Acts 20-21, it blends retrospective reflection upon Paul's past ministry with predictions of his future fate. At a more general level chap. 12 represents the genre of the farewell scene, examples of which can be found from Homer onwards (Bovon, "Saint-Esprit"; and Pervo, *Profit*, 67-69; Pervo, *Acts*, 529-30). In ApocActs scenes of this nature are found in, e.g., *AJn* 58-59, *APet* 1-3, and *AThom* 65-68. Among typical features are assurance that the apostle acts in accordance with the divine will, placement (logically) in the penultimate stage of the apostle's career, with allusions to his coming death, the resultant distress of the faithful, encouraging words, and an escort to the point of departure. A related genre is the testament, the final message of a person approaching death. The testament underwent rich development in early Judaism. See Pervo, *Acts*, 517.

Specific similarities to Acts here are: (1) grief because the faithful will not see Paul again (Acts 20:37-38); (2) Paul speaks of his coming trials (20:23) and fulfillment of his mission (20:24), as well as reflection upon his experiences (20:19); (3) there is a "Gethsemane" at which the apostle rejects seeking to evade martyrdom (21:13-14); (4) the message does not neglect ethical exhortation (20:28); and (5) inspired forecasts embellish the narrative with foreboding (Acts 21:4, 9–11).

The author does not follow his models woodenly. In place of the standard first-person retrospective is a narrative summary. The actual "testament" lasted for a period of forty days. The chapter opens with this summary and devotes much of its space to describing worship in rather more detail than Acts 20:7–12. 1 Corinthians is the chief source of this description. Whereas in Acts danger come from "the Jews" (20:3, 11; 21:11), the adversary here is unspecified but clear: the imperial government.

From Phi[*li*]ppi to Corinth

12.1–6

1. Paul's arrival at Stephen's house in Corinth after his journey from Philippi produced joy on the part of all our people, joy coupled with tears, as he related what he had undergone in the workhouse at Philippi, as well as what had happened to him in every other place, until his tears finally brought relief, and all made fervent prayer for Paul, so that he deemed himself privileged because they daily referred his concerns to the lord in prayer with such spiritual unanimity. As a result the magnitude of his joy was boundless, and Paul's spirits were elevated because of the believers' affection. He taught for forty days about what he had endured, what he had experienced in various places and the sundry marvels accorded to him. In every account he praised God the almighty and Christ Jesus who had been well pleased with Paul in every place.

2. When the time had come for Paul to leave for Rome, grief gripped the believers over when they would see him again. Filled with the Holy Spirit, Paul said: "Sisters and brothers, Devote yourselves to fasting and charity, for I am headed for a fiery furnace—I am speaking of Rome—and I should not be able to endure it if the Lord did not empower me. For David took the same path as Saul [...] overcome with anger he [*would have*] killed Nabal, convinced [...] Nabal; for the God Christ Jesus was with him [...]

this valuable fast. The Grace of the Lord [P.Heid 51 begins here] will be with [*me so that I might accomplish the*] divine plan [*in store for me*] with patient endurance.

3. [*When they heard this*], the believers were troubled and resumed their fasting vigil]. Cleobius, speaking through the Spirit said to them, "Sisters and brothers, Paul must fulfill the entire plan of God and go up to the [*place*] of death [...] with impressive instruction, knowledge, and dissemination of the message, until, having stirred up jealousy, he leaves this world." [P.Heid p. 51 ends] When the believers and Paul heard this, they raised their voices and prayed: "God of our lord, father of Christ, come to the aid of your slave Paul, so that he may remain with us because of our weakness."

4. These words crushed Paul. He brought his fast with them to an end and offered the eucharist (P.Hamb p. 7) [*The bread broke*] into pieces of its own accord [...] When they asked what this [sign] might mean and what he was going to say about it, he [P.Heid. p. 52 begins here] would not respond.

5. But the Spirit fell upon Myrta, who said: "Brothers and sisters, why do you regard this sign with fear? Paul, the slave of the lord, will deliver many in Rome and will nourish so many with his message that their number will exceed calculation and he will become the most noteworthy of the faithful. The glory [of the Lord Christ Jesus] will clothe him with splendor, a magnificent grace in Rome." Once the Spirit within Myrta had subsided, each took some food and they feasted in accordance with the practice of fasting, singing psalms of David and other songs. Even Paul enjoyed himself. [P.Heid. 52 ends]

6. The next day, after they had kept an all night vigil following God's will, Paul said, "My fellow believers, I shall sail out on Friday [P.Heid. 71 begins] and make for Rome. I have no wish to hinder what has been ordained and imposed upon me. This is why I was appointed." All the believers were quite upset at this message; [P.Heid 71 ends] each made as large a contribution as possible so that Paul would not be troubled beyond his separation from them.

Comment

Section 1 is a carefully constructed overture to the final part of Paul's story, marked with a chiastic structure that moves from the particular of Philippi to the general history of his sufferings. The thematic words are the stem *exēg-* ("narrate"; 44.5; 46.13), "joy" (44.3, 9), and the word "place" (44.5; 46.12). These are key terms, for a universal mission involves "telling the story" in every place. The general meaning is clear; individual phrases are uncertain. See the notes *related* and *workhouse*. As stated in the Introduction, the narrative has a testamentary character, which, like that in Acts 20, attends more to adversity than to wonders, although the latter are noted. A forty-day course of autobiographical lectures implies more than an occasional hardship. One function of the length is to imply that the stories narrated in the text are but a sample of a large repertoire. The amount of time devoted to his own story strikes the modern reader as immodest, if not simply narcissistic. For the author and his audience, it was gospel: Paul's life imitated that of his master; only through the power of Christ could the apostle achieve what he had achieved and endure what he had endured. This is the meaning of the final doxology: credit belongs to God. The summary is notable for its lack of polemic or identification of adversaries. One point that hearers are to take away is that Paul endured because of the grace of God; another is more implicit: the path to the future does not follow easy street.

Following the forty days of instruction, the time for Paul's departure for Rome, first identified as his goal here, arrives. Like Jesus (Acts 1:1–11), Paul leaves after a forty-day intensive course. Grief once more rears its head. Paul responds with a brief consolatory address, albeit with a dose of stiff upper lip. "Filled with the Holy Spirit" does not imply that other speeches by Paul lacked divine guidance. These words refer to a charismatic manifestation in Acts 6:15 and may have similar meaning elsewhere. The phrase becomes common, forming a bridge between the D-text of Acts and the ApocActs (Acts 24:10; 26:1; *APet* 2, 6; and R. Pervo, *Acts* 591, n.m.). Here it marks prophetic inspiration.

As Dunn ("Influence") has noted, these sections take 1 Cor 14:26–28 as their model: "When you come together, each one has a hymn, a lesson, a revelation, a tongue, or an interpretation. Let all things be done for building up. If anyone speaks in a tongue, let there be only two or at most three, and each in turn; and let one interpret. But if there is no one to interpret, let them be silent in church and speak to themselves and to God." Paul (12.2), followed by Cleobius in §3 and Myrte in §5, deliver prophecies in intelligible speech. Three may be viewed as the maximum, surely appropriate for a matter of this gravity. The spirit exhibits here a good literary sense. The three form a crescendo of increasing specificity and clarity, ending on a positive note. The lapse of time allowed for reflection. Some of the Pauline spirit, so to speak, still shines, for a woman could prophesy no less than a man. Dunn ("Influence," 452) thinks that 1 Cor 14:34–35 was absent from the author's Pauline text. He may well be right (on this interpolation, see Pervo, *Making of Paul*, 46–48). If the author knew of this passage, he did not accept it.

That author may have wished to do no more than "reconstruct," so to speak, worship of apostolic times based upon apostolic direction and precedent, or he may have wished to promote ideals for his own era. The popularity of the New Prophecy in Asia Minor makes it quite likely that chap. 12 contains a message for its own era, in effect: The spirit should not be quenched, women may prophesy, but . . . please keep within reasonable limits and cherish relevant and intelligible speech. Note the detailed description of the demeanor, role, and function of inspired prophets in *Hermas* 43.8–17.

Paul will require the support of their piety (see *Fasting and charity*). Martyrdom is his destiny. "Fiery furnace" evokes Daniel 3. Cf. 4 Macc 16:21; 1 *Clem* 45:7. The essence of the trope is that the wicked emperor Nebuchadnezzar who condemned Daniel is identified with Nero. (The phrase about Rome is uncertain but logical.) This shows that the strongly anti-imperial orientation of chap. 14 is not restricted to that portion of *APl*. As in §1, Paul attributes his endurance to God. He supports his thesis with two examples from 1 Samuel 24–25. The text is not clear. (See *Nabal*.) The evident meaning is that God twice removed an enemy of David from the scene. An implicit meaning is that one should not seek revenge; that is best left to God. David could trust in God because *God* was with him. See Acts 7:9; 10:38, and Pervo, *Acts*, 172n88. Harrill, *Paul the Apostle*, 101–2, holds that *APl* is not anti-imperial in general, but anti-Nero. Nero is certainly a good target; execution by Nero constituted an honor. The text, however, does not simply denounce bad emperors; believers are soldiers of the great king. This literally militant rhetoric delegitimizes the Roman empire and all emperors. (In picking up on upper-class hatred of Nero second-century Christians adopt a stance that those of lower status in the second half of the first century would not have embraced, for, among the "common people," Nero was popular, sometimes idolized.)

"Patient endurance" (*hypomonē*; 45.11; 46.26) is a traditional Greek virtue. Enduring suffering, mistreatment, and hardship are primary applications. In the Israelite sphere the word acquired in the LXX the connotation of awaiting. It thus became eminently suitable in a martyrological context. See Spicq, *Lexicon* 3:414–20; and F. Hauck, "*hypomenō*," *TDNT* 4:481–88.

The Acts of Paul

References to a divine plan (here *oikonomia*) often appear in the face of misfortune to reassure believers that God remains in charge, that what seems like irredeemable tragedy from the perspective of mere humans will redound to divine glory. See Pervo, "God and Planning."

Since this news was not well received, the spirit turned to Cleobius. His words echo Acts 19:21; 20:22, 29. (See Pervo, *Acts*, 482.) Rome, the imperial capital, will be his city of destiny, as was the religious capital, Jerusalem, for Jesus. Note also 1 *Clement* 5, which identifies jealousy as the cause of Paul's (and Peter's) death and presents Paul as an example of patient endurance. The Roman mission will include substantial instruction. This summary is more pedantic and less dramatic than Acts 28:30–31, but it has the same object. This is a capsule of concentrated Pauline tradition, drawn from several sources. While drawing upon Acts, the author rejects Luke's picture of Paul sent to Rome as a prisoner. (1 *Clement* does not take note of Paul's legal status.)

Several reasons motivated this deviation from Acts. Whereas Luke tends to view imperial officials as less hostile than Jewish authorities, *APl* wishes to depict a direct confrontation with the secular ruler. Rather than recount a long and eventual unsuccessful legal battle, as Acts implies, in this book Paul is able to ignite conflict no less quickly in Rome than elsewhere. In effect, if Paul were to have a successful mission at Rome, he would do it as a free man rather than as an individual under house arrest allowed to entertain visitors. The author of *APl* had logical, theological, and literary reasons for sending Paul to Rome as a free person.

The believers receive Cleobius' revelation with a petition that God spare Paul because of their pastoral needs. Heartbroken, the apostle brought the vigil to an end and began the eucharistic celebration. When the moment came for him to break the loaf into fragments, the action happened without human agency. This evokes the feeding stories (Mark 6:32–44 and parallels). It envisions the unity of the church's growth and social missions. *Did.* 9:4 expresses this message eschatologically: "Just as this broken bread was scattered upon the mountains and then was gathered together and became one, so may your church be gathered together from the ends of the earth into your kingdom" (trans. Holmes, *Apostolic Fathers*, 359).

The action was perceived as a sign, requiring interpretation. Paul did not or would not comment. *Myrta*, however, was inspired to interpret it as a forecast of Paul's work in Rome (§5). His success will be spectacular. This oracle raises the expectations of the reader and the spirits of the dramatic audience. John 12:24 may be in mind, although the sentiment is general. To speak of the Spirit subsiding suggests prior ecstasy. The Coptic translator

Translation, Commentary, and Notes : Chapter

evidently thought so, since the rendering is much blander: "And this is how the Spirit spoke to Myrta" (P.Heid 52.13–14).

With that they turned to a modest feast. The evident ritual sequence is a hard fast, eucharist, nourishing meal. The faithful sang psalms, presumably psalms of praise. See Ferguson, "Music." They pray hard then spend the night in vigil, evidently in accordance with a revelation ("God's will," §6). Paul addresses the assembled formally (see Acts 2:29, e.g.), in solemn terms. His announcement that he will sail on Friday (the Jewish term, "preparation" [for Sabbath], adopted by Christians) indicates divine control, for ships could not sail until the winds were favorable. The verb "make for" is not clear, but context is an adequate guide. Paul is absolutely stalwart in the face of impending death. See Mark 14:32–42 (where the disciples cannot keep vigil), especially vv. 35–36; John 12:27; Acts 21:10–14. He closes with an allusion to the PE: 1 Tim 2:7; 2 Tim 1:11. This solemn first-person declaration should be compared with similar statements attributed to Jesus, such as Mark 1:38. The thrust is upon acceptance of, better, identification with, the mission. It is not self-proclamation.

In response to their grief, the believers took thought for Paul's welfare and raised a purse to ease his travel expenses. The source is 1 Cor 16:1–4. This is another transformation of Pauline history. In the course of gathering his collection for Jerusalem, his attempt to establish a basis for and sign of unity among followers of Jesus, Paul was accused of raising the money for his own benefit, if not for himself. See Georgi, *Remembering*, e.g., 60–61. Since the author of *APl* has dropped the entire story of Paul's trip to Jerusalem, his arrest, and voyage to Rome in custody, he does not have room for the collection and freely adopts a view that may have been circulated by Paul's enemies during his own lifetime. This purse will explain how the apostle will be able to rent a facility in Rome (chap. 14).

Notes

Stephen's. Schmidt and Schubart read "Epiphanius' house." (44) Rordorf (1167) proposes "Stephanas." This name differs from the traditional "Stephen," *Stephanos.* Rordorf's reading conforms to 1 Cor 1:16; 16:15, 17, and is therefore preferable. The ms. is difficult to read. See Dunn, "Influence," 445.

Joy. A regular feature of the opening of chapters.

Our people. This surprising use of the first-person plural looks like what contemporary critics call "metalepsis," in this instance an intrusion of the narrator into the text, but it means here "Christians." Cf. Tit 3:14; *Mart. Polyc.* 9:1.

Related. Translation of this sentence is uncertain. The syntax would best fit a bipartite division: Paul's suffering in Philippi and everywhere as well as what he had experienced (in general). The translation provided aims at what the author evidently meant. For Paul to speak about his mission meant much talk about suffering, but not exclusively so.

Workhouse. The translation of *ergastrois* is quite difficult. Its primary meaning is "the cost of labor." This is impossible. Translators assume that it is a synecdoche, like the modern use of "labor" to mean the cost of labor. On the similar term *ergastulum*, used for a slave prison, see Harrill, *Manumission of Slaves*, 35n92.

Relief. On the term, see 4.12; 2 Cor 7:5.

Prayer. Cf. Acts 12:5, *v.l.*

Boundless. The same expression appears in *AJn* 63.

Forty Days. Cf. Acts 1:3, where the risen Christ is said to have taught for forty days prior to his departure.

Fasting and charity. "Fasting" is a reasonable conjecture. The second term *agapē* could be understood to refer to the "love feast" that follows fasts. Cf. §5. Preferred here is "charity," in the sense of charitable contributions, for example as a result of funds saved through not eating. With prayer, fasting and almsgiving are traditional virtues inspired by Judaism.

Nabal. Schmidt and Schubart supply by "the wife of" Nabal, (*Praxeis*, 46 l. 23), but this does not fit the context of the speech. (Nabal's wife, Abigail, dissuaded David from attacking and was awarded with David's hand in marriage after Nabal's demise.)

God. "The God Jesus Christ" appears to be one of the Monarchian features not edited out of the text.

Vigil. This is a conjectural restoration, first proposed by Schmidt and Schubart, *Praxeis*, 47.

Myrta. This is an attested Greek proper name and should not be taken as a speaking sprig of myrtle, the proper form of which ends in *-os*.

Translation, Commentary, and Notes : Chapter

Bibliography

Bovon, François. "Le Saint-Esprit, l'Église et les relations humaines selon Actes 20,36—21,16." In *Les Actes des Apôtres: Traditions, redaction, théologies*, edited by Jacob Kremer, 339–58. BETL 43. Leuven: Leuven University Press 1979.

Czachesz, István. "The Acts of Paul and the Western Text of Luke's Acts: Paul between Canon and Apocrypha." In *The Apocryphal Acts of Paul and Thecla*, edited by Jan N. Bremmer, 107–25. Kampen: Kok Pharos, 1996.

Dunn, Peter W. "The Influence of 1 Corinthians on the *Acts of Paul*." In SBLSP, 438–54. Atlanta: Scholars, 1996.

Ferguson, Everett. "Music." In *Encyclopedia of Early Christianity*, edited by Everett Ferguson et al., 629–32. New York: Garland, 1990.

Georgi, Dieter. *Remembering the Poor: The History of Paul's Collection for Jerusalem*. Nashville: Abingdon, 1992.

Glancy, Jennifer A. "Boasting of Beatings (2 Corinthians 11:23–25)." *JBL* 123 (2004) 99–135

Harrill, J. Albert. *The Manumission of Slaves in Early Christianity*. HUT 32. Tübingen: Mohr/Siebeck, 1995.

———. *Paul the Apostle*. Cambridge: Cambridge University Press, 2012.

Pervo, Richard I. "God and Planning: Footprints of Providence in Acts and in the *Acts of Paul*." In *Method and Meaning: Festschrift for Harold Attridge*, edited by Andrew McGowan, 259–77. Atlanta: SBL, 2011.

———. "A Hard Act to Follow: The Acts of Paul and the Canonical Acts." *Journal of Higher Criticism* 2, no. 2 (1995) 3–32.

———. *The Making of Paul: Constructions of Paul in Early Christianity*. Minneapolis: Fortress, 2010.

Chapter 13

Sources: P.Hamb. 7–8, P.Heid. 79–80, P.Mich. inv. 1317, 3788, P. Berlin 13893.

Introduction. The introduction to chap. 12 argued that it was the beginning of the "Pauline passion narrative." The major continuous ms., P.Hamb., has no division between the chapters. The text of this segment shows signs of subsequent editing, including marks of third-century theological positions and, most notably, evident interaction with *APet*.

Until the emergence of P.Hamb., scholarship tended to follow Schmidt in assigning priority to *APl*. That papyrus tilted Schmidt, followed by many others, in the other direction. (See Rordorf, "Relation," 178–80). 13.2 reports a dream appearance of the Lord to Paul the closely resembles *APet* 35 (*Passion* 7). At the urging of others, Peter has left Rome to avoid persecution:

> When he went out of the gate he saw the Lord come into Rome. And when he saw him he said, "Lord, where are you going? And the Lord said to him, "I go to Rome to be crucified." And Peter said to him, "Lord, are you being crucified again?" and he said, "Yes, Peter, again I shall be crucified." And Peter came to himself; and he saw the Lord ascending to heaven. Then he returned to Rome, rejoicing and praising the Lord because he had said, "I am being crucified." This was to happen to Peter. (trans. Elliott, 424)

For scholars born before 1950 Peter's *quo vadis* (where are you going?) experience was a part of general popular culture (Pervo, "Ancient Novel," 704), and its Petrine associations endure. This association generates a strong prejudice. Nonetheless, comparison of the arguments of MacDonald ("Which Came First?," 15–18) and Stoops ("*Acts of Peter*," 77–79), indicates that the episode fits quite well in the story of Peter. It is another story of petrine failure followed by recovery, e.g., Matt 14:22–33. Whether the author of *APet* found and revised or invented this story, he produced an enduring miniature classic.

Formally, each narrates an appearance of the risen Lord to a follower engaged on a journey in furtherance of the Christian mission. Both offer an apophthegm (pronouncement story) in the form of a dialogue based upon a prophetic I-saying of Jesus. Compare Luke 13:31–32 (–35), where the goal is Jerusalem rather than Rome. The sayings are similar, but not identical. Different modes of expressing the future are selected. With Peter the statement about crucifixion is given three times (cf. Mark 14:66–72; John 21:15–17, triple denial and threefold "rehabilitation"). The texts use different words for "again," *palin* in *APet* and the more ambiguous *anōthen* in *APl*. The latter is found in connection with martyrdom in *Mart. Pol.* 1.1.

The claim that the passage was more relevant to Peter because he was crucified whereas Paul was beheaded is not decisive. Historically, the manner of their deaths is not known outside of legends contained within the ApocActs. Barnes argues that the tradition about the death of Peter in John 21 refers to burning rather than to crucifixion (*Hagiography*, 1–41). Origen, whose attribution of the "crucified afresh" saying to *APl* was all that was known of this chapter until the discovery of P.Hamb, preferred to interpret "crucify" as metaphorical. In his comments on John 8 he cites Gal 2:19–20 ("For through the law I died to the law, so that I might live to God. I have been crucified with Christ; 20 and it is no longer I who live, but it is Christ who lives in me. And the life I now live in the flesh I live by faith in the Son of God, who loved me and gave himself for me"). *APet* could have transformed a metaphorical understanding into a literal one, as MacDonald ("Which," 17) and Rordorf ("Relation," 187) allow (although Rordorf prefers a common oral tradition behind both). In fact, the saying does not seem to apply to Paul's fate.

The two texts exhibit structural parallels at beginning, middle, and end:

1. A ship captain baptized by Peter (with differing names: Artemon in *APl* 13; Theon in *APet* 5).

2. A christophany of similar form focused upon the saying "I shall be crucified again." *APl* 13; *APet* 35.

3. The captains introduce the apostles to friends in Italy (Claudius, *APl* 13; Ariston, *APet* 6).

Appeal to coincidence rings hollow here. Contamination has taken place, although clear delineation of responsibility is more or less impossible. Most manuscripts of Mark, for example, have been contaminated by material from other gospels, especially Matthew. One cannot address the Synoptic Problem (the question of priority among Matthew, Mark, and Luke, presuming a literary relation) until a clean text of each Gospel has been determined, although the establishment of a clean text does not take place in a vacuum. The better solution is to regard the current text of *APl* 13 as contaminated by the *APet*. The most logical explanation for borrowing from the *APet* would be the goal of coordinating the ministries of Peter and Paul at Rome and assimilating their martyrdoms, a process that resulted in the celebration of their deaths on the same day. A major force behind this drive to "twin" the apostolic martyrs was the Roman church. See Eastman,

Martyr, 15–69; and Barnes (above). From the perspective of competition—to make Peter as good as Paul and vice-versa—imitation may take either direction. In the case of the martyrdom chapters, imitation of *APl* by *APet* is highly likely. See Pervo, "Egging on."

Intertextual possibilities include: (1) the author of 3 *Cor* imitated the Christology of *APl* 13; (2) the editor responsible for the current shape of *APl* 13 appropriated the theology of 3 *Cor*; or (3) the same editor who inserted 3 *Cor* revised chap. 13. The first of these is the least likely, while the third admits of a hypothesis: the editor responsible for inserting 3 *Cor* wished to underline Paul's "anti-gnostic" orthodoxy and his relation to other apostles (3 *Cor* 4.4). Chapter 13 is not anti-heretical; it, like 3 *Cor*, does show an interest in relating Paul to other apostles. The hypothesis presented here is that the editor responsible for most of chap. 10 (3 *Cor*), also revised chap. 13 in order to allow Paul to provide a summary of Christian belief prior to his final trial and to associate him more closely with other early Christian leaders. This hypothesis cannot serve as a platform for other proposals, but it is a reasonable and economical solution. As in the case of 3 *Cor*, the proposed editor made use of his source. This would account for similarities of language and consistency of thought within *APl*. *APet* is the other major probable source.

Issues of intertextuality aside, chap. 13 is unusual in several ways. This is the only description of a voyage in the extant *APl*. The model of Acts 27 is one good explanation. Acts 27:23–25 also provides the precedent for a vision. The christophany evokes gospel stories. Furthermore, the sermon contains an embedded gospel, like those in *APet* 20 and *AJn* 88–102, although, unlike those apostles, Paul cannot provide a first-person account. Here only the *APl* names two other apostles, Peter and Philip, both of whom had followed Jesus. Finally, the theology expressed in Paul's sermon has affinities with 3 *Cor*, notably its "spirit Christology." (See the comments on chapter 10.) This Christology is not otherwise characteristic of *APl*.

In summary, chap. 13 in its present form is a later reworking of the text. The extant material may well preserve the structure of its presumed predecessor. That structure is clear and simple enough: Paul travels to Rome, is strengthened by an appearance of the Lord, and taken to the home of one Claudius, evidently the host of a house-church, where the apostle preaches a sermon, the last part of which is lost.

13.1–2: Voyage and Christophany

1. When Paul boarded the ship, attended by the prayers of all, its captain, Artemon, who had been baptized by Peter, [*greeted*] Paul with joy... and so, because so many things had been entrusted to Paul [*Artemon treated him as if, in him,*] the lord had come aboard. Once the ship had gotten underway, Artemon, by divine grace, joined Paul to glorify the lord Jesus Christ, who had fashioned in advance his plan for Paul. When they had reached the high sea and quiet prevailed, Paul fell asleep, exhausted by his fasting and nightlong vigils with the believers.

2. At that time the lord came to him, walking on the sea He nudged Paul and said, "Get up and see!" Upon awakening he said, "You are my lord Jesus Christ, the king [...] But why are you so sad and gloomy, Lord? If you are troubled, [*tell me clearly what it is*], lord, for seeing you like this is quite upsetting."

"Paul, I am going to be crucified again."

"God forbid, lord, that I should ever see that!"

"Paul, go to Rome and exhort the believers to remain faithful to their heavenly calling."

[...] walking on the sea the lord went ahead of them, pointing out the way like a [guiding s]tar.

13.3–4: Arrival and Pastoral Address

3. When the voyage was over [...] Paul left the ship, burdened with considerable sadness. [*He saw*] a man in the harbor area who welcomed captain Artemon with a greeting when he saw him: (p. 8) "Claudius, Look at who is here with me [*Paul, the be*]loved of the lord." [P.Mich. 1317 begins here] Claudius greeted Paul with a warm embrace. [Berl 13893 begins here] and promptly, with Artemon, carried the baggage from the boat to his place.

4. Claudius quite joyfully advised the believers about Paul, so that his house was quickly filled with joy and grace. They took

The Acts of Paul

note of how Paul dropped his unhappiness and began to teach the authentic message:

5. "My fellow believers, soldiers of Christ, Hear me out. How often God delivered Israel from some lawless person! So long as they observed what God required, he did not desert them. For example he delivered them from Pharaoh's lawless claws and from the utterly unsanctified king Og, from Arad, and the foreigners. So long as they observed God's requirements, the almighty, since he had promised them the land of the Canaanites, granted them offspring, and subjected the foreigners to them. After all that he had provided for them in the uninhabited country and the waterless territory, (6) he also sent them prophets to announce our lord Jesus Christ. They also received, in accordance with their station, lot, and portion some of the Spirit of the Christ and consequently suffered much and were put to death by the people. Because their lawlessness led them to rebel against the living God, they lost their eternal inheritance.

7. "At present, brothers and sisters, a great trial impends. If we endure it we shall have access to the lord and receive a sanctuary and a source of good will, [P.Mich. 3788 begins] Jesus Christ, who gave himself for us. He is indeed God's son, in accordance with the message you have received. In the last times God sent for us a spirit of power into flesh, that is, into Mary the Galilean, in fulfillment of the prophetic message. He was conceived and carried by her until she delivered and gave birth to Jesus our king, in Judean Bethlehem. He was reared in Nazareth, went to Jerusalem and all Judea teaching, 'The kingdom of heaven is at hand. Abandon the darkness; accept the light, you who haunt the shadows of death. A light has risen for you.'

8. "He did splendid and marvelous things, (and so selected twelve men from the tribes whom he kept with him, men of [intel]ligence [...] and faith), raising the dead, healing the sick, cleansing lepers, healing the blind, curing the crippled, raising up the paralyzed, cleans[ing] the demon-possessed, and, in a word, he went about ministering to the entire region along the shore [...] heal[ing] [...] the river. [Isra]el. For [A] woman with a flow of

blood [came] to him [but I] not other than [...] of our Lord Jesus Christ [...][...] [he/I was brought to a] meeting and [...] cemeteries [...] greatly by [...] glorious king. The other seed that the glorious king [sowed] for the price of/upon [the twelve men] [...] receiv[ing?] Israel [... P.Heid. 79 begins here]

9. "... the deeds [...] wondered considerably and [*pondered*] internally. [*He said to them*] [*After all the powerful deeds and works that he did*] 'Why are you surprised that I raise the dead or make cripples walk or purify lepers or revive the sick or heal paralytics and possessed people or that I distributed a little bread and satisfied a multitude or walked on sea or commanded the winds? If you believe these things, then you [*know*] that they are extraordinary. For truly [*I say*] to you, if you tell [*this mountain*], "Get going and throw yourself [*into the sea*]." This will take place if you do it without a shred of mental reservation. This [...]'

10. "One of them, named Simon, was sufficiently convinced to say, 'Lord, the deeds you accomplish are truly magnificent, for we have never heard nor have we [*ever*] seen someone other than you who raises the dead. [...]'

11. "[The Lord said] '[...], but the other works [...] these I perform as a temporary deliverance, while they are here, so that people may believe in the one who sent me.'

Simon said, 'Lord, direct me to speak.'

'Speak, Peter.' (For thereafter he always addressed them by name.)

'What work is greater than these [...] other than raising the dead [...] [*and*] feeding a multitude?'

'There is something greater than this. Blessed are those who have believed with all their heart.'

Philip then said angrily, 'What sort of stuff are you trying to teach us?'

'You...'"

The Acts of Paul

Comment

The opening evokes Acts 21:5–6, Paul's last trip as a free man. The reference to a captain baptized by Peter is an invitation to read this final part of *APl* in conjunction—or competition—with *APet*. Why the name *Artemon*? The author may be sowing seeds of doubt about *APet* while evoking it. The balance of that sentence is badly damaged. The supplement attempts no more than the probable general sense. The author follows Acts in stressing that Paul's forthcoming death was in accordance with God's will and in furtherance of God's plan. See Pervo, "God and Planning."

The model for Christ's epiphany is the gospel sea-stories: Mark 4:35–41 and 6:45–52. Paul's sleep echoes Luke 8:23, while his exhaustion parallels Luke 9:32; Matt 26:43, and Luke 6:12. The apostle is like his master. Given the ardors and emotional stress of chap. 12, his exhaustion is highly appropriate. Amidst the soothing sound and gentle motion of placid waves Paul can finally fall into a well-deserved sleep.

This rest was not to last. In an evocation of Jesus walking on the water (Mark 6:45–52 and parallels; "walking on the sea" is identical to Mark 6:48) Christ comes to greet him. That story was probably first told as an appearance of the Risen Lord. *APl* has thus "restored" it to the original setting. Details differ: in Mark the sea is stormy and the wind difficult; most notably, Paul does not react in fear; he recognizes his savior, who, like the angel of Acts 12:7, prods him awake. The invitation "Get up and see" is natural and logical enough, but it also refers to rising to new life and seeing with the eyes of faith.

Paul recognizes his nocturnal, walking-on-water visitor and hails him in *creedal* language. (Following "king" was a qualifier, such as "eternal," "heavenly," "of the ages.") Since gods awarding mortals with an epiphany characteristically smiled, Jesus' demeanor upsets Paul. On his initial question, see 5.3 (Nympha); his final declaration is verbally identical to a statement in 3.13. In short, the style is suitable for *APl*.

Description of Jesus' affect sets the stage for the central saying, around which this pronouncement story is set. (See the note *crucified*.) Paul's reply treats this as a literal statement. The contrasting uses of "see" are instructive. Paul is invited to "see" the risen Christ but does not want to contemplate Christ crucified. That view needs to be corrected. The saying relates to martyrdom as imitation of Christ. See, e.g., Moss, *Other Christs*. The Lord ends the dialogue with a commission and direction: Paul is to help the faithful at Rome in the face of impending persecution and martyrdoms. Christ did not appear to warn Paul about his personal fate but to give him a pastoral charge.

The unit ends with an *inclusion*: walking on the water, followed by the image of Christ as the one who always goes ahead of the believers, illuminating the darkness and bringing them to their goal. Nothing could be further from Acts 27, where stars disappear (v. 20). The term *phōstēer* is a title in Rev 21:11. The author may also be playing on the star that led the astrologers to Bethlehem (Matt 2:1–12). See Spicq, *Lexicon* 3:487–88.

With §3 the papyrus fragments from Michigan and Berlin add their witness. These show general stability as well as variety. See the articles by Kilpatrick and Roberts, "Acta Pauli"; Rordorf, "Actes"; and Sanders, "Fragment." The papyri are important because they attest to the popularity of *APl* in Egypt in antiquity. Sections 3 and 4 take Paul to the house of Claudius and set the stage for his subsequent sermon, incomplete as our mss. end.

The destination is not mentioned. Large ships did not disembark at Rome. Acts 28:14 reports that Paul landed at Puteoli and traveled by land to the city. *APet* 6 has Peter land at Puteoli, be handed over by Theon to Ariston, and eventually travel to Rome. Ostia, the port of Rome, is another possibility. The lost ending to this chapter probably noted the journey to Rome. Claudius (a proper Roman name) takes the role here played by Ariston in *APet* (above). Carrying Paul's luggage is a sign of respect, since heads of Roman households did not often act as porters. The epithet "beloved," used by Paul in addressing believers (e.g., Rom 1:7), here indicates his close relationship to Christ, most recently demonstrated on the voyage. (Jesus is identified as God's beloved son at the baptism and transfiguration: Mark 1:11; 9:7). Typically, the assembly opens on a note of joy. As elsewhere, the presence of believers relieves the apostle's depression. *APl* has grasped, from Paul's letters, this sense of believers as his source of encouragement and nurture.

The sermon that begins in §5 and breaks off in §11 is an exhortation to remain true to God, who will remain true to the promises. This is presented primarily through a summary of salvation history, first from the history of Israel in the Exodus and wilderness experiences (§5), followed by a summary of the work of the prophets (§6). The opening and closing sentences of this part make the point: God protected Israel so long as it obeyed; disobedience led to loss of the promise. This is the only final and definitive condemnation of Israel in *APl*. Its basis is general disobedience to the prophets of God and the execution of at least some by "the people" rather than specifically for the condemnation of Jesus.

With this historical example in mind, Paul turns at §7 to the threat of a pending trial and the accompanying promise. This leads to a review of Jesus' conception, birth, and ministry and includes a catalogue of miracles. As the ms. breaks off, some of Jesus' disciples express doubts about his powers.

Those doubts will very likely be repudiated; the ending shows them quite unlike the recalcitrantly disobedient Israelites. The speech does not affirm God's role in creation. No "heresies" are attacked.

The opening words evoke the beginning of Stephen's address to the Sanhedrin, Acts 7:2. "Soldiers of Christ" may be an addition by the later editor. On this concept, see the comments at 13.2. "Lawless" is especially apt for tyrants. An example of that species will play a major role in the next chapter. Pharaoh, a classic persecuting monarch, receives attention, as does Og (P.Hamb. reads "Gog," identifying him with the eschatological foe of Rev 20:8), described as the king of Arad ("Adar" in P.Hamb.). The king of Arad is nameless in Num 21:1–3, while Og was king of Bashan (Num 21:33). For the purposes of fairness it should be stated that Numbers 21 does not comment upon the moral character of either king. The references presumably come from memory. Two examples provide the minimum: one for deliverance from evil and the other for gaining the inheritance. Stage two is the prophetic era, characterized by disobedience. In the end the circle is complete. The heirs become lawless, killing the prophets. Insofar as the prophets possessed "some of the Spirit of the Christ," crimes against them were crimes against the Messiah.

The speech does not distinguish "old" from "new," although the shift from promise to fulfillment is apparent. The next section opens with the warning of a great *trial*, coupled with a promise encompassed in three potent images: an open door to God (or Christ), a refuge from danger, and protection from the powers of evil. These are not concrete in the sense of "believe in Jesus and your life will be trouble-free." Persecution will arrive shortly. The promise is that these torments will no more separate us from God's loving care than Jesus' horrible death meant the failure of his mission. Gal 1:4 ("gave himself") is evoked. "Spirit" into "flesh" superficially resembles the later "Word/Flesh" theology of Alexandria. "Spirit of power" (cf. 3 Cor 2:5) could mean "powerful spirit," but this is unlikely. The Spirit is Christ, not the source through which he was conceived. By his lights the author is affirming the Incarnation. "He [*hos*; relative] was conceived" (cf. Ignatius, *Eph* 18.2) is not logical, as the last subject was neuter (spirit). Jesus is king, a title that will become important in chap. 14.

Three of the categories used by ancient biographers and encomiasts were birth, rearing, and education. See Pervo, *Acts*, 562. That model is adjusted here, instead of describing Jesus' education, the subject is what he taught. The implication is that Jesus required no education. The summary of Jesus' message derives from Matt 4:13–17, expanding the invitation to choose light.

The story of Jesus continues with a summary of Jesus' acts, in particular his miracles. The author lists seven categories, followed by brief specific examples. The twelve chosen form an *inclusio* around §7. The pattern found here: Incarnation followed by wonder-working career is not limited to this text. Hills has shown the same pattern in the *Epistula Apostolorum* 3 and Melito of Sardis' *Homily on the Pascha* frg. 15, among others (*Tradition* 46–48. See his discussion of miracle lists, 37–66). The summary of the woman with a continuous flow derives from Matt 9:18–26; the reference to a *meeting* might refer to a synagogue, but a plot is also possible. Cf. Matt 22:14. "Cemeteries" may refer to Matt 8:28–34 and the so-called "Gerasene Demoniac." The narrative is moving, in a manner that can no longer be recovered, toward a dialogue between Jesus and the disciples.

When Schmidt published the Heidelberg papyrus of *APl*, he denominated p. 79 (=p. 129, Cherix) as a "fragment of an unknown Gospel" (*55–*56). Subsequent discoveries show that this material is part of an "embedded gospel," like those found in other ApocActs (above). It is arguable that this overlaps with the earlier summary and represents another edition of *APl*. Equally possible is the hypothesis that this is an intentional repetition for rhetorical emphasis.

The context shows that Jesus is talking to and with the chosen twelve, challenging their amazement at his marvelous deeds. The master makes a promise based upon Mark 11:23. Note also Luke 17:6. Moving mountains was a proverbial image for the power of prayer. See Grant, *Miracle and Natural Law*, 58, 167. In the background is the view that earthquakes are epiphanies, displays of divine power. See Pervo, *Acts*, 123–24; 411. Cf. 1 Cor 13:2.

In §10 Peter, first called "Simon," offers praise. This is a kind of Petrine confession, more like John 6:60–69 than Mark 8:27–30. It is sufficient to authorize his new, "real" name. cf. Matt 16:13–20. The change of name reflects a changed understanding. Peter's faith is strong, but he still does not fully understand. His view is: "It doesn't get any better than this." The speech is modeled on units like John 14:7–14. (Note the role of Philip in John 6:7; 14:8.) Jesus' deeds are means for provoking faith. Their immediate earthly effect is temporary. All those healed, exorcised, and raised will die. The greatest gift is the power of faith. Philip remains unconvinced. At this point the text breaks off. Philip will be shown the truth. Paul will make the proper application: the believers must trust in God throughout the impending ordeal.

The Acts of Paul

Notes

Artemon. This is a known Greek name. The noun (with a different stress) means "foresail." Cf. Acts 27:40. The author may be displaying a sense of humor.

Joy. This is Rordorf's reasonable restoration.

Creedal Forms. Greek verbs have endings that express person and number, such as "I am" and "we are." Pronouns can be added for emphasis: "*I* am." Such first-person forms can be found in the self revelation of a god: "I am (*egō eimi*) the bread of life" (John 6:35). Second-person forms ("*you* are") are quite suitable for hymns of praise directed to the god. An example is the ancient Latin hymn *Te Deum Laudamus* ("You are God; we praise you"), which has the features of a Christian creed. A cogent example is the "Confession of Peter": "*You* are (*su ei*) the Messiah" (Mark 8:29). The introductory formula, *su ei*, is that used by Paul in 52.29. Cf. also Mark 1:11//Luke 3:22: "*You* are my son" (if so read in Luke). Matt 3:17 uses the third person: "This (*houtos estin*) is my son." That is suitable for community confessions, such as creeds. On these forms, see Norden, *Agnostos Theos*, 177–201.

Crucified. As noted in the introduction to this chapter, this saying was cited by Origen in his commentary on John. The copyist of P.Hamb accidently omitted it and had to append it in what amounts to a footnote (Schmidt and Schubart, *Praxeis*, 52).

Quo Vadis. In chap. 15 of the Ethiopic *History of the Contending of Saint Paul* (trans. Budge, 572), the Blessed Virgin Mary appears to exhort Paul, who has taken refuge in a cave, with the words, "O Paul, whither goest thou?"

Grace. See Sanders, "Fragment," 82.

Unhappiness. This rendition follows the Michigan Papyrus.

Offspring. Cf. Ps 132:11; Acts 2:30.

Station, lot, and portion. The evident implication is that the more messianic the prophecy was, the more of Christ's spirit the prophet had received. The language can be understood as deterministic; it tends to reassure the faithful of their standing in God's sight. In the background is the inheritance of the land. See Deut 10:9; 12:12; 14:27, 29; Acts 8:21; Col 1:22; Heb 2:4; 1QH 11.11–12. Note 3 *Cor* 2:10. On the text, see Sanders, "Fragment," 84.

By the People. cf. Acts 7:52. *3 Cor* 2:11. Examples of killing prophets are found in the small collection, *Lives of the Prophets*, the base of which is presumably Jewish, although the texts bear marks of Christianization.

Lawlessness. P. Berl and P. Mich read a plural, which is probably superior to the proposed singular.

Trial. The word *peirasmos* is that usually rendered "temptation" in the Our Father. Here it refers to a test of ultimate significance, as does the petition in the prayer taught by Jesus. Two basic studies are Heinrich Seesemann, "peira, k.t.l.", *TDNT* 6:23–36; and Spicq, *Theological Lexicon*, 3:80–90.

Source of Good Will. Literally "instrument" or "weapon" (*hoplon*) of good will. The motif of "weapons of righteousness" is Pauline (2 Cor 6:7). This phrase, which looks paradoxical, evidently views Christ as the means through which believers receive God's good will. Cf. Luke 2:14.

In the last times or similar words often introduces a soteriological summary. See 2 Peter 1:20; *3 Cor* 2:13 (Armenian).

Mary the Galilean identifies Jesus' mother in terms of her native region rather than, as is customary for women, by reference to husband or father. Cf. *3 Cor* 2.13.

Shadows. See Sanders, "Fragment," 87.

Intelligence . . . The text is evidently corrupt. The Michigan and Berlin papyri read, according to Sanders, 80: ". . . marvelous things, so that he chose, from the twelve tribes men whom in [intel]ligence, unction [nom.] and faith he had with himself" (author's trans.).

Demon-possessed. See Matt 10:8 and the *Martyrium Petri et Pauli* 20.

Shore. The following is obscure. Sanders ("Fragment," 89) proposes *meileissomenos*, "speak kindly," without any confidence. The entire line is obscure.

River. This is uncertain. Other than in John 3:22–23 Jesus is not associated with a/the river after his baptism by John.

Meeting. This follows Sanders, "Fragment," 89. The noun *symboulion* with *agesthai* means "convene a council or meeting." See Ignatius, *Polyc.* 7.2. In the Gospels the noun refers to plots (metonymy: the result of a meeting) against Jesus.

Glorious King. This phrase "king of glory" occurs five times in Ps 24:7–10.

Bibliography

Baldwin, Matthew C. *Whose* Acts of Peter? *Text and Historical Context of the Actus Vercellenses*. WUNT 2/196. Tübingen: Mohr/Siebeck, 2005.

Barnes, Timothy D. *Early Christian Hagiography and Roman History*. Tübingen: Mohr/Siebeck, 2010.

Eastman, David L. *Paul the Martyr: The Cult of the Apostle Paul the Martyr in the Latin West*. WGRWS 4. Atlanta: SBL, 2011.

Grant, Robert M. *Miracle and Natural Law in Graeco-Roman and Early Christian Thought*. Amsterdam: North-Holland, 1952.

Hills, Julian V. *Tradition and Composition in the* Epistula Apostolorum. HTS 57. Cambridge, MA: Harvard University Press, 2008.

Kilpatrick, G. D., and C. H. Roberts. "The Acta Pauli: A New Fragment." *JTS* 47 (1946) 196–99.

MacDonald, Dennis R. "Which Came First? Intertextual Relationships among the Apocryphal Acts of the Apostles." *Semeia* 80 (1997) 11–41.

Moss, Candida, R. *The Other Christs: Imitating Jesus in Ancient Christian Ideologies of Martyrdom*. New York: Oxford, 2010.

Norden, Eduard. *Agnostos Theos. Untersuchungen zur Formengeschichte religiöser Rede*. Leipzig: Teubner, 1913.

Pervo, Richard I. "The Ancient Novel Becomes Christian." In *The Novel in the Ancient World*, ed. G. Schmeling, 685–711. Mnemosyne Supplementum 159. Leiden: Brill, 1996.

———. "Egging on the Chickens: A Cowardly Response to Dennis MacDonald and Then Some." *Semeia* 80 (1997) 43–56.

———. "God and Planning: Footprints of Providence in Acts and in the *Acts of Paul*." In *Method and Meaning: Festschrift for Harold Attridge*, edited by Andrew McGowan, 259–77. Atlanta: SBL, 2011.

Poupon, Gérard. "Les Actes de Pierre et leur remaniement." *ANRW* 2.25.6 (1988) 4363–82.

Rordorf, Willy. "Les Actes de Paul sur papyrus: problèmes aux Pmich. Inv. 1317 et 3788." In *Proceedings of the XVIII International Congress of Papyrology: Athens*, edited by Basileios G. Mandēlaras, 1:453–61. Athens: 1988.

———. "The Relation between the *Acts of Peter* and the *Acts of Paul*: State of the Question." In *The Apocryphal Acts of Peter: Magic, Miracles and Gnosticism*, edited by Jan N. Bremmer, 178–91. Leuven: Peeters, 1998.

Sanders, H. A. "A Fragment of the Acta Pauli in the Michigan Collection." *HTR* 31 (1939) 73–90.

———. "Three Theological Fragments." *HTR* 36 (1943) 165–67.

Stoops, Robert F. "The *Acts of Peter* in Intertextual Context." *Semeia* 80 (1997) 57–86.

Chapter 14: The Martyrdom of the Holy Apostle Paul

Sources: Three complete Greek mss, one of the ninth and two of the eleventh centuries. P.Hamb, Latin, Coptic (P.Heid, which is fragmentary), Syriac, Arabic, Ethiopic, Armenian, and Georgian versions; secondary source: Nicetas of Paphlagonia.

Introduction. Like the story of Thecla (chaps. 3–4) and *3 Cor* (chap. 10), chap. 14 enjoyed a separate existence. As with the Thecla material, liturgical usage guaranteed preservation, since reading the martyrdom was a part of the monastic liturgy of the hours on the occasion of that commemoration. Such preservation brought challenges: propensities toward abbreviation, embellishment, and modification for doctrinal reasons. The chief threat to the integrity of *APl* was the desire to amalgamate his martyrdom with that of Peter, a shift arguably present in the current state of chap. 13. The result of this would be the demise of the classic model of ApocActs, attention to the ministry of one apostle. (On this phenomenon, see Pervo, *Making*, 184–85.) Real and imagined rivalry between these two apostles was swallowed up in the victory of Christianity.

That same triumph witnessed the transformation of Paul from Nero's antagonist to Constantine's colleague and collaborator. (See Eastman, *Paul*.) On traditions about Paul's death, see Snyder, "Remembering," 10–26.) The star witness to the "before" part of this story is *APl*. See Pervo, "(Not) Appealing." Readers may be somewhat surprised to discover that chap. 14 presents a militant, in both style and imagery, Paul who roundly condemns both emperor and empire. This raises the question of whether chap. 14 was composed separately and later incorporated into the larger work. Snyder evidently views the martyrdom as an originally independent story ("Remembering," 56–66). The view adopted here is that chap. 14 is essentially the work of the basic author of *APl*, who utilized some sources and may well have appropriated traditions, welding them into a unit that is congruous with the work as a whole. Congruity is manifest in the use of sex as the device that springs the plot and the presentation of the apostle as a Christ figure. (See Pervo: "Christ Figure.") One might object that these features are common in ApocActs. True, but the *APl* is generally viewed as the generative model for other ApocActs.

At first glimpse the Paul of chap. 14 appears quite different. The uncompromising teacher of rigorous ethics has become a political agitator. Granted that the Paul of chap. 14 is more of an apocalyptic militant, but the discontinuity is less than may initially appear to be the case. The theme of believers as *militia Christi*, soldiers of Christ, is taken from the PE (2 Tim

303

2:3) and found at *APl* 13.5. The image of fiery judgment appeared in 9.13, 17. The difference is that in chap. 14 Paul is entangled with a cruel and murderous tyrant. This is the climax of his trials. The proconsul Castellius had him whipped and driven from Iconium (3.14–21); at Ephesus Hieronymos agreed to death by wild beasts. Both acted against their wills at the behest of a mob. The third time will bring the climax. (This is in accordance with the extant text. Other judgments, dire as they seem, appear to have been local actions rather than the judgments of imperial officials. Missing portions may have included trials by other officials.) Nero does not seek merely to punish Paul; he is attempting to eradicate the community. Paul responds with threats of equally universal scope. *APl* 14 does not introduce an alien theology; it reveals an element of the author's theology.

Although this theology would not have been out of place around the end of the first century, it was by no means unheard of in the middle third of the second, as discussions of the New Prophecy demonstrate. The author makes use of Mark and John, as well as Acts and the PE. This array of texts suggests a date not earlier than 150. Chap. 14 was in its present form by c. 190 at latest, since it was utilized by *APet*. See MacDonald, "Which?" To summarize: chap. 14 has the characteristics of the *APl* in general and, in its present form, is the work of the author, who may have had access to some traditions, but has given his own imprint to the work, once more demonstrating mastery over the sources. Use of Acts and the PE, is, as often, ingenious, both lending credit to *APl* while casting doubt upon the reliability of the other texts.

Improvement upon Acts is the major goal. The canonical author had left his lead character dangling and many readers unsatisfied. *APl* sets the entire Lucan apparatus of Jewish machinations aside. Paul arrives in Rome as an unhindered (cf. Acts 28:31) missionary, albeit with no illusions about his personal fate. The narrator nonetheless evokes Acts, notably by having Paul rent a facility. The mission follows a standard course. Growth is phenomenal. Paul revives a young follower who had fallen to his death while listening to the apostle. This restoration will lead to Paul's death, as in the case of Lazarus' benefactor, Jesus (John 12:10). Although Nero learned of the boy, Patroclus,' death and discovered that he had been restored, he would no longer be able to enjoy the youth's sexual favors. The narrative is not explicit about this matter, but intelligent readers will grasp the point. The nature of the situation generates an explosion: general persecution of all the soldiers of Christ. Although not, as is usually the case, a specific target, Paul is singled out after his arrest and engages in a debate with the Emperor. At this point *Longinus and Cescus*, who will represent the total victory of the *militia Christi*, appear. The latter represents the centurion who affirmed Jesus at the time of his death (Mark 15:39 and parallels). Longinus is characterized as "the prefect," a title with various meanings, here probably intended as the urban prefect (*praefectus urbis*), who was something like the appointed mayor of Rome. He stands, *pars pro toto* (as a synecdoche), for the conversion of Rome. The narrative of this chapter presents three pairs of characters: Luke and Titus, Longinus and Cescus, and Parthenius and Pheres.

The passion thus plays out. A number of "improvements" upon the canonical Gospels are apparent. The disciples do not flee at Paul's arrest, the witnesses are men rather than flighty, "hysterical" women, Paul appears post-mortem to people of the highest standing, and the ending is hopeful and devoid of ambiguity. A trajectory can be described, from uncertain Mark to John 20, to Matthew and Luke, to John 21, and here. *APl* was in its day the "best yet" of "gospels" for those not fond of the ambiguous.

The opening section properly connects with what has gone before and provides the incident, a resurrection, that will, ironically, lead to Paul's death. According to Acts 28:16 unnamed believers from Rome traveled some distance (over sixty kilometers) to meet Paul. This is the only mention of believers at Rome in Acts. *APl* includes two long-time companions, Titus and Luke. The former, according to *ATit* 4, joined Paul prior to his work with Barnabas in Antioch. Here, as in Iconium, Titus served as a kind of advance man for Paul, which, according to *ATit* 4, he did everywhere. According to *ATit* 6, Titus, Timothy, and Luke stayed with Paul until his death. In fact, the narrative does not report their arrest. Why was Timothy included on that list? Presumably because in 2 Tim 4:9 the apostle urges Timothy to come quickly. That verse may well have come to mind because 2 Tim 4:10 is the basis of the first sentence of §1: "Crescens has gone to Galatia, Titus to Dalmatia." The author locates this chapter—in defiance of all reasonable chronology—after the request in 2 Timothy. "Gaul" is a variant here that has contaminated the text of 2 Timothy. See the note. The otherwise otiose Crescens has been replaced by "Luke." This choice was evidently motivated by the subsequent verse (2 Tim 4:11): at that time Luke was Paul's sole companion. The author appears to play a double game with the PE. The relationship is not solely oppositional. The author draws data from the PE both to enhance the appearance of authenticity—these characters are familiar, and to discredit the PE by pointing out where it has not got things right. The approach to Acts is similar. Whereas the contrast with the PE is mainly social and theological, as the demand for celibacy and the authorization of a woman teacher emphatically illustrate, the contrast with Acts is mainly historical and biographical. Paul's voyage to Rome as a free person has been a major factor supporting the view that the author either ignored or did not know of Acts. (See Rordorf, "Verhältnis"; and Schneemelcher, "Apostelgeschichte.") Yet traces of borrowing from Acts permeate chaps. 12–14. *APl* places Luke in Rome with Paul throughout his sojourn. This raises an interesting question. Briefly stated, the leading options are: Did the author not yet know of the tradition that Luke wrote Acts, or did he wish to discredit Acts by showing the author present on the scene of incidents that he did not correctly report, or seek to show that Acts was not written by Luke, a companion of Paul? Irenaeus and *APl* are the earliest certain witnesses to Acts. Irenaeus' *Against Heresies* can be dated c. 175, i.e., while Eleutheros was bishop of Rome. Irenaeus identifies the author of the Third Gospel and Acts as Luke, a companion of Paul. See Pervo, *Acts*, 5–7.

The simplest and least speculative hypothesis is that the author of *APl* was not aware of the attribution of Acts to Luke but knew it as an anonymous book, just as it is still found in the manuscripts. This would heighten the possibility that Irenaeus originated the tradition of Lucan authorship.[2] The attraction of the other hypotheses is that they attribute to *APl* motives and techniques similar to those employed with regard to the PE. Choice between the two basic alternatives is difficult. The problem reveals that the status of Acts was not as secure as Irenaeus might have wished his readers to think.

The author was the first person known to have integrated information from Acts and the PE. The basis for this is an assumption that the case against Paul was dropped because his accusers failed to appear. See *Second Imprisonment*. After Paul's release came more evangelism, possibly including a visit to Spain, and a return to the east, reflected in the PE. Upon a return to Rome Paul was re-arrested and condemned by Nero. For a brief form of this hypothesis, see Tajra, *Martyrdom*, 73–76. A longer account is available in Murphy-O'Connor, *Paul*, 356–71, for example. The ancient authority for this hypothesis is Eusebius (*H.E.* 2.22). The ultimate source of Eusebius' claim could well be the martyrdom story found in *APl*. (In *H.E.* 3.1.3 the historian states that that Paul was martyred in Rome under Nero, according to the third book of Origen's commentary on Genesis. Origen knew the *APl*, including its "Passion Narrative.") *APl* does not utilize the PE to construct a release and second imprisonment, but prefers to take data from the Pastorals to illustrate the imprisonment and lend his account verisimilitude.

---

2. This does not imply that Irenaeus "invented" Lucan authorship, but that he reached that conclusion on the basis of Col 4:14; 2 Tim 4:11; and the "we passages" in Acts. (January 2014. It seems more probable that the author was unaware of the view that Luke wrote Acts.)

Translation, Commentary, and Notes : Chapter

14.1–3 New Life Brings the Threat of Death to Believers

1. Awaiting Paul at Rome were Luke, who had come from Gaul, and Titus, from Dalmatia. The sight of them brought joy to Paul. He therefore rented a barn outside of Rome in which he taught, along with the believers, the message that introduces truth. He achieved fame; many persons joined the community. The word reverberated through Rome. A large number of the imperial staff came to him and became believers. Joy abounded.

Patroclus, an imperial cupbearer came late to the barn and, since he could not get close to Paul because of the crowd, perched in a high window and listened to him as he taught God's word. Because the Devil, that wicked creature, was aroused to jealousy by the believers' love for one another, Patroclus fell from the window and died. News of this quickly reached Nero.

When Paul learned of this through the Spirit, he said, "My fellow believers, the evil one has contrived an opportunity to test you. Go outside to find a boy fallen from a height. He is about to expire. Pick him up and bring him to me here. They went and did as he said. The sight of the body wrenched the attendant crowds. Paul said, "Brothers and sisters, show your faith. Come, let us implore our Lord Jesus Christ with tears that he may live and we remain unmolested." After all had uttered profound sighs, the boy began to breathe again. They put him upon an animal and sent him home alive with the other members of the imperial staff.

2. News of Patroclus' death upset Nero a great deal. Upon returning from the bath he directed someone else to serve the wine. His servants, however, said, "Caesar; Patroclus is alive and has taken his place at the table." This information made the emperor initially hesitant to go in. When he finally did so, he saw the lad and said, "Are you alive, Patroclus?"

"I am, your majesty."

"Who brought you back to life?"

Uplifted by the enthusiasm of his faith, the youth said, "Christ Jesus the king of the ages."

307

The Acts of Paul

Upset, Caesar said, "Is he therefore going to rule the ages and abolish every kingdom?"

"Yes. He will destroy all kingdoms. He alone will be eternal and no kingdom will elude him."

Nero struck him on the face, saying, "Patroclus, are you also a soldier of that king?"

"Yes, Lord Caesar, for he raised me after I had died." Then Barsabas "Flatfoot" Justus, Orion the Cappadocian, and Festus the Galatian, Nero's leading men, said, "We too serve in the army of the king of the ages."

Despite his great affection for them, Nero imprisoned these men and subjected them to brutal torture. He directed that all the soldiers of the great king be sought out and promulgated an edict that all exposed as Christians and soldiers of Christ were to be killed.

3. Among the many taken into custody was Paul. The other prisoners paid careful attention to him. Observing this, Caesar concluded that he was in charge of the soldiers and addressed him, "Agent [P.Hamb 9 begins] of the great king, albeit my prisoner, why did you come up with the idea of surreptitiously entering Roman territory and recruiting from my dominion?"

Inspired, Paul responded, with the entire audience in mind, "Caesar, we do not recruit from your dominion alone, but from every inhabited place, for we have been directed to exclude no one who wishes to enlist in the service of my king. If enrolling in his service should actually appeal to you, neither wealth nor the splendors of present existence will avail you, but if you submit and entreat him, you will experience deliverance. For on a single day he will destroy the world."

Caesar thereupon ordered that all the prisoners be burned at the stake, excepting Paul, who was to be decapitated, in accordance with Roman law. This did not silence Paul, who continued to share the message with Longinus the prefect and Cescus the centurion. Because of the machinations of the evil one many Christians were being executed at Rome without trial, so many in fact that the citizenry gathered in front of the palace shouting, "Enough, Caesar.

These are our people! You are ruining Roman power!" He desisted on the grounds that no Christian should be touched until he had investigated the facts of the case.

Comments

The text testifies to its original state, for it presumes that Paul had arrived at Rome. This would have been at the no-longer-extant conclusion of chap. 13. Paul immediately launches into a mission at Rome. With a nod to Acts 28:30 he rents a barn *outside the city*. Paul's work is described as teaching rather than, for example, evangelism. The term is common in Acts, e.g., 28:31. The narrator implies that Luke and Titus, at least, assisted in this task. (*Ps.-Linus* adds "and others." On this work, see the note. The Greek ms. A reports that Paul lived in the barn with the believers, relieving them of teaching duty. See Vouaux, 279.) They taught, lit., "the word of truth," a phrase taken from the PE (e.g., 2 Tim 2:15) and other early writings. Ms. A. adds "welcoming and entertaining all," a phrase inspired by Acts 28:31. The language evokes the opening of Jesus' ministry, the Jerusalem mission in Acts 2, and the success at Antioch in Acts 11. On "fame," see Mark 1:28; Luke 4:14. The word *ēchos* (Luke 4:37) is related to "echo" (thus "reverberated"). "Many persons" (lit. "many souls") comes from Acts 2:41. The verb "add" occurs there and in 11:24. Latin and Syriac witnesses expand the summary with references to numerous signs and wonders. "Large number" appears in Mark 3:7 and Acts 14:1, while "imperial staff" (lit., "household of Caesar") is based upon Phil 4:22, probably presumed by the author to have been written at Rome. The reference prepares the way for Patroclus. On "joy," an almost fixed feature of the beginning of Paul›s enterprises, see the note at 3.5. At this point Ps.-Linus introduces the story of Paul's relations with Seneca. (See the note. On the correspondence, see, e.g., Pervo, *Making*, 110–16; and Klauck, *Bibel*, 199–228.)

The experience of Patroclus will ignite the persecution. His resurrection will, with that of Paul, form a bracket around the chapter. The major source was the story of Eutychus (Acts 20:7–12). The author also includes allusions to Mark 2:1–12, evoking Jesus' early ministry and great popularity and to the story of Thecla, to which this constitutes a parallel. Arguments for dependence upon Acts are nearly insuperable. See Bovon, "La vie," 150; MacDonald, "Luke's Eutychus"; Pervo, "Hard Act," 10–12; Pervo, *Acts* 511n64 (with additional references); and Bauckham, "Sequel," 134. Each story has a child (*pais*) sitting in a window (*thyris*) who falls to his death while listening to Paul preach. Both involve some ambiguity about whether the youth is dead. In each story others go to lift the corpse, Paul soothes his hearers, and the living child is sent home. The account in *APl* includes some improvements over its model. On these, see MacDonald, "Eutychus"; and Pervo, "Hard Act." This is not a case of variant forms of a similar legend.

Mark 2:4 provides the motive for Patroclus' seat in the window: the crowd was too large to permit him to get any closer. (Syriac recognizes this and calls the place a house, as in Mark.) Paul's spiritual insight (pedantically expanded in the Latin and Syriac) is inspired by Mark 2:8. Paul has filled the place to the bursting point. His omniscience resembles that of his master. Patroclus' listening post in a window brings Thecla to mind. Both of these young people embraced Paul's message and shared it with disapproving authorities. Both faced certain death but were delivered. Recognition of such correspondences pleases the attentive reader, helps to integrate the narrative, and, not least, provides foreshadowing. People who listen to Paul while perched in a window are likely to get into trouble.

Readers do not learn if this is Patroclus' first visit to hear Paul. He encapsulates salvation history. Prodded by the devil, he "falls," but is revived and given new life in Christ. By attributing the fall to the Devil the narrator makes the evil one responsible for the persecution. On the relation of envy to the fall, see Wis 2:24. Satan's envy is aroused by the believers' care for one another. (The variants include redirecting this love toward the Lord.) Their love may be contrasted with Nero's affection for Patroclus. Nero's grief over the loss of Patroclus and his rage at the boy's adherence to Christ are sexual in nature. Like Thamyris (chap. 3) he has been deprived of a romantic interest. See *Patroclus*. Although it is unstated, the sexual motive strengthens the case that the shape of chap. 14 comes from the author, who has done more than touch up a pre-existing legend.

The narrative is more complex than Acts 20:7–12. *APl* preserves, apparently intensifies, the ambiguity, for the narrator here flatly states that Patroclus died. (Witnesses expand the text at this point. See Vouaux, 282.) In neither case does the narrator intimate that Paul's medical insight prevented a premature declaration of death. Even if alive the patients would have suffered from fractures and other traumas. In both cases Paul can see beyond the merely transitory barrier of mortality. See Pervo, *Acts*, 510–14. Another task undertaken by the narrator is to have the Emperor advised of Patroclus' death prior to his revivification. The focus of the community's anxiety is the expected reaction of Nero to the loss of his favorite.

Paul quickly takes charge, correctly assigning blame to the devil and interpreting the calamity as a test of faith. In contrast to Acts 20, he has the corpse brought into his presence. This produces appropriate pathos (and allows for the edifying sight of a public revivication). Paul exhorts the community to show the power of faith. Prayer will have two goals: life for Patroclus and freedom from persecution for the community. The second is deleted by some witnesses, probably because it remained unfulfilled.

Insofar as the narrative is concerned, the restoration occurred through the collective prayer of the community. This probably conforms to actual practice. No words, gestures, touches, or other acts are mentioned. One reason for neglect of procedural details is that the resuscitation of Eutychus in Acts 20, which is based upon a biblical precedent (2 Kgs 4:18–37), has an indelicate appearance and would not be the ideal means for relating the restoration of Nero's boy toy to a new and chaste life. (On the therapeutic technique employed in Acts 20, see Pervo, *Acts*, 512.) Unlike other miracle reports, the narrator says nothing about the community response. Patroclus is sent home on an animal, with other imperial slaves. The possible dire consequences of his accidental death and subsequent charges of criminal negligence have been averted. The story has come to a happy ending.

This reasonable judgment was premature. Nero, reacting superstitiously to the report of Patroclus' revival, inquired about its cause. Discovery that this was the work of a competitor was exacerbated by the revelation that some of the chief courtiers also confessed Christ. The general persecution feared because of Patroclus' death did break out—because of his life.

§2 begins with a fine circumstantial description of Nero's grief and his appointment of a new cupbearer *pro tem*. (Witnesses often abbreviate these details.) When advised that Patroclus was alive and back on duty, Nero hesitated. This fear resembles that of Jesus' followers in the face of resurrection (Mark 16:8; Luke 24:37). At least one editor did not regard this as unintentional. Ms. A reads: "When Caesar heard and while he marveled at the unbelievable report that *Patroclus* lived, he did not want to go to dinner." In the resultant dialogue (A again expands; see Vouaux, 286) Nero assumes that Patroclus had died and been revivified. The more logical approach would be to conclude that the reports of his death had been exaggerated. In the end it may not have mattered. The narrative assumes that the emperor accepts the possibility of return from the dead. His subsequent queries allow for rapid confession of the faith. If, for example, the conversation had followed the line of Rom 13:1–7 (see Pervo, "Appealing"), Nero would have been told that all monarchs owe their power to God. Narrative paths not taken underline that followed, which here opposes the reign of God to that of Caesar.

Threatened, Nero responds with a tyrannical act of undisciplined petulance. John 18:22 comes to mind. Every martyr follows the way taken by Jesus. With his question Nero lobs Patroclus a ball he can smash. The theme of *militia Christi*, comparison of Christian life to military service, is at a low ebb just now, but it has a long and often distinguished history, ranging in background from the concrete understanding of some Qumran texts (such as 1QM; 1Q33; 4Q 491–7; 4Q471; 4Q285; 11Q14), which are nonetheless about spiritual warfare directed against Rome, to philosophers from at least the time of Plato (*Apol.* 28), who liked the military metaphor because it represented philosophy as a way of life demanding gravity, order and discipline. For references and discussion, see Pervo, "(Not) Appealing"; and Moss, *Other Christs,* 87–97. In *APl* 14 "soldier" and related terms occur fourteen times. See Bolyki, "Events." With some impetus from the undisputed letters (e.g., 1 Cor 9:7; 2 Cor 10:1–6; Phlm 2) the view of the Christian life as military service thrived in the Deutero-Pauline world: *1 Clem* 37; 1 Tim 1:18–19; 6:12; 2 Tim 2:3–7; Ign. *Pol.* 6.2. Note the references from the PE, which constitute the closest parallels to *APl,* although the PE stand in the non-violent metaphorical tradition. Once more, the *APl* utilize the PE to show authenticity while radically altering the message.

Patroclus' confession motivates three chief courtiers to acknowledge their faith. Christianity has made substantial inroads into the household of Caesar! The first has an Aramaic first name ("Saturday's child"), a vulgar nickname, and a Latin surname. See the note. Cappadocia and Galatia were not the sorts of regions from which an aficionado of culture would draw his prominent officials. Was the author making fun of Nero? This is unlikely since these persons are Christian confessors. At the time of composition persons with such names were quite likely to be Christians; by calling such the chiefs of Nero's cabinet the narrator was flaunting his invincible ignorance.

Dearly did Nero love Flatfoot and friends, but, as a model monarch, he loved national security more. Incarceration and torture were the lot of these officials, while a decree went forth directing that followers of Jesus were to pay for their crime with their lives. In this way the narrative coincides with Tacitus (see Rordorf, "Verfolgung"), but their crime is explicitly political rather than literal incendiarism. Nero is a round character, who develops and acts upon a range of feelings, including grief, fear, fury and implacable rage. See Vouaux, 291.

Section 3 will narrate both the "trial" of Paul and the collapse of the persecution due to concerns about national security. Narration is through showing more than telling. Caught in a general roundup of Christians, Paul's prominence and power emerge in the deference shown him by other believers (none of whom are depicted as even given a chance to confess their faith), while Nero's pettiness emerges in his visit to the prison and his tyranny through the absence of even the faintest vestige of the appearance of justice.

The dialogue resembles John 18 and 19, where the leaders' blindness is represented through their inability to penetrate the literal surface. Various witnesses show that this tactic was intolerable by supplying doctrinal data. Unable to refrain from a bit of sarcasm, Nero asks Paul, the group's manifest leader, why he has engaged in secret recruiting. Rather than deny the implied charge of subversive behavior, the apostle assures the tyrant that Christians are equal-opportunity subversives, recruiting ubiquitously and universally accepting. As elsewhere (e.g., 9.17), the apostle insists that wealth and earthly glory will be of no use against the coming fire of destruction. (P.Hamb expands this section, probably secondarily.)

That was enough for Nero, who ordered that all the captives be put to the torch without benefit of trial. This is, as Ps.-Linus already recognized, poetic justice. Those who held that the world would be condemned by fire were condemned to fire. Nero had, according to Tacitus, *Annals* 15.44, made living torches of Christians because he blamed them for burning Rome. *APl* deflects this incendiary, as it were, charge. The single exception is Paul, who will be beheaded, as the law prescribes. Respect for laws about the mode of death suitable to Roman citizens is all well and good, but some other legal technicalities, such as the requirement of a proper trial, would also have helped. The author may have learned of Paul's Roman citizenship from Acts, the only extant source of this claim. See Pervo, *Acts*, 554–56. This distinction makes Paul stand out; the narrator has, alas, forgotten that many Roman citizens had been condemned, including Nero's leading ministers. Ps.-Linus specifies that Paul was condemned for *laesa maiestas*, a crime against the majesty of the emperor. (Historians would like to know the legal grounds for Paul's execution.)

Undeterred, Paul continues his ministry while condemned, as did Jesus while on the cross (Luke 23:39–43). Longinus and Cescus (see the note) will play an important role at the climax of the story. Meanwhile, participatory democracy intervenes. The public assembles outside of the palace to beseech Nero to call off the persecution, which threatens to bring down the empire. Irony builds on irony. Through such unison shouts (e.g., "Crucify him!") the public could make its will known and sometimes impose the same. See Pervo, *Acts*, 55. Massacring the forces of the great king reduces Roman power. Nero imagines that he is killing enemies. Persecution injures the empire. Nero took their point and stipulated the legal basis for subsequent persecution.

The Acts of Paul

Notes

Title. This is the shortest form of the title, precisely parallel with the final chapter of *APet*. Other forms, many of which mention the date, may be found in Lipsius 1:104. This distinct title witnesses to the chapter's circulation as a separate work.

Gaul (Gallia and Galatia were used as names for ancient France.). Gallia is read at 2 Tim 4:10 by a number of authorities (Sin C 81. 104. 326 pc mss of Vulgate, Sahidic some Bohairic mss, the ancient theologians Eusebius and Epiphanius). At this point the Syriac (Vouaux, 278–79) adds a passage that brings the account into closer harmony with the canonical Acts (although not directly addressing issue of Paul's legal status), and coordinates the stories of Peter and Paul, concluding with the claim that Nero was absent from Rome.

Outside the city. Words from the Greek stem *misth-* can have the same ambiguity as "rent" and "hire" in American English. Acts 28:16 is uncertain, but the author of *APl* took it to mean "rent." He has Paul rent a facility for the storage of grain, a much larger building than a rented urban apartment. "Outside the city" modifies "outside of the barracks" (a D-Text reading at Acts 28:16). The narrator probably does not intend to suggest that Paul sought to avoid legal entanglement, but that one could get a larger facility for a modest price beyond the city limits. The *sight* of Luke and Titus alludes to Acts 28:15. Polycarp has two farms outside the city (of Smyrna; *Mart. Polyc.* 5:1; 6:1).

Patroclus. The name (Syriac alters it to "Patricius") is a clue, for Patroclus was regarded in post-Homeric Greece as Achilles' lover (e.g., Aeschylus, fr. 134a.). Even more telling is his role, cupbearer to Nero. Patroclus played Ganymede to the empire's Zeus. The general view held that Zeus kidnapped Ganymede for sexual purposes, e.g., Theognis 1345–48. See Drexler, "Ganymedes." Although no sexual impropriety was too gross to attribute to Nero (Suetonius, *Nero* 29), "Ganymedes" were popular even with the "Good Emperors." See Birley, *Hadrian*, 29 (presuming that Antinous, Hadrian's lover, requires no mention). Ps.-Linus makes the sexual relationship explicit by labeling the boy as *deliciosus* ("adorable" or, perhaps, his "darling"). The audience would have assumed that Patroclus was a sexual object of Nero. He may also be seen as the antithesis to Pharaoh's cupbearer in Genesis 40, who forgets his benefactor, Joseph.

Seneca. Here is the relevant portion of Ps.-Linus:

Yet even the very preceptor of the emperor was joined to Paul in friendship because he saw divine learning in him, so that he could scarcely wait to engage in conversation with him. In as much as face-to-face conversation was not possible, they engaged in a most pleasant, friendly, and bountiful epistolary conversation of mutual benefit. By this means Paul's message, through the agency of the Holy Spirit, gained an increasing impact and admiration, so that the preceptor freely presented it to many who received it quite happily. Indeed, he disputed with polytheist philosophers and refuted them, with the result that a great number of them conceded his victory. (Lipsius, 1:24; author's trans.)

Test you. V.l. "us." L. expands with a prediction: "But the Lord Jesus Christ will, as is his wont, transform this wickedness into his own glory."

Height. Vouaux, 283, omits "from a height." See his n11.

Ps.-Linus. This work, *The Passion of the Holy Apostle* Paul, derives from the late fourth or early fifth century and is attributed to a putative early bishop of Rome. The text is in Lipsius 1:23–44. See Vouaux, 281n2; and Tajra, *Martyrdom*, 138–42.

Faith. Ps.-Linus expands: "toward the Lord Jesus Christ, for it is time that the seed of eternal life might fall on good ground and produce a hundredfold." Cf. Luke 8:8. This presumes that martyrdom will result.

He may live. "Boy" is a variant. Ps.-Linus expands: "that his life might be restored into that young cadaver and that he might live better than he has lived." This probably reveals awareness of his sexual life.

Sigh. This may be thaumaturgic, or it may reflect the community's anxiety. See the note on chap. 11.

Animal. Some Latin and Syriac witnesses omit this clause, while others simplify. It could be taken as evidence that the youth was not fully recovered and would benefit from riding rather than walking.

Caesar. Later witnesses make the address more formal, the equivalent of "your majesty." The simpler form is earlier.

Servants . . . said. This verb (*appangellō*) is used to announce the resurrection of Jesus, e.g., Matt 28:8; Luke 24:9.

The Acts of Paul

Revivified. The Greek employed throughout this text is the present tense of *zaō* ("live"). This allows some ambiguity, as in Nero's question, lit., "Who made you live?" Underlying this use of the verb stands the view of eternal life as a present possession.

King of the Ages. The phrase has its background in Jewish thought. Cf. Tob 13; 1 *Enoch* 9:4; 1 Tim 1:17; *Gospel of Bartholomew* 2:13. A reads "the king of the entire universe of human beings." The noun "ages" can be construed as temporal, spatial, or, often preferably, both.

Destroy all kingdoms. Witnesses tend to expand and clarify the declarations in this dialogue, adding theological correctness and sabotaging its literary power. A, with its typical love for expansion, takes notice of Patroclus' joy.

Nero's leading men. This vague term (*prōtoi*), often used for the leading citizens of a municipality, is omitted by P.Heid and altered into more likely roles. For patristic views on the conversion of members of the imperial household, see the examples from John Chrysostom given by Tajra, *Martyrdom*, 128n40.

Barsabas. For the name, see Acts 1:23. In the tradition this person is confused/identified with Barnabas. See Lipsius' note, 1:109. Joseph Barsabbas reportedly was one of the seventy disciples (Eusebius, *H.E.* 1:12; see Luke 10:1). He allegedly drank snake venom in the name of Jesus without suffering any ill effects (Eusebius, *H.E.* 3:39; see Ps.-Mark 16:18).

Great king. Cf. 2 Tim 2:3. This title is equivalent to "king of kings," the ruler above all other rulers.

Inspired. Some witnesses omit, probably because they presumed that Paul was always inspired.

Entreat him. Witnesses modify and expand this promise. Forgiveness is offered to all, but in some cases qualification is desirable.

Destroy the world. This conjectures *apollyein* rather than *polemein* ("make war upon," "assault"), which caused problems for ancient translators. In defense of "make war upon" is continuation of the metaphor. Vouaux, 293, also proposes *porthein* ("devastate"), which retains a sense of the military metaphor. S offers "judge," in conformity with Acts 17:31. "With fire" (cf. 1 Cor 3:13) is probably a secondary expansion, possibly generated by the longer text of P.Hamb. 9.8–12.

Longinus and Cescus. The names vary. M reads Longinus and Egestius; L notes two prefects: Longinus and Megistus, and a centurion Acescus; while Coptic offers Longinus and Cescus. Rordorf accepts the last pairing, which is found in P.Hamb.

Without trial. The text of the Greek ms. P is apparently corrupt. The restoration proposed derives in part from P. Hamb. and in part from the lengthy paraphrase of A: "At that time the dreadful and utterly cruel wild beast Nero, driven by the great potency of the evil one, so that many Christians were killed through his commands." See Vouaux 294–95; and Rordorf, 1175, whose text is close to that of A. Polycarp also does not receive a trial. See Parvis, "*Martyrdom,*" 138–39.

Facts of the case. The text appears to be corrupt. The final clause looks like a reference to the (alleged) "Rescript of Hadrian," cited in Eusebius, *H. E.* 4.8–9. (Christians probably revised the wording. See Birley, *Hadrian,* 127.) The demand for lawful procedures was consistently pressed by apologists (e.g., Justin, *1 Apology* 68) and endorsed by Trajan (Pliny, *Ep.* 10.97). It seems that Paul has been reprieved.

14.4–7: The Execution and Vindication of Paul

4. Subsequent to this direction Paul was brought forward. Nero persisted in his claim that he should be decapitated. Paul said: "Caesar, my life for my king is not ephemeral. Even if you decapitate me, I shall do this: rise and appear to you, because I shall not have died but remain alive in my Lord Christ Jesus, who will come to judge the earth."

[*After Paul had been sent off to be executed*] Longinus and Cescus said to Paul: "Where do you get this king from, in whom you so trust that even death will not change your mind?" Paul shared the message with them, "Gentlemen, living in ignorance and deceit, change your minds and be saved from the conflagration that will inundate the world. We are not enrolled, as you imagine, in the service of a terrestrial king, but one from heaven, the living God, who because of the lawless things done in this world is coming as judge. Blessed are those who will have trust in him and live forever, when he comes to purify the world with fire!"

The Acts of Paul

They thereupon begged him, "Please, please help us and we shall let you go."

"I am no deserter from Christ, but a loyal soldier of the living God. If I knew that I was going to die, I would have tried to save myself, Longinus and Cescus, but since I live for God and love myself, I am going to the lord, so that I might come back with him in the glory of his father."

"How shall we live if you have been beheaded?" asked the two.

5. Nero sent one Parthenion and Feritas to learn whether Paul had been decapitated. They arrived to find him alive, still speaking with the two officers. He invited them: "Believe in the living God, who raises me and all who believe in him, from the dead!"

"We're returning to Nero now," they replied. "We'll believe in your God after you have died and arisen."

To the inquiries of Longinus and Cescus about salvation, he said: "Come promptly here to my tomb at dawn. You will find two men praying, Titus and Luke. They will seal you in the Lord." Paul stood, facing east and prayed at some length, communing via prayer, in Hebrew with his forebears. Without another word he stretched out his neck. When the executioner lopped off his head, milk spewed out onto the soldier's clothes. When the soldier and all the bystanders saw this, they praised the God who had given Paul such glory. They then returned to report to the emperor what had happened.

6. While he was amazed at this report and still at a loss for words, Paul came, at 1500, when many philosophers, as well as the centurion, were assembled with the emperor. Visible to all, he said to the Emperor, "Caesar, behold Paul, the soldier of God. I have not died, but live. Many dreadful things will happen to you because of the righteous you have killed." Nero was upset and directed that the prisoners be released, including Patroclus and Barsabbas' circle.

7. Longinus and the centurion Cescus set out with anxiety for Paul's tomb as he had told them. Upon their rival they saw two men at prayer, Paul between them. The sight astonished them. Titus and Luke, swept away by mortal fear, turned and ran

away. Their pursuers cried, "We are not chasing you with death in view but life, as Paul—who was praying between you a moment ago—promised."

Titus and Luke were glad to hear this and sealed them in the Lord.

Comments

§4 reveals that Nero's abatement of the massacre did not apply to the leader of the Christians. Paul's response is an expanded form of his earlier words, raising the question of whether one of these two scenes is secondary to the other. On this, see Snyder, 10–66, esp. 58–59. The author has created narrative unity; all of the pieces fit together, original or otherwise. This chapter was particularly vulnerable to expansion—witness ms. A and versions. The Notes identify some of these interpolations, which tend to heighten pathos. In the end such expansions raise one's appreciation for the original narrator. Still, there are points, notably the beginning of the second paragraph, where it is arguable that the text has been abbreviated.

The second appearance before Nero may be regarded as motivated by the amnesty. The emperor did not change his mind, perhaps on the grounds that their first interview had satisfied legal requirements. Paul explains that death is not the end and that he will prove the point by making a postmortem appearance. His speech ends with the implied threat of judgment.

Nero thereupon effectively disappears, and Paul engages in a long conversation with the officers Longinus and Cescus. As much of the tradition implies, this conversation took place on the way to the place of execution, or at it. §5 confirms this. The officers are certainly taken with Paul's courage in the face of death. He urges them to repent, in language reminiscent of the style of John the Baptizer (Luke 3:2–9). For them the apostle clarifies that the military language is metaphorical. Longinus and Cescus cannot fully grasp the message. They offer to let Paul escape if he will render them assistance. Evidently they desire magic formulae or similar means that will allow them to evade eschatological condemnation.

This gives Paul the opportunity to affirm, in military metaphors, his steadfastness. (On the "deserter" language, see MacDonald, "Which," 11.) "Live for God and love (*agapō*) myself" may strike some as sub-Christian. Aristotle (*Nicomachean Ethics* 9.4) discusses love of self in the context of friendship. To state the thesis in pedestrian terms, those who do not love themselves will have difficulty loving others. Such self-love is not to be

The Acts of Paul

confused with narcissism, which places the self at the center of the known universe. Martyrdom does not obviate love for self. The sentence closes with the standard picture of the triumphant Christ returning in glory. The two are distraught at the thought of losing their preceptor. Behind this is the assurance that the successors of the apostles continue to communicate the apostolic faith.

With §5, following suitable retardation, the execution finally takes place. In the style of popular literature, Nero, who does not expect to rest easily until assured that Paul has been removed, dispatches a pair of two named but otherwise unidentified men to get the news. Paul makes the same missionary overture to them as to Longinus and Cescus (expanded in various witnesses). They take the role made famous by Thomas (John 20:25) and return to the emperor. The scene is quite awkward, possibly abbreviated. It is certainly expanded in the tradition. Syriac has them report that Paul is still alive. Ps.-Linus takes the opportunity to insert the legend of Plautilla, who plays a role like that of Veronica in the story of Jesus' passion (see Tajra, *Martyrdom*, 149). The narrator's problem is that he has to whisk these two away so that they will not see the wonder accompanying Paul's execution. One wonders why they have been introduced. The next paragraph picks up, and not smoothly, where §4 left off. See the note on *inquiries*.

Paul instructs them to come to his tomb at dawn. The narrator has said nothing about a place of burial or the act. It is taken for granted. See *tomb*. Just as he promised Nero that he would appear, so he promises baptism to the pair. (They could, to be sure, have been baptized then and there, but that would ruin the ending.)

The execution is stylized, like that of Jesus in Luke and John and of Stephen in Acts. The preliminaries may have been abbreviated. Later traditions expand them considerably. Prayer in "Hebrew" (which often means "Aramaic" in early Christian texts) is a parallel with Jesus (Mark 15:44). The forebears ("fathers"=patriarchs) are the leading figures of the Hebrew Bible, with whom Paul stands as a peer. Milk gushed from his severed body. Tajra rightly calls this "a beautifully poetic creation" (*Martyrdom* 130). The primary function of this event is the obvious parallel with John 19:34 (blood and water flow from the side of the dead Jesus). Paul is a Christ figure. See Pervo, "Christ Figure." His death is a soteriological event.

Milk has a rich symbolism. Because it is humans' first nourishment, it is primary, in two senses: something from which to be weaned, and the ultimate nourishment, food requiring no labor or preparation, sustenance given out of love. Two figurative applications are educational and sacramental. In the former sense milk can be criticized as "kid stuff" or viewed positively as nurture in general. For detailed references, see the note. Sacramental imagery builds upon the primary as utopian and ultimate. As Heinrich Schlier ("*gala*," *TDNT* 1:645–47) summarizes, this can be expressed mythologically (milk as food of the gods), eschatologically (milk as celestial nourishment), and magically (milk mediates life: after the womb and before the tomb). 1 Pet 2:2 has at least some affinity with the sacramental sense. Milk took a logical place in initiatory rites. The educational and the sacramental could become commingled in that wisdom/education was itself the means of initiation. The ritual expression of the sacramental sense this is the delivery of a chalice containing milk mixed with honey, described in the *Apostolic Tradition* and still practiced in the Coptic and Ethiopic rites.

The primary referent to milk here is educational: Paul is the teacher of the church. See Pervo, *Making*, 18–19; Snyder, "Remembering," 16. His message was not restricted to neophytes, but his provision of milk was appropriate because of the numbers converted by his mission. It also has a sacramental dimension, because it is the basis for the initiation of the two officers. Clothes soaked with this blood were not among the hardships observers of executions had to endure. These were primary relics of the martyred apostle. Syriac apostrophizes upon this wonder (to which blood is added). Ps.-Linus, not for the first time, goes overboard, adding the odor of sanctity and a vision of heavenly splendor.

The reaction of the "soldier" (the centurion) evokes the response to Jesus' death by the centurion (Mark 15:39) and other bystanders (Luke 23:47–48; Matt 27:54). (The text is not clear, but the general sense is. P.Hamb lacks this sentence.) With a prefect (Longinus) as well as the centurion Cescus, Paul is equipped with a higher class of witnesses to the events surrounding his death. For that matter, the milk was superior to Jesus' discharge in John 19:34, for, while some explanations for a rush of blood and its breakdown into water and (?) plasma can be advanced, a gush of milk cannot be attributed to natural causation.

Another improvement over the Jesus tradition emerges in the quality of spectators to Paul's post-resurrection appearance (§6). At that "ninth hour" (on which, see Vouaux, 309) Nero happened to be passing the time with many philosophers. A member of that guild, Celsus, issued a work entitled *The True Doctrine* at roughly the same time as the appearance of *APl*. One of the extant fragments—all quotations preserved by Origen in his refutation, *Contra Celsum*—ridicules the stories of Jesus' resurrection appearances by focusing upon a "hysterical woman" (*C. Cels.* 2.55. Women were often viewed as poor witnesses in antiquity, because of their lack of education, experience, and alleged emotional balance. See MacDonald, *Early Christian Women*, 94–115). At 2.63 of *Contra Celsum* Origen says:

The Acts of Paul

> After this Celsus speaks evil of the biblical story in a way that cannot be lightly passed over, when he says that *if Jesus really wanted to show forth divine power, he ought to have appeared to the very men who treated him despitefully and to the man who condemned him and to everyone everywhere.* (trans. Chadwick, 114)

Celsus could have made no such allegations about this appearance, the apologetic function of which is blatant. Witnesses tend to expand this brief account, and not effectively. For example, Slavic expands the audience to include nobles. A. adds friends of Nero. P.Heid reads "he stood" (*estē*), which is customary in epiphanies, e.g., John 20:19. Syriac says that Paul was "revealed by the Spirit and appeared to the emperor, all the philosophers, and the generals gathered about the throne." Cescus, the centurion, provides continuity, as he is present in every episode from Paul's trial on (§3–7). The text assumes that this is a bodily appearance, like those of the risen Jesus, since a phantom or ghost would serve rather as a proof of death.

Proof is no more than a secondary element of the canonical post-resurrection appearances. Demonstration that Paul is alive is an element of this account, but its primary function is as an oracle of judgment. This does not lead to an explicit admission of wrongdoing, but produces fear that motivates Nero to release those incarcerated, including his own courtiers, who, fortunately, still awaited execution. Paul's death brings life to others.

The standard pattern follows a tomb scene with appearances. This "gospel" reverses the procedure. The basis is Mark 16:1–8 and the goal is, once again, improvement. The two officers, in faithful, albeit anxious, obedience to Paul's directions come "very early" (cf. Mark 16:1) to the tomb, where they find Titus and Luke praying; between them stands Paul. Wherever two or three gather, there is Paul in their midst. (Syriac notes Paul's ethereal radiance.) Paul had mentioned just two persons. The officers were astonished at the celestial visitor, while, for their part, Titus and Luke were terrified by the sight of two Roman soldiers and ran for their lives. Titus and Luke take the role played by Jesus' women followers in Mark 16 and parallels. Unlike the male disciples of Jesus, they had not deserted. (The narrator has not done a tidy job with these two. Readers do not know if they were arrested and released, although that is probable. Did they come in hopes of an appearance, or as a pious gesture?) Loyal they are, but far from perfect, although Paul might have mentioned that two candidates for baptism would be arriving. That would have ruined the story and deprived their pursuers of their fine words: we do not wish to kill you but for you to give us life. The apostle has vanished, as those risen may do, leaving his followers to find

Translation, Commentary, and Notes : Chapter

their own way through the web of deceit and appearance, confusion and grace that characterize the life of faith.

This chapter began and ended with Titus and Luke meeting Paul. Much has changed and everything goes on as before. As promised (12.5) Paul's life and death in Rome have brought about much new life, epitomized in the baptism of two Roman officials. The soldiers of Christ are ultimately victorious.

The mss. end with conventional doxologies. Both P.Heid and P.Hamb have the subscript "Acts of Paul," affirming that this is not the end of a separate story about Paul's martyrdom, but a longer work. P.Heid. makes Paul the authority behind the text, adding "according to the apostle." The preposition is *kata*, a Greek word often equivalent to "of" or "by," as in "The Gospel according to Matthew."

Notes

Brought forward. A has Paul in chains.

Decapitated. A: "They continued beseeching him not to harm Paul, Nero held rigidly to his former position, that Paul should be delivered to the punishment of the sword." The versions also expand.

Do this. A reassures: "By the power of God."

Alive . . . Christ. Cf. Rom 14:8.

Judge the earth. Cf. Acts 17:31; John 3:17. A adds "with total righteousness." Ps.-Linus expands:

> "So that you, Nero, might know that, after my decapitation, I shall live eternally for my unconquered king, but you, who imagine that you now conquer, will be conquered. After my head has been removed I shall appear alive to you and you will be able to recognize that death and life serve my Lord Jesus Christ, to whom belongs every kingdom."

Syriac (with an eye to 2 Tim 4:1; Matt 16:27) adds, at the close, "who will come to judge the living and the dead and will reward all in accordance with their deeds."

Change your Mind. Cf. Rom 8:38. A qualifies: "We are quite astonished at this." Syr and Ps.-Linus expand.

Inundate the world. Syriac adds "and will burn all the liars such as yourselves who have not served their good Lord and good Jesus Christ, who is forgotten in the world." This presumes a universal mission that has produced many nominal believers.

Save myself. The contrary-to-fact statement is difficult—the Greek apodosis reads "I would have done it"—and witnesses seek improvement. A adds, after "die," "for my king, as you think," and, at the close: "so that I might be rescued by you and evade dying." Syriac says, in effect, "When I must die, I would not run away, as you advise me." On rescue, see Matt 26:53.

Live for God. Cf. Rom 6:10. A: "But since I am confident that I shall live . . ."

Parthenion. Syriac omits the names of this pair.

Raises. The participle is present and probably embraces both present and future. "Is going to raise" is a legitimate translation.

Inquiries. A. improves by having the three resume their journey to the place of execution, during which the two demand initiation.

Prayer. P.Hamb. gives the content of the prayer, a blend of Luke 23:46 and Acts 7:59, e.g., *I call upon the* father [into his ha]nds I commend [*my*] spirit [. . . *re*]ceive it. After finishing this prayer he communed with the forebears in Hebrew, without another . . ." A. also expands. Ps.-Linus has a simple ending linked to the Plautilla episode. Syriac proposes a sermon with many conversions, culminating in the arrival of another delegation from Nero.

Milk. Elementary education: 1 Cor 3:3; Heb 5:12–13; cf. Philo, *Agric* 9; *Omn prob lib* 160; Epict., *Diss.* 3.24.9; Ignatius, *Trall.* 5.1; *AJn* 45. Nurture in general: cf. Irenaeus, *Adv. Haer.* 4.38.1–2; Clem. Al. *Paed.* 1.6.25–27. On the sacramental significance in general, see Lehman, "Sakral." A famous example of the use of milk at initiations can be seen in Sallustius' (fourth-century) interpretation of the myth/mystery of Attis (Nock, *Sallustius*, 8–9): "After this [fast] we are fed on milk as though being reborn (*anagennōmenōn*); that is followed by rejoicings and garlands and as it were a new ascent to the gods." For milk as wisdom conveying a redeeming message cf. Hippolytus, *Ref.* 5.8.30 ("Gnostic") and the *Odes of Solomon* 8.16; 19.1–5. On milk in so-called "primitive religions," see L. Gomme, "Milk," *ERE* 8:633–34.

The Latin text of the *Apostolic Tradition* gives this prayer over the cup of milk and honey administered to first communicants: ". . . milk and honey mixed together for the fulfillment of the promise that was to the fathers, which he said, 'a land flowing [with] milk and honey' and which Christ gave, his flesh, through which like little children, those who believe are nourished" (Bradshaw, 120). On "milk and honey," see George A. Barton, "Milk," *ERE* 8: 635-37.

Not died. Cf. Ps 118:17.

Within a Few Days. Cf. Acts 1:5.

Second Imprisonment. The hypothesis of a return to Rome from the East is not only without support from Acts; it positively contradicts Acts 20-21. According to Romans 15 Paul did not intend to engage in a mission at Rome. The Second Imprisonment hypothesis must presume that Paul, for reasons only to be conjectured, reversed all of his previous plans. This is not impossible, but it requires construction of a house of hypotheses built upon a foundation of conjectures. For a learned and thoughtful attempt to fit *APl* within the framework of a return to Rome, see Bauckham, "Sequel."

Tomb. Paul's statement to the officers implies that his tomb will be located at the place of his execution. That the account presumes the existence of a tomb is interesting, but there is no reason for thinking that the author was familiar with Rome, let alone the location of Paul's remains. The first extant reference to them comes from the mid-third century. See Eastman, *Paul.* For the importance of tombs in hero cults, see Koester, "On Heroes."

Turned and ran. The text may be corrupt here.

Bibliography

Bauckham, Richard, "The Acts of Paul as a Sequel to Acts." In *The Book of Acts in its First Century Setting.* Vol 1. *The Book of Acts in its Ancient Literary Setting*, edited by Bruce W. Winter and A. D. Clarke, 105-52. Grand Rapids: Eerdmans, 1993.

Birley, Anthony R. *Hadrian: The Restless Emperor.* London: Routledge, 1997.

Bolyki, János. "Events after the Martyrdom: Missionary Transformation of an Apocalyptical Metaphor in Martyrium Pauli." In *The Apocryphal Acts of Paul and Thecla*, edited by Jan N. Bremmer, 92-106. Kampen: Kok Pharos, 1996.

Bovon, François. "La vie des apotres. Traditions bibliques et narrations apocryphes." In *Les Actes apocryphes des Apôtres: christianisme et monde païen*, edited by François Bovon et al., 141-58. Publications de la Faculté de Théologie de l'Université de Genève 4. Geneva: Labor et Fides, 1981.

Drexler, Wilhelm. "Ganymedes." In *Ausführliches Lexicon der Griechischen und Römischen Mythologie*, edited by Wilhelm H. Roscher, 1:1595-1603. Leipzig: Teubner, 1886-1890.

Eastman, David L. *Paul the Martyr: The Cult of the Apostle Paul the Martyr in the Latin West.* WGRWS 4. Atlanta: SBL, 2011.

The Acts of Paul

Harrill, J. Albert. *Paul the Apostle*. Cambridge: Cambridge University Press, 2012.

Klauck, Hans-Josef. *Die apokryphe Bibel: Ein anderer Zugang zum frühen Christentum*. Tria Corda. Tübingen: Mohr/Siebeck, 2008.

Koester, Helmut. "On Heroes, Tombs, and Early Christianity: An Epilogue." In *Flavius Philostratus Heroikos*, edited by Jennifer K. B. Maclean and Ellen B Aitken, 257–64. WGRW. Atlanta: SBL, 2001.

Lalleman, Pieter J. "The Resurrection in the Acts of Paul." In *The Apocryphal Acts of Paul and Thecla*, edited by Jan N. Bremmer, 126–41. Kampen: Kok Pharos, 1996.

Lehman, F. "Die Entstehung der sakralen bedeutungender Milch." *Zeitschrift für Missionskunde und Religionswisssenschaft* 22 (1917) 1–12; 33–45.

MacDonald, Dennis R. "Luke's Eutychus and Homer's Elpenor: Acts 20:7–12 and *Odyssey*, 10–12." *JHC* 1 (1994) 5–24.

———. "Which Came First? Intertextual Relationships among the Apocryphal Acts of the Apostles." *Semeia* 80 (1997) 11–41.

MacDonald, Margaret Y. *Early Christian Women and Pagan Opinion: The Power of the Hysterical Woman*. Cambridge: Cambridge University Press, 1996

Murphy-O'Connor, Jerome. *Paul: A Critical Life*. Oxford: Clarendon, 1996.

Nock, Arthur Darby. *Sallustius, Concerning the Gods and the Universe*. Cambridge: Cambridge University Press, 1926.

Origen. *Contra Celsum*. Translated by Henry Chadwick. Cambridge: Cambridge University Press, 1953.

Parvis, Sara. "The *Martyrdom of Polycarp*." In *The Writings of the Apostolic Fathers*, ed. Paul Foster, 126–46. London: T. & T. Clark, 2007.

Pervo, Richard I. "(Not) Appealing to the Emperor: Acts (and The *Acts of Paul*)." In *Paul and the Heritage of Israel: Paul's Claim upon Isarael's Legacy in Luke and Acts in Light of the Pauline Letters*, edited by D. Moessner et al., 165–79. London: T. & T. Clark, 2012.

———. "Shepherd of the Lamb: Paul as a Christ-Figure in the *Acts of Paul*." In *Portraits of Jesus: Studies in Christology*, edited by Susan E. Myers, 355–69. WUNT 321. Tübingen: Mohr/Siebeck, 2012.

Rordorf, Willy. "Die neronische Christenverfolgung im Spiegel der Apokryphen Paulusakten." *NTS* 28 (1981–1982) 365–74. Reprinted in Rordorf, *Lex Orandi—Lex Credendi*, 368–77.

———. "In welchem Verhältnis stehen die apokryphen Paulusakten zur kanonischen Apostelgeschichte und zu den Pastoralbriefen?" In *Text and Testimony: Essays on New Testament and Apocryphal Literature in Honour of A. F. J. Klijn*, edited by Tjitze Baarda et al., 225–41. Kampen, Netherlands: Kok, 1988. (= *Lex Orandi—Lex Credendi*, 449–69.)

Schneemelcher, Wilhelm. "Die Apostelgeschichte des Lukas und die *Acta Pauli*." In *Apophoreta: Festschrift für Ernst Haenchen zu seinem siebzigsten Geburtstag am 10. Dezember 1964*, edited by Walther Eltester and Franz Heinrich Kettler, 236–50. BZNW 30. Berlin: Töpelmann, 1964. (= Schneemelcher, *Gesammelte Aufsätze*, 204–22.)

Tajra, Harry W. *The Martyrdom of St. Paul*. WUNT 67. Tübingen: Mohr/Siebeck, 1994.

Appendix 1

Fragments of Uncertain Location

1. Origen, *On First Principles* 1, 2, 3. The theme is the relation of personified Wisdom to Word. Origen states that they are the same "because she [*Wisdom*] is as it were an interpreter of the mind's secrets. Hence I consider that to be a true saying which is written in the Acts of Paul, 'He is the word, a living being' [*unde et recte mihi dictus videtur sermo ille qui in Actibus Pauli scriptus est, qui 'hic est verbum animal vivens*]. John, however, uses yet more exalted and wonderful language" (trans. Butterworth, *Origen on First Principles*, 16–17).

As stated in the Introduction, this quotation most likely came from a speech or sermon. A missionary or pastoral address would be likely. Brief as it is, it reveals the connection of *APl* to the Logos theology of various apologists.

2. A fragmentary papyrus from Yale. P.Yale 87 (inv. 1376, in Stephens, ed., *Yale Papyri*, 3–7).

This material is from an apocryphon dealing with Paul. That it is from a lost part of *APl* is probable. The recto appears to be from a speech or, perhaps more likely, a conversation. L. 3 can be construed as "I praise y[ou]." In l.4 "the Lord Jesus" is possible (Stephens, ed., *Yale Papyri*, 5). Ll. 6–7 refer to "Alexander." If this is from *APl*, the Alexander in view may be he of 1 Tim 1:20; 2 Tim 4:14, since the author takes a number of his characters from the PE. In l.6 the genitive "of Alexander" is followed by *pist*-. The word could mean "faithful," "faith," or represent a form of "believe," "trust." Ll. 7–8 evidently have "s/he [Alexander, God?] saved both [?] messenger/angel . . . Paul said to him." A sentence in l.11 closes with "We have done." The following sentence includes "God . . . of the earth . . . the father . . . his [?] son/

Appendix 1

servant Jesus Christ from him . . ." The speaker, almost certainly Paul, has moved into a creedal statement, summarizing creation and redemption. For a similar speech see 3.24, where Thecla says: "Father, the maker of heaven and earth, the father of your beloved son Jesus Christ, *I praise you* because you have delivered me from fire so that I might see Paul."

The verso appears to deal with Paul's "conversion." The narrative is third person, i.e., Paul is not telling his own story. L. 2 contains "mighty" or "strong" (neuter pl.); ll. 3–4, "to Damascus . . . s/he sent to Jerusalem." L.5 may be "he found now an apostle . . ." L. 8 mentions Damascus (acc.) followed by letters that might mean "He saw a novel" (fem.); l.10, "Paul to him"; l.11, "the appearance (*epiphaneia*) of the lord"; l.12 "and he stayed, but . . ."; l. 13, "Damascus and from there from . . ."

It is not certain whether the recto or the verso is prior, as no page numbers survive. The content and language make it quite likely that this fragment derives from the *APL*. Can it be located? One possibility is chap. 1. After narrating the conversion the story turned to an attempt to persuade Alexander, perhaps one of Paul's companions, of his newfound faith. Another would be in the catch-all designated as chap. 8.

Appendix 2

The Continuation of Thecla's Story

Chapter 4 closes the story of Thecla firmly and succinctly: "Following this exhortation she went to Seleucia, where, after enlightening many with God's word, she enjoyed a noble death." With these words the author of *APl* intended to remove her from the scene. When her story was detached for service in her cult at Seleucia, this brief closure was deemed inadequate. Eventually her story was revised into a more elegant preface to a collection of miracles experienced at her shrine (Dagron, *Vie*; and Johnson, *Life*). Prior to that longer endings were supplied. Lipsius 1:269–72 is a fine lesson in the growth of tradition. The Latin tradition includes a clear resolution to the story of her mother Theocleia, left open in the Greek text.

Some Greek mss. insert in 4.18, prior to the notice that she enlightened many:

> She lived in a cave for seventy-two years on a diet of vegetables and water.
>
> 19. Some men of the city, pagans in religion and physicians in profession, sent some arrogant young men to corrupt [i.e., rape] her. They claimed: "She is a virgin dedicated to Artemis. That is why she can master illnesses." By divine foresight she went into the rock and underground. She went to Rome to see Paul but found that he had died. After a short stay she died gloriously and is buried no more than a third of a mile from her teacher Paul.
>
> 45. She was thrown to the flames when she was seventeen, at eighteen she was condemned to the beasts, and she lived an ascetic life for seventy-two years, as noted, in the cave, for a total of ninety years. After accomplishing a vast number of healings

329

Appendix 2

she is at rest with the saints, having died on 24 September in Jesus Christ our Lord, to whom be glory and power for evermore. (author's trans.)

Comment

This addition seeks to justify the cult of Thecla at Rome, particularly a church dedicated to her. See Davis, *Cult*, 46–47. It appears to be based upon a much longer account found in Lipsius 1:271–72; trans. Elliott, 372–74. This circumstantial story clarifies what is obscure in §44: if Thecla loses her virginity she will lose her power to heal, which is having a ruinous effect upon the income of the local physicians. After a display of piety and the development of considerable suspense, she saw the rock opened widely enough for her to enter, which she did. It then closed without a seam, leaving them with nothing more than a piece of her dress (which could thereafter serve as a relic of the second class). Elizabeth and the young John the Baptizer escape murderers by the same device (*Protevangelium of James* 22.8). (24 September is her Eastern feast day; in the West it was 23 September.)

For other additions to the story, see the Bibliography. English translations are available in Talbot and Johnson, *Miracle Tales*.

Bibliography

Bovon, François, and Bertrand Bouvier. "Miracles additionnels de Thècle dans le manuscrit de Rome, *Angelicus graecus 108*." *Apocrypha* (forthcoming, 2013).

Dagron, Gilbert, ed. *Vie et miracles de Sainte Thècle: Texte grec, traduction, et commentaire*. Subsidia Hagiographica 62. Brussels: Société des Bollandistes, 1978.

Davis, Stephen J., *The Cult of Saint Thecla: A Tradition of Women's Piety in Late Antiquity*. Oxford Early Christian Studies. Oxford: Oxford University Press, 2001.

Johnson, Scott F. *The Life and Miracles of Thekla: A Literary Study*. Washington, DC: Center for Hellenic Studies, 2006.

Talbot, Alice-Mary, and Scott F. Johnson, *Miracle Tales from Byzantium*. Cambridge, MA: Harvard University Press, 2012.

Appendix 3

The *Acts of Titus*

The *Acts of Titus* is an ecclesiastical text of the sixth century that made use of *APl*. See Czachesz, *Commission Narratives*, 208–23; and Pervo, "*Acts of Titus*." This Middle Byzantine text made use of *APl*, as well as the canonical Acts and the Pauline letters in its construction of a life of Titus designed to support and defend the claims of Crete in church politics. Here follows a translation of chaps 1–7, used in reconstruction of *APl*. For details, see Pervo, "*Acts of Titus*."

Sigla:
underlined words = Borrowings from *APl*.
italicized words = Possible Borrowings from or imitations of *APl*.

Of the Holy Apostle Titus, a Disciple of the Holy Apostle Paul, Who Became Bishop of Gortyna in Crete.

1. Zenas the Lawyer, whom the Holy Apostle Paul mentions (Tit 3:13), is the one who wrote his (Titus's) life as set forth below:

The most holy Titus stemmed from the lineage of Minos, king of Crete. At age twenty, when he was quite devoted to the poems and dramas of Homer and the other philosophers, he heard a voice saying, "Titus, you must depart from here and save your soul, for this learning will be of no benefit to you" (cf. 2 Tim 3:16). He wanted to hear the same voice once more, for he was familiar with the deceptions issued vocally from statues. After remaining resistant for nine years, he was instructed in a vision to read the book of the Hebrews. Taking up the book of Isaiah, he came upon the following passage: "Dedicate yourselves to me, you many islands. Israel is saved by the Lord with everlasting salvation," etc.

Appendix 3

2. Now when the Proconsul of Crete, who was the uncle of St Titus, heard of the salutary birth and baptism of Christ the Master and of the marvelous deeds he performed in Jerusalem and elsewhere, he took counsel with the leading people of Crete and then dispatched Titus with some others to Jerusalem so that he would be able to hear the message and speak and teach those things that he was going to see. Titus arrived, saw, and worshipped Christ the Master. He observed all of his marvelous deeds and also witnessed the Master's salutary sufferings, his burial, resurrection, and divine ascension, as well as the arrival of the all-holy Spirit upon the divine apostles. He became a believer.

3. He was numbered with the one-hundred twenty and among the 3,000 who came to believe in Christ through Peter, the chief, as indeed it is written, "Cretans and Arabs" (Acts 1:15; 2:41; 2:11). Titus was ardent and always zealous in the Spirit (cf. Acts 18:25). Three years later 5,000 men had been added to the faith (cf. Acts 4:4). Two years later, after the cripple had been healed by Peter and John, the apostles were persecuted and charged not to speak in the name of the Lord Jesus. When the priests were intent upon putting them to death, Gamaliel, the teacher of the law, deterred their plan (cf. Acts 3–5). After seven years had passed, Stephen was stoned (cf. Acts 7). Thereafter occurred Paul's experiences in Damascus: i.e., his blinding and recovery of sight (cf. Acts 9).

Paul preached the message about Christ first in Damascus.

He healed Aphphia (*v. l.* Amphia), the wife of Chrysippus, who had been possessed by a demon. After a fast of seven days he cast down the idol of Apollo. Then he went to Jerusalem and in turn [or again] to Caesarea.

4. St Titus was ordained by the apostles and sent with Paul to teach and to ordain whomever Paul might designate. Arriving at Antioch, they found Barnabas, the son of Panchares whom Paul had raised. Herod the Tetrarch (cf. Acts 12:1) killed James the brother of John with a sword. After this they traveled to Seleucia, Cyprus, Salamis, and Paphos. From there they went to Perga in Pamphylia and again to Pisidian Antioch, then to Iconium, to the household of Onesiphorus, to whom Titus had previously reported the facts about Paul, since he was Paul's precursor in every city. From there he [Titus?] went to Lystra and Derbe. The divinely inspired Titus both preached the word of God with Paul in every city and endured persecutions and whippings. Both nonetheless enlightened the hearts of unbelievers by working signs and wonders just as [these] all are reported in the Acts of the Apostles.

The Acts of Titus:

When Paul was in custody while at Philippi and an earthquake occurred in the prison work-house, he was freed.

[Now some write "Titus Justus," but others "Titus Pistos."]

5. At that time Rustillus, who was married to Titus's sister, had completed a second period in the governorship of Crete. Paul and Titus arrived there. When the ruler saw the divinely inspired Titus weighed down with tears, he attempted to compel him to live with him, but St Titus did not obey him. Rustillus advised him not to speak against the pagan gods. St Titus expounded the gospel of Christ to him, claiming, "If you believe my message, you will be exalted on earth and in the city of Rome." Shortly thereafter his son died. He brought him to Paul at night. Following prayer, Paul raised him. After they had spent three months (cf. Acts 19:8; 20:3) there, Rustillus sent them on with ample rewards. He went to Rome and was designated consul. Thereafter, because Rustillus was a relative of Titus, those of the circumcision only engaged in verbal combat, not daring to do anything else to the proclaimers of God's word.

6. Leaving Crete, they went to Asia. In the course of Paul's teaching at Ephesus 12,000 persons came to believe. There the apostle also fought with beasts, being cast to a lion. Titus, Timothy, and Erastus delivered the second epistle to the Corinthians.

Titus, Timothy, and Luke remained with the apostle until his consummation under Nero. They thereupon returned to Greece and got Luke established there. Titus and Timothy then moved on to Colossae. Timothy subsequently returned to Ephesus while Titus proceeded to Crete (cf. 1 Tim 1:3; Tit 1:5).

7. The Cretans greeted his arrival joyfully, like that of a relative, and decreed a holiday. They adorned the temples of their idols, took in hand the sacred swords, and, clad in [or carrying] their purple-trimmed ephebic tunics [? possibly: tunics with diagonal purple stripes] they went before him. St Titus addressed them graciously and urged them to be responsive to what he said. He began by singing, in Hebrew, "May God be merciful to us and bless us," etc. They responded that they did not know what he was saying. Only the Hebrews present understood. Presently, as they drew near to the idol of Artemis, it cast itself down, breaking forth with a cry: "You [pl.] are acting insolently in ignorance!" St Titus said to them, "Since you are publicly carrying swords, condemnation therefore falls upon you." They thereupon threw down the swords and remained without food until early morning, reciting the psalm in expectation that they would hear something from the

Appendix 3

idol. Then, after numerous marvels, they began to exclaim: "There is one god, the one manifested to us this day!" Five hundred came to believe in Christ.

The diet of the apostle consisted of garden vegetables. He took his rest upon [dined in?] goat's hair and sheepskin.

(Chapters 8–12 are omitted as irrelevant to *APl*. They can be found in Pervo, "*Acts of Titus*.")

Notes and Comments

4. *Acts*. The dative plural *praxesi* is probably a reference to two books: Acts and *APl*. The canonical book cannot by any stretch of imagination serve as a basis for the ministry of Titus, as it does not mention his name.

Prison work house. The text is difficult. Halkin, "La Légende," 246–47n7, states that O reads *ergastēriois*, while in P there appears *eg//a//ois*. He also notes the appearance of *ergastrois* in chap. 11. Here *ergastrois* is equivalent to *ergastērion* (cf. Latin *ergastulum*). The difficulty of this rare word is strong evidence for dependence upon a text of *APl*.

Titius Justus. The sentence may well be a gloss and a mark of omission from the source.

6. Timothy and Erastus derive from Acts 19:22, where they are sent to Macedonia. 2 Tim 4:20 deposits Erastus at Corinth. 2 Cor 2:13; 7:6; and chap. 8 relate Titus to Macedonia. Like modern scholars, the author coordinates data from Acts with those of the epistles.

7. *Went before him.* The text is difficult, possibly corrupt.

Bibliography

Czachesz, István. *Commission Narratives: A Comparative Study of the Canonical and Apocryphal Acts*. SECA 8. Leuven: Peeters, 2007.

Halkin, François. "La légende crétoise de saint tite." *Analecta Bollandia* 79 (1961) 241–256.

Pervo, Richard I. "The 'Acts of Titus': A Preliminary Translation with an Introduction, Notes, and Appendices." In *SBLSP* 35:455–82. Atlanta: Scholars, 1996.

General Bibliography

Aageson, James W. "The Pastoral Epistles and the *Acts of Paul*: A Multiplex Approach to Authority in Paul's Legacy." *Lexington Theological Quarterly* 40 (2005) 237–48.

Achtemeier, Paul J. *1 Peter: A Commentary on First Peter*. Edited by Eldon J. Epp. Hermeneia. Minneapolis: Fortress, 1996.

———. "Jesus and the Disciples as Miracle Workers in the Apocryphal New Testament." In *Aspects of Religious Propaganda*, edited by Elisabeth Schüssler Fiorenza, 149–86. South Bend, IN: University of Notre Dame Press, 1976.

Adamik, Tamás. "The Baptized Lion in the Acts of Paul." In *The Apocryphal Acts of Paul and Thecla*, edited by Jan N. Bremmer, 60–74. Kampen: Kok Pharos, 1996.

Allberry, C. R. C., ed. *A Manichaean Psalm-Book, part II, vol. 2*. Stuttgart: Kohlhammer, 1938.

Aspegren, Kerstin. *The Male Woman: A Feminine Ideal in the Early Church*. Edited by René Kieffer. Acta universitatis Upsaliensis. Uppsala Women's Studies, Women in Religion 4. Uppsala: Gotab, 1990;

Aubin, Melissa. "Reversing Romance? The *Acts of Thecla* and the Ancient Novel." In *Ancient Fiction and Early Christian Narrative*, edited by R. F. Hock, 257–72. SBL Symposium Series 6. Atlanta: Scholars, 1998.

Aubineau, Michel. "Compléments au dossier de sainte Thècle." *Analecta Bollandiana* 93 (1975) 356–62.

———. "Le panégyrique de Thècle, attribué à Jean Chrysostome (BHG 1720): la fin retrouvée d'un texte motile." *Analecta Bollandiana* 93 (1975) 349–62.

Aune, David E. *Prophecy in Early Christianity and the Ancient Mediterranean World*. Grand Rapids: Eerdmans, 1983.

Aymer, M. P. "Hailstorms and Fireballs: Redaction, World Creation, and Resistance in the Acts of Paul and Thecla." *Semeia* 79 (1997) 45–61.

Babcock, William S., ed. *Paul and the Legacies of Paul*. Dallas: Southern Methodist University Press, 1990.

Baldwin, Matthew C. *Whose* Acts of Peter?: *Text and Historical Context of the Actus Vercellenses*. WUNT 2/196. Tübingen: Mohr/Siebeck, 2005.

Barnes, Timothy D. *Early Christian Hagiography and Roman History*. Tübingen: Mohr/Siebeck, 2010.

Barrier, Jeremy W. *The Acts of Paul and Thecla. A Critical Introduction and Commentary*. WUNT 270. Tübingen: Mohr/Siebeck, 2009.

Baslez, M.-F., P. Hoffman, and M. Trédé, eds. *Le Monde du Roman Grec, Actes du colloque international tenu à l'Ecole normale supérieure (Paris 17–19 décembre 1987)*. Études de Littérature Ancienne 4. Paris: Presses de l'École normale supérieure, 1994.

General Bibliography

Bauckham, Richard, "The Acts of Paul as a Sequel to Acts." In *The Book of Acts in its First Century Setting.* Vol 1. *The Book of Acts in its Ancient Literary Setting*, edited by Bruce W. Winter and A. D. Clarke, 105–52. Grand Rapids: Eerdmans, 1993.

———. "The *Acts of Paul*: Replacement of Acts or Sequel to Acts." *Semeia* 80 (1997) 159–68.

Beard, Mary. *The Fires of Vesuvius: Pompeii Lost and Found.* Cambridge, MA: Harvard University Press, 2010.

Berger, Klaus. *Formgeschichte des neuen Testaments.* Heidelberg: Quelle & Meyer, 1984.

Betz, Hans Dieter. *Galatians.* Hermeneia. Philadelphia: Fortress, 1979.

———. *Lukian von Samosata und das Neue Testament.* TU 76. Berlin: Akadamie, 1961.

———. *The Sermon on the Mount.* Edited by Adela Y. Collins. Hermeneia. Minneapolis: Fortress, 1995.

Betz, Monika. "Thekla und die jüngerin Witwen der Pastoralbriefe. Ein Beispiel für die Situationsgebundenheit paulinischer Tradition." *Annali di Studi Religiosi* 6 (2005) 335–56.

———. "Die betörenden Worte des fremden Mannes: Zur Funktion der Paulusbeschreibung in den Theklaakten." NTS 53 (2007) 130–45.

Bieler, Ludwig. ΘΕΙΟΣ ANHP: *Das Bild des "Göttlichen Menschen" in Spätantike und Frühchristentum.* 2 vols. 1935–1936. Reprint, Darmstadt: Wissenschaftliche Buchgesellschaft, 1967.

Birley, Anthony R. *Hadrian. The Restless Emperor.* London: Routledge, 1997.

Bollók, J. "The Description of Paul in the Acta Pauli." In *The Apocryphal Acts of Paul and Thecla*, edited by Jan N. Bremmer, 1–15. Kampen: Kok Pharos, 1996.

Bolyki, János. "Events after the Martyrdom: Missionary Transformation of an Apocalyptical Metaphor in Martyrium Pauli." In *The Apocryphal Acts of Paul and Thecla*, edited by Jan N. Bremmer, 92–106. Kampen: Kok Pharos, 1996.

Boughton, Lynne C. "From Pious Legend to Feminist Fantasy. Distinguishing Hagiographical License from Apostolic Practice in the *Acts of Paul/Acts of Thecla*." *JR* 71 (1991) 362–84.

Bourguet, Pierre du. *Early Christian Art.* Trans. Thomas Burton. New York: Morrow, 1971.

Bovon, François. "Canonical and Noncanonical Acts of the Apostles." In *New Testament and Christian Apocrypha: Collected Studies II*, by François Bovon, edited by Glenn E. Snyder, 197–222. WUNT 237. Tübingen: Mohr-Siebeck, 2009.

———. "The Child and the Beast: Fighting Violence in Ancient Christianity." *HTR* 92 (1999) 369–92.

———. "A New Citation of the *Acts of Paul* in Origen." In *Studies in Early Christianity*, 267–70. Grand Rapids: Baker, 2005. Originally published as "Une nouvelle citation des *Actes de Paul* chez Origène." *Apocrypha* 5 (1994) 113–17.

———. "Paul as Document and Paul as Monument." In *New Testament and Christian Apocrypha: Collected Studies II*, edited by Glenn E. Snyder, 307–17. WUNT 237. Tübingen: Mohr/Siebeck, 2009.

———. "Le Saint-Esprit, l'Église et les relations humaines selon Actes 20,36—21,16." In *Les Actes des Apôtres: Traditions, redaction, théolgies*, edited by Jacob Kremer, 339–58. BETL 43. Leuven: Leuven University Press 1979.

———. "La vie des apotres. Traditions bibliques et narrations apocryphes." In *Les Actes apocryphes des Apôtres: christianisme et monde païen*, edited by François Bovon et al., 141–58. Publications de la Faculté de Théologie de l'Université de Genève 4. Geneva: Labor et Fides, 1981.

———. "The Woman at the Window: A Study in Intertextuality between Aeschylus and the Book of Judges." *Scripture and Interpretation* 4 (2010) 113–20.
Bovon, François, et al., eds. *Les Actes apocryphes des Apôtres: christianisme et monde païen*. Publications de la Faculté de Théologie de l'Université de Genève 4. Geneva: Labor et Fides, 1981.
Bovon, François, and Bertrand Bouvier. "Miracles additionnels de Thècle dans le manuscrit de Rome, *Angelicus graecus 108*." *Apocrypha* (forthcoming).
Bovon, François, Ann G. Brock, and C. R. Matthews, eds. *The Apocryphal Acts of the Apostles*. Cambridge, MA: Harvard University Press, 1999.
Bovon, François, and Pierre Geoltrain, eds. *Écrits apocryphes chrétiens*. 2 vols. Paris: Gallimard, 1997, 2005.
Bradshaw, Paul F., Maxwell E. Johnson, and L. Edward Phillips, eds. *The Apostolic Tradition*. Hermeneia. Minneapolis: Fortress, 2002.
Braun, Martin. *History and Romance in Greco-Oriental Literature*. Oxford: Blackwell, 1938.
Braun, Willi. "Physiotherapy of Femininity in the Acts of Thecla." In *Text and Artifact in the Religions of Mediterranean Antiquity*, edited by Stephen G. Wilson et al., 209–30. Waterloo, ON: Canadian Corp. for Studies in Religion, 2000.
Bremmer, Jan N. "Magic, martyrdom and women's liberation in the Acts of Paul and Thecla." In *The Apocryphal Acts of Paul and Thecla*, edited by Jan N. Bremmer, 36–59. Kampen: Kok Pharos, 1996.
———. "The Novel and the Apocryphal Acts: Place, Time and Readership." In *Groningen Colloquia on the Novel* IX, edited by H. Hofmann and M. Zimmerman, 157–80. Groningen: Forsten, 1998.
Bremmer, Jan N., ed. *The Apocryphal Acts of Paul and Thecla*. Vol. 2 of *Studies on the Apocryphal Acts of the Apostles*. Kampen: Kok Pharos, 1996.
———. *The Apocryphal Acts of Peter: Magic, Miracles and Gnosticism*. Vol. 3 of *Studies on the Apocryphal Acts of the Apostles*. Leuven: Peeters, 1998.
Brock, Ann G. "Genre of the Acts of Paul: One Tradition Enhancing Another." *Apocrypha* 5 (1994) 119–36.
———. "Political Authority and Cultural Accomodation: Social Diversity in the *Acts of Paul* and *The Acts of Peter*." In *Les Actes apocryphes des Apôtres: christianisme et monde païen*, edited by François Bovon et al., 145–69. Publications de la Faculté de Théologie de l'Université de Genève 4. Geneva: Labor et Fides, 1981.
Brown, Peter. *The Body and Society*. New York: Columbia University Press, 1988.
Budge, E. A. Wallis. *The Contendings of the Apostles: Being the Histories and the Lives and Martyrdoms and Deaths of the Twelve Apostles and Evangelists*. 2nd ed. London: Oxford University Press, 1935.
Büllesbach, Claudia. "Das Verhältnis der Acta Pauli zur Apostelgeschichte des Lukas. Darstellung und Kritik der Forschungsgeschichte." In *Das Ende des Paulus: Historische, theologische und literaturgeschichtliche Aspekte*, edited by F. W. Horn, 215–37. BZNW 106. Berlin, Töpelmann, 2001.
———. "'Ich will mich rundherum scheren und dir folgen': Begegnungen zwischen Paulus und Thekla in den Acta Paula et Theclae." In *Körper und Kommunikation: Beiträge aus der theologischen Genderforschung*, edited by K. Greschat and H. Omerzu, 125–46. Leipzig: Teubner, 2003.
Bultmann, Rudolf. *Das Evangelium des Johannes*. 10th ed.. KEK. Göttingen: Vandenhoeck & Ruprecht, 1964.

General Bibliography

———. *The History of the Synoptic Tradition*. Trans. John Marsh. Rev. ed. New York: Harper & Row, 1968.

Bundy, David. "The Pseudo-Ephremian *Commentary on Third Corinthians*: A Study in Exegesis and Anti-Bardaisanite Polemic." In *After Bardaisan: Studies on Continuity and Change in Syriac Christianity in Honour of Professor Han J. W. Drijvers*, edited by Gerrit J. Reinink and Alexander Cornelis Klugkist, 51–63. Orientalia Lovaniensia Analecta 89. Louvain: Peeters, 1999.

Burrus, Virginia. *Chastity as Autonomy: Women in the Stories of the Apocryphal Acts*. Studies in Women and Religion 23. Lewiston, NY: Mellen, 1987.

———. *The Sex Lives of Saints: An Erotics of Ancient Hagiography*. Philadelphia: University of Pennsylvania Press, 2004.

Butterworth, G. W. *Origen on First Principles*. 1936. Reprint, New York: Harper & Row, 1966.

Bynum, Caroline Walker. *The Resurrection of the Body in Western Christendom, 200–1336*. New York: Columbia University Press, 1995.

Calef, Susan A. "Thecla 'Tried and True' and the Inversion of Romance." In *A Feminist Companion to the New Testament Apocrypha*, edited by A.-J. Levine, 163–85. Feminist Companion to the New Testament and Early Christian Writings 11. New York: T. & T. Clark, 2006.

Calhoun, Robert Matthew. "The Resurrection of the Flesh in *Third Corinthians*." In *Christian Body, Christian Self: Concepts of Early Christian Personhood*, edited by Clare K. Rothschild and Trevor W. Thompson, 235–57. WUNT 284. Tübingen: Mohr/Siebeck, 2011.

Callahan, Allen Dwight. "Dead Paul: The Apostle as Martyr in Philippi." In *Philippi at the Time of Paul and after His Death*, edited by Charlambos Bakirtzi and Helmut Koester, 67–84. Harrisburg, PA: Trinity, 1998.

Campenhausen, Hans von. "Bearbeitungen und Interpolationen des Polykarpmartyriums." In *Aus der Frühzeit des Christentums*, 253–301. Tübingen: Mohr/Siebeck, 1963.

Carrington, Philip. *The Early Christian Church*. Vol. 2, *The Second Christian Century*. Cambridge: Cambridge University Press, 1957.

Cartlidge, David R., and J. Keith Elliott. *Art and the Christian Apocrypha*. London: Routledge, 2001.

Cartlidge, David R. "Transfigurations of Metamorphosis Traditions in the Acts of John, Thomas, and Peter." *Semeia* 38 (1986) 53–66.

Castelli, Elizabeth. *Martyrdom and Memory. Early Christian Culture Making*. New York: Columbia University Press, 2004.

———. "Virginity and its Meaning for Women's Sexuality in Early Christianity." *Journal of Feminist Studies in Religion* 2 (1986) 61–88.

Chariton. *Callirhoe*. Edited and translated by George P. Goold. LCL. Cambridge, MA: Harvard University Press, 1995.

Charlesworth, James H., with James R. Mueller. *The New Testament Apocrypha and Pseudepigrapha: A Guide to Publications, with Excursuses on Apocalypses*. No. 59. London: ATLA / Scarecrow, 1987.

Clark, Elizabeth. "Antifamilial Tendencies in Ancient Christianity." *Journal of the History of Sexuality* 5 (1995) 356–80.

Clarke, John R. *Roman Sex. 100 BC–AD 250*. New York: Abrams, 2003.

Coleman, K. M. "Fatal Charades: Roman Executions Staged as Mythological Enactments." *JRS* 80 (1990) 44–73.

Conybeare, Frederick C. *The Apology and Acts of Appolonius and Other Monuments of Early Christianity*. London: Swan Sonnenschein, 1894.
———. "Commentary of Ephrem on Acts." In *The Beginnings of Christianity*, edited by F. J. Foakes-Jackson and K. Lake, 3:373–453. London: Macmillan, 1926.
Conzelmann, Hans. *First Corinthians*. Trans. J. W. Leitch. Hermeneia. Philadelphia: Fortress, 1975.
Cook, Arthur B. *Zeus. A Study in Ancient Religion*. Vol. 3. Cambridge: Cambridge University Press, 1940.
Cooper, Kate. *The Virgin and the Bride: Idealized Womanhood in Late Antiquity*. Cambridge, MA: Harvard University Press, 1996.
Corssen, P. "Die Urgestalt der Paulusakten." ZNW 4 (1903) 22–47.
———. "Der Schluss der Paulusakten." ZNW 6 (1905) 317–38.
Cothenet, É. "Les Actes de Paul." *Esprit & Vie* 117 (2007) 17–23.
Crossan, John D. *In Fragments: the Aphorisms of Jesus*. New York: Harper & Row, 1983.
Crum, W. E. *Coptic Dictionary*. Oxford: Clarendon, 1939.
———. "New Coptic Manuscripts in the John Rylands Library." *BJRL* 5 (1920) 497–503.
Czachesz, István. *Commission Narratives. A Comparative Study of the Canonical and Apocryphal Acts*. SECA 8. Leuven: Peeters, 2007.
———. "The Acts of Paul and the Western Text of Luke's Acts: Paul between Canon and Apocrypha." In *The Apocryphal Acts of Paul and Thecla*, edited by Jan N. Bremmer, 107–25. Kampen: Kok Pharos, 1996.
Dagron, Gilbert, ed. *Vie et miracles de Sainte Thècle: Texte grec, traduction, et commentaire*. Subsidia Hagiographica 62. Brusells: Société des Bollandistes, 1978.
D'Anna, Alberto. *Terza lettera ai Corinzi. La risurrezione*. Letture cristiane del primo millennio 44. Milan: Paoline, 2009.
Davies, Stevan L. *The Revolt of the Widows: The Social World of the Apocryphal Acts*. Carbondale: University of Southern Illinois Press, 1980.
———. "Women, Tertullian and the Acts of Paul." *Semeia* 38 (1986) 39–44.
Davis, Stephen J. *The Cult of Saint Thecla. A Tradition of Women's Piety in Late Antiquity*. Oxford Early Christian Studies. Oxford: Oxford University Press, 2001.
Dobschütz, Ernst von. "Der Roman in der altchristlichen Literatur." *Deutsche Rundschau* 111 (1902) 87–106.
Dormeyer, Detlev. *The New Testament among the Writings of Antiquity*. Translated by R. Kossov. Sheffield: Sheffield Academic, 1998.
Dover, Kenneth J. *Greek Homosexuality*. New York: Random House, 1980.
Drijvers, Han J. W. "Der getaufte Löwe und die Theologie der Acta Pauli." In *Carl-Schmidt-Kolloquium an der Martin-Luther Universität 1998*, edited by P. Nagel, 181–89. Wissenschaftliche Beiträge 9. Halle: Salle, 1990.
Dunderberg, Ismo. "The School of Valentinus." In *A Companion to Second-Century Christian "Heretics,"* ed. Antti Marjanen and Petri Luomanen, 64–99. Leiden: Brill, 2008.
Dunn, Peter W. "The *Acts of Paul* and the Pauline Legacy in the Second Century." PhD diss., Queens College, Cambridge University, 1996.
———. "The Influence of 1 Corinthians on the *Acts of Paul*." In SBLSP, 438–54. Atlanta: Scholars, 1996.
———. "Women's Liberation, the *Acts of Paul*, and Other Apocryphal Acts of the Apostles. A Review of Some Recent Interpretations" *Apocrypha* 4 (1993) 245–61.

Eastman, David L. *Paul the Martyr: The Cult of the Apostle Paul the Martyr in the Latin West*. WGRWS 4. Atlanta: SBL, 2011.

Ebner Martin. "Gemeindestrukturen in Exempeln: Eine eindeutig frauenfreundliche Kompromisslössung." In *Aus Liebe zu Paulus? Die Akte Thekla neu aufgerollt*, edited by Martin Ebner, 180–86. SBS 206. Stuttgart: Katholisches Bibelwerk, 2005.

———. "Sein und Schein auf dem 'Königsweg,': Figurenaufstellung und 'Einspurung' des Lesers (ActThecl 1–4)." In *Aus Liebe zu Paulus? Die Akte Thekla neu aufgerollt*, edited by Martin Ebner, 52–63. SBS 206. Stuttgart: Katholisches Bibelwerk, 2005.

———. "Paulinische Seligpreisungen à la Thekla: Narrative Relecture der Makarismenreihe in ActThecl 5." In *Aus Liebe zu Paulus? Die Akte Thekla neu aufgerollt*, edited by Martin Ebner, 64–79. SBS 206. Stuttgart: Katholisches Bibelwerk, 2005.

Ebner Martin, ed. *Aus Liebe zu Paulus? Die Akte Thekla neu aufgerollt*. SBS 206. Stuttgart: Katholisches Bibelwerk, 2005.

Elliott, James Keith., ed. *The Apocryphal New Testament: A Collection of Apocryphal Christian Literature in an English Translation*. Oxford: Clarendon, 1993.

Ephrem Syrus. *Commentary on Acts*. Quoted in *The Beginnings of Christianity*, edited by Frederick J. Foakes Jackson, and Kirsopp Lake, 3:373–453. New York: Macmillan, 1920–1933.

Esch, Elisabeth. "Thekla und die Tiere, oder: Die Zähmung der Widerspenstigen." In *Aus Liebe zu Paulus? Die Akte Thekla neu aufgerollt*, edited by Martin Ebner, 159–79. SBS 206. Stuttgart: Katholisches Bibelwerk, 2005.

Esch, Elisabeth, and Andreas Leinhüpl-Wilke. "Auf die Spur gekommen: Plädoyer für eine leserorientierte Literarkritik." In *Aus Liebe zu Paulus? Die Akte Thekla neu aufgerollt*, edited by Martin Ebner, 30–51. SBS 206. Stuttgart: Katholisches Bibelwerk, 2005.

Esch-Wermeling, Elisabeth. *Thekla—Paulusschülerin wider Willen? Strategien der Leserlenkung in den Theklaakten*. Neutestamentliche Abhandlungen. Neue Folge 53. Münster: Aschendorff, 2008.

Faraone, Christopher A. *Ancient Greek Love Magic*. Cambridge, MA: Harvard University Press, 1999.

Faure, Paul. *Magie der Düfte. Eine Kulturgeschichte der Wohlgerüche. Von den Pharaonen zu den Römern*. Munich: Taschen, 1990.

Fitzmyer, Joseph A. *The Letter to Philemon*. AB 34c. Doubleday: New York, 2000.

Foster, Paul. "Polymorphic Christology: Its Origins and Development in Early Christianity." *JTS* 58 (2007) 90–93.

Francis, James A. *Subversive Virtue: Asceticism and Authority in the Second-Century Pagan World*. University Park: Pennsylvania State University Press, 1995.

Fredriksen, Paula. "Mandatory Retirement." *Studies in Religion/Sciences religieuses* 35 (2006) 231–46.

French, David H. "Acts and the Roman Roads of Asia Minor." In *The Book of Acts in Its Graeco-Roman Setting*, edited by David W. J. Gill and Conrad Gempf, 49–58. BIFCS 2. Grand Rapids: Eerdmans, 1994.

Garland, Robert. *The Greek Way of Death*. Ithaca, NY: Cornell Univesity Press, 1985.

Geerard, Maurice. *Clavis apocryphorum Novi Testamenti*. Corpus Christianorum. Turnhout: Brepols, 1992.

Georgi, Dieter. *Remembering the Poor: The History of Paul's Collection for Jerusalem*. Nashville: Abingdon, 1992.

———. *The Opponents of Paul in Second Corinthians*. Philadelphia: Fortress, 1986.
Glancy, Jennifer A. "Boasting of Beatings (2 Corinthians 11:23–25)." *JBL* 123 (2004) 99–135.
Goulet, Richard. "Les *Vies* de philosophes dans l'Antiquité tardive et leur portée Mystère." In *Les Actes apocryphes des Apôtres: christianisme et monde païen*, edited by François Bovon et al., 161–208. Publications de la Faculté de Théologie de l'Université de Genève 4. Geneva: Labor et Fides, 1981.
Gounelle, Rémi. "Actes Apocryphes des Apôtres et Actes des Apôtres Canoniques: État de la recherche et perspectives nouvelles (II)." *RHPR* 84 (2004) 419–41.
Glaser, Timo. *Paulus als Briefroman erzählt*. SUNT 76. Göttingen: Vandenhoeck & Reprecht, 2009.
Goodspeed, Edward J. "The Book of Thekla." *American Journal of Semitic Languages and Literatures* 17 (1901) 65–95.
———. "The Epistle of Pelagia." *AJSL* 20 (1903–1904) 95–108.
Grant, Robert M. "The Description of Paul in the Acta Pauli." *VC* 36 (1982) 1–4.
———. *Miracle and Natural Law in Graeco-Roman and Early Christian Thought*. Amsterdam: North-Holland, 1952.
Gregory, Andrew. "The Acts of Paul and the Legacy of Paul." In *Paul and the Second Century*, edited by Michael F. Bird and Joseph R. Dodson, 169–89. LNTS 412. London: T. & T. Clark, 2011.
Grillmeier, Aloys. *Christ in Christian Tradition*. Trans. John Bowden. Vol. 1. Atlanta: Knox, 1975.
Guéraud, Octave, and Pierre Nautin. *Origène. Sur la Pâque*. Christianisme Antique 2. Paris: Beauchesne, 1979.
Haines-Eitzen, Kim. "Engendering Palimpsests: Reading the Textual Tradition of the Acts of Paul and Thecla." In *The Early Christian Book*, edited by William E. Klingshirn and Linda Safran, 177–93. Washington, DC: Catholic University of America Press, 2007.
———. *The Gendered Palimpsest: Women, Writing, and Representation in Early Christianity*. New York: Oxford University Press, 2012.
Halkin, François. "La légende crétoise de saint Tite." *Analecta Bollandial* 79 (1961) 241–56.
Hansen, William, ed. *Anthology of Ancient Greek Popular Literature*. Bloomington: Indiana University Press, 1998.
Hanson, R. P. C. *Origen's Doctrine of Tradition*. London: SPCK, 1954.
———. *Tradition in the Early Church*. Philadelphia: Westminster, 1962.
Harnack, Adolf. "Drei wenig beachtete cyprianische Schriften und die Acta Pauli." TU n.f., 4:3–34. Leipzig: Teubner, 1899.
———. *Geschichte der altchristlichen literatur bis Eusebius*. 2 vols. in 4. Leipzig: Hinrichs, 1893–1904.
Harrill, J. Albert. *The Manumission of Slaves in Early Christianity*. HUT 32. Tübingen: Mohr/Siebeck, 1995.
———. *Paul the Apostle*. Cambridge: Cambridge University Press, 2012.
Harrison, S. J. *Apuleius. A Latin Sophist*. Oxford: Oxford University Press, 2000.
Hayne, Léonie. "Thecla and the Church Fathers." *VC* 48 (1994) 209–18.
Head, Peter. "Acts and the Problem of Its Texts." In *The Book of Acts in Its Ancient Literary Setting*, edited by Bruce W. Winter and Andrew D. Clarke, 1:415–44. Grand Rapids: Eerdmans, 1993.

General Bibliography

Hilhorst, A. "Tertullian on the Acts of Paul." In *The Apocryphal Acts of Paul and Thecla*, edited by Jan N. Bremmer, 150–63. Kampen: Kok Pharos, 1996.

Hills, Julian V. "The *Acts of Paul* and the Legacy of the Lukan Acts." *Semeia* 80 (1997) 145–58.

———. "The Acts of the Apostles in the Acts of Paul." In SBLSP, 24–54. Atlanta: Scholars, 1994.

———. *The Epistle of the Apostles*. Early Christian Apocrypha. Santa Rosa, CA: Polebridge, 2009.

———. *Tradition and Composition in the* Epistula Apostolorum. HTS 57. Cambridge, MA: Harvard University Press, 2008.

Hoek, Annewies van den, and John J. Herrmann. "Thecla the Beast Fighter: A Female Emblem of Deliverance in Early Christian Popular Art." *Studia Philonica Annual* 13 (2001) 212–49.

Holmes, Michael W. *The Apostolic Fathers. Greek Texts and English Translations*. 3rd ed. Grand Rapids: Baker, 2007.

Holzhey, Carl. *Die Thekla-Akten. Ihre Verbreitung und Beurteilung in der Kirche*. München: Lentner, 1905.

Horn, Cornelia B. "Suffering Children, Parental Authority and the Quest for Liberation? A Tale of Three Girls in the *Acts of Paul (and Thecla)*, The *Act(s) of Peter,* The *Acts of Nerseus and Achilleus* and the *Epistle of Pseudo-Titus*." In *A Feminist Companion to the New Testament Apocrypha*, edited by A.-J. Levine, 118–45. Feminist Companion to the New Testament and Early Christian Writings 11. New York: T. & T. Clark, 2006.

Hovhanessian, Vahan. *Third Corinthians: Reclaiming Paul for Christian Orthodoxy*. Studies in Biblical Literature 18. New York: Lang, 2000.

Howe, Margaret E. "Interpretations of Paul in the Acts of Paul and Thecla." In *Pauline Studies*, edited by Donald A. Hagner and Murry J. Harris, 33–49. FS F. F. Bruce. Grand Rapids: Eerdmans, 1980.

Jackson-McCabe, Mattthew. "Women and Eros in Greek Magic and the *Acts of Paul and Thecla*." In *Women and Gender in Ancient Religions: Interdisciplinary Approaches*, edited by Stephen P. Ahearne-Kroll et al., 267–78. Tübingen: Mohr/Siebeck, 2010.

Jacobs, Andrew S. "A Family Affair." *JECS* 7 (1999) 105–38.

———. "'Her Own Proper Kinship': Marriage, Class and Women in the Apocryphal Acts of the Apostles." In *A Feminist Companion to the New Testament Apocrypha*, edited by A.-J. Levine, 18–46. Feminist Companion to the New Testament and Early Christian Writings 11. New York: T. & T. Clark, 2006.

James, Montague Rhodes. *Apocrypha Anecdota*. Vol. 2. TextsS. Cambridge: Cambridge University Press, 1893.

———. *The Apocryphal New Testament*. Oxford: Oxford University Press, 1924.

Jensen, Anne. *Gottes selbstbewusste Töchter: Frauenemanzipation im frühen Christentum?* Freiburg: Herder, 1992.

———. *Thekla—Die Apostolin: Ein apokrypher Text neu entdeckt*. KT 172. Basel: Herder, 1995.

Johnson, Scott F. *The Life and Miracles of Thekla: A Literary Study*. Washington, DC: Center for Hellenic Studies, 2006.

Johnston, Steve, and Paul-Hubert Poirier. "Nouvelles citations chez Éphrem et Aphraate de la correspondance entre Paul et les Corinthiens." *Apocrypha* 16 (2005) 137–45.

Jones, F. Stanley. "Principal orientations on the Relations between the Apocryphal Acts (*Acts of Paul* and *Acts of John; Acts of Peter* and *Acts of John*)." In 1993 SBLSP, 485–505. Atlanta: Scholars, 1993.

Kaestli, Jean-Daniel. "Les principales orientations de la recherche sur les Actes Apocryphes des Apôtres." In *Les Actes apocryphes des Apôtres: christianisme et monde païen*, edited by François Bovon et al., 49–67. Publications de la Faculté de Théologie de l'Université de Genève 4. Geneva: Labor et Fides, 1981.

Kasser, Rodolphe. "Acta Pauli 1959." *RHPR* 40 (1960) 45–57.

Kasser, Rodolphe, and Philippe Luisier. "Le Papyrus Bodmer XLI en Édition Princeps l'Épisode d'Éphèse des *Acta Pauli* en Copte et en Traduction." *Le Muséon* 117 (2004) 281–384.

Kelly, J. N. D. *Early Christian Creeds*. 3rd ed. London: Longmans, 1972.

Kilpatrick, George D., and C. H. Roberts. "The Acta Pauli: A New Fragment." *JTS* 47 (1946) 196–99.

Klauck, Hans-Josef. *Die apokryphe Bibel. Ein anderer Zugang zum frühen Christentum*. Tübingen: Mohr/Siebeck, 2008.

———. *The Apocyphal Acts of the Apostles. An Introduction*. Trans. Brian McNeil. Waco: Baylor University Press, 2008.

Klijn, Albertus F. J. *The Acts of Thomas: Introduction, Text, and Commentary*. 2nd ed. NovTSup 108. Leiden: Brill, 2003.

———. "The Apocryphal Correspondence between Paul and the Corinthians." *VC* 17 (1963) 2–23.

Koester, Helmut. "On Heroes, Tombs, and Early Christianity: An Epilogue." In *Flavius Philostratus: Heroikos*, edited by Jennifer K. B. Maclean and Ellen B Aitken, 257–64. WGRW. Atlanta: SBL, 2001.

Konstan, David. "Acts of Love: A Narrative Pattern in the Apocryphal Acts." *JECS* 6 (1998) 15–36.

Kötzel, Michael. "Thekla und Alexander—oder Kleider machen Leute: Dramatische Ouvertüre des Antiochia-Zyklus." In *Aus Liebe zu Paulus? Die Akte Thekla neu aufgerollt*, edited by Martin Ebner, 91–109. SBS 206. Stuttgart: Katholisches Bibelwerk, 2005.

Kraemer, Ross S. *Unreliable Witnesses. Religion, Gender, and History in the Greco-Roman Mediterranean*. New York: Oxford University Press, 2011.

Kurfess, Alfons. "Zu dem Hamburger Papyrus der ΠΡΑΞΕΙΣ ΠΑΥΛΟΥ." *ZNW* 38 (1939) 164–70.

Lake, Kirsop, and J. de Zwaan. "Acts of the Apostles (Apocryphal)." In *Dictionary of the Apostolic Church*, edited by James Hastings, 1:29–39. Edinburgh: T. & T. Clark, 1919.

Lalleman, Pieter J. "The Canonical and the Apocryphal Acts of the Apostles." In *Groningen Colloquia on the Novel IX*, edited by H. Hofmann and M. Zimmerman, 181–92. Groningen: Forsten, 1998.

———. "The Resurrection in the Acts of Paul." In *The Apocryphal Acts of Paul and Thecla*, edited by Jan N. Bremmer, 126–41. Kampen: Kok Pharos, 1996.

Lampe, G. W. H. *A Patristic Greek Lexicon*. Oxford: Clarendon, 1961.

Lampe, Peter. *From Paul to Valentinus: Christians at Rome in the First Two Centuries*. Edited by Marshall D. Johnson. Translated by Michael Steinhauser. Minneapolis: Fortress, 2003.

Lapham, Fred. *An Introduction to the New Testament Apocrypha*. London: T. & T. Clark, 2003.

General Bibliography

Lattimore, Richmond. *Themes in Greek and Latin Epitaphs*. Urbana: University of Illinois Press, 1962.

Lattke, Michael. *The Odes of Solomon*. Translated by Marianne Ehrhardt. Hermeneia. Minneapolis: Fortress, 2009.

Lau, Markus. "Enthaltsamkeit und Auferstehung: Narrative Auseindersetzungen in der Paulusschule." In *Aus Liebe zu Paulus? Die Akte Thekla neu aufgerollt*, edited by Martin Ebner, 80–90. Stuttgart: Katholisches Bibelwerk, 2005.

Layton, Bentley. *The Gnostic Scriptures: A New Translation with Annotations and Introductions*. ABRL. New York: Doubleday, 1987.

Lehman, F. "Die Entstehung der sakralen bedeutungender Milch." *Zeitschrift für Missionskunde und Religionswisssenschaft* 22 (1917) 1–12; 33–45.

Leinhäupl-Wilke, Andreas. "Vom Einfluss des lebendigen Gottes: Zwei Bekenntnisreden gegen den Strich gelesen." In *Aus Liebe zu Paulus? Die Akte Thekla neu aufgerollt*, edited by Martin Ebner, 139–58. Stuttgart: Katholisches Bibelwerk, 2005.

Lequeux, X. "La circulation des Actes apocryphes des apôtres." *Apocrypha* 18 (2007) 87–108.

Le Saint, William P. *Tertullian: Treatises on Penance*. Westminster, MD: Newman, 1959.

Levine, Amy-Jill, ed., with Maria M. Robbins. *A Feminist Companion to the New Testament Apocrypha*. Feminist Companion to the New Testament and Early Christian Writings 11. New York: T. & T. Clark, 2006.

Lightfoot, Joseph Barber. *The Apostolic Fathers*. 5 vols. in 2 parts. 2nd ed. London: Macmillan, 1889–1890.

Lindemann, Andreas. *Paulus im ältesten Christentum: Das Bild des Apostels und die Rezeption der paulinischen Theologie in der frühchristlichen Literatur bis Marcion*. BHT 58. Tübingen: Mohr/Siebeck, 1979.

Lipsius, Richard A., and Maximilien Bonnet, eds. *Acta Apostolorum Apocrypha*. 2 vols. in 3. Lipsiae: Mendelssohn, 1891–1903 (1990).

Lipsett, B. Diane. *Desiring Conversion: Hermas, Thecla, Aseneth*. New York: Oxford University Press, 2011.

Long, A. A. *Hellenistic Philosophy: Stoics, Epicureans, Sceptics*. 2nd ed. New York: Scribners, 1974.

Luke, T. S. "The Parousia of Paul at Iconium." *Religion and Theology* 15 (2008) 225–51.

Luttikhuizen, Gerard. "The Apocryphal Correspondence with the Corinthians and the Acts of Paul." In *The Apocryphal Acts of Paul and Thecla*, edited by Jan Bremmer, 75–91. Kampen: Kok Pharos, 1996.

Lutz, Cora E. "Musonius Rufus 'The Roman Socrates.'" In *Yale Classical Studies*, 10:3–147. New Haven: Yale University Press, 1947.

MacDonald, Dennis R. "The *Acts of Paul* and the *Acts of Peter*: Which Came First?" *SBLSP* 31 (1992) 214–24.

———. "Apocryphal and Canonical Narratives about Paul." In *Paul and the Legacies of Paul*, edited by William S. Babcock, 55–70. Dallas: Southern Methodist University Press: 1990.

———. "A Conjectural Emendation of 1 Cor 15:31–32: Or the Case of the Misplaced Lion Fight." *HTR* 73 (1980) 265–78.

———. *The Legend and the Apostle*. Philadelphia: Westminster, 1983.

———. *There is No Male and Female. The Fate of a Dominical Saying in pox and Gnosticism*. HDR 20. Philadelphia: Fortress, 1987.

———. "Which Came First? Intertextual Relationships among the Apocryphal Acts of the Apostles." *Semeia* 80 (1997) 11–41.

MacDonald, Dennis R., ed. *The Apocryphal Acts of the Apostles.* Semeia 38 (1986)
MacDonald, Dennis R., and Andrew D. Scrimgeour. "Pseudo-Chrysostom's *Panegyric to Thecla*: The Heroine of the *Acts of Paul* in Homily and Art." *Semeia* 38 (1986) 151-59.
MacDonald, Margaret Y. *Early Christian Women and Pagan Opinion: The Power of the Hysterical Woman.* Cambridge: Cambridge University Press, 1996.
Mackay, Thomas W. "Observations on P. Bodmer X (Apocryphal Correspondence Between Paul and the Corinthians)." In *Papyrologica Bruxellensia* 16-19 (1977) 119-28.
———. "Response [to S. Davies]." *Semeia* 38 (1986) 145-49.
Malherbe, Abraham J. *Paul and the Popular Philosophers.* Minneapolis: Fortress, 1989.
Malina, Bruce J., and Jerome H. Neyrey. *Portraits of Paul: An Archaeology of Ancient Personality.* Louisville: Westminster John Knox, 1996.
Mara, M. G. "I macarismi di Paolo." *Augustinianum* 47 (2007) 87-108.
Marguerat, Daniel. "The *Acts of Paul* and the Canonical Acts: A Phenomenon of Rereading." *Semeia* 80 (1997) 169-83.
———. "Paul après Paul: une histoire de reception." *NTS* 54 (2008) 317-37.
Marguerat, Daniel, and Walter Rebell. "Les *Actes des Paul.* Un portrait inhabituel de l'apôtre." In *Le mystère apocryphe,* edited by Jean-Daniel Kaestli and Daniel Marguerat, 107-24. Essais bibliques 26. Geneva: Labor et Fides, 1995.
Marjanen, Antti, and Petri Luomanen, eds. *A Companion to Second-Century Christian "Heretics."* Leiden: Brill, 2008.
Mathews, Thomas F. *The Clash of Gods. A Reinterpretation of Early Christian Art.* 2nd ed. Princeton: Princeton University Press, 2003.
Matthews, Christopher R. "Articulate Animals: A Multivalent Motif in the Apocryphal Acts of the Apostles." In *The Apocryphal Acts of the Apostles,* edited by François Bovon, Ann G. Brock, and C. R. Matthews, 205-32. Cambridge, MA: Harvard University Press, 1999.
Matthews, Shelly. "Thinking of Thecla: Issues in Feminist Historiography." *JFemStudRel* 17 (2002) 39-55.
McGinn, Sheila E. "The Acts of Thecla." In *Searching the Scriptures,* edited by E. Schüssler Fiorenza, 1:800-828. New York: Crossroad, 1995.
McGowan, Andrew. *Ascetic Eucharists. Food and Drink in Early Christian Ritual Meals.* OECS. Oxford: Oxford University Press, 1999.
McInerney, Maud B. *Eloquent Virgins from Thecla to Joan of Arc.* New York: Palgrave MacMillan, 2003.
Meinardus, Otto F. A. "Cretan Traditions about St Paul's Mission to the Island." *Ostkirchliche Studien* 22 (1973) 172-83.
Merz, Annette. *Die fictive Selbstauslegung des Paulus. Intertextuelle Studien zur Intention und Rezeption der Pastralbriefe.* NTOA 52. Göttingen: Vandenhoeck & Ruprecht, 2004.
———. "Tränken und Nähren mit dem Wort." In *"Eine gewöhnliche und harmlose Speise?" von den Entwicklungen frühchristlicher Abendmahlstraditionen,* edited by Judith Hartenstein, Silke Petersen, and Angela Standhartinger, 269-95. Gütersloh: Gütersloher, 2009.
Metzger, Bruce M. "St. Paul and the Baptized Lion." *Princeton Seminary Bulletin* 39 (1945) 11-21.
Meyer, Marvin W. "Making Mary Male: The Categories 'Male' and 'Female' in the Gospel of Thomas." *NTS* 31 (1985) 554-70.

General Bibliography

Misset-van de Weg, Magda. "Answers to the Plights of an Ascetic Woman Named Thecla." In *A Feminist Companion to the New Testament Apocrypha*, edited by Amy-Jill Levine, 146–62. Feminist Companion to the New Testament and Early Christian Writings 11. New York: T. & T. Clark, 2006.

———. "Magic, Miracle and Miracle Workers in the Acts of Thecla." In *Women and Miracle Stories: A Multidisciplinary Exploration*, edited by Anne-Marie Korte, 29–52. Studies in the History of Religion 88. Leiden: Brill, 2001.

Mitchell, Margaret M. *The Heavenly Trumpet. John Crysostom and the Art of Pauline Interpretation*. HUT 40. Tübingen: Mohr/Siebeck, 2000.

Mitchell, Stephen. *Anatolia*. 2 vols. Oxford: Oxford University Press, 1993.

Modesto, Christine. *Studien zur Cena Cypriani und zu deren Reeption*. Classica Monacensia 3. Tübingen: Narr, 1992.

Moraldi, Luigi. *Apocrifi del Nuovo Testamento*. 2 vols. Classici delle religioni. Torino: Unione tipografico-editrice torinese, 1971.

Moreschini, Claudio, and Enrico Norelli. *Early Christian Greek and Latin Literature: A Literary History*. Trans M. J. O'Connell. 2 vols. Peabody, MA: Hendrickson, 2005.

Morris, J. B, et al., trans. *The Homilies of St. John Chrysostom on the Epistle of St. Paul the Apostle to the Romans*. In *A Select Library of the Nicene and Post-Nicene Fathers*, edited by P. Schaff, series 1, 11:329–564. Reprint, Grand Rapids: Eerdmans, 1979.

Moss, Candida, R. "On the Dating of Polycarp: Rethinking the Place of the Martyrdom of Polycarp in the History of Christianity." *Early Christianity* 1 (2010) 539–74.

———. *The Other Christs: Imitating Jesus in Ancient Christian Ideologies of Martyrdom*. New York: Oxford, 2010.

Murphy-O'Connor, Jerome. *Paul: A Critical Life*. Oxford: Clarendon, 1996.

Musurillo, Herbert, ed. *The Acts of the Christian Martyrs*. Oxford: Clarendon, 1972.

———. *Acts of the Pagan Martyrs*. Oxford: Oxford University Press, 1954.

Nagel, Peter. "Die apokryphen Apostelakten des 2. und 3. Jahrhunderts in der manichäischen Literatur." In *Gnosis und Neues Testament*, edited by Karl-Wolfgang Tröger, 149–82. Gütersloh: Mohn, 1973.

Nauerth, Claudia, and Rudiger Warns. *Thekla, Ihre Bilder in der fruchristliche Kunst*. Göttinger Orientforschungen II. Studien zur spätantiken und frühchristlichen Kunst 3. Wiesbaden: Otto Harrassowitz, 1981.

Nautin, Pierre. *Origène. Sa vie et son oeuvre*. Christianisme antique 1. Paris: Beauchesne, 1977.

Ng, Esther Y. "Acts of Paul and Thecla. Women's Stories and Precedent." *JTS* 55 (2004) 1–29.

Niederwimmer, Kurt. *The Didache*. Translated by Linda M. Maloney. Hermeneia. Minneapolis: Fortress, 1998.

Nippel, Wilfred. *Public Order in Ancient Rome*. Cambridge: Cambridge University Press, 1995.

Nock, Arthur Darby. *Sallustius, Concerning the Gods and the Universe*. Cambridge: Cambridge University Press, 1926.

Norden, Eduard. *Agnostos Theos. Untersuchungen zur Formengeschichte religiöser Rede*. Leipzig: Teubner, 1913.

Omerzu, H. "The Portrait of Paul's Outer Appearance in the *Acts of Paul and Thecla*: Re-considering the Correspondence between Body and Personality in Ancient Literature." *Religion and Theology* 15 (2008) 252–79.

Osiek, Carolyn, and David L. Balch. *Families in the New Testament World: Households and House Churches*. Philadelphia: Westminster John Knox, 1997.

Parsons, Mikeal C., and Richard I. Pervo. *Rethinking the Unity of Luke and Acts.* Minneapolis: Fortress, 1993.
Parvis, Paul. "*2 Clement* and the Meaning of the Christian Homily." In *The Writings of the Apostolic Fathers*, edited by Paul Foster, 32–41. London: T. & T. Clark, 2007.
Parvis, Sara. "The *Martyrdom of Polycarp*." In *The Writings of the Apostolic Fathers*, edited by Paul Foster, 126–46. London: T. & T. Clark, 2007.
Patlagean, E. "L'histoire de la femme désguisée en moine et l'évolution de la sainteté à Byzance." *Studie Medievalis* 3, no. 17 (1976) 597–623
Patterson, Stephen J. *The Gospel of Thomas and Jesus*. Sonoma, CA: Polebridge, 1993.
Pecere, Oronzo, and Antonio Stramaglia, eds. *La letteratura di consumo nel mondo greco-latino*. Cassino: Università degli studi di Cassino, 1996.
Penny, Donald N. "The Pseudo-Pauline Letters of the First Two Centuries." PhD diss., Emory University, 1979.
Perkins, Judith. *The Suffering Self: Pain and Narrative Representation in Early Christianity*. New York: Routledge, 1995.
Perry, B. E., ed. *Babrius and Phaedrus*. LCL. Cambridge, MA: Harvard University Press, 1965.
Pervo, Richard I. *Acts: A Commentary*. Edited by Harold W. Attridge. Hermeneia. Minneapolis: Fortress, 2009.
———. "The 'Acts of Titus': A Preliminary Translation with an Introduction, Notes, and Appendices." In *SBLSP* 35:455–82. Atlanta: Scholars, 1996.
———. "The Ancient Novel becomes Christian." In *The Novel in the Ancient World*, edited by Gareth Schmeling, 685–711. Rev. ed. Leiden: Brill, 2003.
———. *Dating Acts: Between the Evangelists and the Apologists*. Santa Rosa, CA: Polebridge, 2006.
———. "Early Christian Fiction." In *Greek Fiction: The Greek Novel in Context*, edited by J. R. Morgan and R. Stoneman, 239–54. London. Routledge, 1994.
———. "God and Planning: Footprints of Providence in Acts and in the *Acts of Paul*." In *Method and Meaning: Festschrift for Harold Attridge*, edited by Andrew McGowan, 259–77. Atlanta: SBL, 2011.
———. "A Hard Act to Follow: The *Acts of Paul* and the Canonical Acts," *Journal of Higher Criticism* 2, no. 2 (1995) 3–32.
———. "The Hospitality of Onesiphorus: Missionary Styles and Support in the Acts of Paul." In *The Rise and Expansion of Christianity in the First Three Centuries of the Common Era*, edited by Clare K. Rothschild and Jens Schroter, 341–51. Tübingen: Mohr/Siebeck, 2013.
———. "Johannine Trajectories in the *Acts of John*." *Apocrypha* 3 (1992) 47–68.
———. *The Making of Paul: Constructions of the Apostle in Early Christianity*. Fortress, 2010.
———. "Meet Right—and Our Bounden Duty." *Forum* N.S. 4, no. 1, (2000) 45–62.
———. "(Not) Appealing to the Emperor: Acts (and The *Acts of Paul*)." In *Paul and the Heritage of Israel: Paul's Claim upon Isarael's Legacy in Luke and Acts in Light of the Pauline Letters*, edited by D. Moessner et al., 165–79. London: T. & T. Clark, 2012.
———. *Profit with Delight: The Literary Genre of the Acts of the Apostles*. Philadelphia: Fortress, 1987.
———. "Shepherd of the Lamb: Paul as a Christ-Figure in the *Acts of Paul*." In *Portraits of Jesus: Studies in Christology*, edited by Susan E. Myers, 355–69. WUNT 321. Tübingen: Mohr/Siebeck, 2012.

General Bibliography

———. "The *Testament of Joseph* and Greek Romance." *Studies on the Testament of Joseph*, edited by G. Nickelsburg Jr., 15–28. Missoula, MT: Scholars, 1975.
Pesthy, Monika. "Thecla among the Fathers of the Church." In *The Apocryphal Acts of Paul and Thecla*, edited by Jan N. Bremmer, 164–78. Kampen: Kok Pharos, 1996.
Peterson, Erik. "Einige Bermerkungen zum Hamburger Papyrus-Fragment der Acta, Pauli." In *Frühkirche, Judentum und Gnosis*, 183–208. Freiburg: Herder.
Pherigo, Lindsey P. "Paul's Life after the Close of Acts." *JBL* 70 (1951) 277–84.
Pick, Bernhard. *Apocryphal Acts of Paul, Peter, John, Andrew and Thomas*. Chicago: Open Court, 1909.
Piñero, Antonio, and Gonzalo del Cerro, eds. *Hechos Apócrifos de Los Apóstoles*. 2 vols. Madrid: Biblioteca de Autores Cristianos, 2004–2005.
Potter, David. "Martyrdom as Spectacle." In *Theater and Society in the Classical World*, edited by R. Scodel, 53–88. Ann Arbor: University of Michigan Press, 1993.
Poupon, Gérard. "L'accusation de magie dans les Actes Apocryphes." In *Les Actes apocryphes des Apôtres: christianisme et monde païen*, edited by François Bovon et al., 71–93. Publications de la Faculté de Théologie de l'Université de Genève 4. Geneva: Labor et Fides, 1981.
———. "Les Actes de Pierre et leur remaniement." *ANRW* 2.25.6 (1988) 4363–83.
———. "Encore une fois: Tertullien, De baptismo 17,5." In *Nomen Latinum: Mélanges de langue, de littérature et de civilisation latines offerts au professeur André Schneider à l'occasion de son départ à la retraite; textes recueillis et ed. par Denis Knoepfer; en collab. avec Michel Boillat, Marianne Gendre Loutsch et Catherine Jacobi*, 199–205. Neuchâtel: Faculté de lettres, 1997.
Price, Robert M. *The Widow Traditions in Luke-Acts: A Feminist-Critical Scrutiny*. SBLDS 155. Atlanta: Scholars, 1997.
Price, Simon R. F. *Rituals and Power: The Roman Imperial Cult in Asia Minor*. Cambridge: Cambridge University Press, 1984.
Radermacher, Ludwig. *Hippolytus und Thekla. Studien zur Geschichte von Legende und Kultus*. Vienna. Hölder, 1916.
Ramsay, William M. *The Church in the Roman Empire*. London: Hodder and Stoughton, 1897.
Reardon, Bryan P., ed. *Collected Ancient Greek Novels*. Berkeley: University of California Press, 1989.
Reitzenstein, Richard. *Hellenistische Wundererzählungen*. Leipzig: Teubner, 1906.
Rensberger, David K. "As the Apostle Teaches: The Development of the Use of Paul's Letters in Second-Century Christianity." PhD diss., Yale University, 1981.
Riemer, Ulrike. "Miracle Stories and Their Narrative Intent in the Context of the Ruler Cult of Classical Antiquity." In *Wonders Never Cease: The Purpose of Narrating Miracle Stories in the New Testament and Its Religious Environment*, edited by Michael Labahn and Bertjan L. Peerbolte, 32–47. Library of New Testament Studies 288. London: T. & T. Clark.
Rigsby, Kent J. "Missing Places." *Classical Philology* 91 (1996) 254–60.
Rist, Martin. "III Corinthians as a Pseudepigraphic Refutation of Marcionism." *Iliff Review* 26 (1969) 49–58.
———. "Pseudepigraphic Refutations of Marcionism." *JR* 22 (1942) 36–62.
Rohde, Joachim. "Pastoralbriefe und Acta Pauli." *Studia Evangelica V* (TU 103/2), 303–10. Berlin: Topelman, 1968.
Rordorf, Willy. "Actes de Paul." In *Écrits apocryphes chrétiens*, edited by F. Bovon and P. Geoltrain, 1:1115–77. Paris: Gallimard, 1997.

---. "Les Actes de Paul sur papyrus: problèmes aux PMich. Inv. 1317 et 3788." In *Proceedings of the XVIII International Congress of Papyrology: Athens*, edited by Basileios G. Mandēlaras, 1:453-61. Athens: 1988.

---. "Hérésie et Orthodoxie selon la Correspondance apocryphe entre les Corinthiens et l'apôtre Paul." In *Lex Orandi, Lex Credendi: Gesammelte Aufsätze zum 60. Geburtstag*, 380-431. Paradosis 36. Freiburg: Universtitätsverlag Freiburg, 1993.

---. "In welchem Verhältnis stehen die apokryphen Paulus akten zur kanonischen Apostelgeschichte und zu den Pastoralbriefen?" In *Text and Testimony. Essays on New Testament and Apocryphal Literature in Honour of A. F. J. Klijn*, edited by T. Baarda et al., 225-41. Kampen: Kok, 1988.

---. *Lex Orandi, Lex Credendi: Gesammelte Aufsätze zum 60. Geburtstag*. Paradosis 36. Freiburg: Universtitätsverlag Freiburg, 1993.

---. "Die neronische Christenverfolgung im Spiegel der Apokryphen Paulusakten." *NTS* 28 (1981-1982) 365-74. Reprinted in *Lex Orandi, Lex Credendi: Gesammelte Aufsätze zum 60. Geburtstag*, 368-77. Paradosis 36. Freiburg: Universtitätsverlag Freiburg, 1993.

---. "Nochmals: Paulusakten und Pastoralbriefe." In *Tradition and Interpretation in the New Testament*, edited by G. F. Hawthorne and O. Betz, 319-327. FS E. E. Ellis. Grand Rapids: Eerdmans, 1987.

---. "Paul's Conversion in the Canonical Acts and in the *Acts of Paul*." *Semeia* 80 (1997) 137-44.

---. "Quelques jalons pour une interprétation symbolique des Actes de Paul." *Early Christian Voices: In Texts, Traditions, and Symbols*. FS F. Bovon. BIS 66. Leiden: Brill, 2003, 251-65.

---. "The Relation between the *Acts of Peter* and the *Acts of Paul*: State of the Question." In *The Apocryphal Acts of Peter: Magic, Miracles and Gnosticism*, edited by Jan N. Bremmer, 178-91. Leuven: Peeters, 1998.

---. "Tertullien et les *Actes de Paul*." In *Lex Orandi, Lex Credendi: Gesammelte Aufsätze zum 60. Geburtstag*, 475-84. Paradosis 36. Freiburg: Universtitätsverlag Freiburg, 1993.

---. "Was wissen wir über Plan und Absicht der Paulusakten?" In *Oecumenica et Patristica: Festschrift für Wilhelm Schneemelcher zum 75. Geburtstag*, edited by Damaskinos Papandreou, Wolfgang Bienert, and A. Schäferdiek, 485-96. Stuttgart: Kohlhammer, 1989, 71-82.

Sanchez, Hector. "Paulus nachfolgen—aber wie? Die Bedeutung des 'Hauses' in den Theklakten." In *Aus Liebe zu Paulus? Die Akte Thekla neu aufgerollt*, edited by Martin Ebner, 124-38. SBS 206. Stuttgart: Katholisches Bibelwerk, 2005.

Sanders, H. A. "A Fragment of the Acta Pauli in the Michigan Collection." *HTR* 31 (1939) 73-90.

---. "Three Theological Fragments." *HTR* 36 (1943) 165-67.

Schäfer, Dorothea. "Frauen in der Arena." In *Fünfzig Jahre Forschungen zur Antiken Sklaverei an der Mainzer Akademie, 1950-2000*, edited by Heinz Bellen and Heinz Heinen, 243-68. Stuttgart: Steiner, 2001.

Schäferdiek, Knut. "The Manichean Collection of Apocryphal Acts ascribed to Leucius Charinus." In *New Testament Apocrypha*, edited by Wilhelm Schneemelcher, translated by R. McL. Wilson, 2:87-100. Louisville: Westminster John Knox, 1991-1992.

General Bibliography

Scherer, Hildegard. "Haus-Frauen-Geschichten: Die beiden Mutterfiguren in den Theklaakten." In *Aus Liebe zu Paulus? Die Akte Thekla neu aufgerollt*, edited by Martin Ebner, 110–123. SBS 206. Stuttgart: Katholisches Bibelwerk, 2005.

Schmidt, Carl. *Acta Pauli: Aus der heidelberger koptischen Papyrushandschrift nr. 1*. 2 vols. Leipzig: Hinrichs, 1905. Reprint, Hildesheim: Olms, 1965.

———. "Ein Berliner Fragment der alten ΠΡΑΞΕΙΣ ΠΑΥΛΟΥ." *Sitzungsberichte der bayerischen Akadamie der Wissenschaften* (1931) 37–40.

Schmidt, Carl, with Wilhelm Schubart. *PRAXEIS PAULOU: Acta Pauli*. Glückstadt: Augustin, 1936.

Schneemelcher, Wilhelm. "The Acts of Paul." In *New Testament Apocrypha*, edited by Wilhelm Schneemelcher, translated by R. McL. Wilson, 2:213–270. Louisville, Westminster John Knox, 1991–1992.

———. "Die Apostelgeschichte des Lukas und die Acta Pauli." In *Apophoreta: Festschrift für Earnst Haenchen*, edited by W. Elster and F. H. Kettler, 236–50. BZNW 30. Berlin: Topelmann, 1964.

———. *Gesammelte Aufsätze zum Neuen Testament und zur Patristik*. Analecta Vlatadon 22. Thessaloniki: Patriarchal Institute for Patristic Studies, 1974.

———. "Der Getaufte Löwe." *Gesammelte Aufsätze zum Neuen Testament und zur Patristik*, 223–29. Analecta Vlatadon 22. Thessaloniki: Patriarchal Institute for Patristic Studies, 1974.

———. "Paulus in der griechischen Kirche des zweiten Jahrhunderts." *Zeitschrift für Kirchengeschichte* 75 (1964) 1–20.

Schneemelcher, Wilhelm, ed. *New Testament Apocrypha*. Translated by R. McL. Wilson. 2 vols. Louisville: Westminster John Knox, 1991–1992.

Schneider, H. "Thekla und die Robben." *VC* 55 (2001) 45–57.

Schwartz, Daniel R. "The End of the Line: Paul in the Canonical Book of Acts." In *Paul and the Legacies of Paul*, edited by William S. Babcock, 3–24. Dallas: Southern Methodist University Press, 1990.

Setzer, Claudia. *Resurrection of the Body in Early Judaism and Early Christianity*. Boston: Brill, 2004.

Smallwood, E. Mary. *The Jews under Roman Rule*. SJLA 20. Leiden: Brill, 1981.

Snyder, Glenn E. "Remembering the *Acts of Paul*." PhD diss., Harvard University, 2010. (See now *Acts of Paul: The Formation of a Pauline Corpus*. WUNT 352. Tübingen: Mohr Siebeck, 2013.)

Söder, Rosa. *Die apokryphen Apostelgeschichten und die romanhafte Literatur der Antike*. Würzburger Studien zür Altertumswissenschaft 3. Stuttgart: Kohlhammer, 1932.

Souter, Alexander. *The Earliest Latin Commentaries on the Epistles of St. Paul. A Study*. Oxford: Clarendon, 1927.

Spicq, Ceslas. *Theological Lexicon of the New Testament*. Translated and edited by J. D. Ernest. 3 vols. Peabody, MA: Hendrickson, 1994.

Spittler, Janet, E. *Animals in the Apocryphal Acts of the Apostles*. WUNT 247. Tübingen, Mohr/Siebeck, 2008.

Stephens, Susan A., edited by *Yale Papyri in the Beinecke Rare Book and Manuscript Library II*. Chico, CA: Scholars 1985.

Stoops, Robert F., Jr. "The *Acts of Peter* in Intertextual Context."*Semeia* 80 (1997) 57–86.

Stoops, Robert F., Jr., ed. "The Apocryphal Acts of the Apostles in Intertextual Perspective." Special issue, *Semeia* 80 (1997).

Streete, Gail P. Corrington. "Authority and Authorship: The Acts of Paul and Thecla a Disputed Pauline Text." *LTQ* 40 (2005) 265–76.
———. "Buying the Stairway to Heaven: Perpetua and Thecla as Early Christian Heroines." In *A Feminist Companion to the New Testament Apocrypha*, edited by A.-J. Levine, 186–206. Feminist Companion to the New Testament and Early Christian Writings 11. New York: T. & T. Clark, 2006.
Szepessy, T. "Les Actes d'Apotres Apocryphes et le Roman Antique." *Acta Ant. Hung* 36 (1995) 133–61.
Tajra, Harry W. *The Martyrdom of St. Paul*. WUNT 67. Tübingen: Mohr/Siebeck, 1994.
Talbot, Alice-Mary, and Scott F. Johnson. *Miracle Tales from Byzantium*. Cambridge, MA: Harvard University Press, 2012.
Taylor, Joseph. "St Paul and the Roman Empire: Acts of the Apostles 13–14." *ANRW* 2.26.2 (1995) 1190–1231.
Testuz, Michel. *Papyrus Bodmer X-XII*. Cologny-Geneve: Bibliotheque Bodmer, 1959.
———. "La correspondance apocryphe de Saint Paul et des Corinthiens." *Litterature et Theologie Paulinienes*, 217–23. Paris: de Brouwer, 1960.
Theissen, Gerd. *The Miracle Stories of the Early Christian Tradition*. Translated by Francis McDonagh. Philadelphia: Fortress, 1983.
Thurston, Bonnie Bowman. *The Widows: A Women's Ministry in the Early Church*. Minneapolis: Fortress, 1989.
Toohey, Peter. "Love, Lovesickness, and Melancholia." *Illinois Classical Studies* 17 (1992) 265–86.
Toynbee, Jocelyn M. C. *Death and Burial in the Roman World*. Ithaca, NY: Cornell University Press, 1971.
Trall, A. "Knocking on Knemon's Door." *TAPA* 131 (2001) 87–108.
Trebilco, Paul. *The Early Christians in Ephesus from Paul to Ignatius*. WUNT 166. Tübingen: Mohr/Siebeck, 2004.
Valantasis, Richard. "The Question of Early Christian Identity: Three Strategies Exploring a Third *Genos*." In *A Feminist Companion to the New Testament Apocrypha*, edited by A.-J. Levine, 60–76. Feminist Companion to the New Testament and Early Christian Writings 11. New York: T. & T. Clark, 2006.
van den Hoek, Annewies, and John J. Herrmann, Jr. "Thecla the Beast Fighter: A Female Emblem of Deliverance in early Christian Popular Art." *Studia Philonica Annual* 13 (2001) 212–49.
Vermaseren, Maarten J. *Cybele and Attis. The Myth and the Cult*. Trans. A. Leemers. London: Thames and Hudson, 1977.
Vetter, Paul. *Der apocryphe dritte Korintherbrief*. Vienna: Mechitharisten, 1894.
Vielhauer, Philipp. "Apokryphe Apostelgeschichten." In idem, *Geschichte der urchristlichen Literatur*. Berlin: de Gruyter, 1975.
Vogt, A., ed. "Panégyrique de St. Pierre; Panégyrique de St. Paul. Deux discours inédits de Nicétas de Paphlagonie, disiple de Photius." *Orientalia Christiana* 23 (1931) 5–97.
Vorster, Johannes N. "Construction of Culture through the Construction of Person: The Construction of Thecla in the *Acts of Thecla*." In *A Feminist Companion to the New Testament Apocrypha*, edited by A.-J. Levine, 98–117. Feminist Companion to the New Testament and Early Christian Writings 11. New York: T. & T. Clark, 2006.
Vouaux, Léon. *Les Actes de Paul et ses letters apocryphes*. ANT, Paris: Letouzey, 1913.

General Bibliography

Weaver, John B. *Plots of Epiphany: Prison Escape in Acts of the Apostles.* BZNW 131. Berlin: de Gruyter, 2004.

White, B. L. "Reclaiming Paul? Reconfiguration as Reclamation in *3 Corinthians*." *JECS* 17 (2009) 497–523.

White, John L. *The Form and Structure of The Official Petition.* SBLDS 5. Missoula, MT: Scholars, 1972.

Wiles, Maurice F. *The Divine Apostle: The Interpretation of St. Paul's Epistles in the Early Church.* Cambridge: Cambridge University Press, 1967.

Wilkinson, John. *Egeria's Travels.* 3rd ed. Oxford: Aris & Phillips, 1999.

Warren, David H., Ann Graham Brock, and David H. Pao, eds. *Early Christian Voices in Texts, Traditions, and Symbols: Essays in Honor of François Bovon.* Biblical Interpretation Series 66. Boston: Brill Academic, 2003.

Wehn, Beate. "'Blessed Are the Bodies of Those Who Are Virgins': Reflections on the Image of Paul in the Acts of Thecla." Translated by Brian McNeil. *JSNT* 79 (2000) 149–64.

Williams, Michael A. *Rethinking "Gnosticism": An Argument for Dismantling a Dubious Category.* Princeton: Princeton University Press, 1996.

Wills, Lawrence M. *The Jewish Novel in the Ancient World.* Ithaca, NY: Cornell University Press, 1995.

Wright, Ruth Ohm. "Rendez-vous with Thekla and Paul in Ephesos: Excavating the Evidence." In *Distant Voices Drawing Near: Essays in Honor of Antoinette Clark Wire*, edited by Holly E. Hearon, 227–42. Collegeville, MN: Liturgical, 2004.

Wright, William. *Apocryphal Acts of the Apostles: Edited from Syriac Manuscripts in the British Museum and Other Libraries.* 2 vols. London: Williams and Norgate, 1871.

Yarbro Collins, Adela. *Crisis and Catharsis: The Power of the Apocalypse.* Philadelphia: Westminster, 1984.

Zahn, Theodor. *Geschichte des neutestamentlichen Kanons.* 2 vols. in 4 parts. Erlangen: Deichert, 1888–1891.

Zanker, Paul. *The Mask of Socrates: The Image of the Intellectual in Antiquity.* Trans. A. Shapiro. Berkeley: University of California Press, 1995.

Index of Ancient Sources

1 Clement

	260, 264
5	286
9.3	159
24–25	272
24–26	269
27.2	189
30.1	229
37	312
38.2	103
45.7	285
49.1	272

1 Corinthians

	102, 260, 263
1:13–17	223
1:16, 263	287
1:22	205
3:2	243
3:3	324
3:6	241
3:13	316
3:16–17	103, 269
3:22	260
4:9	202
4:12	211
6:3	104
6:19	103, 269
7:1	254
7:2–5	72
7:12–16	186
7:29	45, 103
7:31	104, 106
7:33–34	143
8–10	200
8:1—10:21	199
8:4	113
9:7	312
10:7	118
11:2–16	144
11:30	200
12:2	230
13:1	217
13:2	299
14:26–28	217, 284
14:34–35	284
15	269–70
15:3	221, 267
15:24	229
15:32	44, 55, 57, 213, 231
15:33	175
15:44	261
15:50	261
16:1–4	287
16:15	287
16:19	221, 287

1 Enoch

9.4	316
38.4	97

1 Kings

17:17–24	270

353

Index of Ancient Sources

1 Peter
	47
1:10–12	272
1:14	81
2:2	321
3:1–6	186

1 Thessalonians
1:8	90
2:2	275
2:9	109, 211, 242
5:17	236

1 Timothy
	42
1:3	333
1:13	81
1:15	272
1:17	316
1:18–19	312
1:20	327
2:2	113
2:7	287
4:3	117
4:10	211
4:12	124
5:22	181
6:12	312
6:17–19	126

1Q
	33, 312

1QM
	312

1QS
3.18—4.26	227
8:5–9	103

2 Baruch
51:3	97
73:6	220

1 Samuel
24–25	285

2 Clement
	70, 73, 75
2.9	272
4.3	103
6.5	103
6.9	104
7.6	104
8.4	103
8.6	104
9	268
9.3	103
9.4	272
14.3	103
15.1	103
16.2	103
17.1	124

2 Corinthians
	48, 90, 93
1:8–11	213
1:8–9	231
2:4	262
2:13	334
2:14	248
6:5	213
6:7	301
6:12	106
7:2	106
7:5	288
7:6	334
10–13	108
10:1–6	312
10:10	93
11:23	213
11:24–28	48

2 Kings
4:18–37	311
5	233
9:30	126
13:21	270

2 Enoch
50.1–4	86

2 Peter

	47
1:20	301

2 Samuel

6:16	108

2 Maccabees

6:18	97
8:13	144

2 Thessalonians

	42, 102
1:7	177
2:8	264

2 Timothy

	42, 49
1:5	208
1:11	287
1:15	49, 89
1:16	90
2:3	303, 316
2:3–7	312
2:15	309
2:17–18	49, 90
2:18	117, 264
3:5	269
3:11	48
3:16	331
4:1	323
4:8	89
4:9	264, 305
4:10	305, 314
4:11	305, 306
4:13	139
4:14	49, 90, 96, 327
4:18	124
4:19	48, 90
4:20	334

3 Maccabees

5:1–12	170

4 Maccabees

16:21	285

4Q	285, 312
4Q	471, 312
4Q	491–97, 312

5 Ezra

2:8	203

11Q	
14	312

Acts

1:1–11	284
1:3	288
1:5	325
1:15	332
1:22	271
1:23	316
2	309
2:3	217, 268
2:4	222
2:10	210
2:11	96, 332
2:29	287
2:30	300
2:38	237
3–5	332
3:6	188
2:41	332
4:4	332
4:8	222
4:8–12	175
4:9	123
4:12	229, 242
4:13	127
4:23–31	228
4:29	127, 201
4:31	127
4:36	84

Index of Ancient Sources

Acts (*cont.*)

5	200
5:1–11	190
5:5	176
5:10	176
5:15	137
6:8	94
6:9	210
6:15	94, 284
7	332
7:2	298
7:9	285
7:52	301
7:55	136, 222
7:58	63
7:59	324
8	185
8:1	63, 211
8:18	116
8:20	188
8:21	300
8:26–40	220
8:39	221
9	1, 52, 79, 81, 192, 193, 195, 217, 218, 332
9:5	82
9:6	81
9:11	80, 218
9:12	195
9–15	56
9:1–2	63
9:17	195
9:19	111
9:27	84
9:30	66, 219
10:3	85
10:17–18	192
10:30	85
10:38	285
11	309
11:19—14:23	85
11:20	210
11:25–26	84, 210
11:26	210
11:27–30	50
11:24	222
12	233, 238
12:1	332
12:1–3	211
12:1–10	237
12:5	288
12:7	296
12:23	176
13	55
13:1	210
13:5	181
13:8	132
13:9	222
13:50	86, 129, 136, 151
13–14	66
14	223, 229
14:1	309
14:1–6	95, 201
14:6	86
14:15	123
14:18–20	85, 86
14:25	197
15	205, 207
15:10	210–11
15:21	210
15:29	260
15:39	147
16	197, 201, 233, 240, 262
16:11–12	255
16:11–40	275
16:17	175, 177
16:19–21	121
16:25	236
16:25–39	200
16:33	237
16:35–36	203
16:38–40	245
17	53, 223, 229
17:6–9	121
17:22	45
17:22–31	268
17:25	124
17:30	81

Index of Ancient Sources

Acts (*cont.*)
17:31	316, 323
18:9–10	192
18:11	178
18:12–13	121
18:12–18	245
18:18	97, 144
18:22–23	205
18:25	332
19	56, 66, 90, 213–14, 223, 225, 228, 231
19:1	205, 286
19:8	333
19:10	223
19:13	229
19:21	250, 286
19:22	334
19:23–40	230–31
19:26	223
20–21	281, 325
	20, 283
20:1	231, 245, 248
20:3	333, 282
20:7–12	190, 278, 281, 309–11
21:10–14	287
20:11	282
20:11–12	279
20:17—21:14	281, 282
20:19	281
20:22	286
20:23	281
20:24	281
20:28	282
20:29	286
20:31	211
20:35	211
20:37–38	281
21	50
21:4	9–11, 282
21:5–6	296
21:8	97
21:11	282
21:13–14	281
21:36	131, 247
22	51, 217
22:2–3	247
22:3	128
22:7	185
22:9	217
22:10	81
22:32	131
23:11	192
23:33—26:32	213
24	122
24:8	122
24:10	94, 284
24:21	123
24:25	101
25:12	132
25:12—26:32	154
26	51, 217
26:1	94, 222, 284
26:7	242
26:16	97
27	292, 297
27–28	54, 65
27:1—28:6	175
27:4	186
27:5–6	182
27:23–24	192
27:40	300
28	66, 213
28:14	297
28:15	314
28:16	305, 314 (*bis*)
28:16–31	90
28:30	309
28:30–31	286
28:31	127, 304, 309

Acts of Andrew
	ix, 51, 185

Gregory, Epitome
11	94
16	97
19	181

357

Index of Ancient Sources

Gregory, Epitome (*cont.*)
28	181
46	181

Acts of Andrew and Matthias among the Cannibals
	200

Acts of Barnabas
	14, 202

Acts of Carpus et al.
4.5	154
6.4	137

Acts of John
	47, 51, 57, 234
18	255
37.4	96
39	243
44	230
45	324
58–59	281
59	199
63	288
73.1	97, 234
88–102	292
88–89	242

Acts of Mariana and James
	9.2, 97

Acts of the Martyrs of Lyons
	133
41	137
164	42

Acts of Perpetua et al.
3	131
3.7	128
4	158
5	131, 237

6	131
7	158
9.1	137
10	158
11	158
14	158
17	200
19	164
20.2	135
21.1	164, 165

Acts of Peter
	51, 260, 290–92, 296, 304, 314
1–3	281
2	284
3	255
5	234, 239, 291
5.19	96
6	284, 291, 297
6.13	97
11–12	218
13	291
15	218
20	292
24	272
27–28	278
31–32	278
34	224
35	290, 291

Acts of Peter and Andrew
	96

Acts of Philip
	41
4.6	142
12	218

Acts of Polyxena and Zanthippe
	54
7	238

Index of Ancient Sources

Acts of Thomas

	41, 48, 51, 80, 234
9	128
11	134
13	128
37	234, 235
49	239
65–68	281
88	234–37, 241
114	142
117	234
118–22	234, 235, 238
121	239
122	241
140	229
152	149
163	149

Acts of Titus

	54, 90, 304, 331–34
3	202, 205–7
4	151, 305
6	305

Aelian

Varia Historia

13.46	248

The Nature of Animals

7.48	247

Aeschylus

Frg. 134a	134

Apocalypse of Paul (Coptic)

	86

Apocalypse of Paul (Latin)

	39, 203

Apocalypse of Peter

	47

Apostolic Constitutions

6.8	255
6.16	255

Apostolic Tradition

	324
17.1	145
21	175
21.1	240
21.13–17	257
21.14–18	221
21.33	220
29c	194
30a	194

Apuleius

Florida

	19, 278

Metamorphoses

4.25—5.27	279
10	133
10.29	157

Aristides

Apology

1.3	229
5.4	229

Aristotle

Nicomachean Ethics

9.4	319

Aseneth

6.1	109
9.1—10.2	111
10	242
13.12	162
21.21	184
27.10	162

359

Index of Ancient Sources

Augustine

Contra Faustum
30–31 — 51

De Sancta Virginitate
45 — 51

Tractate on John
80.3 — 164

Aulus Gellius

Attic Nights
5.14 — 247

Barnabas
— 47, 48
1.7 — 103
2.24 — 103
11 — 103
19.5 — 103
20.2 — 103

Callirhoe
1.1.2 — 107
1.1.3 — 91
2.2.2 — 136

Calpurnius Siculus

Eclogues
7.64–66 — 164

Celsus

On Medicine
2.6 — 278

True Doctrine
— 321

Cena Cypriani
— 51, 52, 59
20.12b — 188
26.16 — 188

John Chrysostom

Against the Opponents of Monastic Life
1.3 — 50

Homilies on Acts
— 50
46 — 50

Homily on 2 Timothy
10 — 50

Cicero

Verrines
2.5.112 — 128

Clement of Alexandria

Excerpta ex Theodoto
78.2 — 242

Paed.
1.6.25–27 — 324

Strom.
2.11 — 68

Colossians
— 42, 48, 73, 213
1:16 — 229
1:22 — 300
1:26 — 210
1:27–28 — 124
2:10 — 229
2:15 — 229
3:5 — 114
4:10–14 — 89
4:14 — 306
4:15 — 264

Commodian

Carmen apologeticum
624–30 — 46, 218, 249

Index of Ancient Sources

Cyril of Jerusalem
Catechetical Lectures
19.9	220

Daniel
	3, 285

Deuteronomy
10:9	300
12:12	300
14:27	29, 300

Didache
	47
1–6	227
6.2	73
7.1	220
7.2	220
9.4	286

Didascalia
	46
19	97

Dio of Prusa ("Chrysostom")
Or.
13.9	122

Diognetus
2.2	230
2.8	242
3.5	242
4.1	229
5.1	229
6.1–3	229
9.1	230
10.2	229

Ecclesiastes
8:15	118

An Ephesian Tale
1.1	91
1.2.5–7	108
2.4.3	229
2.5.6	149
2.7.5	128, 131
3.11	153
4.2.7–10	135
5.1.7	142
5.14.1–2	184

Ephesians
	42, 48, 213
1:5	268
1:6	96
1:21	229
2:20–21	103
3:5	210
3:10	229
4:18	81
5:26	243
6:11	264
6:12	229

An Ethiopian Story
7.25.2	149
8.5.10—6.2	149

Epictetus
Diss. 3.24.9	324

Epiphanius
	314

Panarion
30.16	71
30.13	240

Epistula Apostolorum
3	299
32	81

Index of Ancient Sources

Esther
5:2 (Greek)   97

Euripides
Alcestis
788   118
Bacchae
439   97
Hecuba
612   132

Eusebius of Caesarea,
Ecclesiastical History
1.12   316
2.22   306
2.25.5   48
3.3–4   47
3.25   47
3.39   316
4.8–9   317
5.1.35   97

Exodus
9:13–35   202
12:11   44
19:16   165
20:5   123
21:33   298

Ezekiel
7:16   222
37   222
37:1–9   219

Galatians
    48, 80, 81, 210, 270
1   81, 218
1–2   207, 211, 218
1:4   298
1:11–12   218
1:13   210
1:14   210
1:16   218
1:17   65, 267
1:18   207
1:21   66, 210
1:23   210
2   207, 211
2:1   207
2:2   210
2:8   181
2:11–14   211
2:18–20   218
2:19–20   291
3:26–28   180
3:28   142
4:4   124
4:5   268
4:6   124
5:1   210
5:20–21   229
6:6   178
6:17   271, 272

Genesis
    149
1–2   86
3   218, 269
19   200
20:1–18   148
40   314

Gospel of Bartholomew
2.13   316

Gospel of Philip
2   272
21   178

Gospel of Thomas
    222
22.5   142

Index of Ancient Sources

Gregory Nazianzus

Against Julian
1.69 — 47

Gregory of Nyssa

Baptismal Diff.
— 220

Hebrews
— 47, 48
2:4 — 300
4:14 — 124
5:12–13 — 324
11:5 — 159

Hermas
— 47, 48, 73, 75
35 — 103
36 — 103
37 — 103
40 — 103
43.8–17 — 285
59 — 268
72.3 — 104

Hippolytus (attrib.)

Commentary on Daniel
— 43
29.3 — 43, 249

Refutation
5.8 — 324
6.24 — 272
9.12 — 276

History of the Contending of Saint Paul
— 57–58
15 — 300

Homer

Odyssey
16.476 — 97
20.201 — 97

Homeric Hymns
7 — 242
10.3 — 242

Hosea
2:18 — 220

Ignatius

Eph
18.2 — 298
19 — 272

Magn.
8 — 272

Phil.
7.2 — 103
11.2 — 260

Polyc.
7.2 — 301

Rom.
5.2 — 164
6.3 — 124

Trall.
5.1 — 324

Irenaeus
— 257

Adversus Haereseis
1.22.4 — 272
1.24.1–2 — 261–62
1.27.3 — 272
2.22 — 134
3.7.2 — 264
4.20.3 — 272
4.33.9 — 272
4.38.1–2 — 324
5.15.1 — 222
5.21.2–3 — 268

Index of Ancient Sources

Isaiah
11:6–9 — 220
22:13 — 198
65:25 — 220

Jeremiah
48:28 — 222

Jerome
Commentary on Titus pref. — 68
Ep.
22.41 — 51
Vir. Ill.
7 — 50

John
2:1–12 — 51
3:17 — 323
3:22–23 — 301
5:1–7 — 250
5:24 — 124
6:7 — 299
6:35 — 300
6:60–69 — 299
8 — 291
9:29 — 122
11:25–26 — 175
11:48 — 173
12:10 — 304
12:24 — 269, 286
12:27 — 287
14:7–14 — 299
14:22 — 255
18–19 — 313
18:11 — 192
18:22 — 311
18:26 — 248
19:11–12 — 229
19:34 — 65, 320–21
19:41 — 143
20 — 305
20:19 — 322
20:25 — 320
21 — 291, 305
21:15–17 — 290

Jonah
2 — 270

Joseph and Aseneth.
See *Aseneth*

Josephus
Against Apion — 247
Ant.
7.380 — 144
8.280 — 243
14.306–22 — 206

Judges
5:28 — 128

Justin
1 Apology
52.5 — 222
2 Apology — 186
Dialogue
80.4 — 272
88.3 — 165, 240

Juvenal
Satires
6 — 117
6.235 — 128

Leontius of Neapolis
Sermon Against the Jews — 159

Index of Ancient Sources

Letter of Pelagia

    58

Leucippe

6.19   149

Life of Aesop

1.2–6   93

Life of Pachomius

21   222

Life of Polycarp

    51, 60, 208
1–2   221
2   203

Lives of the Prophets

    301

Luke

    68
1:2   97
1:35   137
1:37   189
1:64   144
2:14   301
2:28   144
3:2–9   319
3:16   268
3:22   300
4:14   309
4:16–30   65
4:37   309
6   101
6:12   296
7:11–17   85, 278
7:38   128
8:1–3   197
8:8   315
8:23   296
9:32   296
9:57   142
9:58   139
10:1–12   139
10:1   65, 316
10:14   197
10:39   128
11:14   206
12:19   118
12:49–53   186
12:53   108
13:31–35   290
14:33   143
17:6   299
20:34–36   101
20:36   103
22:51   250
23:5   113
23:18   247
23:25   167
23:27–31   157
23:39–43   313
23:46   324
23:47–48   321
24:1   240
28:18   131
24   65
24:1   161
24:9   315
24:13–35   134
24:37   311
24:53   144

Lucian

Halcyon

3   189

Dialogues of the Gods

20   158

Lexiphanes

19   170

Peregrinus

12   128

Philopseudes

13   179

Index of Ancient Sources

Lucian (*cont.*)

Toxaris

30	128

Manichean Psalms

	54

Mark

	63, 65–68
1:6	45
1:9–13	219
1:11	175, 297, 300
1:12–13	80
1:13	220
1:16–20	139
1:21–34	206
1:26	250
1:28	309
1:31	188
1:38	287
2:1–12	309
2:4	310
2:8	310
3:7	309
3:8	205
3:12	152
4:35–41	296
5:1–20	85
5:3	143, 206
5:7	250
5:13	206
5:42	250
5:43	188
6:1–12	41
6:6–13	139
6:20	131
6:30–44	141
6:31	97
6:32–44	286
6:34	134
6:45–52	296
7:24	205
7:31	205
7:31–37	206
8:22	192
8:27–30	299
8:29	300
9:2	231
9:7	297
10:14–27	188
10:27	189
10:28	176
10:46	192
11:23	299
12:8	173
14:1	237
14:3–9	170
14:4–5	130
14:17	152
14:32–42	287
14:43	121, 192
14:47	248
14:48	192
14:61	246
14:66–72	290
14:68	116
15:6–14	228, 230
15:11	113
15:15	136, 228
15:21	210
15:26	159
15:34	85
15:39	305, 321
15:44	320
16:1	322
16:1–8	322
16:8	311

(Ps.–Mark)

16:8	279
16:12	134
16:16	175
16:18	316

Index of Ancient Sources

Martial

De Spectaculis

33.1-7	166

Martyrdom of Apollonius

16	230

Martyrdom of Justin

5	228

Martyrdom of Polycarp

	70
1.1	291
5.1	314
6.1	314
7.3	97
8.3	168
9.1	288
12.1	97
12.2	154
13.2	134
13.3–14.1	135
14.2	144
15	170
15–16	135

Martyrdom of Potamiaena and Basilides

3	150

Martyrium Petri et Pauli

20	301

Matthew

	63–68, 101, 291, 305
2:1–12	297
3:17	300
4:5–7	278
4:13–17	298
4:20	143
5	101
5–7	100
5:1–11	102
5:3	103
5:3–12	65
5:4	104
5:7	104
5:8	103
5:9	104
8:28–34	299
9:18–26	299
10:8	301
10:16	149
10:17–25	65
10:28	229
12:33–37	271
14:22–33	290
16:13–20	299
16:27	323
17:5	137
22:14	299
26:43	296
26:52	192
26:53	324
27:19	136
27:24–26	167
27:26	136
27:54	321
28	65
28:4	240
28:8	315
28:16–20	182

Melito of Sardis

Homily on Pascha

frg 15	299

Nicetas of Paphlagonia

	55–57, 61, 81, 84, 151, 209, 211, 255

Nicephorus Callistus, *Ecclesiastical History*

	i2.55, 51, 56–57, 230, 239

Index of Ancient Sources

Numbers
46

Odes of Solomon
8.16   324
17.8   238
19   272, 324

Origen
Commentary on John
20.12   45
Commentary on Matthew
36   134
Contra Celsum
2.55   321
2.63   321
De Pascha
44
On First Principles
1.2.3   45
Sel in Gen
2.13   220

Papyri Graecae Magicae (PGM)
IV 2506–7   279
XIII 326–344   127

Peregrinatio Egeriae
23.5   53

Philo
Agr. 9   324
Migr. Abr.
112   189
146   91
Moses
1.174   189
Omn prob lib
160   324

Poster C.
101   91
Spec. leg.
1.282   189

Plato
Apology
21–23   122;
28   312
Phaedo
97
Symposium
46   215d–217a, 93

Pliny
Natural History
2.146   169
7.37   278
8.42   221
12.41045   169
26.8   278

Pliny the Younger
Ep. 10.97   317

Plutarch
De genio Socratis
97

Proverbs
16:24   250
17:3   86

Philemon
48, 213
1   267
2   312
24   89

Index of Ancient Sources

Philippians

	48, 213
1:7	271
1:11	97
1:12–26	213
1:23	262
2:27	264
3	270
3:8	271
3:11	271
4:22	309

Philostratus

On Apollonius

4.45	278

Physiologus

	17, 46

Polycarp

Philippians

	260
7.1	96

Psalms

118:117	325
132:11	300
143:9	162

Protevangelium of James

	281
19-20	272
22.8	320

Pseudo-Chrysostom

Homily on St. Thecla

	140–41

Pseudo-Clementines

Homilies

2.50.1	97
8.21	242
9.19	239

Recognitions

1.47.3	97
4.37	279

Ps.-Linus

Passion of the Holy Apostle Paul
309, 313–15, 320–21, 323, 324

Revelation

9:20	230
20:8	298
21:11	297

Romans

	48
1:1	175
1:3	96, 267
1:7	297
6:1–23	242
6:3–11	240
6:10	324
8:15	268
8:17	105
8:19–23	220
8:23	268
8:38	229, 323
9:4	268
9:5	97
9:29	203
10:14	227
12:17	86
13:1–7	311
13:4	97
13:13	229
14:8	323
15	325
15:26	275
16	50
16:7	264
16:11	50

Index of Ancient Sources

Sallustius

Concerning the Gods and the Universe
    324

Seneca

Ep. 14.5   134

S.I.G.3

1173   251

Song of Songs

2:14   222

Suetonius

Nero
29   314

Tacitus

Annals
5.9   150
15.44   713

Tatian

Oration
17   242

Tertullian

Against Marcion
5.21   68
On Baptism
16   165
17.5   43, 257
On Penitence
9.4   194
10.5   196
On Purity
3.5   196
13.7   196
On the Resurrection
12   272
30–32   222, 270
Prescription of Heretics
13   272

Testament of Job

48.3   217
49.2   217
50.2   217

Testament of Naphtali

8.4   222

Theognis

1345–48   314

Theophilus

Ad Autolycum
1.13   272

Theophrastus

Hist. Plant.
9.5   169
9.11.3   250
18.8   250
De Odoribus
32   169

Thomas the Contender (Athlete)

     222

Titus

     42
1:5   333
1:10   113
3:13   331
3:14   288

Treatise on the Resurrection

1.4   272

Wisdom

2:24   310

Index of Modern Authors

Achtemeier, P., 188
Adamik, T., 221
Allberry, C., 54
Aubin, M., 64, 88, 112, 126
Aubineau, M., 140
Aune, D., 192

Balch, D., 100
Barnes, T. D., 134, 291, 292
Barrier, J. W., 93, 102, 109, 117,
    119, 124, 128, 132, 136, 137,
    144, 148, 152, 153, 161, 164,
    166, 167, 170, 175–77, 182,
    184
Bauckham, R., 67, 309, 325
Beard, M., 143
Berger, K., 141
Betz, H. D., 97, 101, 229
Bierler, L., 166, 220
Birley, A., 314, 317
Bollók, J., 92
Bolyki, J. 312
Bourguet, P., 270
Bovon, F., 44, 62, 108, 177, 281, 309
Bradshaw, P., 184, 257, 325
Braun, M., 63
Bremmer, J., 92, 154, 159, 180
Brock, A., 62, 64
Brown, P., 63–64
Budge, W., 300
Bultmann, R., 175, 188, 206

Bundy, D., 253
Butterworth, G., 45, 327

Callahan, A., 276
Campenhausen, H., 70
Cartlidge, D., 54, 55, 93, 94, 134,
    144, 168
Castelli, E., 55, 142
Cherix, P., 1, 2, 19, 79, 80, 82, 83,
    195, 207, 211, 259, 299
Clark, E., 112
Clarke, J., 126
Coleman, K., 170
Conybeare, F., 59, 128, 143, 153,
    158, 169, 170, 182, 183, 230,
    231
Conzelmann, H., 202
Cook, A. B., 135, 167, 200, 201
Crossan, J., 141
Crum, W., 1, 60, 79, 81, 82, 195,
    263
Czachesz, I., 69, 81, 82, 201, 203,
    230, 331

Dagron, G., 185, 329
Davies, S., 167
Davis, S., 87, 141, 147, 154, 170,
    180, 185, 330
Dormeyer, D., 141
Dover, K., 64
Drijvers, H., 219

Index of Modern Authors

Dunderberg, I., 272
Dunn, P., 64, 67, 70, 152, 253, 260, 284, 285, 287

Eastman, D., 147, 291, 303, 325
Ebner, M., 91, 93, 97, 101–3
Elliott, J. K., 54, 55, 60, 93, 114, 144, 168, 235, 290, 330
Esch (-Wermeling), E., 69, 91, 126, 146, 150, 152–54, 156–58, 163, 165–67, 169, 170

Faraone, C., 112, 122
Faure, P., 169
Fitzmyer, J., 92
Francis, J., 112
Fredriksen, P., 66n6
French, D., 91

Garland, R., 276
Geerard, M., 59
Georgi, D., 222, 287
Glaser, T., 254
Goodspeed, E., 58
Grant, R., 93, 189, 272, 299
Grillmeier, A., 272

Haines-Eitzen, K., 88
Halkin, F., 334
Hansen, W., 70, 146
Hanson, R., 44
Harnack, A., x, 51
Harrill, J., 285, 288
Harrison, S., 122
Hayne, L.,
Head, P., 68
Hermann, J., 55, 177
Hilhorst, A., 43, 257
Hills, J., 67, 68, 131, 136, 144, 299
Hoek, A. van den, 55, 177
Holmes, M., 103, 104, 136. 286
Holzhey, C., 42
Horn, C., 109

Hovhanessian, V., 253, 254, 256, 263, 267, 269–71, 272

Jackson-McCabe, M., 112
Jacobs, A., 112
James, M. R., 46, 57, 195, 239
Jensen, A., 69, 150, 152
Johnson, F., 95, 141, 329, 330
Johnston, S., 253

Kasser, R., 60, 222–24, 230, 231, 238, 243, 246, 247
Kelly, J. N. D., 257
Kilpatrick, G., 257
Klauck, H.-J., 105, 309
Klijn, A., 234, 242, 268
Koester, H., 325
Kraemer, R., 152, 168
Kurfess, A., 220

Lake, K., 71–72
Lalleman, P., 49, 117, 118
Lampe, G., 96, 169, 221, 222, 263
Lattimore, R., 118
Lattke, M., 238
Lau, M., 116, 117, 119
Layton, B., 142
Lehman, F., 324
Leinhäupl-Wilke, A., 173, 175
Lightfoot, J. B., 51, 208
Lipsett, B. D., 87, 91, 143, 151 161
Lipsius, R., 95, 109, 152, 170, 241, 314–16, 329, 330
Luisier, P., 60, 222–24, 230, 231, 238, 243, 246, 247
Lutz, C., 86

MacDonald, D., 68, 90, 140, 142, 151, 290, 291, 304, 309, 310, 319
MacDonald, M., 321
Mackay, T., 43
Malherbe, A., 92, 93, 118, 249
Malina, B., 92, 93

Index of Modern Authors

Marguerat, D., 67
Mathews, T., 242
Matthews, C., 218
Matthews, S., 95
McGowan, A., 117
Merz, A., 102, 117
Metzger, B., 247
Meyer, M., 142
Misset-van de Weg, M., 151
Mitchell, M., 50
Mitchell, S., 90
Moreschini, C., 46
Morris, J., 50
Moss, C., 136, 296, 312
Murphy-O'Connor, J., 306
Musurillo, H., 135, 137

Nauerth, C., 140
Nautin, P., 44, 45
Neyrey, J., 92, 93
Niederwimmer, K., 73, 229
Nippel, W., 221
Nock, A. D., 324
Norden, E., 300
Norelli, E., 46

Osiek, C., 100

Parsons, M., 92, 169
Parvis, S., 317
Patterson, S., 142
Pecere, O., 70
Penny, D., 258, 267, 269, 270
Perry, B. E., 247, 248
Pervo, R., 42, 50, 54, 63–65, 67, 68, 72, 79, 81, 87, 94, 95, 101, 103, 118, 121, 122, 124, 126, 131, 137, 139, 141, 144, 159, 161, 169, 173, 175, 190, 192, 200, 202, 203, 206, 207, 210, 211, 213, 219, 230, 231, 233, 240, 254, 260, 262, 270, 278, 281, 284, 285, 286, 290, 292, 296, 298, 299, 303, 306, 309–13, 320, 331, 334

Pesthy, M., 95
Peterson, E., 235, 236, 242, 243
Poirier, P.-H., 253
Poupon, G., 85, 122, 233, 237, 238, 240, 242
Price, R., 194
Price, S., 150, 159

Ramsay, W., 69, 90, 91, 95, 148, 152
Reitzenstein, R., 127
Riemer, U., 166, 248
Rigsby, K., 197
Roberts, C. H., 257
Rordorf, W., 1, 43, 51, 64, 67, 69, 79, 80, 81, 96, 109, 128, 146, 152, 190, 195, 207, 211, 242, 251, 259, 269, 279, 287, 290, 291, 297, 300, 306, 312, 317

Sanders, H., 297, 300, 301
Schäfer, D., 170
Schmidt, C., 1, 42, 58, 59, 64, 67, 70, 72, 79n1, 146, 152, 190, 195, 196, 210, 230, 231, 238, 241–43, 246, 249, 259, 275, 283, 287, 288, 290, 299, 300
Schneemelcher, W., 67, 218, 220
Schneider, H., 164
Schubart, W., 59, 230, 231, 238, 241–43, 246, 249, 275, 287, 288, 300
Smallwood, M., 206
Snyder, G., 43, 61, 68, 148, 236, 253, 254, 256–58, 261, 268, 273, 281, 303, 319, 321
Spicq, C., 97, 211, 243, 285, 297, 301
Spittler, J., 164, 166, 167, 170, 177, 218, 248
Stephens, S., 327
Stoops, R., 290

Tajra, H., 54, 306, 315, 316, 320
Talbot, A., 330
Testuz, M., 253

Index of Modern Authors

Theissen, G., 188
Thurston, B., 194
Toynbee, J., 276
Trall, A., 127
Trebilco, P., 221

Van den Hoek, A., 55, 177
Vermaseren, M., 157, 158, 166
Vogt, A., 55
Vouaux, L., 42, 50, 51, 54, 57, 67, 70, 96, 97, 109, 136, 152, 158, 169, 170, 182, 196, 309–12, 314–17, 329, 321

Warns, R., 140
Weaver, J., 200
White, J., 264
Wiles, M., 207
Wills, L., 93
Wright, W., 60, 91, 97, 105, 106, 109, 113, 114, 118, 123, 124, 127–30, 135, 137, 143, 144, 151, 153, 154, 156, 166–70, 176, 177, 178, 182–84

Zahn, T., 61
Zanker, P., 93

www.ingramcontent.com/pod-product-compliance
Lightning Source LLC
Chambersburg PA
CBHW020605300426
44113CB00007B/521